DIS

WORDSWORTH CLASSICS
OF WORLD LITERATURE

General Editor: Tom Griffith MA, MPhil

KEY PHILOSOPHICAL WRITINGS

Descartes

Key Philosophical Writings

Translated by *Elizabeth S. Haldane*
and *G. R. T. Ross*

Edited and with an Introduction by
Enrique Chávez-Arvizo

**WORDSWORTH CLASSICS
OF WORLD LITERATURE**

This edition published 1997 by Wordsworth Editions Limited
Cumberland House, Crib Street, Ware, Hertfordshire SG12 9ET

ISBN 1 85326 470 9

Typeset in Great Britain by Antony Gray
Printed and bound in Denmark by Nørhaven

CONTENTS

INTRODUCTION:
Descartes' Life and the Evolution of his Philosophy　　vii

RULES FOR THE DIRECTION OF THE MIND (*Extracts*)

RULE ONE　　　　　　　3
RULE TWO　　　　　　　5
RULE THREE　　　　　　8
RULE FOUR　　　　　　11
RULE FIVE　　　　　　17
RULE SIX　　　　　　　18
RULE SEVEN　　　　　22
RULE EIGHT　　　　　26
RULE NINE　　　　　　31
RULE TEN　　　　　　33
RULE ELEVEN　　　　36
RULE TWELVE　　　　39
RULE THIRTEEN　　　53
RULE FOURTEEN　　　59

DISCOURSE ON THE METHOD

PART ONE　　　　　　71
PART TWO　　　　　　77
PART THREE　　　　　85
PART FOUR　　　　　91
PART FIVE　　　　　97
PART SIX　　　　　　109

MEDITATIONS ON FIRST PHILOSOPHY

Dedicatory Letter to the Sorbonne   123

Preface to the Reader   127

Synopsis of the Six Following Meditations   130

FIRST MEDITATION:
Of the things as to which we may doubt   134

SECOND MEDITATION:
Of the nature of the human mind   139

THIRD MEDITATION:
Of God's existence   147

FOURTH MEDITATION:
Of the true and the false   162

FIFTH MEDITATION:
Of God, that He exists   170

SIXTH MEDITATION:
Of the existence of material things, etc.   176

OBJECTIONS AND REPLIES (*Extracts*)   191

PRINCIPLES OF PHILOSOPHY (*Extracts*)

Author's Letter–Preface   261

Dedicatory Letter to Elizabeth   274

FIRST PART: *Of the Principles of Human Knowledge*   277

SECOND PART: *Of the Principles of Material Things*   310

THIRD PART: *Of the Visible World*   322

FOURTH PART: *Of the Earth*   324

NOTES DIRECTED AGAINST A CERTAIN PROGRAMME   338

THE PASSIONS OF THE SOUL (*Extracts*)   358

THE SEARCH AFTER TRUTH   384

INTRODUCTION

René Descartes is unarguably one of the greatest philosophers in the history of Western thought. His achievements, which rank second only to Plato's, are the single most important source of our modern intellectual character. He is deservedly known simply as 'the father of modern philosophy', for notwithstanding that Descartes was notably influenced by ancient, medieval, and scholastic sources, he managed to break away from these traditions, thus influencing other early modern thinkers to emulate the break. Some of the writings he produced during his brief but fertile working life – the *Discourse on the Method,* the *Meditations on First Philosophy,* and the *Principles of Philosophy* – are philosophical classics *par excellence.* And all his works display a lucid and rich literary style equalled by few.

Apart from his remarkable philosophical exploits, Descartes made original contributions to what we now call 'sciences' – for example, he wrote treatises on geometry, algebra, physics, mechanics, cosmology, meteorology, optics, physiology, anatomy, and medicine, to name the principal ones. Although most of his scientific ideas have been superseded and are today of mere historical value, still it is difficult not to feel awe at the wide scope of the Cartesian intellectual enterprise.

Descartes was born in La Haye, a small village near Tours in western France, on 31 March 1596, at his maternal grandmother's house. The town was renamed 'La Haye-Descartes' in 1801 but is now known as 'Descartes'; the house is now a small museum. He came from a minor aristocratic family and for the first half of his life he enjoyed using the title *Seigneur du Perron* attached to the family estate. His father, Joachim Descartes (1563–1640), was a Councillor at the Parliament of Brittany. Jeanne Brochard, his mother, died in 1597. Descartes was subsequently raised by Jeanne Sain (d. 1609/1610), his maternal grandmother.

At the age of ten Descartes was sent to study at 'one of the most famous schools in Europe' (as he would later write in the semi-autobiographical part of the *Discourse)*, the college of La Flèche in Anjou, recently founded by the Jesuit order with the patronage of Henry IV (1553–1610), where he boarded for nine years. Due to his delicate health (one possibility is that he temporarily suffered from tuberculosis), Descartes was lodged in private accommodation and was allowed every day to 'lie in' late into the morning, a period during which he found his mind 'naturally inclined to meditation'. He preserved this habit for the rest of his life, even after having recovered from his illness.

Although throughout his life Descartes consistently remained respect-ful and grateful toward the Jesuits, he soon became disappointed with the education he received from them. He was particularly dissatisfied with the philosophy he had studied at La Flèche which is known as scholastic philosophy – a system of medieval philosophy which com-bined the philosophy of Aristotle (384–322 BC) with Christian religious doctrines. Although scholasticism in the seventeenth century appeared in a bewildering variety of forms, this did not discourage Descartes from tackling it. Particularly important for him was the basis of scholasticism, the common denominator of otherwise very diverse views, namely the doctrine of substantial forms or hylomorphism – from the ancient Greek terms *hylê* ('matter') and *morphê* ('form' or 'shape').

According to Aristotle, things are not constituted by matter – which refers very generally to that which remains constant as a thing undergoes change – alone. In addition to matter they have their own forms which differentiate them from one another according to their type. Form is what matter acquires when an object comes into being. The lump of bronze acquires a form by obtaining the shape and representational features of a statue, and the bronze in a bronze ball has a form in so far as it is in the shape of a ball. Moreover, the form of an object consists in those characteristics that make that object what it is. Aristotle claims that all objects of that sort have in common the said characteristics. For example, the form of sharpness consists of those characteristics that all sharp things have in common and that make a thing sharp. The form of a knife consists of those characteristics that all knives have in common and that make a thing a knife and not, say, a hatchet.

Such too was the opinion of the scholastics of the seventeenth century. However, they took the Aristotelian view a step further. To see what Descartes is likely to have been taught at La Flèche, we need to consider how the scholastics used the idea of substantial forms in explanations of natural phenomena. They argued that natural things are not composed of matter alone, since if that were so, a human being, a stone and a lion, being made of the same matter (in the general Aristotelian sense), would have the same essence and definition. Therefore, in addition to matter, they have their own forms which differentiate them from one another. Furthermore, there are individual and particular functions appropriate to each individual natural thing, as reasoning is to a human being, neighing to a horse, heating to a fire, and so on. But these functions do not arise from matter alone which, according to the scholastics, has no *power* to bring anything about. Thus, they must arise from the substantial forms of things. Consequently, one cannot deny to each and every natural thing its inherent substantial form in which the marks and character of each thing are stamped. This is, briefly, the scholastic doctrine.

The topic of hylomorphism deserves a treatise on its own. What is important for us is to note that Descartes rejected the existence of substantial forms, and to understand how he interpreted the scholastic doctrine. In correspondence, Descartes is careful to define what exactly he is rejecting: ' . . . when we deny substantial forms, we mean by the expression a certain substance joined to matter, making up with it a merely corporeal whole, and which, no less than matter and even more than matter, is a true substance, or self-subsistent thing'. Descartes, then, regards the acceptance of substantial forms as the acceptance of the existence of substances attached to things. And the type of substance they are, according to him, is immaterial or mental substance. So he deems the doctrine of substantial forms an error arising from predicating mental characteristics of physical objects (a form of extreme psychological anthropocentrism). For example, Descartes writes to a correspondent: 'I do not suppose there are in nature any [substantial forms] which are attached [to things], like so many little souls to their bodies'. We can, he argues in the same letter, explain things and their behaviour in purely mechanical terms, by appealing to mathematical physics alone. Explanations of natural phenomena in terms of substantial forms or 'little souls' are to be rejected. We need not posit the existence of souls or minds (he doesn't distinguish between the two terms) in nature. The only beings which possess souls are human beings and supernatural beings such as angels and God. But it would take some years for Descartes to develop fully his views which he hoped would eventually displace scholastic ones.

After he left La Flèche, Descartes went to study at Poitiers where he was awarded a degree in law. Around this time he wrote a little *Treatise on Fencing (Traité d'Escrime)*, now lost. 'Resolving', he writes in the *Discourse,* 'to seek no other science [i.e. knowledge] than that which could be found in the great book of the world', he then set out to travel through Europe. Firstly, in 1618, Descartes went to the Netherlands where he joined the army of the Prince of Orange, Maurice Count of Nassau (1567–1625) – son of William the Silent and leader of the Dutch in their war of independence against Spain – as a gentleman soldier. In Breda, he met the Dutch mathematician and scholar Isaac Beeckman (1588–1637), who became his mentor, leading him through the latest discoveries in mathematics and other sciences. He dedicated his first treatise, the *Compendium of Music (Compendium Musicae),* to Beeckman (who had asked Descartes to write it). Written in Latin, this work deals with the mathematical ratios involved in harmony. In 1619 Descartes transferred to the army of the Catholic Duke of Bavaria, Maximilian 1 (1573–1651). That year, he went to Frankfurt in Germany, where he witnessed the coronation of Ferdinand II (1578–1637) which took place from 20 July to 9 September. Near Ulm on the Danube (between Frankfurt and Vienna), on 10 November, as he was returning from the coronation of the Emperor to join the army, the setting-in of winter detained him in a *poêle* or stove-heated room.

In the solitude of the *poêle,* Descartes experienced three famous dreams which he interpreted as a revelation assigning him the mission to discover the 'foundations of a marvellous science' *(mirabilis scientiae fundamenta).* It is probable that what he had in mind at the time was the unification of many sciences previously thought distinct (such as arithmetic, geometry, music, astronomy, optics, and mechanical physics) under the banner of mathematics, performed by a single individual. (Part 2 of the *Discourse* gives a partial and stylised rendering of his thoughts in the stove-heated room.) On 23 September 1620, he made a vow to Our Lady of Loretto to make a pilgrimage to her shrine; whether he later did so cannot be known. Nor do we know for certain Descartes' destination immediately after he left his winter quarters.

During his years as a soldier Descartes never saw any fighting. In this period, in which he claimed to have made more progress in the pursuit of knowledge than he would have if he had done nothing but read books or mix with men of letters, he recorded some of his thoughts in a small notebook, now lost. Fortunately, a copy – made by the great German philosopher and mathematician Gottfried Wilhelm Leibniz

(1646–1716) – was later discovered and published under the title *Private Thoughts (Cogitationes Privatae)*. The original notebook was divided into several different sections. These included comments on scientific issues, mathematics, personal reflections, concrete observations including a reference to his famous dreams, the imagination, the senses, and the will. One section promises a method to solve all the difficulties in mathematics and proposes the unity of the sciences.

We know that in 1622 Descartes returned to France. While in Paris, he sold the family estate he had inherited, the proceeds of which would provide him with a regular but modest income, which allowed him to conduct his intellectual pursuits. *On Having the Right Mind (De Studio Bonae Mentis)*, a lost treatise dealing with the dispositions of the mind required for scientific thought, probably dates from this period. Between March 1623 and May 1625 he went travelling in Italy. On his return, he settled in Paris for two years, marking both the end of his travelling period and the beginning of fame. In November 1627, at the residence of the French Papal Nuncio (later Cardinal) Giovanni Francesco Guidi di Bagno (*c.* 1565–1641), he made a speech which greatly impressed his audience, especially Cardinal Pierre de Bérulle (1575–1629), head of the Congregation of the Oratory. Bérulle afterwards, in private, made Descartes promise him to dedicate his whole life to philosophical studies 'for the benefit of humanity', a promise duly honoured.

In 1628 Descartes moved to Holland, where he lived until 1649. In this country he was constantly on the move, changing his place of residence on more than twelve occasions; he lived first in Franeker, then in Amsterdam, and later in Leiden. In the *Discourse* he claims he moved to Holland in order to get away from any place where he might have acquaintances and because he welcomed the discreet manners of its inhabitants, among whom he could lead a life 'as solitary and retired as in deserts the most remote'. Borrowing from Ovid (who in turn borrowed from Epicurus), he expressed in correspondence his resolve to live his life under the motto 'to live well you must live unseen' (*'bene vixit, bene qui latuit'*). Notwithstanding his desire to be left alone, Descartes' views attracted a great deal of attention and led to his involvement in various public controversies, the most serious of which dragged on for years, and resulted in a ban on his philosophy at the University of Utrecht in 1643. I will return to this later.

During his first years in Holland, research was all-absorbing. In the autumn of 1628, claiming he had exhausted strict mathematical research,

Descartes diversified his inquiries and turned to philosophical and scientific concerns as well. Probably in this year, or earlier, he began to compose (in Latin) his first major work, the *Rules for the Direction of the Mind (Regulae ad Directionem Ingenii)*, published posthumously in a Dutch translation in 1684. (An extant copy of the original manuscript, which was never found, was bought by Leibniz in 1670. The first original language edition only came out in 1701 at Amsterdam.) The *Regulae* (from which extracts are provided in the present volume) were to be divided into three parts, each composed of twelve rules. The first twelve rules deal with simple propositions, paying particular attention to the cognitive operations of intuition and deduction by which these propositions are known; the next set of rules, which ends in Rule Twenty-One (the set was never completed), is concerned with 'perfectly understood problems' – mainly mathematical problems which can be expressed in the form of equations; and the last set, which is altogether missing, purported to deal with 'imperfectly understood problems' – mostly empirical or 'practical' problems which cannot be expressed in the form of equations. His hope was to show that imperfectly understood problems could be reduced to perfectly understood ones. The work as a whole unveils his first attempts to develop a universal method for discovering the truth. In the early 1630s, Descartes moved to the slaughterhouse district in Amsterdam to pursue more easily his physiological interests. In the *Discourse* he reports many important results which came out of this as well as other research in algebra, optics and physics, on which he worked during this period.

In 1629 a friend asked for Descartes' opinion on the phenomenon of parhelia (rings around the sun) observed that year in Italy. His reflections on this issue led him to compose a single work on meteorology in particular, and physics in general, entitled *The World (Le Monde)*, which did away with the substantial forms of the scholastics. However, in 1633, shortly before his work went to press, Descartes learned of Galileo's condemnation by the Inquisition for rejecting (in the *Dialogue on the Two Chief Systems of the Universe (Sistemi del Mondo)*, published in 1632) the Ptolemaic account of an immovable earth and embracing the Copernican heliocentric theory of the earth's movement, a position central to Descartes' own treatise. 'I almost decided to burn all my papers or at least let no one see them', he wrote in correspondence at the time. In the part of the *Discourse* in which Descartes summarises *The World* he writes: 'I endeavoured to explain the most important of these truths [i.e. truths discovered by considering what follows from certain laws of nature] in a treatise which certain considerations prevented me from publishing.' The surviving treatise, first published in 1664, has two parts, the *Treatise on Light (Traité de la Lumière)* and the *Treatise on Man (L'Homme).* From the extant material and from Descartes' testimony in the *Discourse,* it seems that these two parts were linked by two chapters which are now lost; moreover, the *Treatise on Man* mentions yet a third part of *The World,* which has never been found, dealing with the soul and its relation with the body.

One of the few details of Descartes' private life which is known, belongs to this period. In the 1630s he established a relationship with a servant named Hélène who worked at a house where he was staying as a guest. His illegitimate daughter Françine was born on 19 July 1635; unfortunately she became ill with fever and died prematurely at Amesfort in Holland on 7 September 1640.

Shortly after his decision to withdraw *The World* from the world, Descartes began to pull material out of this work and revise it for eventual publication as a series of self-contained treatises. The first material came to form the *Optics (La Dioptrique).* 'I am planning to have it published on its own', he confides to a correspondent in 1635. In another letter written later in the same year, he writes 'I plan to add the *Meteorology (Les Météores)* to the *Optics.* By the following year he adds yet two further works to the above collection: the *Geometry (La Géométrie)* forming a third scientific essay and the *Discourse on the Method (Discours de la Méthode)* serving as preface to the whole. The *Discourse* was finally published in 1637 with the three scientific treatises appended.

Published anonymously when Descartes was forty-one years old, the *Discourse* appeared with the following full title (itself an abbreviated form of an even longer title which Descartes had originally in mind): *Discourse on the Method of rightly conducting one's reason and seeking the truth in the sciences, and in addition the Optics, the Meteorology and the Geometry, which are essays in this Method (Discours de la Méthode pour bien conduire sa raison, et chercher la vérité dans les sciences. Plus la Dioptrique, les Météores et la Géométrie qui sont des essais de cette Méthode).* Written in French rather than Latin, and therefore addressed directly to the lay person, the work aims to give to give a clear and straightforward account of the Cartesian philosophical method, which is accessible to the unprejudiced person of 'Good sense', while remaining interesting to scholars. A virtue of the work is that it aims to show that 'the power of forming a good judgement and of distinguishing the true from the false, which is properly speaking what is called Good sense or Reason, is by nature equal in all men'. Its goal is to present a novel philosophical method of increasing one's knowledge in the form of a history or a fable, the emphasis being 'not to teach the Method which everyone should follow in order to promote the good conduct of his Reason, but only', as Descartes writes, 'to show in what manner I have endeavoured to conduct my own.'

The work is divided into six parts. The first part airs Descartes' dissatisfaction with his scholastic educational upbringing. The second part presents the rules of the method. The third part sketches a provisional moral code consisting of just a few maxims. The fourth part elegantly and lucidly summarises his metaphysical views, including what is arguably philosophy's most famous argument: 'I am thinking, therefore I exist' *('je pense donc je suis',* or *'cogito ergo sum').* Part five is a synopsis of *The World* which manages to avoid drawing its full implications for the Cartesian account of planetary motion; it also includes the doctrine of the *bête-machine* or animal–machine which asserts that all the functions and movements of non-human animals can be explained without having to suggest that animals have souls like humans do, as if animals were splendid and highly complex natural automata (machines made by nature). One implication of this doctrine is that it denies animals the capacity of abstract thought and freedom of will; it is important to note, contrary to standard interpretation, that it does not in any way imply that animals lack sentience. The final part outlines his views on scientific experimentation and his future research plans. The Discourse and Essays as a whole exemplify the Cartesian unitary view of knowledge *(scientia).* Descartes would later describe this vision, in the *Principles,* using a well-known metaphor of the tree of knowledge: 'Philosophy as a whole is like a tree whose roots are metaphysics, whose trunk is physics, and whose branches, which issue from the trunk, are all the other sciences. These reduce themselves to three principal ones, viz. medicine, mechanics, and moralist.' The *Discourse* fluently and stylishly presents the whole of the tree of knowledge in a nutshell.

Toward the end of the *Discourse* Descartes pleaded: 'I beg all those who have any objections to offer to take the trouble of sending them to my publishers, so that, being made aware of them, I may try at the same time to subjoin my reply.' Although the planned addendum never materialised, feedback from various learned readers of the *Discourse* led him to develop further his metaphysical project, originally outlined in

Part IV of this work. The result was his philosophical *magnum opus,* the *Meditations on First Philosophy (Meditationes de Prima Philosophia),* first published in Latin in 1641. The *Meditations,* perhaps the most written-about philosophical text in history, aims to develop a philosophy which would be as solid and certain as mathematics because it relies on a method – the reliable method for discovering truth expounded in the *Discourse* – analogous to that used by mathematicians. As the term 'Meditations' suggests, the idea is that of a personal exercise in thought one conducts as one reads the text, as opposed to a mere exposition of Descartes' views. Of course he is responsible for these views. But one is responsible for reflecting on these views as if they were one's own. Thus the arguments throughout are couched in the first person. Descartes reasons, in an orderly way, from the most basic principles to the most complex. He begins the project by rooting out of his mind all dubitable opinions. Through the so-called method of doubt, he questions systematically all preconceived views open to the smallest doubt, until he encounters an absolute certainty: I am thinking, therefore I exist – the first principle of the philosophy Descartes seeks. From this Archimedean point, he attempts to prove that he is essentially a soul or thinking thing, and later that God exists and that He is the foundation of all truth and the guarantor of the veracity of everything which we clearly and distinctly perceive. Having allegedly found the source of truth and knowledge, Descartes offers the final major metaphysical theses of his project, namely, that of the existence of the material world and the real distinction between the mind and the body. Let us examine the *Meditations'* thread of argument in more detail.

Descartes' metaphysical project can be likened to a personal journey in search for truth, conducted not by a particular person at a particular time (e.g. René Descartes in the seventeenth century), but by any thinker who is willing to step into the shoes of the nameless and timeless meditator and reflect philosophically through a voyage of truth discovery. In preparation for the journey the voyager must adopt a critical position against all unexamined preconceived opinions bestowed on him (e.g. by parents and teachers in his youth). In the First Meditation, the initial leg of the journey is accomplished by exercising the method of doubt, which involves withholding assent from all previous opinions which fail to be certain and indubitable. The methodic doubt does not carry the meditator through this initial stage in a single leap but is itself subdivided into various stages or levels of doubt, each more powerful and of a wider scope than the previous one. The first level, known as the argument from the senses, casts doubt on the senses (and therefore on all sense-based beliefs), because they sometimes deceive us (e.g. my vision might mislead me into thinking that a straight stick immersed in water is as it appears to me – i.e. bent). However, doubting the reliability of the senses leaves many knowledge claims unscathed, for example, the claim that I might be dreaming (e.g. while asleep I might be convinced that I am sitting by the fire when in fact I am lying in bed). The next level of doubt, labelled the dreaming argument, aims to cast doubt on these type of knowledge claims too. I see plainly, ponders the meditator, that there are never any sure signs by means of which being awake can be distinguished from being asleep. But this sort of doubt does not cover geometrical or mathematical knowledge claims, for whether I am awake or asleep, two plus three equals five. The final stage in the method is reached by considering the possibility that some malicious omnipotent deceiver is employing all his energies in order to deceive me. The sky, the earth, shapes, and colours might well be delusions or dreams the demon has devised to ensnare my judgement. The first part of the journey finishes then with the perplexed traveller unable to rescue any of his former beliefs, doubting the evidence from the senses, whether he is dreaming, geometric and mathematical truths, and the existence of the physical world.

Notwithstanding the uninspiring outcome of the first part of the journey, the voyager presses on undeterred in the Second Meditation, in search of a solid epistemological footing (the ancient Greek term *episteme* means knowledge): just as Archimedes used to demand only one firm and immovable point in order to shift the entire planet, so too the meditator hopes to find at least one truth claim, however slight, that is certain and unshakeable, in order to built on it a comprehensive system of knowledge. This he is able to find (at last) in the Cogito – I am thinking, therefore I exist. Even if there is a deceiver of supreme power and cunning who is deliberately and constantly deceiving me, the demon will never bring it about that I am nothing so long as I think that I am something. Thus the second stage of the journey ends with the discovery of a truth which is indubitable, incorrigible (if one believes it one necessarily has a true belief) and self-verifying (if one asserts it then the assertion must be true), namely, 'I exist'.

Once indubitable knowledge of his own existence has been secured, the meditator then embarks on a thoroughly constructive (epistemologically speaking) path to knowledge by attempting to prove the existence of things beyond himself, thus avoiding solipsism – the view that *only* one's self exists and that 'outside' things exist exclusively as objects or contents of one's consciousness. In order to do this it becomes necessary to prove the existence of an all–perfect God who is not a deceiver. For if He, being omnipotent, created me in such a way as to be systematically mistaken I can never be certain, no matter how evident matters seem, that there is anything outside my thought. If, on the contrary, I can demonstrate that I am the creation of a perfect being then I can be sure that my most basic and manifest epistemological claims are indeed true.

In the Third Meditation the meditator conducts the first of two major attempts to prove God's existence, usually labelled the 'trademark argument', for it cashes in an analogy claiming that God has placed the idea of Himself in one's mind just as the mark of the craftsman is stamped on his work. The meditator reasons along the following lines. I am not perfect (there is more perfection in knowledge than in doubt and since I doubt many matters I am an imperfect being) yet I have in me the idea of supreme perfection (the idea of a supremely perfect being – God). Yet – at this point in the argument the meditator uses two standard scholastic metaphysical principles, 'nothing comes from nothing' and 'there must be as much reality in the cause as in the effect of that cause' – this idea cannot come from myself (for I am not perfect), thus it must come from outside myself. The meditator then reasons that the idea must come from God Himself; therefore he concludes that He exists.

In the Fourth Meditation, the meditator continues his discussion of God's attributes and considers what can be referred to as the problem of error, which is best explained as an epistemological version of the perennial problem of evil in the philosophy of religion. The latter consists of the following apparently incoherent claims: God is all-perfect and benevolent, yet there is evil (e.g. natural and human disasters cause enormous pain and suffering) in our world. The problem of evil rests in reconciling these two claims. Similarly, the meditator claims to have just shown that God is all-perfect and not a deceiver, yet knows that he himself is subject to error (he might go wrong when adding two and three, or counting the sides of a chiliagon – a one-thousand-sided figure). The problem of error lies in reconciling these two seemingly incoherent claims. The meditator's answer to the problem of error is analogous to a celebrated answer to the problem of evil which argues that a diversified world, even if some evil exists, is more perfect than a homogenised world which lacks evil but also lacks variety. In like manner, the meditator propounds that a universe with some of its parts not immune to error, while others are immune, is more perfect than a world whose parts are all exactly alike. Finally he goes on to explain that the source of error lies not in God but in the precipitate application of our will to the objects of reason.

The Fifth Meditation offers a second proof of the existence of God known as the 'ontological argument' – a phrase first coined in the eighteenth century by the eminent German philosopher Immanuel Kant (1724–1804) to refer to a particular kind of reasoning which attempts to prove the existence of God abstracted from all experience, inferring His existence *a priori* exclusively from concepts. Briefly, the argument can be stated as follows: God is supremely perfect; existence is part of supreme perfection; therefore, God exists.

In the Sixth Meditation, the final stage of the journey is covered when the meditator attempts to demonstrate the existence of the material world and the real distinction between the mind and the body. Firstly, he argues that given that God is not a deceiver and that I possess ideas about the physical world, it follows that such a world actually exists and is the cause of such ideas. Secondly, he purports to show that the mind and the body have utterly distinct essences or natures. This issue requires a closer look.

Descartes' claim that there exists a real distinction between the mind and the body is known as 'Cartesian dualism'. His thesis maintains that human beings are made out of the union of two incommensurable substances – *res cogitans,* thinking substance, or mind, and *res extensa,* extended corporeal substance, or body. In Descartes' philosophy, thought and extension are regarded as constituting the natures of intelligent substance and corporeal substance; they must then be considered as nothing else but thinking substance itself, and extended substance itself – that is, as mind and body. Moreover, he claims that the rational soul cannot be derived in any way from the qualities of matter but must be specially created (by God). This is the kernel of the Cartesian metaphysical view of human beings. That which makes us distinctly human, the (immaterial) thinking part of us, is not something which is derivable from, or in any way a function of, our body – nor in particular our brain.

Before publishing the *Meditations,* Descartes gave a copy of the manuscript to Friar Marin Mersenne (1588–1648) – his main correspondent – requesting him to circulate it asking selected scholars for their objections. In a letter, he writes to Mersenne: 'I will be very glad if people put to me many objections, the strongest they can find, for I hope that in consequence the truth will stand out all the better from them.' Descartes' call was heeded by an impressive array of scholars. The first edition of the work was printed with a hefty appendix which included six sets of objections and Descartes' replies (all in Latin). The First Set was written by Johannes Caterus, a Dutch Catholic theologian. The Second Set, even though explicitly attributed to 'theologians and philosophers', originated mainly from Mersenne's pen. The Third Set, attributed to 'a celebrated English philosopher', is by Thomas Hobbes (1588–1679). The Fourth Set is by the French theologian Antoine Arnauld (1612–94), Doctor of Theology at the Sorbonne. The Fifth Set is by the French philosopher Pierre Gassendi (1592–1655). Appended to this set is a letter from Descartes to a disciple, Claude Clerselier (1614– 84), which further discusses some of Gassendi's objections. This item first appeared in the 1647 French translation of the *Meditations* which was printed with Descartes' approval. The Sixth Set was, again, compiled by Mersenne even though it is attributed to 'various theologians and philosophers'. Criticisms of the *Meditations* continued to reach Descartes after its publication. The second (Latin) edition, printed in 1642, came accompanied by the Seventh Set of Objections and Replies composed by the Jesuit Pierre Bourdin (1595–1653). This edition also included an open letter written by Descartes to Father Dinet (1584–1653) – former instructor at La Flèche and head of the Jesuits in France – in the hope that it would win him the backing of the Church. The Objections and Replies (from which selections are included in the present volume) are an invaluable source which no interpretation of Descartes' views can afford to ignore.

It must be noted that the manner of presentation of the Objections and Replies I adopt – by theme – diverges from the one adhered to in the original edition, where each set of objections – except the Third – appears uninterrupted followed by Descartes' corresponding unbroken set of replies. I leave to the reader the task of considering the validity and soundness of Descartes' arguments in the *Meditations* and of judging whether his answers to the criticisms raised by the first readers of this work are satisfactory. (The translation of the *Meditations* in the present volume follows the original Latin edition; where it seems desirable, an alternative reading from the French translation is given in square brackets.)

The spread of Descartes' intellectual influence sparked major controversy.

The theologian Gisbertus Voetius (1589–1676), who later became Rector of the University at Utrecht, had two treatises anonymously printed in 1643 which included attacks on Descartes. Descartes reacted by publishing that same year a long open letter entitled 'Letter of René Descartes to that Most Distinguished Man, Mr Gisbertus Voetius' (*Epistola Renati Descartes ad Celeberrimum Virum D. Gisbertum Voetium*), in which he harshly responds to Voetius' attack on his philosophy. As a consequence of this controversy Utrecht pronounced a prohibition against printing any material in favour of or against Cartesianism.

Furthering his attempt to establish his philosophy and gain wider support for it, Descartes published in 1644 his most extensive and comprehensive account of his philosophical system, the *Principles of Philosophy (Principia Philosophiae),* which contains much of the material from the suppressed treatise *The World.* He hoped the *Principles* would be adopted as a university textbook. The *Principles,* originally published in Latin, appeared in French translation in 1647. The latter version, notwithstanding its considerable divergence from the original, had Descartes' explicit approval. The work (from which selections are included in the present volume) is divided into four parts each divided into a number of concise articles – there are five hundred and four in all. Part One deals with metaphysics although adopting a different approach from that followed in the Meditations; Part Two covers the principles of physics; Part Three examines the nature of the universe seen in the light of the principles expounded in the previous part; and Part Four gives an account of the earth's origins and a variety of terrestrial phenomena, including magnetic and gravitational forces, the nature of tides, and fire. In addition, Descartes planned to include two parts dealing with plants and animals respectively, but he never finished them. (The excerpts from the *Principles* in the present volume are made from the original Latin version collated with the French; when it seems desirable to indicate the difference between them this is done by means of square brackets.)

The *Principles* were dedicated to Princess Elizabeth of Bohemia (1618–80), daughter of Frederick IV of Bohemia and Elizabeth Stuart (daughter of James VI of Scotland and I of England). Descartes began a famous and invaluable correspondence – there are fifty-nine extant letters in total – after finding out in 1642 that the Princess had read the *Meditations* with keen interest. He wrote to her offering to elucidate any difficulties with the metaphysical text. However, from 1643 up until 1649 Descartes strongly stresses the 'practical' aspects of his thought: human (and animal) physiology, conduct and behaviour come to constitute the central problems in the Cartesian writings during this period. And it is in fact Princess Elizabeth who pushes him in this direction. Her name connects, with a strong thread, the *Meditations,* the *Principles* and the *Passions* (of which more later).

In 1647, when presenting the French translation of the *Principles* – in the letter-preface to the translator of this work, the Abbé Claude Picot (c. 1601–68) – Descartes took the opportunity to disapprove publicly of a former pupil based at Utrecht, Henri le Roy or Henricus Regius (1598–1679). In response to his charge, Regius published (anonymously) a broadsheet listing the points of disagreement with his former mentor. Descartes countered by writing his *Comments on a Certain Broadsheet (Notae in Programma Quoddam),* published in Latin in 1648.

Also in 1648, Descartes was the subject of a congenial philosophical interview with Frans Burman (1628–79). Burman was a young Dutchman who was to become Professor of Theology at the University of Utrecht in 1664. He went to see Descartes in Egmond Binnen, near Alkmaar, and recorded a set of questions and answers from his conversation with the French philosopher on issues discussed in the *Discourse,* the *Meditations,* and the *Principles.* Four days after the meeting, John Clauberg (b. 1622), who subsequently published many editions of Descartes' works, made a record (preserved in Göttingen) of the manuscript which was published only much later in 1896 under the title *Conversation with Burman (Entretien avec Burman).* Earlier that year, Descartes worked on the *Description of the Human Body (Description du Corps Humain),* which purports to explain 'the way in which the animal is formed, going back to the start of its development'; the unfinished treatise was published in 1664.

Descartes' last major work, *The Passions of the Soul (Les Passions de l'Ame),* was published in 1649, a few months before his death. It began as a little treatise on the subject that he wrote for Elizabeth in 1646, and developed into a large work of enormous philosophical import. Written in French, the *Passions* (from which extracts are provided in the present volume) is divided into three parts, each consisting of a large number of small articles (two hundred and twelve in all). The work offers a taxonomy of the passions or emotions, and valuable material on Descartes' views on ethics, psychology, physiology, and philosophy of mind. In particular it attempts to elucidate the Cartesian account of the relation between the mind and the body.

Worn down by many fierce public disputes, especially the Utrecht controversy, Descartes (hesitantly) accepted an invitation from young Queen Christina of Sweden to join her court, thus accepting full patronage for the first and only time in his life. He arrived in Stockholm on 1 October 1649. There, he is said to have written the libretto for a ballet, the *Birth of Peace (La Naissance de la Paix)*, in celebration of the end of the Thirty Years War. Whether the extant text is the work of Descartes is a matter of controversy. Probably around this time (the date of composition is very much disputed) he began his unfinished dialogue, the *Search for Truth by Means of the Natural Light (La Recherche de la Vérité par la Lumière Naturelle)*, which covers largely the same ground as the *Meditations*.

Queen Christina required philosophy lessons which started at the extremely demanding time of five o'clock in the morning, drastically altering Descartes' life-long habit of remaining in bed through the morning. This probably made him more vulnerable to the rigours of the Swedish winter, and he suffered an attack of pneumonia which led to his untimely death on 11 February 1650 (just short of his fifty-fourth birthday).

Controversy continued to follow Descartes' thought after his death. In 1663 his works were placed in the (recently abolished) 'Index of Forbidden Books' (*Index Librorum Prohibitorum*) by the Roman Catholic Church. Notwithstanding this, editions and renditions of his texts began to multiply and are still doing so at a faster rate than ever. The present collection appears exactly four hundred years after Descartes' birth, at a time when there is an astonishing revival of interest in what he believed. Readers can hardly do better than examine Descartes' key philosophical writings in order to come to terms with some of the most powerful and influential ideas ever written and see the indelible mark the 'father of modern philosophy' has made on our intellectual identity.

In the margins in the present volume I have given the corresponding page number (in Arabic) of the relevant volume (in Roman numerals at the beginning of each work) of the standard Franco-Latin edition of Descartes' works known as 'AT' – see the suggestions for further reading below. All footnotes are supplied by the translators or the editor, not by Descartes.

DR ENRIQUE CHÁVEZ-ARVIZO
University of Reading

FURTHER READING

The literature on Descartes is enormous. What follows is a very selective list with brief comments added.

Charles Adam and Paul Tannery (eds.), *Oeuvres de Descartes*, revised edition, 12 volumes, Paris: J. Vrin in association with the Centre National de la Recherche Scientifique, 1964–76
The standard Franco–Latin edition of Descartes' original works (known as 'AT').

John Cottingham *et al.* (eds and trans.), *The Philosophical Writings of Descartes*, 3 volumes, Cambridge University Press, Cambridge 1985–91
The most comprehensive English translation of Descartes' philosophical writings.

Adrian Baillet, *La Vie de Monsieur Des-Cartes*, 2 volumes, Horthemels, Paris 1691; reprinted, Garland, New York 1987
Descartes' official biography, which usually details its sources carefully but unfortunately contains many errors and inventions. Lamentably, Baillet's work is available only in French.

Elizabeth S. Haldane, *Descartes: His Life and Times,* Murray, London 1905; reprinted Thoemmes Press, Bristol 1992
An English biography which follows Baillet fairly closely (with errors and inventions perpetuated!).

Stephen Gaukroger, *Descartes: An Intellectual Biography,* Clarendon Press, Oxford 1995
A recent intellectual biography which portrays Descartes predominantly as a scientist and only incidentally as a philosopher (which non-specialists will find a tough but worthwhile read).

Tom Sorell, *Descartes,* Oxford University Press, Oxford 1994
A short and extremely accessible introduction to Descartes' thought aimed at the general reader.

More extensive introductions to Descartes' philosophy, accessible to both non-specialists and philosophy beginners, are by:

John Cottingham, *Descartes,* Basil Blackwell, Oxford 1986

Anthony Kenny, *Descartes: A Study of His Philosophy,* Random House, New York 1968; reprinted Thoemmes Press, Bristol 1993

Bernard Williams, *Descartes: The Project of Pure Enquiry,* Penguin, London 1978

Georges Moyal (ed.), *René Descartes: Critical Assessments,* 4 volumes, Routledge, London and New York 1991
High-fliers can whet their philosophical appetite with this most comprehensive collection of articles – one hundred and sixteen in all – on Descartes' philosophy available in English, addressed to philosophy students and specialists.

Willis Doney (ed.), *Descartes: A Collection of Critical Essays,* Doubleday, New York 1967
A shorter yet valuable collection of articles.

Martial Gueroult, *Descartes Selon l'Ordre des Raisons,* 2 volumes, Montaigne, Paris 1953: English translation by Roger Ariew, *Descartes Interpreted According to the Order of Reason,* University of Minnesota Press, Minnesota 1984
French interpretations of Descartes tend to follow a very different approach from Anglo-American ones. This is an authoritative and meticulous French account of Cartesian metaphysics which has been skilfully translated into English.

Enriquez Chávez-Arvizo, *Tríptico Sobre el Alma* (*Triptych on the Soul*): *Aristóteles; Descartes; Nagel,* Monterrey Press, Monterrey 1993
A comparative account of Descartes' views on the self with those of Aristotle and the contemporary philosopher Thomas Nagel.
In my *Triptych* I follow the 'official' Anglo-American reading of Descartes' philosophy of mind. However, in a work which I am currently preparing for publication, *Descartes on the Substantial Union of Mind and Body,* I argue that the standard Cartesian dualist interpretation of Descartes is ill-founded, and offer a revisionist account of his views on mind and body.

NOTE ON THE TEXT

The text reprinted here is selected from the two-volume edition of *The Philosophical Works of Descartes,* first published by Cambridge University Press in 1911.

KEY PHILOSOPHICAL WRITINGS

RULES FOR THE DIRECTION
OF THE MIND[1]

1 *The end of study should be to direct the mind towards the enunciation of sound and correct judgments on all matters that come before it.*

Whenever men notice some similarity between two things, they are wont to ascribe to each, even in those respects in which the two differ, what they have found to be true of the other. Thus they erroneously compare the sciences, which entirely consist in the cognitive exercise of the mind, with the arts, which depend upon an exercise and disposition of the body. They see that not all the arts can be acquired by the same man, but that he who restricts himself to one, most readily becomes the best executant, since it is not so easy for the same hand to adapt itself both to agricultural operations and to harp–playing, or to the performance of several such tasks as to one alone. Hence they have held the same to be true of the sciences also, and distinguishing them from one another according to their subject matter, they have imagined that they ought to be studied separately, each in isolation from all the rest. But this is certainly wrong. For since the sciences taken all together are identical with human wisdom, which always remains one and the same, however applied to different subjects, and suffers no more differentiation proceeding from them than the light of the sun experiences from the variety of the things which it illumines, there is no need for minds to be confined at all within limits; for neither does the knowing of one truth have an effect like that of the acquisition of one art and prevent us from finding out another, it rather aids us to do so. Certainly it appears to me strange that so many people should investigate human customs with such care, the virtues of plants, the motions of the stars, the transmutations of metals, and the objects of similar sciences, while at the same time practically none bethink themselves about good understanding, or universal wisdom, though

360

1 *ingenii.*

nevertheless all other studies are to be esteemed not so much for their own value as because they contribute something to this. Consequently we are justified in bringing forward this as the first rule of all, since there is nothing more prone to turn us aside from the correct way of seeking out truth than this directing of our inquiries, not towards their general end, but towards certain special investigations. I do not here refer to perverse and censurable pursuits like empty glory or base gain; obviously counterfeit reasonings and quibbles suited to vulgar understanding open up a much more direct route to such a goal than does a sound apprehension of the truth. But I have in view even honourable and laudable pursuits, because these mislead us in a more subtle fashion. For example take our investigations of those sciences conducive to the conveniences of life or which yield that pleasure which is found in the contemplation of truth, practically the only joy in life that is complete and untroubled with any pain. There we may indeed expect to receive the legitimate fruits of scientific inquiry; but if, in the course of our study, we think of them, they frequently cause us to omit many facts which are necessary to the understanding of other matters, because they seem to be either of slight value or of little interest. Hence we must believe that all the sciences are so interconnected, that it is much easier to study them all together than to isolate one from all the others. If, therefore, anyone wishes to search out the truth of things in serious earnest, he ought not to select one special science; for all the sciences are conjoined with each other and interdependent: he ought rather to think how to increase the natural light of reason, not for the purpose of resolving this or that difficulty of scholastic type,[2] but in order that his understanding may light his will to its proper choice in all the contingencies of life. In a short time he will see with amazement that he has made much more progress than those who are eager about particular ends, and that he has not only obtained all that they desire, but even higher results than fall within his expectation.

361

2 *scholae*.

2 *Only those objects should engage our attention, to the sure and*   362
indubitable knowledge of which our mental powers[3] *seem to be adequate.*

Science in its entirety is true and evident cognition. He is no more
learned who has doubts on many matters than the man who has
never thought of them; nay he appears to be less learned if he has
formed wrong opinions on any particulars. Hence it were better not
to study at all than to occupy one's self with objects of such
difficulty, that, owing to our inability to distinguish true from false,
we are forced to regard the doubtful as certain; for in those matters
any hope of augmenting our knowledge is exceeded by the risk of
diminishing it. Thus in accordance with the above maxim we reject
all such merely probable knowledge and make it a rule to trust only
what is completely known and incapable of being doubted. No
doubt men of education may persuade themselves that there is but
little of such certain knowledge, because, forsooth, a common
failing of human nature has made them deem it too easy and open
to everyone, and so led them to neglect to think upon such truths;
but I nevertheless announce that there are more of these than they
think – truths which suffice to give a rigorous demonstration of
innumerable propositions, the discussion of which they have
hitherto been unable to free from the element of probability.
Further, because they have believed that it was unbecoming for a
man of education to confess ignorance on any point, they have so   363
accustomed themselves to trick out their fabricated explanations,
that they have ended by gradually imposing on themselves and thus
have issued them to the public as genuine.

But if we adhere closely to this rule we shall find left but few
objects of legitimate study. For there is scarce any question
occurring in the sciences about which talented men have not
disagreed. But whenever two men come to opposite decisions
about the same matter one of them at least must certainly be in the
wrong, and apparently there is not even one of them who knows;
for if the reasoning of the second was sound and clear he would be
able so to lay it before the other as finally to succeed in convincing
his understanding also. Hence apparently we cannot attain to a
perfect knowledge in any such case of probable opinion, for it
would be rashness to hope for more than others have attained to.

3 *ingenia.*

Consequently if we reckon correctly, of the sciences already discovered, arithmetic and geometry alone are left, to which the observance of this rule reduces us.

Yet we do not therefore condemn that method of philosophising which others have already discovered and those weapons of the schoolmen, probable syllogisms, which are so well suited for polemics. They indeed give practice to the wits of youths and, producing emulation among them, act as a stimulus; and it is much better for their minds to be moulded by opinions of this sort, uncertain though they appear, as being objects of controversy among the learned, than to be left entirely to their own devices. For thus through lack of guidance they might stray into some abyss; but as long as they follow in their masters' footsteps, though they may diverge at times from the truth, they will yet certainly find a path which is at least in this respect safer, that it has been approved of by more prudent people. We ourselves rejoice that we in earlier years experienced this scholastic training; but now, being released from that oath of allegiance which bound us to our old masters, and since, as becomes our riper years, we are no longer subject to the ferule, if we wish in earnest to establish for ourselves those rules which shall aid us in scaling the heights of human knowledge, we must admit assuredly among the primary members of our catalogue that maxim which forbids us to abuse our leisure as many do, who neglect all easy quests and take up their time only with difficult matters; for they, though certainly making all sorts of subtle conjectures and elaborating most plausible arguments with great ingenuity, frequently find too late that after all their labours they have only increased the multitude of their doubts, without acquiring any knowledge whatsoever.

But now let us proceed to explain more carefully our reasons for saying, as we did a little while ago, that of all the sciences known as yet, arithmetic and geometry alone are free from any taint of falsity or uncertainty. We must note then that there are two ways by which we arrive at the knowledge of facts, viz. by experience and by deduction. We must further observe that while our inferences from experience [4] are frequently fallacious, deduction, or the pure

4 *experientias*. This is a technical term used (like *experimentum*) for inductive arguments.

illation of one thing from another, though it may be passed over, if it is not seen through,[5] cannot be erroneous when performed by an understanding that is in the least degree rational. And it seems to me that the operation is profited but little by those constraining bonds by means of which the dialecticians claim to control human reason, though I do not deny that that discipline may be serviceable for other purposes. My reason for saying so is that none of the mistakes which men can make (men, I say, not beasts) are due to faulty inference; they are caused merely by the fact that we found upon a basis of poorly comprehended experiences, or that propositions are posited which are hasty and groundless.

This furnishes us with an evident explanation of the great superiority in certitude of arithmetic and geometry to other sciences. The former alone deal with an object so pure and uncomplicated, that they need make no assumptions at all which experience renders uncertain, but wholly consists in the rational deduction of consequences. They are on that account much the easiest and clearest of all, and possess an object such as we require, for in them it is scarce humanly possible for anyone to err except by inadvertence. And yet we should not be surprised to find that plenty of people of their own accord prefer to apply their intelligence to other studies, or to philosophy. The reason for this is that every person permits himself the liberty of making guesses in the matter of an obscure subject with more confidence than in one which is clear, and that it is much easier to have some vague notion about any subject, no matter what, than to arrive at the real truth about a single question however simple[6] that may be.

366

But one conclusion now emerges out of these considerations, viz. not, indeed, that arithmetic and geometry are the sole sciences to be studied, but only that in our search for the direct road towards truth we should busy ourselves with no object about which we cannot attain a certitude equal to that of the demonstrations of arithmetic and geometry.

---

5 *si non videatur*. Leibniz's manuscript adds in brackets *ea opus esse*. Translation: 'if it is not seen to be necessary'.
6 *facili*.

3 *In the subjects we propose to investigate, our inquiries should be directed, not to what others have thought,[7] nor to what we ourselves conjecture, but to what we can clearly and perspicuously behold and with certainty deduce; for knowledge is not won in any other way.*

To study the writings of the ancients is right, because it is a great boon for us to be able to make use of the labours of so many men; and we should do so, both in order to discover what they have correctly made out in previous ages, and also that we may inform ourselves as to what in the various sciences is still left for investigation. But yet there is a great danger lest in a too absorbed study of these works we should become infected with their errors, guard against them as we may. For it is the way of writers, whenever they have allowed themselves rashly and credulously to take up a position in any controverted matter, to try with the subtlest of arguments to compel us to go along with them. But when, on the contrary, they have happily come upon something certain and evident, in displaying it they never fail to surround it with ambiguities, fearing, it would seem, lest the simplicity of their explanation should make us respect their discovery less, or because they grudge us an open vision of the truth.

367

Further, supposing now that all were wholly open and candid, and never thrust upon us doubtful opinions as true, but expounded every matter in good faith, yet since scarce anything has been asserted by any one man the contrary of which has not been alleged by another, we should be eternally uncertain which of the two to believe. It would be no use to total up the testimonies in favour of each, meaning to follow that opinion which was supported by the greater number of authors; for if it is a question of difficulty that is in dispute, it is more likely that the truth would have been discovered by few than by many. But even though all these men agreed among themselves, what they teach us would not suffice for us. For we shall not, e.g. all turn out to be mathematicians though we know by heart all the proofs that others have elaborated, unless we have an intellectual talent that fits us to resolve difficulties of any kind. Neither, though we have mastered all the arguments of Plato and Aristotle, if yet we have not the capacity for passing a solid judgment on these matters, shall we

7 *senserint.*

become philosophers; we should have acquired the knowledge not of a science, but of history.

I lay down the rule also, that we must wholly refrain from ever mixing up conjectures with our pronouncements on the truth of things. This warning is of no little importance. There is no stronger reason for our finding nothing in the current[8] philosophy which is so evident and certain as not to be capable of being controverted, than the fact that the learned, not content with the recognition of what is clear and certain, in the first instance hazard the assertion of obscure and ill-comprehended theories, at which they have arrived merely by probable conjecture. Then afterwards they gradually attach complete credence to them, and mingling them promiscuously with what is true and evident, they finish by being unable to deduce any conclusion which does not appear to depend upon some proposition of the doubtful sort, and hence is not uncertain.

But lest we in turn should slip into the same error, we shall here take note of all those mental operations by which we are able, wholly without fear of illusion, to arrive at the knowledge of things. Now I admit only two, viz. intuition and deduction.[9]

By intuition I understand, not the fluctuating testimony of the senses, nor the misleading judgment that proceeds from the blundering constructions of imagination, but the conception which an unclouded and attentive mind gives us so readily and distinctly that we are wholly freed from doubt about that which we understand. Or, what comes to the same thing, *intuition* is the undoubting conception of an unclouded[10] and attentive mind, and springs from the light of reason alone; it is more certain than deduction itself, in that it is simpler, though deduction, as we have noted above, cannot by us be erroneously conducted. Thus each individual can mentally have intuition of the fact that he exists, and that he thinks; that the triangle is bounded by three lines only, the sphere by a single superficies, and so on. Facts of such a kind are far more numerous than many people think, disdaining as they do to direct their attention upon such simple matters.

But in case anyone may be put out by this new use of the term

368

369

---

8 *vulgari.*
9 *inductio* reads the Amsterdam edition of 1701, but this is a printing error. It should read *deductio* — Ed.
10 *purae.*

intuition[11] and of other terms which in the following pages I am similarly compelled to dissever from their current meaning, I here make the general announcement that I pay no attention to the way in which particular terms have of late been employed in the schools, because it would have been difficult to employ the same terminology while my theory was wholly different. All that I take note of is the meaning of the Latin of each word, when, in cases where an appropriate term is lacking, I wish to transfer to the vocabulary that expresses my own meaning those that I deem most suitable.

This evidence and certitude, however, which belongs to intuition, is required not only in the enunciation of propositions, but also in discursive reasoning of whatever sort. For example consider this consequence: 2 and 2 amount to the same as 3 and 1. Now we need to see intuitively not only that 2 and 2 make 4, and that likewise 3 and 1 make 4, but further that the third of the above statements is a necessary conclusion from these two.

Hence now we are in a position to raise the question as to why we have, besides intuition, given this supplementary method of knowing, viz. knowing by *deduction,* by which we understand all necessary inference from other facts that are known with certainty. This, however, we could not avoid, because many things are known with certainty, though not by themselves evident, but only deduced from true and known principles by the continuous and uninterrupted action of a mind[12] that has a clear vision of each step in the process. It is in a similar way that we know that the last link in a long chain is connected with the first, even though we do not take in by means of one and the same act of vision all the intermediate links on which that connection depends, but only remember that we have taken them successively under review and that each single one is united to its neighbour, from the first even to the last. Hence we distinguish this mental intuition from deduction by the fact that into the conception of the latter there enters a certain movement or succession, into that of the former there does not. Further deduction does not require an immediately presented evidence such as intuition possesses; its certitude is rather conferred upon it in some way by memory. The upshot of the matter is that it

370

11 *intuitus* is but sparingly used in Descartes' later writings.
12 *cogitationis.*

is possible to say that those propositions indeed which are immediately deduced from first principles are known now by intuition, now by deduction, i.e. in a way that differs according to our point of view. But the first principles themselves are given by intuition alone, while, on the contrary, the remote conclusions are furnished only by deduction.

These two methods are the most certain routes to knowledge, and the mind should admit no others. All the rest should be rejected as suspect of error and dangerous. But this does not prevent us from believing matters that have been divinely revealed as being more certain than our surest knowledge, since belief in these things,[13] as all faith in obscure matters,[14] is an action not of our intelligence,[15] but of our will. They should be heeded also since, if they have any basis in our understanding, they can and ought to be, more than all things else, discovered by one or other of the ways above mentioned, as we hope perhaps to show at greater length on some future opportunity.

4   *There is need of a method for finding out the truth.*

371

So blind is the curiosity by which mortals are possessed, that they often conduct their minds along unexplored routes, having no reason to hope for success, but merely being willing to risk the experiment of finding whether the truth they seek lies there. As well might a man burning with an unintelligent desire to find treasure, continuously roam the streets, seeking to find something that a passer by might have chanced to drop. This is the way in which most chemists, many geometricians, and philosophers not a few prosecute their studies. I do not deny that sometimes in these wanderings they are lucky enough to find something true. But I do not allow that this argues greater industry on their part, but only better luck. But however that may be, it were far better never to think of investigating truth at all, than to do so without a method. For it is very certain that unregulated inquiries and confused reflections of this kind only confound the natural light and blind our

13 'that faith of ours,' Leibniz's manuscript.
14 [*ut*] *quaecunque est de obscuris.*
15 *ingenii.*

mental powers. Those who so become accustomed to walk in darkness weaken their eyesight so much that afterwards they cannot bear the light of day. This is confirmed by experience; for how often do we not see that those who have never taken to letters, give a sounder and clearer decision about obvious matters than those who have spent all their time in the schools? Moreover by a method I mean certain and simple rules, such that, if a man observe them accurately, he shall never assume what is false as true, and will never spend his mental efforts to no purpose, but will always gradually increase his knowledge and so arrive at a true understanding of all that does not surpass his powers.

These two points must be carefully noted, viz. never to assume what is false as true, and to arrive at a knowledge which takes in all things. For, if we are without the knowledge of any of the things which we are capable of understanding, that is only because we have never perceived any way to bring us to this knowledge, or because we have fallen into the contrary error. But if our method rightly explains how our mental vision should be used, so as not to fall into the contrary error, and how deduction should be discovered in order that we may arrive at the knowledge of all things, I do not see what else is needed to make it complete; for I have already said that no science is acquired except by mental intuition or eduction. There is besides no question of extending it further in order to show how these said operations ought to be effected, because they are the most simple and primary of all. Consequently, unless our understanding were already able to employ them, it could comprehend none of the precepts of that very method, not even the simplest. But as for the other mental operations, which dialectic does its best to direct by making use of these prior ones, they are quite useless here; rather they are to be accounted impediments, because nothing can be added to the pure light of reason which does not in some way obscure it

Since then the usefulness of this method is so great that without it study seems to be harmful rather than profitable, I am quite ready to believe that the greater minds of former ages had some knowledge of it, nature even conducting them to it. For the human mind has in it something that we may call divine, wherein are scattered the first germs of useful modes of thought. Consequently it often happens that however much neglected and choked by interfering studies they bear fruit of their own accord. Arithmetic and geometry, the simplest sciences, give us an instance of this; for we have sufficient evidence that the ancient geometricians made use of a certain analysis which they extended to the resolution of all problems, though they grudged the secret to posterity. At the present day also there flourishes a certain kind of arithmetic, called algebra, which designs to effect, when dealing with numbers, what the ancients achieved in the matter of figures. These two methods are nothing else than the spontaneous fruit sprung from the inborn principles of the discipline here in question; and I do not wonder that these sciences with their very simple subject matter[16] should have yielded results so much more satisfactory than others in which greater obstructions choke all growth. But even in the latter case, if only we take care to cultivate them assiduously, fruits will certainly be able to come to full maturity.

This is the chief result which I have had in view in writing this treatise. For I should not think much of these rules, if they had no utility save for the solution of the empty problems with which logicians and geometers have been wont to beguile their leisure; my only achievement thus would have seemed to be an ability to argue about trifles more subtly than others. Further, though much mention is here made of numbers and figures, because no other sciences furnish us with illustrations of such self-evidence and certainty, the reader who follows my drift with sufficient attention will easily see that nothing is less in my mind than ordinary mathematics, and that I am expounding quite another science, of which these illustrations are rather the outer husk than the constituents. Such a science should contain the primary rudiments of human reasons and its province ought to extend to the eliciting of true results in every subject. To speak freely, I am convinced that it is a more powerful instrument of knowledge than any other that has been bequeathed to us by human agency, as being the source of all others. But as for the outer covering I mentioned, I mean not to employ it to cover up and conceal my method for the purpose of warding off the vulgar; rather I hope so to clothe and embellish it that I may make it more suitable for presentation to the human mind.

When first I applied my mind to mathematics I read straight away

374

16 *objecta.*

most of what is usually given by the mathematical writers, and I paid special attention to arithmetic and geometry, because they were said to be the simplest and so to speak the way to all the rest. But in

375   neither case did I then meet with authors who fully satisfied me. I did indeed learn in their works many propositions about numbers which I found on calculation to be true. As to figures, they in a sense exhibited to my eyes a great number of truths and drew conclusions from certain consequences. But they did not seem to make it sufficiently plain to the mind itself that those things are so, and how they discovered them. Consequently I was not surprised that many people, even of talent and scholarship, should, after glancing at these sciences, have either given them up as being empty and childish or, taking them to be very difficult and intricate, been deterred at the very outset from learning them. For really there is nothing more futile than to busy one's self with bare numbers and imaginary figures in such a way as to appear to rest content with such trifles, and so to resort to those superficial demonstrations, which are discovered more frequently by chance than by skill, and are a matter more of the eyes and the imagination than of the understanding, that in a sense one ceases to make use of one's reason. I might add that there is no more intricate task than that of solving by this method of proof new difficulties that arise, involved as they are with numerical confusions. But when I afterwards bethought myself how it could be that the earliest pioneers of philosophy in bygone ages refused to admit to the study of wisdom any one who was not versed in mathematics, evidently believing that this was the easiest and most indispensable mental exercise and preparation for laying hold of other more important sciences, I was confirmed in my suspicion that they had knowledge of a species of mathematics very different from that which passes current in our time. I do not indeed imagine that they had a perfect knowledge of it, for they plainly show how little advanced they were by the insensate rejoicings they display and the pompous thanksgivings[17] they offer for the most trifling discoveries. I am not shaken in my opinion by the fact that historians make a great deal of certain machines of theirs. Possibly these machines were quite simple, and yet the ignorant and wonder-loving multitude might easily have

376

17 *sacrificia*.

lauded them as miraculous. But I am convinced that certain primary germs of truth implanted by nature in human minds – though in our case the daily reading and hearing of innumerable diverse errors stifle them – had a very great vitality in that rude and unsophisticated age of the ancient world. Thus the same mental illumination which let them see that virtue was to be preferred to pleasure, and honour to utility, although they knew not why this was so, made them recognise true notions in philosophy and mathematics, although they were not yet able thoroughly to grasp these sciences. Indeed I seem to recognise certain traces of this true mathematics in Pappus and Diophantus, who though not belonging to the earliest age, yet lived many centuries before our own times. But my opinion is that these writers then with a sort of low cunning, deplorable indeed, suppressed this knowledge. Possibly they acted just as many inventors are known to have done in the case of their discoveries, i.e. they feared that their method being so easy and simple would become cheapened on being divulged, and they preferred to exhibit in its place certain barren truths, deductively demonstrated with show enough of ingenuity, as the results of their art, in order to win from us our admiration for these achievements, rather than to disclose to us that method itself which would have wholly annulled the admiration accorded. Finally there have been certain men of talent who in the present age have tried to revive this same art. For it seems to be precisely that science known by the barbarous name algebra, if only we could extricate it from that vast array of numbers and inexplicable figures by which it is overwhelmed, so that it might display the clearness and simplicity which, we imagine, ought to exist in a genuine mathematics. It was these reflections that recalled me from the particular studies of arithmetic and geometry to a general investigation of mathematics, and thereupon I sought to determine what precisely was universally meant by that term, and why not only the above mentioned sciences, but also astronomy, music, optics, mechanics and several others are styled parts of mathematics. Here indeed it is not enough to look to the origin of the word; for since the name 'mathematics' means exactly the same thing as 'scientific study',[18] these other branches could, with as much right as geometry itself, be called

377

18 *disciplina*.

mathematics. Yet we see that almost anyone who has had the slightest schooling can easily distinguish what relates to mathematics in any question from that which belongs to the other sciences. But as I considered the matter carefully it gradually came to light that all those matters only were referred to mathematics in which order and measurement are investigated, and that it makes no difference whether it be in numbers, figures, stars, sounds or any other object that the question of measurement arises. I saw consequently that there must be some general science to explain that element as a whole which gives rise to problems about order and measurement, restricted as these are to no special subject matter. This, I perceived, was called 'universal mathematics', not a far fetched designation, but one of long standing which has passed into current use, because in this science is contained everything on account of which the others are called parts of mathematics. We can see how much it excels in utility and simplicity the sciences subordinate to it, by the fact that it can deal with all the objects of which they have cognisance and many more besides, and that any difficulties it contains are found in them as well, added to the fact that in them fresh difficulties arise due to their special subject matter which in it do not exist. But now how comes it that though everyone knows the name of this science and understands what is its province even without studying it attentively, so many people laboriously pursue the other dependent sciences, and no one cares to master this one? I should marvel indeed were I not aware that everyone thinks it to be so very easy, and had I not long since observed that the human mind passes over what it thinks it can easily accomplish, and hastens straight away to new and more imposing occupations.

I, however, conscious as I am of my inadequacy, have resolved that in my investigation into truth I shall follow obstinately such an order as will require me first to start with what is simplest and easiest, and never permit me to proceed farther until in the first sphere there seems to be nothing further to be done. This is why up to the present time to the best of my ability I have made a study of this universal mathematics; consequently I believe that when I go on to deal in their turn with more profound sciences, as I hope to do soon, my efforts will not be premature. But before I make this transition I shall try to bring together and arrange in an orderly manner, the facts which in my previous studies I have noted as

378

379

being more worthy of attention. Thus I hope both that at a future date, when through advancing years my memory is enfeebled, I shall, if need be, conveniently be able to recall them by looking in this little book, and that having now disburdened my memory of them I may be free to concentrate my mind on my future studies.

5 *Method consists entirely in the order and disposition of the objects towards which our mental vision must be directed if we would find out any truth. We shall comply with it exactly if we reduce involved and obscure propositions step by step to those that are simpler, and then starting with the intuitive apprehension of all those that are absolutely simple, attempt to ascend to the knowledge of all others by precisely similar steps.*

In this alone lies the sum of all human endeavour, and he who would approach the investigation of truth must hold to this rule as closely as he who enters the labyrinth must follow the thread which guided Theseus. But many people either do not reflect on the precept at all, or ignore it altogether, or presume not to need it. Consequently they often investigate the most difficult questions with so little regard to order, that, to my mind, they act like a man who should attempt to leap with one bound from the base to the summit of a house, either making no account of the ladders provided for his ascent or not noticing them. It is thus that all astrologers behave, who, though in ignorance of the nature of the heavens, and even without having made proper observations of the movements of the heavenly bodies, expect to be able to indicate their effects. This is also what many do who study mechanics apart from physics, and rashly set about devising new instruments for producing motion. Along with them go also those philosophers who, neglecting experience, imagine that truth will spring from their brain like Pallas[19] from the head of Zeus.[20]

380

Now it is obvious that all such people violate the present rule. But since the order here required is often so obscure and intricate that not everyone can make it out, they can scarcely avoid error unless they diligently observe what is laid down in the following proposition.

19 *Minerva.*
20 *Jovis.*

381 **6** *In order to separate out what is quite simple from what is complex, and to arrange these matters methodically, we ought, in the case of every series in which we have deduced certain facts the one from the other, to notice which fact is simple, and to mark the interval, greater, less, or equal, which separates all the others from this.*

Although this proposition seems to teach nothing very new, it contains, nevertheless, the chief secret of method, and none in the whole of this treatise is of greater utility. For it tells us that all facts can be arranged in certain series, not indeed in the sense of being referred to some ontological genus such as the categories employed by philosophers in their classification, but in so far as certain truths can be known from others; and thus, whenever a difficulty occurs we are able at once to perceive whether it will be profitable to examine certain others first, and which, and in what order.

Further, in order to do that correctly, we must note first that for the purpose of our procedure, which does not regard things as isolated realities,[21] but compares them with one another in order to discover the dependence in knowledge of one upon the other, all things can be said to be either absolute or relative.

I call that absolute which contains within itself the pure and simple essence of which we are in quest. Thus the term will be applicable to whatever is considered as being independent, or a cause, or simple, universal, one, equal, like, straight, and so forth;

382 and the absolute I call the simplest and the easiest of all, so that we can make use of it in the solution of questions.

But the relative is that which, while participating in the same nature, or at least sharing in it to some degree which enables us to relate it to the absolute and to deduce it from that by a chain of operations, involves in addition something else in its concept which I call relativity.[22] Examples of this are found in whatever is said to be dependent, or an effect, composite, particular, many, unequal, unlike, oblique, etc. These relatives are the further removed from the absolute, in proportion as they contain more elements of relativity subordinate the one to the other. We state in this rule that these should all be distinguished and their correlative connection and natural order so observed, that we may be able by traversing all

21 *naturas.*
22 *respectus.*

the intermediate steps to proceed from the most remote to that which is in the highest degree absolute.

Herein lies the secret of this whole method, that in all things we should diligently mark that which is most absolute. For some things are from one point of view more absolute than others, but from a different standpoint are more relative. Thus though the universal is more absolute than the particular because its essence is simpler, yet it can be held to be more relative than the latter, because it depends upon individuals for its existence, and so on. Certain things likewise are truly more absolute than others, but yet are not the most absolute of all. Thus relatively to individuals, species is something absolute, but contrasted with genus it is relative. So too, among things that can be measured, extension is something absolute, but among the various aspects of extension[23] it is length that is absolute, and so on. Finally also, in order to bring out more clearly that we are considering here not the nature of each thing taken in isolation, but the series involved in knowing them, we have purposely enumerated cause and equality among our absolutes, though the nature of these terms is really relative. For though philosophers make cause and effect correlative, we find that here even, if we ask what the effect is, we must first know the cause and not conversely. Equals too mutually imply one another, but we can know unequals only by comparing them with equals and not *per contra*.

Secondly we must note that there are but few pure and simple essences,[24] which either our experiences or some sort of light innate in us enable us to behold as primary and existing *per se*, not as depending on any others. These we say should be carefully noticed, for they are just those facts which we have called the simplest in any single series. All the others can only be perceived as deductions from these, either immediate and proximate, or not to be attained save by two or three or more acts of inference. The number of these acts should be noted in order that we may perceive whether the facts are separated from the primary and simplest proposition by a greater or smaller number of steps. And so pronounced is everywhere the inter-connection of ground and consequence, which gives rise, in the objects to be examined, to those series to which every inquiry

383

23 *extensiones*.
24 *naturas*.

384   must be reduced, that it can be investigated by a sure method. But because it is not easy to make a review of them all, and besides, since they have not so much to be kept in the memory as to be detected by a sort of mental penetration, we must seek for something which will so mould our intelligence as to let it perceive these connected sequences immediately whenever it needs to do so. For this purpose I have found nothing so effectual as to accustom ourselves to turn our attention with a sort of penetrative insight[25] on the very minutest of the facts which we have already discovered.

Finally we must in the third place note that our inquiry ought not to start with the investigation of difficult matters. Rather, before setting out to attack any definite problem, it behoves us first, without making any selection, to assemble those truths that are obvious as they present themselves to us, and afterwards, proceeding step by step, to inquire whether any others can be deduced from these, and again any others from these conclusions and so on, in order. This done, we should attentively think over the truths we have discovered and mark with diligence the reasons why we have been able to detect some more easily than others, and which these are. Thus, when we come to attack some definite problem we shall be able to judge what previous questions it were best to settle first. For example, if it comes into my thought that the number 6 is twice 3, I may then ask what is twice 6, viz. 12; again, perhaps I seek for the double of this, viz. 24, and again of this, viz. 48. Thus I may easily deduce that there is the same proportion between 3 and 6, as between 6 and 12, and likewise 12 and 24, and so on, and hence that the numbers 3, 6, 12, 24, 48, etc. are in continued proportion. But though these facts are all so clear as to seem almost childish, I am now able by attentive reflection to understand what is the form

385   involved by all questions that can be propounded about the proportions or relations[26] of things, and the order in which they should be investigated; and this discovery embraces the sum of the entire science of pure mathematics.

For first I perceive that it was not more difficult to discover the double of six than that of three; and that equally in all cases, when we have found a proportion between any two magnitudes, we can

25 *cum quadam sagacitate.*
26 *habitudines.*

find innumerable others which have the same proportion between them. So too there is no increase of difficulty, if three, or four, or more of such magnitudes are sought for, because each has to be found separately and without any relation to the others. But next I notice that though, when the magnitudes 3 and 6 are given, one can easily find a third in continued proportion, viz. 12, it is yet not equally easy, when the two extremes, 3 and 12, are given, to find the mean proportional, viz. 6. When we look into the reason for this, it is clear that here we have a type of difficulty quite different from the former; for, in order to find the mean proportional, we must at the same time attend to the two extremes and to the proportion which exists between these two in order to discover a new ratio by dividing the previous one; and this is a very different thing from finding a third term in continued proportion with two given numbers. I go forward likewise and examine whether, when the numbers 3 and 24 were given, it would have been equally easy to determine one of the two intermediate proportionals, viz. 6 and 12. But here still another sort of difficulty arises more involved than the previous ones, for on this occasion we have to attend not to one or two things only but to three, in order to discover the fourth. We may go still further and inquire whether if only 3 and 48 had been given it would have been still more difficult to discover one of the three mean proportionals, viz. 6, 12, and 24. At the first blush this indeed appears to be so; but immediately afterwards it comes to mind that this difficulty can be split up and lessened, if first of all we ask only for the mean proportional between 3 and 48, viz. 12, and then seek for the other mean proportional between 3 and 12, viz. 6, and the other between 12 and 48, viz. 24. Thus we have reduced the problem to the difficulty of the second type shown above.

These illustrations further lead me to note that the quest for knowledge about the same thing can traverse different routes, the one much more difficult and obscure than the other. Thus to find these four continued proportionals, 3, 6, 12, and 24, if two consecutive numbers be assumed, e.g. 3 and 6, or 6 and 12, or 12 and 24, in order that we may discover the others, our task will be easy. In this case we shall say that the proposition to be discovered is directly examined. But if the two numbers given are alternates, like 3 and 12, or 6 and 24, which are to lead us to the discovery of the others, then we shall call this an indirect investigation of the first

mode. Likewise if we are given two extremes like 3 and 24, in order
to find out from these the intermediates 6 and 12, the investigation
will be indirect and of the second mode. Thus I should be able to
proceed further and deduce many other results from this example;
but these will be sufficient, if the reader follows my meaning when I
say that a proposition is directly deduced, or indirectly, and will
reflect that from a knowledge of each of these matters that are
simplest and primary, much may be discovered in other sciences by
those who bring to them attentive thought and a power of sagacious
analysis.

7 *If we wish our science to be complete, those matters which promote the end
we have in view must one and all be scrutinised by a movement of thought
which is continuous and nowhere interrupted; they must also be included in
an enumeration which is both adequate and methodical.*

It is necessary to obey the injunctions of this rule if we hope to gain
admission among the certain truths for those which, we have
declared above, are not immediate deductions from primary and
self-evident principles. For this deduction frequently involves such a
long series of transitions from ground to consequent that when we
come to the conclusion we have difficulty in recalling the whole of
the route by which we have arrived at it. This is why I say that there
must be a continuous movement of thought to make good this
weakness of the memory. Thus, e.g. if I have first found out by
separate mental operations what the relation is between the
magnitudes A and B, then what between B and C, between C and
D, and finally between D and E, that does not entail my seeing what
the relation is between A and E, nor can the truths previously learnt
give me a precise knowledge of it unless I recall them all. To
remedy this I would run them over from time to time, keeping the
imagination moving continuously in such a way that while it is
intuitively perceiving each fact it simultaneously passes on to the
next; and this I would do until I had learned to pass from the first to
the last so quickly, that no stage in the process was left to the care of
the memory, but I seemed to have the whole in intuition before me
at the same time. This method will both relieve the memory,
diminish the sluggishness of our thinking, and definitely enlarge our
mental capacity.

But we must add that this movement should nowhere be interrupted. Often people who attempt to deduce a conclusion too quickly and from remote principles do not trace the whole chain of intermediate conclusions with sufficient accuracy to prevent them from passing over many steps without due consideration. But it is certain that wherever the smallest link is left out the chain is broken and the whole of the certainty of the conclusion falls to the ground.

Here we maintain that an enumeration [of the steps in a proof] is required as well, if we wish to make our science complete. For resolving most problems other precepts are profitable, but enumeration alone will secure our always passing a true and certain judgment on whatsoever engages our attention; by means of it nothing at all will escape us, but we shall evidently have some knowledge of every step.

This enumeration or induction is thus a review or inventory of all those matters that have a bearing on the problem raised, which is so thorough and accurate that by its means we can clearly and with confidence conclude that we have omitted nothing by mistake. Consequently as often as we have employed it, if the problem defies us, we shall at least be wiser in this respect, viz. that we are quite certain that we know of no way of resolving it. If it chance, as often it does, that we have been able to scan all the routes leading to it which lie open to the human intelligence, we shall be entitled boldly to assert that the solution of the problem lies outside the reach of human knowledge.

Furthermore we must note that by adequate enumeration or induction is only meant that method by which we may attain surer conclusions than by any other type of proof, with the exception of simple intuition. But when the knowledge of some matter cannot be reduced to this, we must cast aside all syllogistic fetters and employ induction, the only method left us, but one in which all confidence should be reposed. For whenever single facts have been immediately deduced the one from the other, they have been already reduced, if the inference was evident, to a true intuition. But if we infer any single thing from various and disconnected facts, often our intellectual capacity is not so great as to be able to embrace them all in a single intuition; in which case our mind should be content with the certitude attaching to this operation. It is in precisely similar fashion that though we cannot with one single gaze

389

distinguish all the links of a lengthy chain, yet if we have seen the connection of each with its neighbour, we shall be entitled to say that we have seen how the first is connected with the last.

I have declared that this operation ought to be adequate, because it is often in danger of being defective and consequently exposed to error. For sometimes, even though in our enumeration we scrutinise many facts which are highly evident, yet if we omit the smallest step the chain is broken and the whole of the certitude of the conclusion falls to the ground. Sometimes also, even though all the facts are included in an accurate enumeration, the single steps are not distinguished from one another, and our knowledge of them all is thus only confused.

Further, while now the enumeration ought to be complete, now distinct, there are times when it need have neither of these characters; it was for this reason that I said only that it should be adequate. For if I want to prove by enumeration how many genera there are of corporeal things, or of those that in any way fall under the senses, I shall not assert that they are just so many and no more, unless I previously have become aware that I have included them all in my enumeration, and have distinguished them each separately from all the others. But if in the same way I wish to prove that the rational soul is not corporeal, I do not need a complete enumeration; it will be sufficient to include all bodies in certain collections in such a way as to be able to demonstrate that the rational soul has nothing to do with any of these. If, finally, I wish to show by enumeration that the area of a circle is greater than the area of all other figures whose perimeter is equal, there is no need for me to call in review all other figures; it is enough to demonstrate this of certain others in particular, in order to get thence by induction[27] the same conclusion about all the others.

I added also that the enumeration ought to be methodical. This is both because we have no more serviceable remedy for the defects already instanced, than to scan all things in an orderly manner; and also because it often happens that if each single matter which concerns the quest in hand were to be investigated separately, no man's life would be long enough for the purpose, whether because they are far too many, or because it would chance that the same

27 This seems to be a different sense of the word *inductio* from that above.

things had to be repeated too often. But if all these facts are arranged in the best order, they will for the most part be reduced to determinate classes, out of which it will be sufficient to take one example for exact inspection, or some one feature in a single case, or certain things rather than others, or at least we shall never have to waste our time in traversing the same ground twice. The advantage of this course is so great that often many particulars can, owing to a well devised arrangement, be gone over in a short space of time and with little trouble, though at first view the matter looked immense.

But this order which we employ in our enumerations can for the most part be varied and depends upon each man's judgment. For this reason, if we would elaborate it in our thought with greater penetration, we must remember what was said in our fifth proposition.[28] There are also many of the trivial things of man's devising, in the discovery of which the whole method lies in the disposal of this order. Thus if you wish to construct a perfect anagram by the transposition of the letters of a name, there is no need to pass from the easy to the difficult, nor to distinguish absolute from relative. Here there is no place for these operations; it will be sufficient to adopt an order to be followed in the transpositions of the letters which we are to examine, such that the same arrangements are never handled twice over. The total number of transpositions should, e.g. be split up into definite classes, so that it may immediately appear in which there is the best hope of finding what is sought. In this way the task is often not tedious but merely child's play.

However, these three propositions should not be separated, because for the most part we have to think of them together, and all equally tend towards the perfecting of our method. There was no great reason for treating one before the other, and we have expounded them but briefly here. The reason for this is that in the rest of the treatise we have practically nothing else left for consideration. Therefore we shall then exhibit in detail what here we have brought together in a general way.

392

28 See p.17.

8 *If in the matters to be examined we come to a step in the series of which our understanding is not sufficiently well able to have an intuitive cognition, we must stop short there. We must make no attempt to examine what follows; thus we shall spare ourselves superfluous labour.*

The three preceding rules prescribe and explain the order to be followed. The present rule, on the other hand, shows when it is wholly necessary and when it is merely useful. Thus it is necessary to examine whatever constitutes a single step in that series, by which we pass from relative to absolute, or conversely, before discussing what follows from it. But if, as often happens, many things pertain to the same step, though it is indeed always profitable to review them in order, in this case we are not forced to apply our method of observation so strictly and rigidly. Frequently it is permissible to proceed farther, even though we have not clear knowledge of all the facts it involves, but know only a few or a single one of them.

393

This rule is a necessary consequence of the reasons brought forward in support of the second. But it must not be thought that the present rule contributes nothing fresh towards the advancement of learning, though it seems only to bid us refrain from further discussion, and apparently does not unfold any truth. For beginners, indeed, it has no further value than to teach them how not to waste time, and it employs nearly the same arguments in doing so as Rule 2. But it shows those who have perfectly mastered the seven preceding maxims, how in the pursuit of any science so to satisfy themselves as not to desire anything further. For the man who faithfully complies with the former rules in the solution of any difficulty, and yet by the present rule is bidden desist at a certain point, will then know for certainty that no amount of application will enable him to attain to the knowledge desired, and that not owing to a defect in his intelligence, but because the nature of the problem itself, or the fact that he is human, prevents him. But this knowledge is not the less science than that which reveals the nature of the thing itself; in fact he would seem to have some mental defect who should extend his curiosity farther.

394

But what we have been saying must be illustrated by one or two examples. If, for example, one who studies only mathematics were to seek to find that curve which in dioptrics is called the anaclastic, that from which parallel rays are so refracted that after the refraction they all meet in one point, it will be easy to see, by applying Rules 5 and 6, that the determination of this line depends upon the relation which the angles of refraction bear to the angles of incidence. But because he is unable to discover this, since it is a matter not of mathematics but of physics, he is here forced to pause at the threshold. Nor will it avail him to try and learn this from the philosophers or to gather it from experience; for this would be to break Rule 3. Furthermore this proposition is both composite and relative; but in the proper place we shall show that experience is unambiguous only when dealing with the wholly simple and absolute. Again, it will be vain for him to assume some relation or other as being that which prevails between such angles, and conjecture that this is the truest to fact; for in that case he would be on the track not of the anaclastic, but merely of that curve which could be deduced from his assumption.

If, however, a man who does not confine his studies to mathematics, but, in accordance with the first rule, tries to discover the truth on all points, meets with the same difficulty, he will find in addition that this ratio between the angles of incidence and of refraction depends upon changes in their relation produced by varying the medium. Again these changes depend upon the manner in which the ray of light traverses the whole transparent body; while the knowledge of the way in which the light thus passes through presupposes a knowledge of the nature of the action of light, to understand which finally we must know what a natural potency is in general, this last being the most absolute term in the whole series in question. When, therefore, by a mental intuition he has clearly comprehended the nature of this, he will, in compliance with Rule 5, proceed backwards by the same steps. And if when he comes to the second step he is unable straightway to determine the nature of light, he will, in accordance with the seventh rule, enumerate all the other natural potencies, in order that the knowledge of some other of them may help him, at least by analogy (of which more anon), to understand this. This done, he will ask how the ray traverses the whole of the transparent body, and will so follow out the other points methodically, that at last he will arrive at the anaclastic itself: Though this has long defied the efforts of many inquirers, I see no reason why a man who fully carried out our method should fail to arrive at a convincing knowledge of the matter.

395

But let us give the most splendid example of all. If a man proposes to himself the problem of examining all the truths for the knowledge of which human reason suffices – and I think that this is a task which should be undertaken once at least in his life by every person who seriously endeavours to attain equilibrium[29] of thought – he will, by the rules given above, certainly discover that nothing can be known prior to the understanding, since the knowledge of all things else depends upon this and not conversely. Then, when he has clearly grasped all those things which follow proximately on the knowledge of the naked understanding, he will enumerate among other things whatever instruments of thought we have other than the understanding; and these are only two, viz. imagination and sense. He will therefore devote all his energies to the distinguishing and examining of these three modes of cognition, and seeing that in the strict sense truth and falsity can be a matter of the understanding alone, though often it derives its origin from the other two faculties, he will attend carefully to every source of deception in order that he may be on his guard. He will also enumerate exactly all the ways leading to truth which lie open to us, in order that he may follow the right way. They are not so many that they cannot all be easily discovered and embraced in an adequate enumeration. And though this will seem marvellous and incredible to the inexpert, as soon as in each matter he has distinguished those cognitions which only fill and embellish the memory, from those which cause one to be deemed really more instructed, which it will be easy for him to do . . . [30] he will feel assured that any absence of further knowledge is not due to lack of intelligence or of skill, and that nothing at all can be known by anyone else which he is not capable of knowing, provided only that he given to it his utmost mental application. And though many problems may present themselves, from the solution of which this rule prohibits him, yet because he will clearly perceive that they pass the limits of human intelligence, he will deem that he is not the more ignorant on that account; rather, if he is reasonable, this very knowledge, that the solution can be discovered by no one, will abundantly satisfy his curiosity.

But lest we should always be uncertain as to the powers of the

---

29 *bonam mentem.*
30 The Amsterdam edition of 1701 indicates an omission here.

mind, and in order that we may not labour wrongly and at random before we set ourselves to think out things in detail, we ought once in our life to inquire diligently what the thoughts are of which the human mind is capable. In order the better to attain this end we ought, when two sets of inquiries are equally simple, to choose the more useful.

397

This method of ours resembles indeed those devices employed by the mechanical crafts, which do not need the aid of anything outside of them, but themselves supply the directions for making their own instruments. Thus if a man wished to practise any one of them, e.g. the craft of a smith, and were destitute of all instruments, he would be forced to use at first a hard stone or a rough lump of iron as an anvil, take a piece of rock in place of the hammer, make pieces of wood serve as tongs, and provide himself with other such tools as necessity required. Thus equipped, he would not then at once attempt to forge swords or helmets or any manufactured article of iron for others to use. He would first of all fashion hammer, anvil, tongs, and the other tools useful for himself. This example teaches us that, since thus at the outset we have been able to discover only some rough precepts, apparently the innate possession of our mind, rather than the product of technical skill, we should not forthwith attempt to settle the controversies of philosophers, or solve the puzzles of the mathematicians, by their help. We must first employ them for searching out with our utmost attention all the other things that are more urgently required in the investigation of truth. And this since there is no reason why it should appear more difficult to discover these than any of the answers which the problems proposed by geometry or physics or the other sciences are wont to demand.

Now no more useful inquiry can be proposed than that which seeks to determine the nature and the scope of human knowledge. This is why we state this very problem succinctly in the single question, which we deem should be answered at the very outset with the aid of the rules which we have already laid down. This investigation should be undertaken once at least in his life by anyone who has the slightest regard for truth, since in pursuing it the true instruments of knowledge and the whole method of inquiry come to light. But nothing seems to me more futile than the conduct of those who boldly dispute about the secrets of nature, the influence of the heavens on these lower regions, the predicting of future events and

398

similar matters, as many do, without yet having ever asked even whether human reason is adequate to the solution of these problems. Neither ought it to seem such a toilsome and difficult matter to define the limits of that understanding[31] of which we are directly aware[32] as being within us, when we often have no hesitation in passing judgment even on things that are without us and quite foreign to us. Neither is it such an immense task to attempt to grasp in thought all the objects comprised within this whole of things, in order to discover how they singly fall under our mental scrutiny. For nothing can prove to be so complex or so vague as to defeat the efforts of the method of enumeration above described, directed towards restraining it within certain limits or arranging it under certain categories.[33] But to put this to the test in the matter of the question above propounded, we first of all divide the whole problem relative to it into two parts; for it ought either to relate to us who are capable of knowledge, or to the things themselves which can be known: and these two factors we discuss separately.

In ourselves we notice that while it is the understanding alone which is capable of knowing, it yet is either helped or hindered by three other faculties, namely imagination, sense, and memory. We must therefore examine these faculties in order, with a view to finding out where each may prove to be an impediment, so that we may be on our guard; or where it may profit us, so that we may use to the full the resources of these powers. This first part of our problem will accordingly be discussed with the aid of a sufficient enumeration, as will be shown in the succeeding proposition.

We come secondly to the things themselves which must be considered only in so far as they are the objects of the understanding. From this point of view we divide them into the class (1) of those whose nature is of the extremest simplicity, and (2) of the complex and composite. Simple natures must be either spiritual or corporeal or at once spiritual and corporeal. Finally among the composites there are some which the understanding realises to be complex before it judges that it can determine anything about them; but there are also others which it itself puts together. All these matters will be expounded at greater length in the twelfth proposition, where it will be shown that there can be no falsity save

399

---

31 *ingenii*. 32 *sentimus*. 33 *capita*.

in the last class – that of the compounds made by the understanding itself. This is why we further subdivide these into the class of those which are deducible from natures which are of the maximum simplicity and are known *per se*, of which we shall treat in the whole of the succeeding book;[34] and into those which presuppose the existence of others which the facts themselves show us to be composite. To the exposition of these we destine the whole of the third[35] book.

But we shall indeed attempt in the whole of this treatise to follow so accurately the paths which conduct men to the knowledge of the truth and to make them so easy, that anyone who has perfectly learned the whole of this method, however moderate may be his talent, may see that no avenue to the truth is closed to him from which everyone else is not also excluded, and that his ignorance is due neither to a deficiency in his capacity nor to his method of procedure. But as often as he applies his mind to the understanding of some matter, he will either be entirely successful, or he will realise that success depends upon a certain experiment which he is unable to perform, and in that case he will not blame his mental capacity although he is compelled to stop short there. Or finally he may show that the knowledge desired wholly exceeds the limits of the human intelligence; and consequently he will believe that he is none the more ignorant on that account. For to have discovered this is knowledge in no less degree than the knowledge of anything else.

400

9 *We ought to give the whole of our attention to the most insignificant and most easily mastered facts, and remain a long time in contemplation of them until we are accustomed to behold the truth clearly and distinctly.*

We have now indicated the two operations of our understanding, intuition and deduction, on which alone we have said we must rely in the acquisition of knowledge. Let us therefore in this and in the following proposition proceed to explain how we can render ourselves more skilful in employing them, and at the same time cultivate the two principal faculties of the mind, to wit perspicacity,

34 This begins at Rule 8. Of the later rules we have the titles only in the case of 19–21, while the last three are entirely lacking.
35 Apparently not even begun.

by viewing single objects distinctly, and sagacity, by the skilful deduction of certain facts from others.

Truly we shall learn how to employ our mental intuition from comparing it with the way in which we employ our eyes. For he who attempts to view a multitude of objects with one and the same glance, sees none of them distinctly; and similarly the man who is wont to attend to many things at the same time by means of a single act of thought is confused in mind. But just as workmen, who are employed in very fine and delicate operations and are accustomed to direct their eyesight attentively to separate points, by practice have acquired a capacity for distinguishing objects of extreme minuteness and subtlety; so likewise people who do not allow their thought to be distracted by various objects at the same time, but always concentrate it in attending to the simplest and easiest particulars, are clear-headed.

But it is a common failing of mortals to deem the more difficult the fairer; and they often think that they have learned nothing when they see a very clear and simple cause for a fact, while at the same time they are lost in admiration of certain sublime and profound philosophical explanations, even though these for the most part are based upon foundations which no one has adequately surveyed – a mental disorder which prizes the darkness higher than the light. But it is notable that those who have real knowledge discern the truth with equal facility whether they evolve it from matter that is simple or that is obscure; they grasp each fact by an act of thought that is similar, single, and distinct, after they have once arrived at the point in question. The whole of the difference between the apprehension of the simple and of the obscure lies in the route taken, which certainly ought to be longer if it conducts us from our initial and most absolute principles to a truth that is somewhat remote.

Everyone ought therefore to accustom himself to grasp in his thought at the same time facts that are at once so few and so simple, that he shall never believe that he has knowledge of anything which he does not mentally behold with a distinctness equal to that of the objects which he knows most distinctly of all. It is true that some men are born with a much greater aptitude for such discernment than others, but the mind can be made much more expert at such work by art and exercise. But there is one fact which I should here emphasise above all others; and that is that everyone should firmly persuade himself that none of the sciences, however abstruse, is to be deduced from lofty and obscure matters, but that they all proceed only from what is easy and more readily understood.

For example if I wish to examine whether it is possible for a natural force to pass at one and the same moment to a spot at a distance and yet to traverse the whole space in between, I shall not begin to study the force of magnetism or the influence of the stars, not even the speed of light, in order to discover whether actions such as these occur instantaneously; for the solution of this question would be more difficult than the problem proposed. I should rather bethink myself of the spatial motions of bodies, because nothing in the sphere of motion can be found more obvious to sense than this. I shall observe that while a storm cannot pass to another place in one and the same moment, because it is a body, yet a force similar to that which moves the stone is communicated exactly instantaneously if it passes unencumbered[36] from one object to another. For instance, if I move one end of a stick of whatever length, I easily understand that the power by which that part of the stick is moved necessarily moves also all its other parts at the same moment, because then the force passes unencumbered and is not imprisoned in any body, e.g. a stone, which bears it along.

In the same way if I wish to understand how one and the same simple cause can produce contrary effects at the same time, I shall not cite the drugs of the doctors which expel certain humours and retain others; nor shall I romance about the moon's power of warming with its light and chilling by means of some occult power. I shall rather cast my eyes upon the balance in which the same weight raises one arm at the same time as it depresses the other, or take some other familiar instance.

10 *In order that it may acquire sagacity the mind should be exercised in pursuing just those inquiries of which the solution has already been found by others; and it ought to traverse in a systematic way even the most trifling of men's inventions, though those ought to be preferred in which order is explained or implied.*

I confess that my natural disposition is such that I have always found, not the following of the arguments of others, but the discovery of

36 *nuda.*

reasons by my own proper efforts, to yield me the highest intellectual satisfaction. It was this alone that attracted me, when I was still a young man, to the study of science. And whenever any book by its title promised some new discovery, before I read further, I tried whether I could achieve something similar by means of some inborn faculty of invention,[37] and I was careful lest a premature perusal of the book might deprive me of this harmless pleasure. So often was I successful that at length I perceived that I no longer came upon the truth by proceeding as others commonly do, viz. by pursuing vague and blind inquiries and relying more on good fortune than on skill. I saw that by long experience I had discovered certain rules which are of no little help in this inquiry, and which I used afterwards in devising further rules. Thus it was that I diligently elaborated the whole of this method and came to the conclusion that I had followed that plan of study which was the most fruitful of all.

404

But because not all minds are so much inclined to puzzle things out unaided, this proposition announces that we ought not immediately to occupy ourselves with the more difficult and arduous problems, but first should discuss those disciplines[38] which are easiest and simplest, and those above all in which order most prevails. Such are the arts of the craftsmen who weave webs and tapestry, or of women who embroider or use in the same work threads with infinite modification of texture. With these are ranked all play with numbers and everything that belongs to arithmetic, and the like. It is wonderful how all these studies discipline our mental powers, provided that we do not know the solutions from others, but invent them ourselves. For since nothing in these arts remains hidden, and they are wholly adjusted to the capacity of human cognition, they reveal to us with the greatest distinctness innumerable orderly systems, all different from each other, but none the less conforming to rule, in the proper observance of which systems of order consists the whole of human sagacity.

It was for this reason that we insisted that method must be employed in studying those matters; and this in those arts of less importance consists wholly in the close observation of the order which is found in the object studied, whether that be an order

37 *sagacitatem.*   38 *artes.*

existing in the thing itself, or due to subtle human devising. Thus if we wish to make out some writing in which the meaning is disguised by the use of a cypher, though the order here fails to present itself, we yet make up an imaginary one, for the purpose both of testing all the conjectures we may make about single letters, words or sentences, and in order to arrange them so that when we sum them up we shall be able to tell all the inferences that we can deduce from them. We must principally beware of wasting our time in such cases by proceeding at random and unmethodically; for even though the solution can often be found without method, and by lucky people sometimes quicker, yet such procedure is likely to enfeeble the faculties and to make people accustomed to the trifling and the childish, so that for the future their minds will stick on the surface of things, incapable of penetrating beyond it. But meanwhile we must not fall into the error of those who, having devoted themselves solely to what is lofty and serious, find that after many years of toil they have acquired, not the profound knowledge they hoped for, but only mental confusion. Hence we must give ourselves practice first in those easier disciplines, but methodically, so that by open and familiar ways we may ceaselessly accustom ourselves to penetrate as easily as though we were at play into the very heart of these subjects. For by this means we shall afterwards gradually feel (and in a space of time shorter than we could at all hope for) that we are in a position with equal facility to deduce from evident first principles many propositions which at first sight are highly intricate and difficult.

It may perhaps strike some with surprise that here, where we are discussing how to improve our power of deducing one truth from another, we have omitted all the precepts of the dialecticians, by which they think to control the human reason. They prescribe certain formulae of argument, which lead to a conclusion with such necessity that, if the reason commits itself to their trust, even though it slackens its interest and no longer pays a heedful and close attention to the very proposition inferred, it can nevertheless at the same time come to a sure conclusion by virtue of the form of the argument alone. Exactly so; the fact is that frequently we notice that often the truth escapes away out of these imprisoning bonds, while the people themselves who have used them in order to capture it remain entangled in them. Other people are not so frequently

405

406

entrapped; and it is a matter of experience that the most ingenious sophisms hardly ever impose on anyone who uses his unaided reason, while they are wont to deceive the sophists themselves.

Wherefore as we wish here to be particularly careful lest our reason should go on holiday while we are examining the truth of any matter, we reject those formulae as being opposed to our project, and look out rather for all the aids by which our thought may be kept attentive, as will be shown in the sequel. But, to say a few words more, that it may appear still more evident that this style of argument contributes nothing at all to the discovery of the truth we must note that the dialecticians are unable to devise any syllogism which has a true conclusion, unless they have first secured the material out of which to construct it, i.e. unless they have already ascertained the very truth which is deduced in that syllogism. Whence it is clear that from a formula of this kind they can gather nothing that is new, and hence the ordinary dialectic is quite valueless for those who desire to investigate the truth of things, Its only possible use is to serve to explain at times more easily to others the truths we have already ascertained; hence it should be transferred from philosophy to rhetoric.

407   11 *If, after we have acquired intuitively a number of simple truths, we wish to draw any inference from them, it is useful to run them over in a continuous and uninterrupted act of thought, to reflect upon their relations to one another, and to group together distinctly a number of these propositions so far as is possible at the same time. For this is a way of making our knowledge much more certain, and of greatly increasing the power of the mind.*

Here we have an opportunity of expounding more clearly what has been already said of mental intuition in the third and seventh rules.[39] In one passage[40] we opposed it to deduction, while in the other we distinguished it from enumeration only, which we defined as an inference drawn from many and diverse things'.[41] But the simple deduction of one thing from another, we said in the same passage,[42] was effected by intuition.

It was necessary to do this, because two things are requisite for mental intuition. Firstly the proposition intuited must be clear and

39 pp. 8 and 22.   40 pp. 9 and 10.   41 p. 23.   42 pp. 10 and 11.

distinct; secondly it must be grasped in its totality at the same time and not successively. As for deduction, if we are thinking of how the process works, as we were in Rule 3, it appears not to occur all at the same time, but involves a sort of movement on the part of our mind when it infers one thing from another. We were justified therefore in distinguishing deduction in that rule from intuition. But if we wish to consider deduction as an accomplished fact, as we did in what we said relatively to the seventh rule, then it no longer designates a movement, but rather the completion of a movement, and therefore we suppose that it is presented to us by intuition when it is simple and clear, but not when it is complex and involved. When this is the case we give it the name of enumeration or induction, because it cannot then be grasped as a whole at the same time by the mind, and its certainty depends to some extent on the memory, in which our judgments about the various matters enumerated must be retained, if from their assemblage a single fact is to be inferred.

All these distinctions had to be made if we were to elucidate this rule. We treated of mental intuition solely in Rule 9; the tenth dealt with enumeration alone; but now the present rule explains how these two operations aid and complete each other. In doing so they seem to grow into a single process by virtue of a sort of motion of thought which has an attentive and vision-like knowledge of one fact and yet can pass at the very same moment to another.

Now to this co-operation we assign a twofold advantage. Firstly it promotes a more certain knowledge of the conclusion with which we are concerned, and secondly it makes the mind readier to discover fresh truths. In fact the memory, on which we have said depends the certainty of the conclusions which embrace more than we can grasp in a single act of intuition, though weak and liable to fail us, can be renewed and made stronger by this continuous and constantly repeated process of thought. Thus if diverse mental acts have led me to know what is the relation between a first and a second magnitude, next between the second and a third, then between the third and a fourth, and finally the fourth and a fifth, that need not lead me to see what is the relation between the first and the fifth, nor can I deduce it from what I already know, unless I remember all the other relations. Hence what I have to do is to run over them all repeatedly in my mind, until I pass so quickly from the first to the last that practically no step is left to the memory, and I seem to view the whole all at the same time.

Everyone must see that this plan does much to counteract the slowness of the mind and to enlarge its capacity. But in addition we must note that the greatest advantage of this rule consists in the fact that, by reflecting on the mutual dependence of two propositions, we acquire the habit of distinguishing at a glance what is more or less relative, and what the steps are by which a relative fact is related to something absolute. For example, if I run over a number of magnitudes that are in continued proportion, I shall reflect upon all the following facts: viz. that the mental act is entirely similar – and not easier in the one case, more difficult in another – by which I grasp the relation between the first and the second, the second and third, third and fourth, and so on; while yet it is more difficult for me to conceive what the relation of the second is to the first and to the third at the same time, and much more difficult still to tell its relation to the first and fourth, and so on. These considerations then lead me to see why, if the first and second alone are given, I can easily find the third and fourth, and all the others; the reason being that this process requires only single and distinct acts of thought. But if only the first and the third are given, it is not so easy to recognise the mean, because this can only be accomplished by means of a mental operation in which two of the previous acts are involved. If the first and the fourth magnitudes alone are given, it is still more difficult to present to ourselves the two means, because here three acts of thought come in simultaneously. It would seem likely as a consequence that it would be even more difficult to discover the three means between the first and the fifth. The reason why this is not so is due to a fresh fact; viz. even though here four mental acts come together they can yet be disjoined, since four can be divided by another number. Thus I can discover the third by itself from the first and fifth, then the second from the first and third, and so on. If one accustoms one's self to reflect on these and similar problems, as often as a new question arises, at once one recognises what produces its special difficulty, and what is the simplest method of dealing with all cases; and to be able to do so is a valuable aid to the discovery of the truth.

12 *Finally we ought to employ all the aids of understanding, imagination, sense and memory, first for the purpose of having a distinct intuition of simple propositions; partly also in order to compare the propositions to be proved with those we know already, so that we may be able to recognise their truth; partly also in order to discover the truths, which should be compared with each other so that nothing may be left lacking on which human industry may exercise itself.*

This rule states the conclusion of all that we said before, and shows in general outline what had to be explained in detail, in this wise.

411

In the matter of the cognition of facts two things alone have to be considered, ourselves who know and the objects themselves which are to be known. Within us there are four faculties only which we can use for this purpose, viz. understanding, imagination, sense and memory. The understanding is indeed alone capable of perceiving the truth, but yet it ought to be aided by imagination, sense and memory, lest perchance we omit any expedient that lies within our power. On the side of the facts to be known it is enough to examine three things; first that which presents itself spontaneously, secondly how we learn one thing by means of another, and thirdly what (truths) are deduced from what. This enumeration appears to me to be complete, and to omit nothing to which our human powers can apply.

I should have liked therefore to have turned to the first point and to have explained in this passage, what the human mind is, what body, and how it is 'informed' by mind; what the faculties in the complex whole are which serve the attainment of knowledge, and what the agency of each is. But this place[43] seems hardly to give me sufficient room to take in all the matters which must be premised before the truth in this subject can become clear to all. For my desire is in all that I write to assert nothing controversial unless I have already stated the very reasons which have brought me to that conclusion, and by which I think that others also may be convinced.

412

But because at present I am prevented from doing this, it will suffice me to explain as briefly as possible that mode of viewing everything within us which is directed towards the discovery of truth, which most promotes my purpose. You need not believe that the facts are so unless you like. But what prevents us following these

43 [*locus*] is added in another hand in the Hanover manuscript.

suppositions, if it appears that they do no harm to the truth, but only render it all much clearer? In geometry you do precisely the same thing when you make certain assumptions about a quantity which do not in any way weaken the force of your arguments, though often our experience of its nature in physics makes us judge of it quite otherwise.

Let us then conceive of the matter as follows: — all our external senses, in so far as they are part of the body, and despite the fact that we direct them towards objects, so manifesting activity, viz. a movement in space, nevertheless properly speaking perceive in virtue of passivity alone, just in the way that wax receives an impression[44] from a seal. And it should not be thought that all we mean to assert is an analogy between the two. We ought to believe that the way is entirely the same in which the exterior figure of the sentient body is really modified by the object, as that in which the shape of the surface of the wax is altered by the seal. This has to be admitted not only in the case of the figure, hardness, roughness, etc. of a body which we perceive by touch, but even when we are aware of heat, cold, and the like qualities. It is likewise with the other senses. The first opaque structure in the eye receives the figure impressed upon it by the light with its various colours; and the first membrane[45] in the ears, the nose, and the tongue that resists the further passage of the object, thus also acquires a new figure from the sound, the odour, and the savour, as the case may be.

It is exceedingly helpful to conceive all those matters thus, for nothing falls more readily under sense than figure, which can be touched and seen. Moreover that nothing false issues from this supposition more than from any other, is proved by the fact that the concept of figure is so common and simple that it is involved in every object of sense. Thus whatever you suppose colour to be, you cannot deny that it is extended and in consequence possessed of figure. Is there then any disadvantage, if, while taking care not to admit any new entity uselessly, or rashly to imagine that it exists, and not denying indeed the beliefs of others concerning colour, but merely abstracting from every other feature except that it possesses the nature of figure, we conceive the diversity existing between white, blue, and red, etc., as being like the difference

413

46 *figuram*.   45 *cutem*.

between the following similar figures? The same argument applies to all cases;

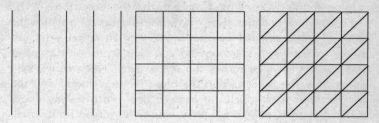

for it is certain that the infinitude of figures suffices to express all the differences in sensible things.

Secondly we must believe that while the external sense is stimulated[46] by the object, the figure which is conveyed to it is carried off to some other part of the body, that part called the common sense,[47] in the very same instant and without the passage of any real entity from one to the other. It is in exactly the same manner that now when I write I recognise that at the very moment when the separate characters are being written down on the paper, not only is the lower end of the pen moved, but every motion in that part is simultaneously shared by the whole pen. All these diverse motions are traced by the upper end of the pen likewise in the air, although I do not conceive of anything real passing from the one extremity to the other. Now who imagines that the connection between the different parts of the human body is slighter than that between the ends of a pen, and what simpler way of expressing this could be found? 414

Thirdly we must believe that the common sense has a function like that of a seal, and impresses on the fancy or imagination, as though on wax, those very figures and ideas which come uncontaminated and without bodily admixture from the external senses. But this fancy is a genuine part of the body, of sufficient size to allow its different parts to assume various figures in distinctness from each other and to let those parts acquire the practice of retaining the

46 *movetur*.
47 *sensus communis*. This theory is indistinguishable from one interpretation of the Aristotelian doctrine of a central sense with a central organ in the body.

impressions for some time. In the latter case we give the faculty the name of memory.

In the fourth place we must conceive that the motor force or the nerves themselves derive their origin from the brain, in which the fancy is located, and that the fancy moves them in various ways, just as the external senses act on the common sense, or the lower extremity of the pen moves the whole pen. This example also shows how the fancy can be the cause of many motions in the nerves, motions of which, however, it does not have the images stamped upon it, possessing only certain other images from which these latter follow. Just so the whole pen does not move exactly in the way in which its lower end does; nay the greater part seems to have a motion that is quite different from and contrary to that of the other. This lets us understand how all the motions of the other animals can come about, though we can ascribe to them no knowledge at all, but only fancy of a purely corporeal kind. We can explain also how in ourselves all those operations occur which we perform without any aid from the reason.

Finally and in the fifth place, we must think that that power by which we are properly said to know things, is purely spiritual, and not less distinct from every part of the body than blood from bone, or hand from eye. It is a single agency, whether it receives impressions from the common sense simultaneously with the fancy, or applies itself to those that are preserved in the memory, or forms new ones. Often the imagination is so beset by these impressions that it is unable at the same time to receive ideas from the common sense, or to transfer them to the motor mechanism in the way befitting its purely corporeal character. In all these operations this cognitive power is at one time passive, at another active, and resembles now the seal and now the wax. But the resemblance on this occasion is only one of analogy, for among corporeal things there is nothing wholly similar to this faculty. It is one and the same agency which, when applying itself along with the imagination to the common sense, is said to see, touch, etc.; if applying itself to the imagination alone in so far as that is endowed with diverse impressions, it is said to remember; if it turn to the imagination in order to create fresh impressions, it is said to imagine or conceive; finally if it act alone it is said to understand. How this latter function takes place I shall explain at greater length in the proper place. Now

415

416

it is the same faculty that in correspondence with those various functions is called either pure understanding, or imagination, or memory, or sense. It is properly called mind[48] when it either forms new ideas in the fancy, or attends to those already formed. We consider it as capable of the above various operations, and this distinction between those terms must in the sequel be borne in mind. But after having grasped these facts the attentive reader will gather what help is to be expected from each particular faculty, and discover how far human effort can avail to supplement the deficiencies of our mental powers.

For, since the understanding can be stimulated by the imagination, or on the contrary act on it; and seeing that the imagination can act on the senses by means of the motor power applying them to objects, while they on the contrary can act on it, depicting on it the images of bodies; considering on the other hand that the memory, at least that which is corporeal and similar to that of the brutes, is in no respect distinct from the imagination; we come to the sure conclusion that, if the understanding deal with matters in which there is nothing corporeal or similar to the corporeal, it cannot be helped by those faculties, but that, on the contrary, to prevent their hampering it, the senses must be banished and the imagination as far as possible divested of every distinct impression. But if the understanding proposes to examine something that can be referred to the body, we must form the idea of that thing as distinctly as possible in the imagination; and in order to effect this with greater ease, the thing itself which this idea is to represent must be exhibited to the external senses. Now when the understanding wishes to have a distinct intuition of particular facts a multitude of objects is of no use to it. But if it wishes to deduce one thing from a number of objects, as often has to be done, we must banish from the ideas of the objects presented whatsoever does not require present attention, in order that the remainder may be the more readily retained in memory. In the same way it is not on those occasions that the objects themselves ought to be presented to the external senses, but rather certain compendious abbreviations which, provided they guard the memory against lapse, are the handier the shorter they are. Whosoever observes all these recom-

417

48 *ingenium.*

mendations, will, in my opinion, omit nothing that relates to the first part of our rule.

Now we must approach the second part of our task. That was to distinguish accurately the notions of simple things from those which are built up out of them; to see in both cases where falsity might come in, so that we might be on our guard and give our attention to those matters only in which certainty was possible. But here, as before, we must make certain assumptions which probably are not agreed on by all. It matters little, however, though they are not believed to be more real than those imaginary circles by means of which astronomers describe their phenomena, provided that you employ them to aid you in discerning in each particular case what sort of knowledge is true and what false.

418   Finally, then, we assert that relatively to our knowledge single things should be taken in an order different from that in which we should regard them when considered in their more real nature. Thus, for example, if we consider a body as having extension and figure, we shall indeed admit that from the point of view of the thing itself it is one and simple. For we cannot from that point of view regard it as compounded of corporeal nature, extension and figure, since these elements have never existed in isolation from each other. But relatively to our understanding we call it a compound constructed out of these three natures, because we have thought of them separately before we were able to judge that all three were found in one and the same subject. Hence here we shall treat of things only in relation to our understanding's awareness of them, and shall call those only simple, the cognition of which is so clear and so distinct that they cannot be analysed by the mind into others more distinctly known. Such are figure, extension, motion, etc.; all others we conceive to be in some way compounded out of these. This principle must be taken so universally as not even to leave out those objects which we sometimes obtain by abstraction from the simple natures themselves. This we do, for example when we say that figure is the limit of an extended thing, conceiving by the term limit something more universal than by the term figure since we can talk of a limit of duration, a limit of motion, and so on. But our contention is right, for then, even though we find the meaning of limit by abstracting it from figure, nevertheless it should
419   not for that reason seem simpler than figure. Rather, since it is

predicated of other things, as for example of the extreme bounds of a space of time or of a motion, etc., things which are wholly different from figure, it must be abstracted from those natures also; consequently it is something compounded out of a number of natures wholly diverse, of which it can be only ambiguously predicated.

Our second assertion is that those things which relatively to our understanding[49] are called simple, are either purely intellectual[50] or purely material, or else common both to intellect and to matter. Those are purely intellectual which our understanding[49] apprehends by means of a certain inborn light, and without the aid of any corporeal image. That a number of such things exist is certain; and it is impossible to construct any corporeal idea which shall represent to us what the act of knowing is, what doubt is, what ignorance, and likewise what the action of the will is which it is possible to term volition, and so with other things. Yet we have a genuine knowledge of all these things, and know them so easily that in order to recognise them it is enough to be endowed with reason. Those things are purely material which we discern only in bodies; e.g. figure, extension, motion, etc. Finally those must be styled common which are ascribed now to corporeal things, now to spirits, without distinction. Such are existence, unity, duration and the like. To this group also we must ascribe those common notions which are, as it were, bonds for connecting together the other simple natures, and on whose evidence all the inferences which we obtain by reasoning depend. The following are examples: things that are the same as a third thing are the same as one another. So too: things which do not bear the same relation to a third thing have some diversity from each other, etc. As a matter of fact these common notions can be discerned by the understanding either unaided[51] or when it is aware of the images of material things.

420

But among these simple natures we must rank the privative and negative terms corresponding to them in so far as our intelligence grasps them. For it is quite as genuinely an act of knowledge by which I am intuitively aware of what nothing is, or an instant, or rest, as that by which I know what existence is, or lapse of time, or motion. This way of viewing the matter will be helpful in enabling

49 *intellectus.*   50 *intellectuales.*   51 *puro.*

us henceforth to say that all the rest of what we know is formed by composition out of these simple natures. Thus, for example, if I pronounce the judgment that some figure is not moving, I shall say that in a certain sense my idea[52] is a complex of figure and rest; and so in other cases.

Thirdly we assert that all these simple natures are known *per se* and are wholly free from falsity. It will be easy to show this, provided we distinguish that faculty of our understanding by which it has intuitive awareness of things and knows them, from that by which it judges, making use of affirmation and denial. For we may imagine ourselves to be ignorant of things which we really know, for example on such occasions as when we believe that in such things, over and above what we have present to us or attain to by thinking, there is something else hidden from us, and when this belief of ours is false. Whence it is evident that we are in error if we judge that any one of these simple natures is not completely known by us. For if our mind attains to the least acquaintance with it, as must be the case, since we are assumed to pass some judgment on it, this fact alone makes us infer that we know it completely. For otherwise it could not be said to be simple, but must be complex – a compound of that which is present in our perception of it, and that of which we think we are ignorant.

In the fourth place we point out that the union of these things one with another is either necessary or contingent. It is necessary when one is so implied in the concept of another in a confused sort of way that we cannot conceive either distinctly, if our thought assigns to them separateness from each other. Thus figure is conjoined with extension, motion with duration or time, and so on, because it is impossible to conceive of a figure that has no extension, nor of a motion that has no duration. Thus likewise if I say 'four and three are seven', this union is necessary. For we do not conceive the number seven distinctly unless we include in it the numbers three and four in some confused way. In the same way whatever is demonstrated of figures or numbers is necessarily united with that of which it is affirmed. Further, this necessity is not restricted to the field of sensible matters alone. The conclusion is necessary also in such a case – If Socrates says he doubts everything, it follows

52 *cogitatio*.

necessarily that he knows this at least – that he doubts. Likewise he knows that something can be either true or false, and so on, for all those consequences necessarily attach to the nature of doubt. The union, however, is contingent in those cases where the things are conjoined by no inseparable bond. Thus when we say a body is animate, a man is clothed, etc. Likewise many things are often necessarily united with one another, though most people, not noticing what their true relation is, reckon them among those that are contingently connected. As example, I give the following proposition: – 'I exist, therefore God exists': also 'I know, therefore I have a mind distinct from my body', etc. Finally we must note that very many necessary propositions become contingent when converted. Thus though from the fact that I exist I may infallibly conclude that God exists, it is not for that reason allowable to affirm that because God exists I also exist.

Fifthly we remark that no knowledge is at any time possible of anything beyond those simple natures and what may be called their intermixture or combination with each other. Indeed it is often easier to be aware of several of them in union with each other, than to separate one of them from the others. For, to illustrate, I am able to know what a triangle is, though I have never thought that in that knowledge was contained the knowledge of an angle, a line, the number three, figure, extension, etc. But that does not prevent me from saying that the nature of the triangle is composed of all these natures, and that they are better known than the triangle since they are the elements which we comprehend in it. It is possible also that in the triangle many other features are involved which escape our notice, such as the magnitude of the angles, which are equal to two right angles, and the innumerable relations which exist between the sides and the angles, or the size of the area, etc.

Sixthly, we say that those natures which we call composite are known by us, either because experience shows us what they are, or because we ourselves are responsible for their composition. Matter of experience consists of what we perceive by sense, what we hear from the lips of others, and generally whatever reaches our understanding either from external sources or from that contemplation which our mind directs backwards on itself. Here it must be noted that no direct experience can ever deceive the understanding if it restrict its attention accurately to the object presented to it, just as it is given to it either at first-hand[53] or by means of an image; and if it moreover refrain from judging that the imagination faithfully reports the objects of the senses, or that the senses take on the true forms of things, or in fine that external things always are as they appear to be; for in all these judgments we are exposed to error. This happens, for example, when we believe as fact what is merely a story that someone has told us; or when one who is ill with jaundice judges everything to be yellow because his eye is tinged with yellow. So finally, too, when the imagination is diseased, as in cases of melancholia, and a man thinks that his own disorderly fallacies represent real things. But the understanding of a wise man will not be deceived by these fancies, since he will judge that whatever comes to him from his imagination is really depicted in it, but yet will never assert that the object has passed complete and without any alteration from the external world to his senses, and from his senses to his imagination, unless he has some previous ground for believing this. Moreover we ourselves are responsible for the composition of the things present to our understanding when we believe that there is something in them which our mind never experiences when exercising direct perception.[54] Thus if a man suffering from jaundice persuades himself that the things he sees are yellow, this thought of his will be composite, consisting partly of what his imagination represents to him, and partly of what he assumes on his own account, namely that the colour looks yellow not owing to the defect in his eye, but because the things he sees really are yellow. Whence the conclusion comes that we can go wrong only when the things we believe are in some way compounded by ourselves.

424   Seventhly, this compounding can come about in other ways, namely by impulse, by conjecture, or by deduction. Impulse sways the formation of judgments about things on the part of those whom their own initiative constrains to believe something, though they can assign no reason for their belief, but are merely determined either by some higher power, or by their own free will, or by their fanciful disposition. The first cause is never a source of error, the

53 *prout illam habet vel in se ipso.*
54 This translation is doubtful. The Latin might at least equally well mean 'which our mind perceives immediately without any experience'.

second rarely, the third almost always. But a consideration of the first does not concern us here because it does not fall within the province of human skill.[55] The working of conjecture is shown, for example, in this: water which is at a greater distance from the centre of the globe than earth, is likewise less dense substance, and likewise the air which is above the water, is still rarer; hence we hazard the guess that above the air nothing exists but a very pure aether, which is much rarer than air itself. Moreover nothing that we construct in this way really deceives us, if we merely judge it to be probable and never affirm it to be true; in fact it makes us better instructed.

Deduction is thus left to us as the only means of putting things together so as to be sure of their truth. Yet in it too there may be many defects. Thus if, in this space which is full of air, there is nothing to be perceived either by sight, touch, or any other sense, we conclude that the space is empty, we are in error, and our synthesis of the nature of a vacuum with that of this space is wrong. This is the result as often as we judge that we can deduce anything universal and necessary from a particular or contingent fact. But it is within our power to avoid this error, if, for example, we never interconnect any objects unless we are directly aware that the conjunction of the one with the other is wholly necessary. Thus we are justified if we deduce that nothing can have figure which has not extension, from the fact that figure and extension are necessarily conjoined.

From all these considerations we conclude firstly – that we have shown distinctly and, as we judge, by an adequate enumeration, what we were originally able to express only confusedly and in a rough and ready way. This was that mankind has no road towards certain knowledge open to it, save those of self-evident intuition and necessary deduction; further, that we have shown what those simple natures are of which we spoke in the eighth proposition. It is also quite clear that this mental vision extends both to all those simple natures, and to the knowledge of the necessary connections between them, and finally to everything else which the understanding accurately experiences either at first hand[56] or in the imagination. Deduction, however, will be further treated in what follows.

Our second conclusion is that in order to know these simple

425

---

55 *artem.*   56 *in se.ipse.*

natures no pains need be taken, because they are of themselves sufficiently well known. Application comes in only in isolating them from each other and scrutinising them separately with steadfast mental gaze. There is no one whose intelligence is so dull as not to perceive that when he is seated he in some way differs from what he is when standing. But not everyone separates with equal distinctness the nature of position[57] from the other elements contained in the cognition in question, or is able to assert that in this case nothing alters save the position. Now it is not without reason that we call attention to the above doctrine; for the learned have a way of being so clever as to contrive to render themselves blind to things that are in their own nature evident, and known by the simplest peasant. This happens when they try to explain by something more evident those things that are self-evident. For what they do is either to explain something else, or nothing at all. Who, for instance, does not perfectly see what that is, whatsoever it may be, in respect of which alteration occurs when we change position[58]? But is there anyone who would grasp that very thing when he was told that *place*[58] *is the surface of the body surrounding us*? This would be strange seeing that that surface can change though I stay still and do not change my place, or that, on the contrary, it can so move along with me that, although it continues to surround me, I am nevertheless no longer in the same place. Do not these people really seem to use magic words which have a hidden force that eludes the grasp of human apprehension? They define *motion*, a fact with which everyone is quite familiar, as *the actualisation of what exists in potentiality, in so far as it is potential*! Now who understands these words? And who at the same time does not know what motion is? Will not everyone admit that those philosophers have been trying to find a knot in a bulrush? We must therefore maintain that no definitions are to be used in explaining things of this kind lest we should take what is complex in place of what is simple. We must be content to isolate them from each other, and to give them, each of us, our individual attention, studying them with that degree of mental illumination which each of us possesses.

Our third conclusion is that the whole of human knowledge consists in a distinct perception of the way in which those simple

57 *situs*.   58 *locum*.

natures combine in order to build up other objects. It is important to note this; because whenever some difficulty is brought forward for examination, almost everyone is brought to a standstill at the very outset, being in doubt as to the nature of the notions he ought to call to mind, and believing that he has to search for some new kind of fact previously unknown to him. Thus, if the question is, 'what is the nature of the magnet?' people like that at once prognosticate difficulty and toil in the inquiry, and dismissing from mind every well-known fact, fasten on whatsoever is most difficult, vaguely hoping that by ranging over the fruitless field where multifarious causes lie, they will find something fresh. But he who reflects that there can be nothing to know in the magnet which does not consist of certain simple natures evident in themselves, will have no doubt how to proceed. He will first collect all the observations with which experience can supply him about this stone, and from these he will next try to deduce the character of that intermixture of simple natures which is necessary to produce all those effects which he has seen to take place in connection with the magnet. This achieved, he can boldly assert that he has discovered the real nature of the magnet in so far as human intelligence and the given experimental observations can supply him with this knowledge.

Finally, it follows fourthly from what has been said that we must not fancy that one kind of knowledge is more obscure than another, since all knowledge is of the same nature throughout, and consists solely in combining what is self-evident. This is a fact recognised by very few. People have their minds already occupied by the contrary opinion, and the more bold among them, indeed, allow themselves to uphold their private conjectures as though they were sound demonstrations, and in matters of which they are wholly ignorant feel premonitions of the vision of truths which seem to present themselves through a cloud. These they have no hesitation in propounding, attaching to their concepts certain words by means of which they are wont to carry on long and reasoned out discussions, but which in reality neither they nor their audience understand. On the other hand more diffident people often refrain from many investigations that are quite easy and are in the first degree necessary to life, merely because they think themselves unequal to the task. They believe that these matters can be discovered by others who are endowed with better mental

428

faculties, and embrace the opinion of those in whose authority they have most confidence.

We assert fifthly[59] that by deduction we can get only things from words, cause from effect, or effect from cause, like from like, or parts or the whole itself from the parts . . . [60]

For the rest, in order that there may be no want of coherence in our series of precepts, we divide the whole matter of knowledge into simple propositions and 'questions'.[61] In connection with simple propositions the only precepts we give are those which prepare our cognitive faculties for fixing distinctly before them any objects, whatsoever they are, and scrutinising them with keen intelligence, since propositions of this type do not arise as the result of inquiry, but present themselves to us spontaneously. This part of our task we have undertaken in the first twelve rules, in which, we believe, we have displayed everything which, in our opinion, can facilitate the exercise of our reason. But as to 'questions' some of them can be perfectly well comprehended, even though we are ignorant of their solution; these we shall treat by themselves in the next twelve rules. Finally there are others, whose meaning is not quite clear, and these we reserve for the last twelve. This division has been made advisedly, both in order to avoid mentioning anything which presupposes all acquaintance with what follows, and also for the purpose of unfolding first what we feel to be most important first to inculcate in cultivating the mental powers. Among the 'questions' whose meaning is quite plain, we must to begin with note that we place those only in which we perceive three things distinctly; to wit, the marks by which we can identify what we are looking for when it occurs; what precisely the fact is from which our answer ought to be deduced; and how it is to be proved that these (the ground and its consequence) so depend one on another that it is impossible for either to change while the other remains

429

59 So Leibniz's manuscript. The Amsterdam edition has 'eighthly' which carries on the previous list of assertions.

60 There seems to be a break here. For a continuation of the doctrine see p. 55.

61 *quaestiones*. Inverted commas have been employed wherever it is important to remember Descartes' special technical of this term.

unchanged. In this way we shall have all the premises we require, and the only thing remaining to be shown will be how to discover the conclusion. This will not be a matter of deducing some one fact from a single simple matter (we have already said that we can do this without the help of rules), but of disentangling so skilfully some one fact that is conditioned by a number of others which all involve one another, that in recognising it there shall be no need to call upon a higher degree of mental power than in making the simplest inference. 'Questions' of this kind, being highly abstract and occurring almost exclusively in arithmetic and geometry, seem to the inexperienced of little value. But I warn them that people ought to busy and exercise themselves a long time in learning this art, who desire to master the subsequent portions of this method, in which all the other types of 'question' are treated.

430

13 *Once a 'question' is perfectly understood, we must free it of every conception superfluous to its meaning, state it in its simplest terms, and, having recourse to an enumeration, split it up into the various sections beyond which analysis cannot go in minuteness.*

This is the only respect in which we imitate the dialecticians; just as they, in teaching their doctrine of the forms of syllogism, assume that the terms or matter of their syllogisms are already known, so also we on this occasion lay it down as a prerequisite that the question to be solved should be perfectly understood. But we do not, as they, distinguish two extremes and a middle term. The following is the way in which we look at the whole matter. Firstly, in every 'question' there must be something of which we are ignorant; otherwise there is no use asking the question. Secondly, this very matter must be designated in some way or other; otherwise there would be nothing to determine us to investigate it rather than anything else. Thirdly, it can only be so designated by the aid of something else which is already known. All three conditions are realised even in questions that are not fully understood. Thus if the problem be the nature of the magnet, we already know what is meant by the two words 'magnet' and 'nature', and this knowledge determines us to seek one sort of answer rather than another, and so on. But over and above this, if the question is to be perfectly stated, we require that it should be wholly determinate, so that we shall have nothing more to seek for than what can be inferred from the data. For example some one might set me the question, what is to

431 be inferred about the nature of the magnet from that set of experiments precisely which Gilbert[62] asserts he has performed, be they trustworthy or not. So again the question may be, what my conclusion is as to the nature of sound, founding my judgment merely on the precise fact that the three strings A, B, and C give out an identical[63] sound, when by hypothesis B, though twice as thick as A, but not longer, is kept in tension by a weight that is twice as heavy; while C, though no thicker than A, but merely twice as long, is nevertheless kept in tension by a weight four times as heavy. Other illustrations might be given; but they all make it quite clear how all imperfectly expressed 'questions' may be reduced to others whose meaning is quite clear, as I shall show at greater length in the proper place. We see also how it is possible to follow this rule in divesting any difficulty, where the problem is properly realised, of every superfluous conception, and in reducing it to a form in which we no longer deem that we are treating of this or that special matter, but are dealing only in a general way with certain magnitudes which have to be fitted together.[64] Thus, to illustrate, after we have limited ourselves to the consideration of this or that set of experiments merely relative to the magnet, there is no difficulty in dismissing from view all other aspects of the case.

432 We add also that the problem[65] ought to be reduced to its simplest statement in accordance with Rules 5 and 6, and resolved into parts in accordance with Rule 7. Thus if I employ a number of experiments in investigating the magnet, I shall run them over successively, taking each by itself. Again if my inquiry is about sound, as in the case above, I shall separately consider the relation between strings A and B, then that between A and C, and so on, so that afterwards my enumeration of results may be sufficient, and may embrace every case. These three rules are the only ones which the pure understanding need observe in dealing with the terms of any proposition before approaching its ultimate solution, though

62 *Gilbertus*, presumably the English physicist W. Gilbert (1510–1603), author of *De Magneto*, 1600.   63 *aequalem*.
64 *componendas*, Amsterdam edition; 'compared with one another', Leibniz's manuscript.   65 *difficultatem*.

that requires us to employ the following eleven rules. The third part of this treatise will show us more clearly how to apply them. Further by a 'question' we understand everything in which either truth or falsity is found; and we must enumerate the different types of 'question' in order to determine what we are able to accomplish in each case.

We have already said that there can be no falsity in the mere intuition of things, whether they are simple or united together. So conceived these are not called 'questions', but they acquire that designation so soon as we prepare to pass some determinate judgment about them. Neither do we limit the title to those questions which are set us by other people. His own ignorance, or more correctly his own doubt, presented a subject of inquiry to Socrates when first he began to study it and to inquire whether it was true that he doubted everything, and maintained that such was indeed the case.

Moreover in our 'questions' we seek to derive either things from words, or causes from effects, or effects from causes, or the whole or other parts from parts, or to infer several of these simultaneously.

433

We are said to seek to derive things from words when the difficulty consists merely in the obscurity of the language employed. To this class we refer firstly all riddles, like that of the Sphinx about the animal which to begin with is four-footed, then two-footed, and finally three-footed. A similar instance is that of the fishers who, standing on the bank with rods and hooks ready for the capture of fish, said that they no longer possessed those creatures which they had caught, but on the other hand had those which they had not yet been able to catch. So in other cases; but besides these, in the majority of matters on which the learned dispute, the question is almost always one of names. We ought not to judge so ill of our great thinkers as to imagine that they conceive the objects themselves wrongly, in cases where they do not employ fit words in explaining them. Thus when people call *place* the *surface of the surrounding body,* there is no real error in their conception; they merely employ wrongly the word *place,* which by common use signifies that simple and self-evident nature in virtue of which a thing is said to be here or there. This consists wholly in a certain relation of the thing said to be in the place towards the parts of the space external to it, and is a feature which certain writers, seeing that the name place was reserved for the surface of the surrounding body, have improperly called the thing's *intrinsic position*.[66] So it is in other cases; indeed these verbal questions are of such frequent occurrence, that almost all controversy would be removed from among philosophers, if they were always to agree as to the meaning of words.

We seek to derive causes from effects when we ask concerning anything, whether it exists or what it is . . .[67]

Since, however, when a 'question' is propounded for solution we are frequently unable at once to discern its type, or to determine whether the problem is to derive things from words, or causes from effects, etc., for this reason it seems to be superfluous to say more here in detail about these matters. It will occupy less space and will be more convenient, if at the same time we go over in order all the steps which must be followed if we are to solve a problem of any sort. After that, when any 'question' is set, we must strive to understand distinctly what the inquiry is about.

For frequently people are in such a hurry in their investigations, that they bring only a blank understanding to their solution, without having settled what the marks are by which they are to recognise the fact of which they are in search, if it chance to occur. This is a proceeding as foolish as that of a boy, who, sent on an errand by his master, should be so eager to obey as to run off without having received his orders or knowing where to go.

However, though in every 'question' something must be unknown, otherwise there is no need to raise it, we should nevertheless so define this unknown element by means of specific conditions that we shall be determined towards the investigation of one thing rather than another. These are conditions to which, we maintain, attention must be paid at the very outset. We shall succeed in this if we so direct our mental vision as to have a distinct and intuitive presentation of each by itself, and inquire diligently how far the unknown fact for which we are in search is limited by each. For the

---

66 *ubi intrinsecum.*

67 There is obviously a lacuna here. The lost manuscript seems to have contained matter which is partly reproduced in a passage by Arnauld in the 2nd edition of the Port-Royal Logic. See Adam and Tannery X, pp. 470 *sqq.*

human mind is wont to fall into error in two ways here; it either assumes more than is really given in determining the question, or, on the other hand, leaves something out.

We must take care to assume neither more nor less than our data furnish us. This applies chiefly to riddles and other problems where the object of the skill employed is to try to puzzle people's wits. But frequently also we must bear it in mind in other 'questions', when it appears as though we could assume as true for the purpose of their solution a certain matter which we have accepted, not because we had a good reason for doing so, but merely because we had always believed it. Thus, for example, in the riddle put by the Sphinx, it is not necessary to believe that the word 'foot' refers merely to the real foot of an animal; we must inquire also whether the term cannot be transferred to other things, as it may be, as it happens, to the hands of an infant, or an old man's staff, because in either case these accessories are employed as feet are in walking. So too, in the fishermen's conundrum, we must beware of letting the thought of fish occupy our minds to the exclusion of those creatures which the poor so often carry about with them unwillingly, and fling away from them when caught. So again, we must be on our guard when inquiring into the construction of a vessel, such as we once saw, in the midst of which stood a column and upon that a figure of Tantalus in the attitude of a man who wants to drink. Water when poured into the vessel remained within without leaking as long as it was not high enough to enter the mouth of Tantalus, but as soon as it touched the unhappy man's lips the whole of it at once flowed out and escaped. Now at the first blush it seems as if the whole of the ingenuity consisted in the construction of this figure of Tantalus, whereas in reality this is a mere accompaniment of the fact requiring explanation, and in no way conditions it. For the whole difficulty consists solely in the problem of how the vessel was constructed so as to let out the whole of the water when that arrived at a certain height, whereas before none escaped. Finally, likewise, if we seek to extract from the recorded observations of the stars an answer to the question as to what we can assert about their motions, it is not to be gratuitously assumed that the earth is immoveable and established in the midst of the universe, as the Ancients would have it, because from our earliest years it appears to be so. We ought to regard this

436

as dubious, in order afterwards to examine what certainty there is in this matter to which we are able to attain. So in other cases.

On the other hand we sin by omission when there is some condition requisite to the determination of the question either expressed in it or in some way to be understood, which we do not bear in mind. This may happen in an inquiry into the subject of perpetual motion, not as we meet with it in nature in the movements of the stars and the flowing of springs, but as a motion contrived by human industry. Numbers of people have believed this to be possible, their idea being that the earth is in perpetual motion in a circle round its own axis, while again the magnet retains all the properties of the earth. A man might then believe that he would discover a perpetual motion if he so contrived it that a magnet should revolve in a circle, or at least that it communicated its own motion along with its other properties to a piece of iron. Now although he were to succeed in this, it would not be a perpetual motion artificially contrived; all he did would be to utilise a natural motion, just as if he were to station a wheel in the current of a river so as to secure an unceasing motion on its part. Thus in his procedure he would have omitted a condition requisite for the resolution of his problem.

When we have once adequately grasped the meaning of a 'question', we ought to try and see exactly wherein the difficulty consists, in order that, by separating it out from all complicating circumstances, we may solve it the more easily. But over and above this we must attend to the various separate problems involved in it, in order that if there are any which are easy to resolve we may omit them; when these are removed, only that will remain of which we are still in ignorance. Thus in that instance of the vessel which was described a short time ago, it is indeed quite easy to see how the vessel should be made; a column must be fixed in its centre, a bird[68] must be painted on it. But all these things will be set aside as not touching the essential point; thus we are left with the difficulty by itself, consisting in the fact that the whole of the water, which had previously remained in the vessel, after reaching a certain height, flows out. It is for this that we have to seek a reason.

68 Leibniz's manuscript has 'axis' and Garnier conjectures *fingenda*. Translate 'a valve must be fitted in it'.

Here therefore we maintain that what is worthwhile doing is simply this – to explore in an orderly way all the data furnished by the proposition, to set aside everything which we see is clearly immaterial, to retain what is necessarily bound up with the problem, and to reserve what is doubtful for a more careful examination.

14 *The same rule is to be applied also to the real extension of bodies. It must be set before the imagination by means of mere figures, for this is the best way to make it clear to the understanding.*

But in proposing to make use of the imagination as an aid to our thinking, we must note that whenever one unknown fact is deduced from another that is already known, that does not show that we discover any new kind of entity, but merely that this whole mass of knowledge is extended in such a way that we perceive that the matter sought for participates in one way or another in the nature of the data given in the proposition.[69] For example if a man has been blind from his birth it is not to be expected that we shall be able by any train of reasoning to make him perceive the true ideas of the colours which we have derived from our senses. But if a man has indeed once perceived the primary colours, though he has never seen the intermediate or mixed tints, it is possible for him to construct the images of those which he has not seen from their likeness to the others, by a sort of deduction. Similarly if in the magnet there be any sort of nature[70] the like of which our mind has never yet known, it is hopeless to expect that reasoning will ever make us grasp it; we should have to be furnished either with some new sense or with a divine intellect.[71] But we shall believe ourselves to have attained whatever in this matter can be achieved by our human faculties, if we discern with all possible distinctness that mixture of entities or natures already known which produces just those effects which we notice in the magnet.

Indeed all these previously known entities, viz. extension, figure, motion and the like, the enumeration of which does not belong to this place, are recognised by means of an idea which is one and the same in the various subject matters. The figure of a silver crown

439

69 Clearly the sense is continuous with that of the last paragraph in the exposition of the previous rule. The formulated rule has in this case at least been inserted later.   70 *entis.*   71 *mente.*

which we imagine, is just the same as that of one that is golden. Further this common idea is transferred from one subject to another, merely by means of the simple comparison by which we affirm that the object sought for is in this or that respect like, or identical with, or equal to a particular datum. Consequently in every train of reasoning it is by comparison merely that we attain to a precise knowledge of the truth. Here is an example: all A is B, all B is C, therefore all A is C. Here we compare with one another a *quaesitum* and a *datum* viz. A and C, in respect of the fact that each is B, and so on. But because, as we have often announced, the syllogistic forms are of no aid in perceiving the truth about objects, it will be for the reader's profit to reject them altogether and to conceive that all knowledge whatsoever, other than that which consists in the simple and naked intuition of single independent objects, is a matter of the comparison of two things or more, with each other. In fact practically the whole of the task set the human reason consists in preparing for this operation; for when it is open and simple, we need no aid from art, but are bound to rely upon the light of nature alone, in beholding the truth which comparison gives us.

440

We must further mark that comparison should be simple and open, only as often as *quaesitum* and *datum* participate equally in a certain nature. Note that the only reason why preparation is required for comparison that is not of this nature is the fact that the common nature we spoke of does not exist equally in both, but is complicated with certain other relations or ratios. The chief part of our human industry consists merely in so transmuting these ratios as to show clearly a uniformity[72] between the matter sought for and something else already known.

Next we must mark that nothing can be reduced to this uniformity,[72] save that which admits of a greater and a less, and that all such matter is included under the term magnitude. Consequently when, in conformity with the previous rule, we have freed the terms of the problem from any reference to a particular subject, we shall discover that all we have left to deal with consists of magnitudes in general.

We shall, however, even in this case make use of our imagination, employing not the naked understanding but the intellect as aided by

72 *aequalitas*.

images of particulars[73] depicted on the fancy. Finally we must note 441 that nothing can be asserted of magnitudes in general that cannot also be ascribed to any particular instance.[74]

This lets us easily conclude that there will be no slight profit in transferring whatsoever we find asserted of magnitudes in general to that particular species of magnitude which is most easily and distinctly depicted in our imagination. But it follows from what we stated about the twelfth rule that this must be the real extension of body abstracted from everything else except the fact that it has figure; for in that place we represented the imagination itself along with the ideas it contains as nothing more than a really material body possessing extension and figure. This is also itself evident; for no other subject displays more distinctly differences in ratio of whatsoever kind. Though one thing can be said to be more or less white than another, or a sound sharper or flatter, and so on, it is yet impossible to determine exactly whether the greater exceeds the less in the proportion two to one, or three to one, etc., unless we treat the quantity as being in a certain way analogous to the extension of a body possessing figure. Let us then take it as fixed and certain that perfectly definite 'questions' are almost free from difficulty other than that of transmuting ratios so that they may be stated as equations.[75] Let us agree too that everything in which we discover precisely this difficulty, can be easily, and ought to be, disengaged from reference to every other subject, and immediately stated in terms of extension and figure. It is about these alone that we shall for this reason henceforth treat, up to and as far as the twenty-fifth rule, omitting the consideration of everything else.

My desire is that here I may find a reader who is an eager student 442 of arithmetic and geometry, though indeed I should prefer him to have had no practice in these arts, rather than to be an adept after the ordinary standard. For the employment of the rules which I here

---

73 *speciebus*.

74 An alternative way of translating this paragraph would be to make the previous sentence follow the present one. We should then have to begin it differently, viz. 'This will teach us even then to make use of our imagination etc.'

75 '*in proportionibus in aequalitates evolvendis*', conjecture by Adam and Tannery; *in aequalitatibus*, Leibniz's manuscript; *inaequalitatis*, Amsterdam edition.

unfold is much easier in the study of arithmetic and geometry (and it is all that is needed in learning them) than in inquiries of any other kind. Further its usefulness as a means towards the attainment of a profounder knowledge is so great, that I have no hesitation in saying that it was not the case that this part of our method was invented for the purpose of dealing with mathematical problems, but rather that mathematics should be studied almost solely for the purpose of training us in this method. I shall presume no knowledge of anything in mathematics except perhaps such facts as are self-evident and obvious to everyone. But the way in which people ordinarily think about them, even though not vitiated by any glaring errors, yet obscures our knowledge with many ambiguous and ill-conceived principles, which we shall try incidentally to correct in the following pages.

By extension we understand whatever has length, breadth, and depth, not inquiring whether it be a real body or merely space; nor does it appear to require further explanation, since there is nothing more easily perceived by our imagination. Yet the learned frequently employ distinctions so subtle that the light of nature is dissipated in attending to them, and even those matters of which no peasant is ever in doubt become invested in obscurity. Hence we announce that by extension we do not here mean anything distinct and separate from the extended object itself; and we make it a rule not to recognise those metaphysical[76] entities which really cannot be presented to the imagination. For even though someone could persuade himself, for example, that supposing every extended object in the universe were annihilated, that would not prevent extension in itself alone existing, this conception of his would not involve the use of any corporeal image,[77] but would be based on a false judgment of the intellect working by itself. He will admit this himself, if he reflect attentively on this very image of extension when, as will then happen, he tries to construct it in his imagination. For he will notice that, as he perceives it, it is not divested of a reference to every object, but that his imagination of it is quite different from his judgment about it. Consequently, whatever our understanding may believe as to the truth of the matter, those abstract entities are never given to our imagination as separate from

76 *philosophica.* 77 *idea.*

the objects in which they inhere.

But since henceforth we are to attempt nothing without the aid of the imagination, it will be worth our while to distinguish carefully the ideas which in each separate case are to convey to the understanding the meaning of the words we employ. To this end we submit for consideration these three forms of expression: — *extension occupies place, body possesses extension, and extension is not body.*

The first statement shows how extension may be substituted for that which is extended. My conception is entirely the same if I say *extension occupies place*, as when I say *that which is extended occupies place*. Yet that is no reason why, in order to avoid ambiguity, it should be better to use the term *that which is extended*; for that does not indicate so distinctly our precise meaning, which is, that a subject occupies place owing to the fact that it is extended. Someone might interpret the expression to mean merely *that which is extended is an object occupying place*, just in the same way as if I had said *that which is animate occupies place*. This explains why we announced that here we would treat of extension,[78] preferring that to 'the extended,'[79] although we believe that there is no difference in the conception of the two.

Let us now take up these words: *body possesses extension*. Here the meaning of *extension* is not identical with that of body, yet we do not construct two distinct ideas in our imagination, one of body, the other of extension, but merely a single image of extended body; and from the point of view of the thing it is exactly as if I had said: *body is extended*, or better, *the extended is extended*. This is a peculiarity of those entities which have their being merely in something else, and can never be conceived without the subject in which they exist. How different is it with those matters which are really distinct from the subjects of which they are predicated. If, for example, I say *Peter has wealth*, my idea of Peter is quite different from that of wealth. So if I say *Paul is wealthy*, my image is quite different from that which I should have if I said *the wealthy man is wealthy*. Failure to distinguish the diversity between these two cases is the cause of the error of those numerous people who believe that extension contains some-thing distinct from that which is extended, in the same way as Paul's wealth is something different from Paul himself.

444

---

78 *extensio.*   79 *extensum.*

Finally, take the expression: *extension is not body*. Here the term extension is taken quite otherwise than as above. When we give it this meaning there is no special idea corresponding to it in the imagination. In fact this entire assertion is the work of the naked understanding, which alone has the power of separating out abstract entities of this type. But this is a stumbling-block for many, who, not perceiving that extension so taken, cannot be grasped by the imagination, represent it to themselves by means of a genuine image. Now such an idea necessarily involves the concept of body, and if they say that extension so conceived is not body, their heedlessness involves them in the contradiction of saying that *the same thing is at the same time body and not body*. It is likewise of great moment to distinguish the meaning of the enunciations in which such names as *extension, figure, number, superficies, line, point, unity*, etc. are used in so restricted a way as to exclude matters from which they are not really distinct. Thus when we say: *extension or figure is not body; number is not the thing that is counted; a superficies is the boundary of a body, the line the limit of a surface, the point of a line; unity is not a quantity*, etc.; all these and similar propositions must be taken altogether outside the bounds of the imagination, if they are to be true. Consequently we shall not discuss them in the sequel.

But we should carefully note that in all other propositions in which these terms, though retaining the same signification and employed in abstraction from their subject matter, do not exclude or deny anything from which they are not really distinct, it is both possible and necessary to use the imagination as an aid. The reason is that even though the understanding in the strict sense attends merely to what is signified by the name, the imagination nevertheless ought to fashion a correct image[80] of the object, in order that the very understanding itself may be able to fix upon other features belonging to it that are not expressed by the name in question whenever there is occasion to do so, and may never imprudently believe that they have been excluded. Thus, if number be the question, we imagine an object which we can measure by summing a plurality of units. Now though it is allowable for the understanding to confine its attention for the present solely to the multiplicity displayed by the object, we must be on our guard nevertheless not

80 *ideam*.

on that account afterwards to come to any conclusion which implies that the object which we have described numerically has been excluded from our concept. But this is what those people do who ascribe mysterious properties to number, empty inanities in which they certainly would not believe so strongly, unless they conceived that number was something distinct from the things we number. In the same way, if we are dealing with figure, let us remember that we are concerned with an extended subject, though we restrict ourselves to conceiving it merely as possessing figure. When body is the object let us reflect that we are dealing with the very same thing taken as possessing length, breadth and depth. Where superficies comes in, our object will still be the same[81] though we conceive it as having length and breadth, and we shall leave out the element of depth, without denying it. The line will be considered as having length merely, while in the case of the point the object, though still the same, will be divested in our thought of every characteristic save that of being something existent.

In spite of the way in which I have dwelt on this topic, I fear that men's minds are so dominated by prejudice that very few are free from the danger of losing their way here, and that, notwithstanding the length of my discourse, I shall be found to have explained myself too briefly. Those very disciplines arithmetic and geometry, though the most certain of all the sciences, nevertheless lead us astray here. For is there a single arithmetician who does not believe that the numbers with which he deals are not merely held in abstraction from any subject matter by the understanding, but are really distinct objects of the imagination? Does not your geometrician obscure the clearness of his subject by employing irreconcilable principles? He tells you that lines have no breadth, surfaces no depth; yet he subsequently wishes to generate the one out of the other, not noticing that a line, the movement of which is conceived to create a surface, is really a body; or that, on the other hand, the line which has no breadth, is merely a mode of body. But, not to take more time in going over these matters, it will be more expeditious for us to expound the way in which we assume our object should be taken, in order that we may most easily give a proof of whatsoever is true in arithmetic and geometry.

81 Adopting Adam and Tannery's conjecture of *idem* for *item*.

Here therefore we deal with an extended object, considering nothing at all involved in it save extension, and purposely refraining from using the word quantity, because there are certain philosophers so subtle as to distinguish it also from extension. We assume such a simplification of our problems as to leave nothing else to be inquired about except the determination of a certain extension by comparing it with a certain other extension that is already determinately known. For here we do not look to discover any new sort of fact; we merely wish to make a simplification of ratios, be they ever so involved, such that we may discover some equation[82] between what is unknown and something known. Since this is so, it is certain that whatsoever differences in ratio exist in these subjects can be found to prevail also between two or more extensions. Hence our purpose is sufficiently served if in extension itself we consider everything that can aid us in setting out differences in ratio; but there are only three such features, viz. dimension, unity and figure.

By dimension I understand nothing but the mode and aspect according to which a subject is considered to be measurable. Thus it is not merely the case that length, breadth and depth are dimensions; but weight also is a dimension in terms of which the heaviness of objects is estimated. So, too, speed is a dimension of motion, and there are an infinite number of similar instances. For that very division of the whole into a number of parts of identical nature, whether it exist in the real order of things or be merely the work of the understanding, gives us exactly that dimension in terms of which we apply number to objects. Again that mode which constitutes number is properly said to be a species of dimension, though there is not an absolute identity between the meaning of the two terms. For if we proceed by taking part after part until we reach the whole, the operation is then said to be counting, whereas if conversely we look upon the whole as something split up into parts, it is an object which we measure. Thus we measure centuries by years, days, hours and moments, while if we count up moments, hours, days and years, we shall finish with a total of centuries.

It clearly follows that there may be an infinite number of dimensions in the same subject, which make no addition at all to the objects which possess them, but have the same meaning whether

448

82 *ut illud, quod est ignotum, aequale cuidam cognito reperiatur.*

they are based on anything real in the objects themselves, or are the arbitrary inventions of our own mind. Weight is indeed something real existing in a body, and the speed of motion is a reality, and so with the division of a century into years and days. But it is otherwise with the division of the day into hours and moments, etc. Yet all these subdivisions are exactly similar if considered merely from the point of view of dimension, as we ought to regard them both here and in the science of mathematics. It falls rather to physics to inquire whether they are founded on anything real.

Recognition of this fact throws much light on geometry, since in that science almost everyone goes wrong in conceiving that quantity has three species, the line, the superficies, and the solid. But we have already stated that the line and the superficies are not conceived as being really distinct from solid body, or from one another. Moreover if they are taken in their bare essence as abstractions of the understanding, they are no more diverse species of quantity than the 'animal' and 'living creature' in man are diverse species of substance. Incidentally also we have to note that the three dimensions of body, length, breadth and depth, are only in name distinct from one another. For there is nothing to prevent us, in any solid body with which we are dealing, from taking any of the extensions it presents as the length, or any other as its depth, and so on. And though these three dimensions have a real basis in every extended object quâ extended, we have nevertheless no special concern in this science with them more than with countless others, which are either mental creations or have some other ground in objects. For example in the case of the triangle, if we wish to measure it exactly, we must acquaint ourselves with three features of its existence, viz. either its three sides, or two sides and an angle, or two angles and its area, and so forth. Now these can all be styled dimensions. Similarly in a trapezium five facts have to be noted, in a tetrahedron six, and so on. But if we wish to choose here those dimensions which shall give most aid to our imagination, we shall never attend at the same time to more than one or two of those depicted in our imagination, even though we know that in the matter set before us with which we are dealing several others are involved. For the art of our method consists in distinguishing as many elements as possible, so that though we attend to only a few simultaneously, we shall yet cover them all in time, taking one after the other.

449

The unit is that common element in which, as above remarked, all the things compared with each other should equally participate. If this be not already settled in our problems, we can represent it by one of the magnitudes already presented to us, or by any other magnitude we like, and it will be the common measure of all the others. We shall understand that in it there exists every dimension found in those very widely sundered facts which are to be compared with each other, and we shall conceive it either (1) merely as something extended, omitting every other more precise determination — and then it will be identical with the point of geometry, considered as generating a line by its movement; or (2) we shall conceive it as a line, or (3) as a square.

To come to figures, we have already shown above how it is they alone that give us a means of constructing the images of all objects whatsoever. It remains to give notice in this place, that of the innumerable diverse species of figure, we shall employ only those which most readily express differences of relation or proportion. Moreover there are two sorts of objects only which are compared with each other, viz. numerical assemblages[83] and magnitudes. Now there are also two sorts of figures by means of which these may be presented to our conception. For example we have the points

.

.   .

.   .   .

which represent a triangular[84] number, or again the 'tree' which illustrates genealogical relation as in such a case —

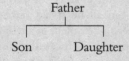

Father

Son   Daughter

---

83 *multitudines*.
84 *triangularis*, conjecture Adam and Tannery. Previous versions give *triangulorum*. Triangular numbers are the sums of the natural numbers, viz. 1, 3, 6, 10, etc., and thus can be constructed from any number n according to the formula $\dfrac{n\,(n+1)}{2}$.

So in similar instances. Now these are figures designed to express   451
numerical assemblages; but those which are continuous and undivided
like the triangle, the square, etc.,

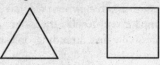

explain the nature of magnitudes.

But in order that we may point out which of all these figures we
are going to use, it ought to be known that all the relations which
can exist between things of this kind, must be referred to two heads,
viz. either to order or to measurement.

We must further realise that while the discovery of an order is no
light task, as may be seen throughout this treatise, which makes this
practically its sole subject, yet once the order has been discovered
there is no difficulty at all in knowing it. The seventh rule shows us
how we may easily review in sequence mentally the separate
elements which have been arranged in order, for the reason that in
this class of relation the bond between the terms is a direct one
involving nothing but the terms themselves, and not requiring
mediation by means of a third term, as is the case in measurement.
The unfolding of relations of measurement will therefore be all that
we shall treat of here. For I recognise the order in which A and B
stand, without considering anything except these two – the extreme
terms of the relation. But I can recognise the ratio of the magnitude
of two to that of three, only by considering some third thing,
namely unity, which is the common measure of both.

We must likewise bear in mind that, by the help of the unit we   452
have assumed, continuous magnitudes can sometimes be reduced in
their entirety to numerical expressions, and that this can always be
partly realised. Further it is possible to arrange our assemblage of
units in such an order that the problem which previously[85] was one
requiring the solution of a question in measurement, is now a matter
merely involving an inspection of order. Now our method helps us
greatly in making the progress which this transformation effects.

Finally remember that of the dimensions of continuous magnitude

[85] *pertinebat*, conjecture by Adam and Tannery; editors and manuscript
pertineat.

none are more distinctly conceived than length and breadth, and that we ought not to attend to more than these two simultaneously in the same figure, if we are to compare two diverse things with each other. The reason is, that when we have more than two diverse things to compare with each other, our method consists in reviewing them successively and attending only to two of them at the same time.

Observation of these facts leads us easily to our conclusion. This is that there is no less reason for abstracting our propositions from those figures of which geometry treats, if the inquiry is one involving them, than from any other subject matter. Further, in doing so we need retain nothing but rectilinear and rectangular superficies, or else straight lines, which we also call figures, because they serve quite as well as surfaces in aiding us to imagine an object which actually has extension, as we have already said. Finally those same figures have to represent for us now continuous magnitudes, again a plurality of units or number also. Human ingenuity can devise nothing simpler for the complete expression of differences of relation.

The remaining rules, 15–21, are here omitted. – (Ed.)

DISCOURSE ON THE METHOD OF RIGHTLY CONDUCTING THE REASON AND SEEKING FOR TRUTH IN THE SCIENCES

If this Discourse appears too long to be read all at once it may be separated into six portions. And in the first there will be found various considerations respecting the sciences; in the second the principal rules regarding the method which the author has sought out; while in the third are some of the rules of morality which he has derived from this method. In the fourth are the reasons by which he proves the existence of God and of the human soul which form the foundation of his metaphysic. In the fifth, the order of the questions regarding physics which he has investigated and particularly the explanation of the movement of the heart, and of some other difficulties which pertain to medicine, as also the difference between the soul of man and that of the brutes. And in the last part the questions raised relate to those matters which the author believes to be requisite in order to advance further in the investigation of nature, in addition to the reasons that caused him to write.

Part 1

Good sense is of all things in the world the most equally distributed, for everybody thinks himself so abundantly provided with it, that even those most difficult to please in all other matters do not commonly desire more of it than they already possess. It is unlikely that this is an error on their part; it seems rather to be evidence in support of the view that the power of forming a good judgment and of distinguishing the true from the false, which is properly speaking what is called good sense or reason, is by nature equal in all men. Hence too it will show that the diversity of our opinions does not proceed from some men being more rational than others, but solely from the fact that our thoughts pass through diverse channels and the same objects are not considered by all. For to be possessed of good mental powers is not sufficient; the principal matter is to apply them well. The greatest minds are capable of the greatest vices as

well as of the greatest virtues, and those who proceed very slowly
may, provided they always follow the straight road, really advance
much faster than those who, though they run, forsake it.

For myself I have never ventured to presume that my mind was in
any way more perfect than that of the ordinary man; I have even
longed to possess thought as quick, or an imagination as accurate
and distinct, or a memory as comprehensive or ready, as some
others. And besides these I do not know any other qualities that
make for the perfection of the human mind. For as to reason or
sense, inasmuch as it is the only thing that constitutes us men and
distinguishes us from the brutes, I would fain believe that it is to be
found complete in each individual, and in this I follow the common
opinion of the philosophers, who say that the question of more or
3   less occurs only in the sphere of the *accidents* and does not affect the
forms or natures of the *individuals* in the same *species*.

But I shall not hesitate to say that I have had great good fortune
from my youth up, in lighting upon and pursuing certain paths
which have conducted me to considerations and maxims from
which I have formed a method, by whose assistance it appears to me
I have the means of gradually increasing my knowledge and of little
by little raising it to the highest possible point which the mediocrity
of my talents and the brief duration of my life can permit me to
reach. For I have already reaped from it fruits of such a nature that,
even though I always try in the judgments I make on myself to lean
to the side of self-depreciation rather than to that of arrogance, and
though, looking with the eye of a philosopher on the diverse actions
and enterprises of all mankind, I find scarcely any which do not
seem to me vain and useless, I do not cease to receive extreme
satisfaction in the progress which I seem to have already made in the
search after truth, and to form such hopes for the future as to
venture to believe that, if amongst the occupations of men, simply
as men, there is some one in particular that is excellent and
important, that is the one which I have selected.

It must always be recollected, however, that possibly I deceive
myself, and that what I take to be gold and diamonds is perhaps no
more than copper and glass. I know how subject we are to delusion
in whatever touches ourselves, and also how much the judgments of
our friends ought to be suspected when they are in our favour. But
4   in this Discourse I shall be very happy to show the paths I have

followed, and to set forth my life as in a picture, so that everyone may judge of it for himself; and thus in learning from the common talk what are the opinions which are held of it, a new means of obtaining self-instruction will be reached, which I shall add to those which I have been in the habit of using.

Thus my design is not here to teach the method which everyone should following in order to promote the good conduct of his reason, but only to show in what manner I have endeavoured to conduct my own. Those who set about giving precepts must esteem themselves more skilful than those to whom they advance them, and if they fall short in the smallest matter they must of course take the blame for it. But regarding this treatise simply as a history, or, if you prefer it, a fable in which, amongst certain things which may be imitated, there are possibly others also which it would not be right to follow, I hope that it will be of use to some without being hurtful to any, and that all will thank me for my frankness.

I have been nourished on letters since my childhood, and since I was given to believe that by their means a clear and certain knowledge could be obtained of all that is useful in life, I had an extreme desire to acquire instruction. But so soon as I had achieved the entire course of study at the close of which one is usually received into the ranks of the learned, I entirely changed my opinion. For I found myself embarrassed with so many doubts and errors that it seemed to me that the effort to instruct myself had no effect other than the increasing discovery of my own ignorance. And yet I was studying at one of the must celebrated schools in Europe, where I thought that there must be men of learning if they were to be found anywhere in the world. I learned there all that others learned; and not being satisfied with the sciences that we were taught, I even read through all the books which fell into my hands, treating of what is considered most curious and rare. Along with this I knew the judgments that others had formed of me, and I did not feel that I was esteemed inferior to my fellow-students, although there were amongst them some destined to fill the places of our masters. And finally our century seemed to me as flourishing, and as fertile in great minds, as any which had preceded. And this made me take the liberty of judging all others by myself and of coming to the conclusion that there was no learning in the world such as I was formerly led to believe it to be.

5

I did not omit, however, always to hold in esteem those exercises which are the occupation of the schools. I knew that the languages which one learns there are essential for the understanding of all ancient literature; that fables with their charm stimulate the mind and histories of memorable deeds exalt it; and that, when read with discretion, these books assist in forming a sound judgment. I was aware that the reading of all good books is indeed like a conversation with the noblest men of past centuries who were the authors of them, nay a carefully studied conversation, in which they reveal to us none but the best of their thoughts. I deemed eloquence to have a power and beauty beyond compare; that poesy has most ravishing delicacy and sweetness; that in mathematics there are the subtlest discoveries and inventions which may accomplish much, both in satisfying the curious, and in furthering all the arts, and in diminishing man's labour; that those writings that deal with morals contain much that is instructive, and many exhortations to virtue which are most useful; that theology points out the way to Heaven; that philosophy teaches us to speak with an appearance of truth on all things, and causes us to be admired by the less learned; that jurisprudence, medicine and all other sciences bring honour and riches to those who cultivate them; and finally that it is good to have examined all things, even those most full of superstition and falsehood, in order that we may know their just value, and avoid being deceived by them.

But I considered that I had already given sufficient time to languages and likewise even to the reading of the literature of the ancients, both their histories and their fables. For to converse with those of other centuries is almost the same thing as to travel. It is good to know something of the customs of different peoples in order to judge more sanely of our own, and not to think that everything of a fashion not ours is absurd and contrary to reason, as do those who have seen nothing. But when one employs too much time in travelling, one becomes a stranger in one's own country, and when one is too curious about things which were practised in past centuries, one is usually very ignorant about those which are practised in our own time. Besides, fables make one imagine many events possible which in reality are not so, and even the most accurate of histories, if they do not exactly misrepresent or exaggerate the value of things in order to render them more worthy of being read, at least omit in them all the circumstances which are basest and least notable; and from this fact it follows that what is retained is not portrayed as it really is, and that those who regulate their conduct by examples which they derive from such a source, are liable to fall into the extravagances of the knights-errant of romance, and form projects beyond their power of performance.

I esteemed eloquence most highly and I was enamoured of poesy, but I thought that both were gifts of the mind rather than fruits of study. Those who have the strongest power of reasoning, and who most skilfully arrange their thoughts in order to render them clear and intelligible, have the best power of persuasion even if they can but speak the language of Lower Brittany and have never learned rhetoric. And those who have the most delightful original ideas and who know how to express them with the maximum of style and suavity, would not fail to be the best poets even if the art of poetry were unknown to them.

Most of all was I delighted with mathematics because of the certainty of its demonstrations and the evidence of its reasoning; but I did not yet understand its true use, and, believing that it was of service only in the mechanical arts, I was astonished that, seeing how firm and solid was its basis, no loftier edifice had been reared thereupon. On the other hand I compared the works of the ancient pagans which deal with morals to palaces most superb and magnificent, which are yet built on sand and mud alone. They praise the virtues most highly and show them to be more worthy of being prized than anything else in the world, but they do not sufficiently teach us to become acquainted with them, and often that which is called by a fine name is nothing but insensibility, or pride, or despair, or parricide.

I honoured our theology and aspired as much as anyone to reach to heaven, but having learned to regard it as a most highly assured fact that the road is not less open to the most ignorant than to the most learned, and that the revealed truths which conduct thither are quite above our intelligence, I should not have dared to submit them to the feebleness of my reasonings; and I thought that, in order to undertake to examine them and succeed in so doing, it was necessary to have some extraordinary assistance from above and to be more than a mere man.

I shall not say anything about philosophy, but that, seeing that it has been cultivated for many centuries by the best minds that have ever lived, and that nevertheless no single thing is to be found in it which is not subject of dispute, and in consequence which is not dubious, I had not enough presumption to hope to fare better there than other men had done. And also, considering how many conflicting opinions there may be regarding the self-same matter, all supported by learned people, while there can never be more than one which is true, I esteemed as well-nigh false all that only went as far as being probable.

Then as to the other sciences, inasmuch as they derive their principles from philosophy, I judged that one could have built nothing solid on foundations so far from firm. And neither the honour nor the promised gain was sufficient to persuade me to cultivate them, for, thanks be to God, I did not find myself in a condition which obliged me to make a merchandise of science for the improvement of my fortune; and, although I did not pretend to scorn all glory like the Cynics, I yet had very small esteem for what I could not hope to acquire, excepting through fictitious titles. And, finally, as to false doctrines, I thought that I already knew well enough what they were worth to be subject to deception neither by the promises of an alchemist, the predictions of an astrologer, the impostures of a magician, the artifices or the empty boastings of any of those who make a profession of knowing that of which they are ignorant.

This is why, as soon as age permitted me to emerge from the control of my tutors, I entirely quitted the study of letters. And resolving to seek no other science than that which could be found in myself, or at least in the great book of the world, I employed the rest of my youth in travel, in seeing courts and armies, in intercourse with men of diverse temperaments and conditions, in collecting varied experiences, in proving myself in the various predicaments in which I was placed by fortune, and under all circumstances bringing my mind to bear on the things which came before it, so that I might derive some profit from my experience. For it seemed to me that I might meet with much more truth in the reasonings that each man makes on the matters that specially concern him, and the issue of which would very soon punish him if he made a wrong judgment, than in the case of those made by a man of letters in his study touching speculations which lead to no result, and which bring about no other consequences to himself excepting that he will be all the more vain the more they are removed from common sense, since in this case it proves him to have employed so much the more ingenuity and skill in trying to make them seem probable. And I always had an excessive desire to learn to distinguish the true from the false, in order to see clearly in my actions and to walk with confidence in this life.

It is true that while I only considered the manners of other men I found in them nothing to give me settled convictions; and I remarked in them almost as much diversity as I had formerly seen in the opinions of philosophers. So much was this the case that the greatest profit which I derived from their study was that, in seeing many things which, although they seem to us very extravagant and ridiculous, were yet commonly received and approved by other great nations, I learned to believe nothing too certainly of which I had only been convinced by example and custom. Thus little by little I was delivered from many errors which might have obscured our natural vision and rendered us less capable of listening to reason. But after I had employed several years in thus studying the book of the world and trying to acquire some experience, I one day formed the resolution of also making myself an object of study and of employing all the strength of my mind in choosing the road I should follow. This succeeded much better, it appeared to me, than if I had never departed either from my country or my books.

Part 2

I was then in Germany, to which country I had been attracted by the wars which are not yet at an end. And as I was returning from the coronation of the Emperor to join the army, the setting in of winter detained me in a quarter where, since I found no society to divert me, while fortunately I had also no cares or passions to trouble me, I remained the whole day shut up alone in a stove-heated room, where I had complete leisure to occupy myself with my own thoughts. One of the first of the considerations that occurred to me was that there is very often less perfection in works composed of several portions, and carried out by the hands of various masters, than in those on which one individual alone has worked. Thus we see that buildings planned and carried out by one architect alone are usually more beautiful and better proportioned than those which many have tried to put in order and improve, making use of old walls which were built with other ends in view. In the same way also, those ancient cities which, originally mere villages, have become in the process of time great towns, are usually badly constructed in comparison with those which are regularly laid out on a plain by a surveyor who is free to follow his own ideas. Even though, considering their buildings each one apart, there is often as much or more display of skill in the one case than in the other, the former have large buildings and small buildings indiscriminately placed together, thus rendering the streets crooked and irregular, so that it might be said that it was chance rather than the will of men guided by reason that led to such an arrangement. And if we consider that this happens despite the fact that from all time there have been certain officials who have had the special duty of looking after the buildings of private individuals in order that they may be public ornaments, we shall understand how difficult it is to bring about much that is satisfactory in operating only upon the works of others. Thus I imagined that those people who were once half-savage, and who have become civilised only by slow degrees, merely forming their laws as the disagreeable necessities of their crimes and quarrels constrained them, could not succeed in establishing so good a system of government as those who, from the time they first came together as communities, carried into effect the constitution laid down by some prudent legislator. Thus it is quite certain that the constitution of the true religion whose ordinances are of God alone is incomparably better regulated than any other. And, to come down to human affairs, I believe that if Sparta was very flourishing in former times, this was not because of the excellence of each and every one of its laws, seeing that many were very strange and even contrary to good morals, but because, being drawn up by one individual, they all tended towards the same end. And similarly I thought that the sciences found in books — in those at least whose reasonings are only probable and which have no demonstrations, composed as they are of the gradually accumulated opinions of many different individuals — do not approach so near to the truth as the simple reasoning which a man of common sense can quite naturally carry out respecting the things which come immediately before him. Again I thought that since we have all been

12

13

children before being men, and since it has for long fallen to us to be governed by our appetites and by our teachers (who often enough contradicted one another, and none of whom perhaps counselled us always for the best), it is almost impossible that our judgments should be so excellent or solid as they should have been had we had complete use of our reason since our birth, and had we been guided by its means alone.

It is true that we do not find that all the houses in a town are rased to the ground for the sole reason that the town is to be rebuilt in another fashion, with streets made more beautiful; but at the same time we see that many people cause their own houses to be knocked down in order to rebuild them, and that sometimes they are forced so to do where there is danger of the houses falling of themselves, and when the foundations are not secure. From such examples I argued to myself that there was no plausibility in the claim of any private individual to reform a state by altering everything, and by overturning it throughout, in order to set it right again. Nor is it likewise probable that the whole body of the sciences, or the order of teaching established by the schools, should be reformed. But as regards all the opinions which up to this time I had embraced, I thought I could not do better than endeavour once for all to sweep them completely away, so that they might later on be replaced, either by others which were better, or by the same, when I had made them conform to the uniformity of a rational scheme. And I firmly believed that by this means I should succeed in directing my life much better than if I had only built on old foundations, and relied on principles of which I allowed myself to be in youth persuaded without having inquired into their truth. For although in so doing I recognised various difficulties, these were at the same time not unsurmountable, nor comparable to those which are found in reformation of the most insignificant kind in matters which concern the public. In the case of great bodies it is too difficult a task to raise them again when they are once thrown down, or even to keep them in their places when once thoroughly shaken; and their fall cannot be otherwise than very violent. Then as to any imperfections that they may possess (and the very diversity that is found between them is sufficient to tell us that these in many cases exist) custom has doubtless greatly mitigated them, while it has also helped us to avoid, or insensibly corrected a number against

14

which mere foresight would have found it difficult to guard. And finally the imperfections are almost always more supportable than would be the process of removing them, just as the great roads which wind about amongst the mountains become, because of being frequented, little by little so well-beaten and easy that it is much better to follow them than to try to go more directly by climbing over rocks and descending to the foot of precipices.

This is the reason why I cannot in any way approve of those turbulent and unrestful spirits who, being called neither by birth nor fortune to the management of public affairs, never fail to have always in their minds some new reforms. And if I thought that in this treatise there was contained the smallest justification for this folly, I should be very sorry to allow it to be published. My design has never extended beyond trying to reform my own opinion and to build on a foundation which is entirely my own. If my work has given me a certain satisfaction, so that I here present to you a draft of it, I do not so do because I wish to advise anybody to imitate it. Those to whom God has been most beneficent in the bestowal of His graces will perhaps form designs which are more elevated; but I fear much that this particular one will seem too venturesome for many. The simple resolve to strip oneself of all opinions and beliefs formerly received is not to be regarded as an example that each man should follow, and the world may be said to be mainly composed of two classes of minds neither of which could prudently adopt it. There are those who, believing themselves to be cleverer than they are, cannot restrain themselves from being precipitate in judgment and have not sufficient patience to arrange their thoughts in proper order; hence, once a man of this description had taken the liberty of doubting the principles he formerly accepted, and had deviated from the beaten track, he would never be able to maintain the path which must be followed to reach the appointed end more quickly, and he would hence remain wandering astray all through his life. Secondly, there are those who having reason or modesty enough to judge that they are less capable of distinguishing truth from falsehood than some others from whom instruction might be obtained, are right in contenting themselves with following the opinions of these others rather than in searching better ones for themselves.

For myself I should doubtless have been of these last if I had never had more than a single master, or had I never known the diversities which have from all time existed between the opinions of men of the greatest learning. But I had been taught, even in my college days, that there is nothing imaginable so strange or so little credible that it has not been maintained by one philosopher or other, and I further recognised in the course of my travels that all those whose sentiments are very contrary to ours are yet not necessarily barbarians or savages, but may be possessed of reason in as great or even a greater degree than ourselves. I also considered how very different the self-same man, identical in mind and spirit, may become, according as he is brought up from childhood amongst the French or Germans, or has passed his whole life amongst Chinese or cannibals. I likewise noticed how even in the fashions of one's clothing the same thing that pleased us ten years ago, and which will perhaps please us once again before ten years are passed, seems at the present time extravagant and ridiculous. I thus concluded that it is much more custom and example that persuade us than any certain knowledge, and yet in spite of this the voice of the majority does not afford a proof of any value in truths a little difficult to discover, because such truths are much more likely to have been discovered by one man than by a nation. I could not, however, put my finger on a single person whose opinions seemed preferable to those of others, and I found that I was, so to speak, constrained myself to undertake the direction of my procedure.

But like one who walks alone and in the twilight I resolved to go so slowly, and to use so much circumspection in all things, that if my advance was but very small, at least I guarded myself well from falling. I did not wish to set about the final rejection of any single opinion which might formerly have crept into my beliefs without having been introduced there by means of reason, until I had first of all employed sufficient time in planning out the task which I had undertaken, and in seeking the true method of arriving at a knowledge of all the things of which my mind was capable.

Among the different branches of philosophy, I had in my younger days to a certain extent studied logic; and in those of mathematics, geometrical analysis and algebra — three arts or sciences which seemed as though they ought to contribute something to the design I had in view. But in examining them I observed in respect to logic that the syllogisms and the greater part of the other teaching served

17

better in explaining to others those things that one knows (or like the art of Lully, in enabling one to speak without judgment of those things of which one is ignorant) than in learning what is new. And although in reality logic contains many precepts which are very true and very good, there are at the same time mingled with them so many others which are hurtful or superfluous that it is almost as difficult to separate the two as to draw a Diana or a Minerva out of a block of marble which is not yet roughly hewn. And as to the analysis of the ancients and the algebra of the moderns, besides the fact that they embrace only matters the most abstract, such as appear to have no actual use, the former is always so restricted to the consideration of symbols that it cannot exercise the understanding without greatly fatiguing the imagination; and in the latter one is so subjected to certain rules and formulas that the result is the construction of an art which is confused and obscure, and which embarrasses the mind, instead of a science which contributes to its cultivation. This made me feel that some other method must be found, which, comprising the advantages of the three, is yet exempt from their faults. And as a multiplicity of laws often furnishes excuses for evil-doing, and as a State is hence much better ruled when, having but very few laws, these are most strictly observed; so, instead of the great number of precepts of which logic is composed, I believed that I should find the four which I shall state quite sufficient, provided that I adhered to a firm and constant resolve never on any single occasion to fail in their observance.

The first of these was to accept nothing as true which I did not clearly recognise to be so: that is to say, carefully to avoid precipitation and prejudice in judgments, and to accept in them nothing more than what was presented to my mind so clearly and distinctly that I could have no occasion to doubt it.

The second was to divide up each of the difficulties which I examined into as many parts as possible, and as seemed requisite in order that it might be resolved in the best manner possible.

The third was to carry on my reflections in due order, commencing with objects that were the most simple and easy to understand, in order to rise little by little, or by degrees, to knowledge of the most complex, assuming an order, even if a fictitious one, among those which do not follow a natural sequence relatively to one another.

The last was in all cases to make enumerations so complete and reviews so general that I should be certain of having omitted nothing.

Those long chains of reasoning, simple and easy as they are, of which geometricians make use in order to arrive at the most difficult demonstrations, had caused me to imagine that all those things which fall under the cognisance of man might very likely be mutually related in the same fashion; and that, provided only that we abstain from receiving anything as true which is not so, and always retain the order which is necessary in order to deduce the one conclusion from the other, there can be nothing so remote that we cannot reach to it, nor so recondite that we cannot discover it. And I had not much trouble in discovering which objects it was necessary to begin with, for I already knew that it was with the most simple and those most easy to apprehend. Considering also that of all those who have hitherto sought for the truth in the sciences, it has been the mathematicians alone who have been able to succeed in making any demonstrations, that is to say producing reasons which are evident and certain, I did not doubt that it had been by means of a similar kind that they carried on their investigations. I did not at the same time hope for any practical result in so doing, except that my mind would become accustomed to the nourishment of truth and would not content itself with false reasoning. But for all that I had no intention of trying to master all those particular sciences that receive in common the name of mathematics; but observing that, although their objects are different, they do not fail to agree in this, that they take nothing under consideration but the various relationships or proportions which are present in these objects, I thought that it would be better if I only examined these proportions in their general aspect, and without viewing them otherwise than in the objects which would serve most to facilitate a knowledge of them. Not that I should in any way restrict them to these objects, for I might later on all the more easily apply them to all other objects to which they were applicable. Then, having carefully noted that in order to comprehend the proportions I should sometimes require to consider each one in particular, and sometimes merely keep them in mind, or take them in groups, I thought that, in order the better to consider them in detail, I should picture them in the form of lines, because I could find no method

20

more simple nor more capable of being distinctly represented to my imagination and senses. I considered, however, that in order to keep them in my memory or to embrace several at once, it would be essential that I should explain them by means of certain formulas, the shorter the better. And for this purpose it was requisite that I should borrow all that is best in geometrical analysis and algebra, and correct the errors of the one by the other.

As a matter of fact, I can venture to say that the exact observation of the few precepts which I had chosen gave me so much facility in sifting out all the questions embraced in these two sciences, that in the two or three months which I employed in examining them – commencing with the most simple and general, and making each truth that I discovered a rule for helping me to find others – not only did I arrive at the solution of many questions which I had hitherto regarded as most difficult, but, towards the end, it seemed to me that I was able to determine in the case of those of which I was still ignorant, by what means, and in how far, it was possible to solve them. In this I might perhaps appear to you to be very vain if you did not remember that having but one truth to discover in respect to each matter, whoever succeeds in finding it knows in its regard as much as can be known. It is the same as with a child, for instance, who has been instructed in arithmetic and has made an addition according to the rule prescribed; he may be sure of having found as regards the sum of figures given to him all that the human mind can know. For, in conclusion, the method which teaches us to follow the true order and enumerate exactly every term in the matter under investigation contains everything which gives certainty to the rules of arithmetic.

But what pleased me most in this method was that I was certain by its means of exercising my reason in all things, if not perfectly, at least as well as was in my power. And besides this, I felt in making use of it that my mind gradually accustomed itself to conceive of its objects more accurately and distinctly; and not having restricted this method to any particular matter, I promised myself to apply it as usefully to the difficulties of other sciences as I had done to those of algebra. Not that on this account I dared undertake to examine just at once all those that might present themselves; for that would itself have been contrary to the order which the method prescribes. But having noticed that the knowledge of these difficulties must be

dependent on principles derived from philosophy in which I yet
found nothing to be certain, I thought that it was requisite above all   22
to try to establish certainty in it. I considered also that since this
endeavour is the most important in all the world, and that in which
precipitation and prejudice were most to be feared, I should not try
to grapple with it till I had attained to a much riper age than that of
three and twenty, which was the age I had reached. I thought, too,
that I should first of all employ much time in preparing myself for
the work by eradicating from my mind all the wrong opinions
which I had up to this time accepted, and accumulating a variety of
experiences fitted later on to afford matter for my reasonings, and by
ever exercising myself in the method which I had prescribed, in
order more and more to fortify myself in the power of using it.

Part 3

And finally, as it is not sufficient, before commencing to rebuild the
house which we inhabit, to pull it down and provide materials and
an architect (or to act in this capacity ourselves, and make a careful
drawing of its design), unless we have also provided ourselves with
some other house where we can be comfortably lodged during the
time of rebuilding, so in order that I should not remain irresolute in
my actions while reason obliged me to be so in my judgments, and
that I might not omit to carry on my life as happily as I could, I
formed for myself a code of morals for the time being which did not
consist of more than three or four maxims, which maxims I should
like to enumerate to you.

The first was to obey the laws and customs of my country,   23
adhering constantly to the religion in which by God's grace I had
been instructed since my childhood, and in all other things directing
my conduct by opinions the most moderate in nature, and the
farthest removed from excess in all those which are commonly
received and acted on by the most judicious of those with whom I
might come in contact. For since I began to count my own
opinions as nought, because I desired to place all under examination, I was convinced that I could not do better than follow those
held by people on whose judgment reliance could be placed. And
although such persons may possibly exist amongst the Persians and
Chinese as well as amongst ourselves, it seemed to me that it was

most expedient to bring my conduct into harmony with the ideas of those with whom I should have to live; and that, in order to ascertain that these were their real opinions, I should observe what they did rather than what they said, not only because in the corrupt state of our manners there are few people who desire to say all that they believe, but also because many are themselves ignorant of their beliefs. For since the act of thought by which we believe a thing is different from that by which we know that we believe it, the one often exists without the other. And amongst many opinions all equally received, I chose only the most moderate, both because these are always most suited for putting into practice, and probably the best (for all excess has a tendency to be bad), and also because I should have in a less degree turned aside from the right path, supposing that I was wrong, than if, having chosen an extreme

24   course, I found that I had chosen amiss. I also made a point of counting as excess all the engagements by means of which we limit in some degree our liberty. Not that I hold in low esteem those laws which, in order to remedy the inconstancy of feeble souls, permit, when we have a good object in our view, that certain vows be taken, or contracts made, which oblige us to carry out that object. This sanction is even given for security in commerce where designs are wholly indifferent. But because I saw nothing in all the world remaining constant, and because for my own part I promised myself gradually to get my judgments to grow better and never to grow worse, I should have thought that I had committed a serious sin against common sense if, because I approved of something at one time, I was obliged to regard it similarly at a later time, after it had possibly ceased to meet my approval, or after I had ceased to regard it in a favourable light.

My second maxim was that of being as firm and resolute in my actions as I could be, and not to follow less faithfully opinions the most dubious, when my mind was once made up regarding them, than if these had been beyond doubt. In this I should be following the example of travellers, who, finding themselves lost in a forest, know that they ought not to wander first to one side and then to the other, nor, still less, to stop in one place, but understand that they should continue to walk as straight as they can in one direction, not diverging for any slight reason, even though it was possibly

25   chance alone that first determined them in their choice. By this means if they do not go exactly where they wish, they will at least arrive somewhere at the end, where probably they will be better off than in the middle of a forest. And thus since often enough in the actions of life no delay is permissible, it is very certain that, when it is beyond our power to discern the opinions which carry most truth, we should follow the most probable; and even although we notice no greater probability in the one opinion than in the other, we at least should make up our minds to follow a particular one and afterwards consider it as no longer doubtful in its relationship to practice, but as very true and very certain, inasmuch as the reason which caused us to determine upon it is known to be so. And henceforward this principle was sufficient to deliver me from all the penitence and remorse which usually affect the mind and agitate the conscience of those weak and vacillating creatures who allow themselves to keep changing their procedure, and practise as good, things which they afterwards judge to be evil.

My third maxim was to try always to conquer myself rather than fortune, and to alter my desires rather than change the order of the world, and generally to accustom myself to believe that there is nothing entirely within our power but our own thoughts: so that after we have done our best in regard to the things that are without us, our ill-success cannot possibly be failure on our part.[1] And this alone seemed to me sufficient to prevent my desiring anything in the future beyond that I could actually obtain, hence rendering me content; for since our will does not naturally induce us to desire anything but what our understanding represents to it as in some way possible of attainment, it is certain that if we consider all good things which are outside of us as equally outside of our power, we should not have more regret in resigning those goods which appear to pertain to our birth, when we are deprived of them for no fault of our own, than we have in not possessing the kingdoms of China or Mexico. In the same way, making what is called a virtue out of a necessity, we should no more desire to be well if ill, or free, if in prison, than we now do to have our bodies formed of a substance as

26

---

1 'So that whatever does not eventuate after we have done all in our power that it should happen is to be accounted by us as among the things which evidently cannot be done and which in philosophical phrase are called impossible.' Latin version.

little corruptible as diamonds, or to have wings to fly with like birds. I allow, however, that to accustom oneself to regard all things from this point of view requires long exercise and meditation often repeated and I believe that it is principally in this that is to be found the secret of those philosophers who, in ancient times, were able to free themselves from the empire of fortune, or, despite suffering or poverty, to rival their gods in their happiness. For, ceaselessly occupying themselves in considering the limits which were prescribed to them by nature, they persuaded themselves so completely that nothing was within their own power but their thoughts, that this conviction alone was sufficient to prevent their having any longing for other things. And they had so absolute a mastery over their thoughts that they had some reason for esteeming themselves as more rich and more powerful, and more free and more happy than other men, who, however favoured by nature or fortune they might be, if devoid of this philosophy, never could arrive at all at which they aim.

And last of all, to conclude this moral code, I felt it incumbent on me to make a review of the various occupations of men in this life in order to try to choose out the best: and without wishing to say anything of the employment of others I thought that I could not do better than continue in the one in which I found myself engaged, that is to say, in occupying my whole life in cultivating my reason, and in advancing myself as much as possible in the knowledge of the truth in accordance with the method which I had prescribed myself. I have experienced so much satisfaction since beginning to use this method, that I did not believe that any sweeter or more innocent could in this life be found — every day discovering by its means some truths which seemed to me sufficiently important, although commonly ignored by other men. The satisfaction which I had so filled my mind that all else seemed of no account. And, besides, the three preceding maxims were founded solely on the plan which I had formed of continuing to instruct myself. For since God has given to each of us some light with which to distinguish truth from error, I could not believe that I ought for a single moment to content myself with accepting the opinions held by others unless I had in view the employment of my own judgment in examining them at the proper time; and I could not have held myself free of scruple in following such opinions, if nevertheless I had not intended to lose no occasion of finding superior opinions, supposing them to exist; and finally, I should not have been able to restrain my desires nor to remain content, if I had not followed a road by which, thinking that I should by certain to be able to acquire all the knowledge of which I was capable, I also thought I should likewise be certain of obtaining all the best things which could ever come within my power. And inasmuch as our will impels us neither to follow after nor to flee from anything, excepting as our understanding represents it as good or evil, it is sufficient to judge wisely in order to act well, and the best judgment brings the best action — that is to say, the acquisition of all the virtues and all the other good things that it is possible to obtain. When one is certain that this point is reached, one cannot fail to be contented.

Having thus assured myself of these maxims, and having set them on one side along with the truths of religion which have always taken the first place in my creed, I judged that as far as the rest of my opinions were concerned, I could safely undertake to rid myself of them. And inasmuch as I hoped to be able to reach my end more successfully in converse with man than in living longer shut up in the warm room where these reflections had come to me, I hardly awaited the end of winter before I once more set myself to travel. And in all the nine following years I did nought but roam hither and thither, trying to be a spectator rather than an actor in all the comedies the world displays. More especially did I reflect in each matter that came before me as to anything which could make it subject to suspicion or doubt, and give occasion for mistake, and I rooted out of my mind all the errors which might have formerly crept in. Not that indeed I imitated the sceptics, who only doubt for the sake of doubting, and pretend to be always uncertain; for, on the contrary, my design was only to provide myself with good ground for assurance, and to reject the quicksand and mud in order to find the rock or clay. In this task it seems to me, I succeeded pretty well, since in trying to discover the error or uncertainty of the propositions which I examined, not by feeble conjectures, but by clear and assured reasonings, I encountered nothing so dubious that I could not draw from it some conclusion that was tolerably secure, if this were no more than the inference that it contained in it nothing that was certain. And just as in pulling down an old house we usually preserve the debris to serve in building up another, so in

29

destroying all those opinions which I considered to be ill-founded, I made various observations and acquired many experiences, which have since been of use to me in establishing those which are more certain. And more than this, I continued to exercise myself in the method which I have laid down for my use; for besides the fact that I was careful as a rule to conduct all my thoughts according to its maxims, I set aside some hours from time to time which I more especially employed in practising myself in the solution of mathematical problems according to the method, or in the solution of other problems which though pertaining to other sciences, I was able to make almost similar to those of mathematics, by detaching them from all principles of other sciences which I found to be not sufficiently secure. You will see the result in many examples which are expounded in this volume.[2] And hence, without living to all appearance in any way differently from those who, having no occupation beyond spending their lives in ease and innocence, study to separate pleasure from vice, and who, in order to enjoy their leisure without weariness, make use of all distractions that are innocent and good, I did not cease to prosecute my design, and to profit perhaps even more in my study of truth than if I had done nothing but read books or associate with literary people.

These nine years thus passed away before I had taken any definite part in regard to the difficulties as to which the learned are in the habit of disputing, or had commenced to seek the foundation of any philosophy more certain than the vulgar. And the example of many excellent men who had tried to do the same before me, but, as it appears to me, without success, made me imagine it to be so hard that possibly I should not have dared to undertake the task, had I not discovered that someone had spread abroad the report that I had already reached its conclusion. I cannot tell on what they based this opinion; if my conversation has contributed anything to it, this must have arisen from my confessing my ignorance more ingenuously than those who have studied a little usually do. And perhaps it was also due to my having shown forth my reasons for doubting many things which were held by others to be certain, rather than from having boasted of any special philosophic system. But being at heart

2 The *Dioptrics, Meteors* and *Geometry* were published originally in the same volume.

honest enough not to desire to be esteemed as different from what I am, I thought that I must try by every means in my power to render myself worthy of the reputation which I had gained. And it is just eight years ago that this desire made me resolve to remove myself from all places where any acquaintances were possible, and to retire to a country such as this,[3] where the long-continued war has caused such order to be established that the armies which are maintained seem only to be of use in allowing the inhabitants to enjoy the fruits of peace with so much the more security; and where, in the crowded throng of a great and very active nation, which is more concerned with its own affairs than curious about those of others, without missing any of the conveniences of the most populous towns, I can live as solitary and retired as in deserts the most remote.

Part 4

I do not know that I ought to tell you of the first meditations there made by me, for they are so metaphysical and so unusual that they may perhaps not be acceptable to everyone. And yet at the same time, in order that one may judge whether the foundations which I have laid are sufficiently secure, I find myself constrained in some measure to refer to them. For a long time I had remarked that it is sometimes requisite in common life to follow opinions which one knows to be most uncertain, exactly as though they were indisputable, as has been said above. But because in this case I wished to give myself entirely to the search after truth, I thought that it was necessary for me to take an apparently opposite course, and to reject as absolutely false everything as to which I could imagine the least ground of doubt, in order to see if afterwards there remained anything in my belief that was entirely certain. Thus, because our senses sometimes deceive us, I wished to suppose that nothing is just as they cause us to imagine it to be; and because there are men who deceive themselves in their reasoning and fall into paralogisms, even concerning the simplest matters of geometry, and judging that I was as subject to error as was any other, I rejected as false all the reasons formerly accepted by me as demonstrations. And since all the same thoughts and conceptions which we have while awake may also come to us in sleep, without any of them being at that time true, I

31

32

3 i.e. Holland, where Descartes settled in 1629.

resolved to assume that everything that ever entered into my mind was no more true than the illusions of my dreams. But immediately afterwards I noticed that whilst I thus wished to think all things false, it was absolutely essential that the 'I' who thought this should be somewhat, and remarking that this truth '*I think, therefore I am*' was so certain and so assured that all the most extravagant suppositions brought forward by the sceptics were incapable of shaking it, I came to the conclusion that I could receive it without scruple as the first principle of the philosophy for which I was seeking.

And then, examining attentively that which I was, I saw that I could conceive that I had no body, and that there was no world nor place where I might be; but yet that I could not for all that conceive that I was not. On the contrary, I saw from the very fact that I thought of doubting the truth of other things, it very evidently and certainly followed that I was; on the other hand if I had only ceased from thinking, even if all the rest of what I had ever imagined had really existed, I should have no reason for thinking that I had existed. From that I knew that I was a substance the whole essence or nature of which is to think, and that for its existence there is no need of any place, nor does it depend on any material thing; so that this 'me', that is to say, the soul by which I am what I am, is entirely distinct from body, and is even more easy to know than is the latter; and even if body were not, the soul would not cease to be what it is.

After this I considered generally what in a proposition is requisite in order to be true and certain; for since I had just discovered one which I knew to be such, I thought that I ought also to know in what this certainty consisted. And having remarked that there was nothing at all in the statement '*I think, therefore I am*' which assures me of having thereby made a true assertion, excepting that I see very clearly that to think it is necessary to be, I came to the conclusion that I might assume, as a general rule, that the things which we conceive very clearly and distinctly are all true – remembering, however, that there is some difficulty in ascertaining which are those that we distinctly conceive.

Following upon this, and reflecting on the fact that I doubted, and that consequently my existence was not quite perfect (for I saw clearly that it was a greater perfection to know than to doubt), I resolved to inquire whence I had learnt to think of anything more perfect than I myself was; and I recognised very clearly that this

33

34

conception must proceed from some nature which was really more perfect. As to the thoughts which I had of many other things outside of me, like the heavens, the earth, light, heat, and a thousand others, I had not so much difficulty in knowing whence they came, because, remarking nothing in them which seemed to render them superior to me, I could believe that, if they were true, they were dependencies upon my nature, in so far as it possessed some perfection; and if they were not true, that I held them from nought, that is to say, that they were in me because I had something lacking in my nature. But this could not apply to the idea of a Being more perfect than my own, for to hold it from nought would be manifestly impossible; and because it is no less contradictory to say of the more perfect that it is what results from and depends on the less perfect, than to say that there is something which proceeds from nothing, it was equally impossible that I should hold it from myself. In this way it could but follow that it had been placed in me by a Nature which was really more perfect than mine could be, and which even had within itself all the perfections of which I could form any idea — that is to say, to put it in a word, which was God. To which I added that since I knew some perfections which I did not possess, I was not the only being in existence (I shall here use freely, if you will allow, the terms of the school); but that there was necessarily some other more perfect Being on which I depended, or from which I acquired all that I had. For if I had existed alone and independent of any others, so that I should have had from myself all that perfection of being in which I participated to however small an extent, I should have been able for the same reason to have had all the remainder which I knew that I lacked; and thus I myself should have been infinite, eternal, immutable, omniscient, all-powerful, and, finally, I should have all the perfections which I could discern in God. For, in pursuance of the reasonings which I have just carried on, in order to know the nature of God as far as my nature is capable of knowing it, I had only to consider in reference to all these things of which I found some idea in myself, whether it was a perfection to possess them or not. And I was assured that none of those which indicated some imperfection were in Him, but that all else was present; and I saw that doubt, inconstancy, sadness, and such things, could not be in Him considering that I myself should have been glad to be without them. In addition to this, I had ideas

35

of many things which are sensible and corporeal, for, although I might suppose that I was dreaming, and that all that I saw or imagined was false, I could not at the same time deny that the ideas were really in my thoughts. But because I had already recognised very clearly in myself that the nature of the intelligence is distinct from that of the body, and observing that all composition gives evidence of dependency, and that dependency is manifestly an imperfection, I came to the conclusion that it could not be a perfection in God to be composed of these two natures, and that consequently He was not so composed. I judged, however, that if there were any bodies in the world, or even any intelligences or other natures which were not wholly perfect, their existence must depend on His power in such a way that they could not subsist without Him for a single moment.

After that I desired to seek for other truths, and having put before myself the object of the geometricians, which I conceived to be a continuous body, or a space indefinitely extended in length, breadth, height or depth, which was divisible into various parts, and which might have various figures and sizes, and might be moved or transposed in all sorts of ways (for all this the geometricians suppose to be in the object of their contemplation), I went through some of their simplest demonstrations, and having noticed that this great certainty which everyone attributes to these demonstrations is founded solely on the fact that they are conceived of with clearness, in accordance with the rule which I have just laid down, I also noticed that there was nothing at all in them to assure me of the existence of their object. For, to take an example, I saw very well that if we suppose a triangle to be given, the three angles must certainly be equal to two right angles; but for all that I saw no reason to be assured that there was any such triangle in existence, while on the contrary, on reverting to the examination of the idea which I had of a Perfect Being, I found that in this case existence was implied in it in the same manner in which the equality of its three angles to two right angles is implied in the idea of a triangle; or in the idea of a sphere, that all the points on its surface are equidistant from its centre, or even more evidently still. Consequently it is at least as certain that God, who is a Being so perfect, is, or exists, as any demonstration of geometry can possibly be.

What causes many, however, to persuade themselves that there is difficulty in knowing this truth, and even in knowing the nature of their soul, is the fact that they never raise their minds above the things of sense, or that they are so accustomed to consider nothing excepting by imagining it, which is a mode of thought specially adapted to material objects, that all that is not capable of being imagined appears to them not to be intelligible at all. This is manifest enough from the fact that even the philosophers in the schools hold it as a maxim that there is nothing in the understanding which has not first of all been in the senses, in which there is certainly no doubt that the ideas of God and of the soul have never been. And it seems to me that those who desire to make use of their imagination in order to understand these ideas, act in the same way as if, to hear sounds or smell odours, they should wish to make use of their eyes: excepting that there is indeed this difference, that the sense of sight does not give us less assistance of the truth of its objects, than do those of sight or of hearing, while neither our imagination nor our senses can ever assure us of anything, if our understanding does not intervene.

If there are finally any persons who are not sufficiently persuaded of the existence of God and of their soul by the reasons which I have brought forward, I wish that they should know that all other things of which they perhaps think themselves more assured (such as possessing a body, and that there are stars and an earth and so on) are less certain. For, although we have a moral assurance of these things which is such that it seems that it would be extravagant in us to doubt them, at the same time no one, unless he is devoid of reason, can deny, when a metaphysical certainty is in question, that there is sufficient cause for our not having complete assurance, by observing the fact that when asleep we may similarly imagine that we have another body, and that we see other stars and another earth, without there being anything of the kind. For how do we know that the thoughts that come in dreams are more false than those that we have when we are awake, seeing that often enough the former are not less lively and vivid than the latter? And though the wisest minds may study the matter as much as they will, I do not believe that they will be able to give any sufficient reason for removing this doubt, unless they presuppose the existence of God. For to begin with, that which I have just taken as a rule, that is to say, that all the things that we very clearly and very distinctly conceive of are true, is certain

38

only because God is or exists, and that He is a perfect Being, and that all that is in us issues from Him. From this it follows that our ideas or notions, which to the extent of their being clear or distinct are ideas of real things issuing from God, cannot but to that extent be true. So that though we often enough have ideas which have an element of falsity, this can only be the case in regard to those which have in them somewhat that is confused or obscure, because in so far as they have this character they participate in negation – that is, they exist in us as confused only because we are not quite perfect. And it is evident that there is no less repugnance in the idea that error or imperfection, inasmuch as it is imperfection, proceeds from God, than there is in the idea of truth or perfection proceeding from nought. But if we did not know that all that is in us of reality and truth proceeds from a perfect and infinite Being, however clear and distinct were our ideas, we should not have any reason to assure ourselves that they had the perfection of being true.

But after the knowledge of God and of the soul has thus rendered us certain of this rule, it is very easy to understand that the dreams which we imagine in our sleep should not make us in any way doubt the truth of the thoughts which we have when awake. For even if in sleep we had some very distinct idea such as a geometrician might have who discovered some new demonstration, the fact of being asleep would not militate against its truth. And as to the most ordinary error in our dreams, which consists in their representing to us various objects in the same way as do our external senses, it does not matter that this should give us occasion to suspect the truth of such ideas, because we may be likewise often enough deceived in them without our sleeping at all, just as when those who have the jaundice see everything as yellow, or when stars or other bodies which are very remote appear much smaller than they really are. For, finally, whether we are awake or asleep, we should never allow ourselves to be persuaded excepting by the evidence of our reason. And it must be remarked that I speak of our reason and not of our imagination nor of our senses; just as though we see the sun very clearly, we should not for that reason judge that it is of the size of which it appears to be; likewise we could quite well distinctly imagine the head of a lion on the body of a goat, without necessarily concluding that a chimera exists. For reason does not insist that whatever we see or imagine thus is a truth, but it tells us clearly that all our ideas or notions must have some foundation of truth. For otherwise it could not be possible that God, who is all perfection and truth, should have placed them within us. And because our reasonings are never so evident nor so complete during sleep as during wakefulness, although sometimes our imaginations are then just as lively and acute, or even more so, reason tells us that since our thoughts cannot possibly be all true, because we are not altogether perfect, that which they have of truth must infallibly be met with in our waking experience rather than in that of our dreams.

Part 5

I should be very glad to proceed to show forth the complete chain of truths which I have deduced from these first, but because to do this it would have been necessary now to speak of many matters of dispute among the learned, with whom I have no desire to embroil myself, I think that it will be better to abstain. I shall only state generally what these truths are, so that it may be left to the decision of those best able to judge whether it would be of use for the public to be more particularly informed of them or not. I always remained firm in the resolution which I had made, not to assume any other principle than that of which I have just made use, in order to demonstrate the existence of God and of the Soul, and to accept nothing as true which did not appear to be more clear and more certain than the demonstrations of the geometricians had formerly seemed. And nevertheless I venture to say that not only have I found the means of satisfying myself in a short time as to the more important of those difficulties usually dealt with in philosophy, but I have also observed certain laws which God has so established in nature, and of which He has imprinted such ideas on our minds, that, after having reflected sufficiently upon the matter, we cannot doubt their being accurately observed in all that exists or is done in the world. Further, in considering the sequence of these laws, it seems to me that I have discovered many truths more useful and more important than all that I had formerly learned or even hoped to learn.

But because I tried to explain the most important of these in a treatise[4] which certain considerations prevented me from publishing,

4 i.e. *Le Monde*, suppressed on hearing of Galileo's condemnation.

I cannot do better, in making them known, than here summarise briefly what that treatise contains. I had planned to comprise in it all that I believed myself to know regarding the nature of material objects, before I set myself to write. However, just as the painters who cannot represent equally well on a plain surface all the various sides of a solid body, make selection of one of the most important, 42 which alone is set in the light, while the others are put in shadow and made to appear only as they may be seen in looking at the former, so, fearing that I could not put in my treatise all that I had in my mind, I undertook only to show very fully my conceptions of light. Later on, when occasion occurred, I resolved to add something about the sun and fixed stars, because light proceeds almost entirely from them; the heavens would be dealt with because they transmit light, the planets, the comets and the earth because they reflect it, and more particularly would all bodies which are on the earth, because they are either coloured or transparent, or else luminous; and finally I should deal with man because he is the spectator of all. For the very purpose of putting all these topics somewhat in shadow, and being able to express myself freely about them, without being obliged to adopt or to refute the opinions which are accepted by the learned, I resolved to leave all this world to their disputes, and to speak only of what would happen in a new world if God now created, somewhere in an imaginary space, matter sufficient wherewith to form it, and if He agitated in diverse ways, and without any order, the diverse portions of this matter, so that there resulted a chaos as confused as the poets ever feigned, and concluded His work by merely lending His concurrence to nature in the usual way, leaving her to act in accordance with the laws which He had established. So, to begin with, I described this matter and tried to represent it in such a way, that it seems to me that nothing in the world could be more clear or intelligible, excepting 43 what has just been said of God and the Soul. For I even went so far as expressly to assume that there was in it none of these forms or qualities which are so debated in the schools, nor anything at all the knowledge of which is not so natural to our minds that none could even pretend to be ignorant of it. Further I pointed out what are the laws of nature, and, without resting my reasons on any other principle than the infinite perfections of God, I tried to demonstrate all those of which one could have any doubt, and to show that they are of such a nature that even if God had created other worlds, He could not have created any in which these laws would fail to be observed. After that, I showed how the greatest part of the matter of which this chaos is constituted, must, in accordance with these laws, dispose and arrange itself in such a fashion as to render it similar to our heavens; and how meantime some of its parts must form an earth, some planets and comets, and some others a sun and fixed stars. And, enlarging on the subject of light, I here explained at length the nature of the light which would be found in the sun and stars, and how from these it crossed in an instant the immense space of the heavens, and how it was reflected from the planets and comets to the earth. To this I also added many things touching the substance, situation, movements, and all the different qualities of these heavens and stars, so that I thought I had said enough to make it clear that there is nothing to be seen in the heavens and stars pertaining to our system which must not, or at least may not, appear exactly the same in those of the system which I described. From this point I came to speak more particularly of the earth, showing how, though I had expressly presupposed that God had not placed any weight in the matter of which it is composed, its parts did not fail all to gravitate exactly to its centre; and how, having water and air on its surface, the disposition of the heavens and of the stars, more particularly of the moon, must cause a flux or reflux, which in all its circumstances is similar to that which is observed in our seas, and besides that, a certain current both of water and air from east to west, such as may also be observed in the tropics. I also showed how the mountains, seas, fountains and rivers, could naturally be formed in it, how the metals came to be in the mines and the plants to grow in the fields; and generally how all bodies, called mixed or composite, might arise. And because I knew nothing but fire which could produce light, excepting the stars, I studied amongst other things to make very clear all that pertains to its nature, how it is formed, how nourished, how there is sometimes only heat without light, and sometimes light without heat; I showed, too, how different colours might by it be induced upon different bodies and qualities of diverse kinds, how some of these were liquefied and others solidified, how nearly all can be consumed or converted into ashes and smoke by its means, and finally how of these ashes, by the intensity of its action alone, it forms glass. Since this transformation

44

45 of ashes into glass seemed to me as wonderful as any other process in nature, I took particular pleasure in describing it.

I did not at the same time wish to infer from all these facts that this world has been created in the manner which I described; for it is much more probable that at the beginning God made it such as it was to be. But it is certain, and it is an opinion commonly received by the theologians, that the action by which He now preserves it is just the same as that by which He at first created it. In this way, although He had not, to begin with, given this world any other form than that of chaos, provided that the laws of nature had once been established and that He had lent His aid in order that its action should be according to its wont, we may well believe, without doing outrage to the miracle of creation, that by this means alone all things which are purely material might in course of time have become such as we observe them to be at present; and their nature is much easier to understand when we see them coming to pass little by little in this manner, than were we to consider them as all complete to begin with.

From a description of inanimate bodies and plants I passed on to that of animals, and particularly to that of men. But since I had not yet sufficient knowledge to speak of them in the same style as of the rest, that is to say, demonstrating the effects from the causes, and showing from what beginning, and in what fashion nature must produce them, I contented myself with supposing that God formed
46 the body of man altogether like one of ours, in the outward figure of its members as well as in the interior conformation of its organs, without making use of any matter other than that which I had described, and without at the first placing in it a rational soul, or any other thing which might serve as a vegetative or as a sensitive soul; excepting that He kindled in the heart one of these fires without light, which I have already described, and which I did not conceive of as in any way different from that which makes the hay heat when shut up before it is dry, and which makes new wine grow frothy when it is left to ferment over the limit. For, examining the functions which might in accordance with this supposition exist in this body, I found precisely all those which might exist in us without our having the power of thought, and consequently without our soul – that is to say, this part of us, distinct from the body, of which it has just been said that its nature is to think –

contributing to it, functions which are identically the same as those in which animals lacking reason may be said to resemble us. For all that, I could not find in these functions any which, being dependent on thought, pertain to us alone, inasmuch as we are men; while I found all of them afterwards, when I assumed that God had created a rational soul and that He had united it to this body in a particular manner which I described.

But in order to show how I there treated of this matter, I wish here to set forth the explanation of the movement of heart and arteries which, being the first and most general movement that is observed in animals, will give us the means of easily judging as to what we ought to think about all the rest. And so that there may be less difficulty in understanding what I shall say on this matter, I should like that those not versed in anatomy should take the trouble, before reading this, of having cut up before their eyes the heart of some large animal which has lungs (for it is in all respects sufficiently similar to the heart of a man), and cause that there be demonstrated to them the two chambers or cavities which are within it. There is first of all that which is on the right side, with which two very large tubes or channels correspond, viz. the *vena cava*, which is the principal receptacle of the blood, and so to speak the trunk of a tree of which all the other veins of the body are the branches; and there is the arterial vein which has been badly named because it is nothing but an artery which, taking its origin from the heart, divides, after having issued from it, into many branches which proceed to disperse themselves all through the lungs. Then there is secondly the cavity on the left side with which there again correspond two tubes which are as large or larger than the preceding, viz. the venous artery, which has also been badly named, because it is nothing but a vein which comes from the lungs, where it is divided into many branches, interlaced with those of the arterial vein, and with those of the tube which is called the windpipe, through which enters the air which we breathe; and the great artery which, issuing from the heart, sends its branches throughout the body. I should also wish that the eleven little membranes, which like so many doors, open and shut the four entrances which are in these two cavities, should be carefully shown. There are of these three at the entrance of the *vena cava*, where they are so arranged that they can in nowise prevent the blood which it contains from flowing into the right cavity of the heart and yet exactly prevent its issuing out; there are three at the entrance to the arterial vein, which, being arranged quite the other way, easily allow the blood which is in this cavity to pass into the lungs, but not that which is already in the lungs to return to this cavity. There are also two others at the entrance of the venous artery, which allow the blood in the lungs to flow towards the left cavity of the heart, but do not permit its return; and three at the entrance of the great artery, which allow the blood to flow from the heart, but prevent its return. There is then no cause to seek for any other reason for the number of these membranes, except, that the opening of the venous artery being oval, because of the situation where it is met with, may be conveniently closed with two membranes, while the others, being round, can be better closed with three. Further, I should have my readers consider that the grand artery and the arterial vein are much harder and firmer than are the venous artery and the *vena cava;* and that these two last expand before entering the heart, and there form so to speak two pockets called the auricles of the heart, which are composed of a tissue similar to its own; and also that there is always more heat in the heart than in any other part of the body; and finally that this heat is capable of causing any drop of blood that enters into its cavities promptly to expand and dilate, as liquids usually do when they are allowed to fall drop by drop into some very hot vessel.

49

After this I do not need to say anything, with a view to explaining the movement of the heart, except that when its cavities are not full of blood there necessarily flows from the *vena cava* into the right cavity, and from the venous artery into the left, enough blood to keep these two vessels always full, and being full, that their orifices, which are turned towards the heart, cannot then be closed. But as soon as two drops of blood have thus entered, one into each of the cavities, these drops, which cannot be otherwise than very large, because the openings by which they enter are very wide and the vessels from whence they come are very full of blood, rarefy and dilate because of the heat which they find there. By this means, causing the whole heart to expand, they force home and close the five little doors which are at the entrances of the two vessels whence they flow, thus preventing any more blood from coming down into the heart; and becoming more and more rarefied, they push open the six doors which are in the entrances of the two other vessels through which they make their exit, by this means causing all the branches of the arterial vein and of the great artery to expand almost at the same instant as the heart. This last immediately afterward contracts as do also the arteries, because the blood which has entered them has cooled; and the six little doors close up again, and the five doors of the *vena cava* and of the venous artery re-open and make a way for two other drops of blood which cause the heart and the arteries once more to expand, just as we saw before, and because the blood which then enters the heart passes through these two pouches which are called auricles, it comes to pass that their movement is contrary to the movement of the heart, and that they contract when it expands. For the rest, in order that those who do not know the force of mathematical demonstration and are unaccustomed to distinguish true reasons from merely probable reasons, should not venture to deny what has been said without examination, I wish to acquaint them with the fact that this movement which I have just explained follows as necessarily from the very disposition of the organs, as can be seen by looking at the heart, and from the heat which can be felt with the fingers, and from the nature of the blood of which we can learn by experience, as does that of a clock from the power, the situation, and the form, of its counterpoise and of its wheels.

But if we ask how the blood in the veins does not exhaust itself in thus flowing continually into the heart, and how the arteries do not become too full of blood, since all that passes through the heart flows into them, I need only reply by stating what has already been written by an English physician,[5] to whom the credit of having broken the ice in this matter must be ascribed, as also of being the first to teach that there are many little tubes at the extremities of the arteries whereby the blood that they receive from the heart enters the little branches of the veins, whence it returns once more to the heart; in this way its course is just a perpetual circulation. He proves this very clearly by the common experience of surgeons, who, by binding the arm moderately firmly above the place where they open the vein, cause the blood to issue more abundantly than it would have done if they had not bound it at all; while quite a contrary result would occur if they bound it below, between the hand and

5 Harvey.

50

51

the opening, or if they bound it very firmly above. For it is clear that when the bandage is moderately tight, though it may prevent the blood already in the arm from returning to the heart by the veins, it cannot for all that prevent more blood from coming anew by the arteries, because these are situated below the veins, and their walls, being stronger, are less easy to compress; and also that the blood which comes from the heart tends to pass by means of the arteries to the hand with greater force than it does to return from the hand to the heart by the veins. And because this blood escapes from the arm by the opening which is made in one of the veins, there must necessarily be some passages below the ligature, that is to say, towards the extremities of the arm, through which it can come thither from the arteries. This physician likewise proves very clearly the truth of that which he says of the course of the blood, by the existence of certain little membranes or valves which are so arranged in different places along the course of the veins, that they do not permit the blood to pass from the middle of the body towards the extremities, but only to return from the extremities to the heart; and further by the experiment which shows that all the blood which is in the body may issue from it in a very short time by means of one single artery that has been cut, and this is so even when it is very tightly bound very near the heart, and cut between it and the ligature, so that there could be no ground for supposing that the blood which flowed out of it could proceed from any other place but the heart.

But there are many other things which demonstrate that the true cause of this motion of the blood is that which I have stated. To begin with, the difference which is seen between the blood which issues from the veins, and that which issues from the arteries, can only proceed from the fact, that, being rarefied, and so to speak distilled by passing through the heart, it is more subtle and lively and warmer immediately after leaving the heart (that is to say, when in the arteries) than it is a little while before entering it (that is, when in the veins). And if attention be paid, we shall find that this difference does not appear clearly, excepting in the vicinity of the heart, and is not so clear in those parts which are further removed from it. Further, the consistency of the coverings of which the arterial vein and the great artery are composed, shows clearly enough that the blood beats against them with more force than it does in the case of the veins. And why should the left cavity of the heart and the great artery be larger and wider than the right cavity and the arterial vein, if it is not that the blood of the venous artery having only been in the lungs since it had passed through the heart, is more subtle and rarefies more effectively and easily than that which proceeds immediately from the *vena cava?* And what is it that the physicians can discover in feeling the pulse, unless they know that, according as the blood changes its nature, it may be rarefied by the warmth of the heart in a greater or less degree, and more or less quickly than before? And if we inquire how this heat is communicated to the other members, must it not be allowed that it is by means of the blood which, passing through the heart, is heated once again and thence is spread throughout all the body? From this it happens that if we take away the blood from any particular part, by that same means we take away from it the heat; even if the heart were as ardent as red hot iron it would not suffice to heat up the feet and hands as it actually does, unless it continually sent out to them new blood. We further understand from this that the true use of respiration is to carry sufficient fresh air into the lungs to cause the blood, which comes there from the right cavity of the heart, where it has been rarefied and so to speak transformed into vapours, to thicken, and become anew converted into blood before falling into the left cavity, without which process it would not be fit to serve as fuel for the fire which there exists. We are confirmed in this statement by seeing that the animals which have no lungs have also but one cavity in their hearts, and that in children, who cannot use them while still within their mother's wombs, there is an opening by which the blood flows from the *vena cava* into the left cavity of the heart, and a conduit through which it passes from the arterial vein into the great artery without passing through the lung. Again, how could digestion be carried on in the stomach if the heart did not send heat there by the arteries, and along with this some of the more fluid parts of the blood which aid in dissolving the foods which have been there placed? And is not the action which converts the juice of foods into blood easy to understand if we consider that it is distilled by passing and repassing through the heart possibly more than one or two hundred times in a day? What further need is there to explain the process of nutrition and the production of the different humours which are in the body, if we

53

54

can say that the force with which the blood, in being rarefied, passes from the heart towards the extremities of the arteries, causes some of its parts to remain among those of the members where they are found and there to take the place of others which they oust; and that according to the situation or form or smallness of the little pores which they encounter, certain ones proceed to certain parts rather than others, just as a number of different sieves variously perforated, as everyone has probably seen, are capable of separating different species of grain? And finally what in all this is most remarkable of all, is the generation of the animal spirits, which resemble a very subtle wind, or rather a flame which is very pure and very vivid, and which, continually rising up in great abundance from the heart to the brain, thence proceeds through the nerves to the muscles, thereby giving the power of motion to all the members. And it is not necessary to suppose any other cause to explain how the particles of blood, which, being most agitated and most penetrating, are the most proper to constitute these spirits, proceed towards the brain rather than elsewhere, than that the arteries which carry them thither are those which proceed from the heart in the most direct lines, and that according to the laws of mechanics, which are identical with those of nature, when many objects tend to move together to the same point, where there is not room for all (as is the case with the particles of blood which issue from the left cavity of the heart and tend to go towards the brain), the weakest and least agitated parts must necessarily be turned aside by those that are stronger, which by this means are the only ones to reach it.

55

I had explained all these matters in some detail in the treatise which I formerly intended to publish. And afterwards I had shown there, what must be the fabric of the nerves and muscles of the human body in order that the animal spirits therein contained should have the power to move the members, just as the heads of animals, a little while after decapitation, are still observed to move and bite the earth, notwithstanding that they are no longer animate; what changes are necessary in the brain to cause wakefulness, sleep and dreams; how light, sounds, smells, tastes, heat and all other qualities pertaining to external objects are able to imprint on it various ideas by the intervention of the senses; how hunger, thirst and other internal affections can also convey their impressions upon it; what should be regarded as the 'common sense' by which these ideas are received, and what is meant by the memory which retains them, by the fancy which can change them in diverse ways and out of them constitute new ideas, and which, by the same means, distributing the animal spirits through the muscles, can cause the members of such a body to move in as many diverse ways, and in a manner as suitable to the objects which present themselves to its senses and to its internal passions, as can happen in our own case apart from the direction of our free will. And this will not seem strange to those, who, knowing how many different *automata* or moving machines can be made by the industry of man, without employing in so doing more than a very few parts in comparison with the great multitude of bones, muscles, nerves, arteries, veins, or other parts that are found in the body of each animal. From this aspect the body is regarded as a machine which, having been made by the hands of God, is incomparably better arranged, and possesses in itself movements which are much more admirable, than any of those which can be invented by man. Here I specially stopped to show that if there had been such machines, possessing the organs and outward form of a monkey or some other animal without reason, we should not have had any means of ascertaining that they were not of the same nature as those animals. On the other hand, if there were machines which bore a resemblance to our body and imitated our actions as far as it was morally possible to do so, we should always have two very certain tests by which to recognise that, for all that, they were not real men. The first is, that they could never use speech or other signs as we do when placing our thoughts on record for the benefit of others. For we can easily understand a machine's being constituted so that it can utter words, and even emit some responses to action on it of a corporeal kind, which brings about a change in its organs; for instance, if it is touched in a particular part it may ask what we wish to say to it; if in another part it may exclaim that it is being hurt, and so on. But it never happens that it arranges its speech in various ways, in order to reply appropriately to everything that may be said in its presence, as even the lowest type of man can do. And the second difference is, that although machines can perform certain things as well as or perhaps better than any of us can do, they infallibly fall short in others, by the which means we may discover that they did not act from knowledge, but only from the disposition of their organs. For while reason is a universal instrument which can

56

57

serve for all contingencies, these organs have need of some special adaptation for every particular action. From this it follows that it is morally impossible that there should be sufficient diversity in any machine to allow it to act in all the events of life in the same way as our reason causes us to act.

By these two methods we may also recognise the difference that exists between men and brutes. For it is a very remarkable fact that there are none so depraved and stupid, without even excepting idiots, that they cannot arrange different words together forming of them a statement by which they make known their thoughts; while, on the other hand, there is no other animal, however perfect and fortunately circumstanced it may be, which can do the same. It is not the want of organs that brings this to pass, for it is evident that magpies and parrots are able to utter words just like ourselves, and yet they cannot speak as we do, that is, so as to give evidence that they think of what they say. On the other hand, men who, being born deaf and dumb, are in the same degree, or even more than the brutes, destitute of the organs which serve the others for talking, are in the habit of themselves inventing certain signs by which they make themselves understood by those who, being usually in their company, have leisure to learn their language. And this does not merely show that the brutes have less reason than men, but that they have none at all, since it is clear that very little is required in order to be able to talk. And when we notice the inequality that exists between animals of the same species, as well as between men, and observe that some are more capable of receiving instruction than others, it is not credible that a monkey or a parrot, selected as the most perfect of its species, should not in these matters equal the stupidest child to be found, or at least a child whose mind is clouded, unless in the case of the brute the soul were of an entirely different nature from ours. And we ought not to confound speech with natural movements which betray passions and may be imitated by machines as well as be manifested by animals; nor must we think, as did some of the ancients, that brutes talk, although we do not understand their language. For if this were true, since they have many organs which are allied to our own, they could communicate their thoughts to us just as easily as to those of their own race. It is also a very remarkable fact that although there are many animals which exhibit more dexterity than we do in some of their actions, we at the same time observe that they do not manifest any dexterity at all in many others. Hence the fact that they do better than we do, does not prove that they are endowed with mind, for in this case they would have more reason than any of us, and would surpass us in all other things. It rather shows that they have no reason at all, and that it is nature which acts in them according to the disposition of their organs, just as a clock, which is only composed of wheels and weights is able to tell the hours and measure the time more correctly than we can do with all our wisdom.

59

I had described after this the rational soul and shown that it could not be in any way derived from the power of matter, like the other things of which I had spoken, but that it must be expressly created. I showed, too, that it is not sufficient that it should be lodged in the human body like a pilot in his ship, unless perhaps for the moving of its members, but that it is necessary that it should also be joined and united more closely to the body in order to have sensations and appetites similar to our own, and thus to form a true man. In conclusion, I have here enlarged a little on the subject of the soul, because it is one of the greatest importance. For next to the error of those who deny God, which I think I have already sufficiently refuted, there is none which is more effectual in leading feeble spirits from the straight path of virtue, than to imagine that the soul of the brute is of the same nature as our own, and that in consequence, after this life we have nothing to fear or to hope for, any more than the flies and ants. As a matter of fact, when one comes to know how greatly they differ, we understand much better the reasons which go to prove that our soul is in its nature entirely independent of body, and in consequence that it is not liable to die with it. And then, inasmuch as we observe no other causes capable of destroying it, we are naturally inclined to judge that it is immortal.

60

Part 6

It is three years since I arrived at the end of the treatise which contained all these things; and I was commencing to revise it in order to place it in the hands of a printer, when I learned that certain persons, to whose opinions I defer, and whose authority cannot have less weight with my actions than my own reason has over my thoughts, had disapproved of a physical theory published a little while before by another person.[6] I will not say that I agreed with this opinion, but only that before their censure I observed in it nothing which I could possibly imagine to be prejudicial either to religion or the State, or consequently which could have prevented me from giving expression to it in writing, if my reason had persuaded me to do so: and this made me fear that among my own opinions one might be found which should be misunderstood, notwithstanding the great care which I have always taken not to accept any new beliefs unless I had very certain proof of their truth, and not to give expression to what could tend to the disadvantage of any person. This sufficed to cause me to alter the resolution which I had made to publish. For, although the reasons for my former resolution were very strong, my inclination, which always made me hate the profession of writing books, caused me immediately to find plenty of other reasons for excusing myself from doing so. And these reasons, on the one side and on the other, are of such a nature that not only have I here some interest in giving expression to them, but possibly the public may also have some interest in knowing them.

61

I have never made much of those things which proceed from my own mind, and so long as I culled no other fruits from the method which I use, beyond that of satisfying myself respecting certain difficulties which pertain to the speculative sciences, or trying to regulate my conduct by the reasons which it has taught me, I never believed myself to be obliged to write anything about it. For as regards that which concerns conduct, everyone is so confident of his own common sense, that there might be found as many reformers as heads, if it were permitted that others than those whom God has established as the sovereigns of his people, or at least to whom He has given sufficient grace and zeal to be prophets, should be allowed to make any changes in that. And, although my speculations give me the greatest pleasure, I believed that others also had speculations which possibly pleased them even more. But so soon as I had acquired some general notions concerning physics, and as, beginning to make use of them in various special difficulties, I observed to what point they might lead us, and how much they differ from the principles of which we have made use up to the present time, I believed that I could not keep them concealed without greatly

6 i.e. Galileo.

sinning against the law which obliges us to procure, as much as in us lies, the general good of all mankind. For they caused me to see that it is possible to attain knowledge which is very useful in life, and that, instead of that speculative philosophy which is taught in the schools, we may find a practical philosophy by means of which, knowing the force and the action of fire, water, air, the stars, heavens and all other bodies that environ us, as distinctly as we know the different crafts of our artisans, we can in the same way employ them in all those uses to which they are adapted, and thus render ourselves the masters and possessors of nature. This is not merely to be desired with a view to the invention of an infinity of arts and crafts which enable us to enjoy without any trouble the fruits of the earth and all the good things which are to be found there, but also principally because it brings about the preservation of health, which is without doubt the chief blessing and the foundation of all other blessings in this life. For the mind depends so much on the temperament and disposition of the bodily organs that, if it is possible to find a means of rendering men wiser and cleverer than they have hitherto been, I believe that it is in medicine that it must be sought. It is true that the medicine which is now in vogue contains little of which the utility is remarkable; but, without having any intention of decrying it, I am sure that there is no one, even among those who make its study a profession, who does not confess that all that men know is almost nothing in comparison with what remains to be known; and that we could be free of an infinitude of maladies both of body and mind, and even also possibly of the infirmities of age, if we had sufficient knowledge of their causes, and of all the remedies with which nature has provided us. But, having the intention of devoting all my life to the investigation of a knowledge which is so essential, and having discovered a path which appears to me to be of such a nature that we must by its means infallibly reach our end if we pursue it unless, indeed, we are prevented by the shortness of life or by lack of experience, I judged that there was no better provision against these two impediments than faithfully to communicate to the public the little which I should myself have discovered, and to beg all well-inclined persons to proceed further by contributing, each one according to his own inclination and ability, to the experiments which must be made, and then to communicate to the public all the things which they might discover, in order that the last should commence where the preceding had left off; and thus, by joining together the lives and labours of many, we should collectively proceed much further than any one in particular could succeed in doing.

I remarked also respecting experiments, that they become so much the more necessary the more one is advanced in knowledge, for to begin with it is better to make use simply of those which present themselves spontaneously to our senses, and of which we could not be ignorant provided that we reflected ever so little, rather than to seek out those which are more rare and recondite; the reason of this is that those which are more rare often mislead us so long as we do not know the causes of the more common, and the fact that the circumstances on which they depend are almost always so particular and so minute that it is very difficult to observe them.

64 But in this the order which I have followed is as follows: I have first tried to discover generally the principles or first causes of everything that is or that can be in the world, without considering anything that might accomplish this end but God Himself who has created the world, or deriving them from any source excepting from certain germs of truths which are naturally existent in our souls. After that I considered which were the primary and most ordinary effects which might be deduced from these causes, and it seems to me that in this way I discovered the heavens, the stars, an earth, and even on the earth, water, air, fire, the minerals and some other such things, which are the most common and simple of any that exist, and consequently the easiest to know. Then, when I wished to descend to those which were more particular, so many objects of various kinds presented themselves to me, that I did not think it was possible for the human mind to distinguish the forms or species of bodies which are on the earth from an infinitude of others which might have been so if it had been the will of God to place them there, or consequently to apply them to our use, if it were not that we arrive at the causes by the effects, and avail ourselves of many particular experiments. In subsequently passing over in my mind all the objects which have ever been presented to my senses, I can truly venture to say that I have not there observed anything which I could not easily explain by the principles which I had discovered. But I must also confess that the power of nature is so ample and so vast, and these principles are so simple and general, that I observed

hardly any particular effect as to which I could not at once recognise
that it might be deduced from the principles in many different ways;
and my greatest difficulty is usually to discover in which of these
ways the effect does depend upon them. As to that, I do not know
any other plan but again to try to find experiments of such a nature
that their result is not the same if it has to be explained by one of the
methods, as it would be if explained by the other. For the rest, I
have now reached a position in which I discern, as it seems to me,
sufficiently clearly what course must be adopted in order to make
the majority of the experiments which may conduce to carry out
this end. But I also perceive that they are of such a nature, and of so
great a number, that neither my hands nor my income, though the
latter were a thousand times larger than it is, could suffice for the
whole; so that just in proportion as henceforth I shall have the
power of carrying out more of them or less, shall I make more or
less progress in arriving at a knowledge of nature. This is what I had
promised myself to make known by the treatise which I had
written, and to demonstrate in it so clearly the advantage which the
public might receive from it, that I should induce all those who
have the good of mankind at heart – that is to say, all those who are
really virtuous in fact, and not only by a false semblance or by
opinion – both to communicate to me those experiments that they
have already carried out, and to help me in the investigation of
those that still remain to be accomplished.

But I have since that time found other reasons which caused me
to change my opinion, and consider that I should indeed continue
to put in writing all the things which I judged to be of importance
whenever I discovered them to be true, and that I should bestow
on them the same care as I should have done had I wished to have
them printed. I did this because it would give me so much the
more occasion to examine them carefully (for there is no doubt that
we always scrutinise more closely what we think will be seen by
many, than what is done simply for ourselves, and often the things
which have seemed true to me when I began to think about them,
seemed false when I tried to place them on paper); and because I
did not desire to lose any opportunity of benefiting the public if I
were able to do so, and in order that if my works have any value,
those into whose hands they will fall after my death, might have the
power of making use of them as seems best to them. I, however,

resolved that I should not consent to their being published during my lifetime, so that neither the contradictions and controversies to which they might possibly give rise, nor even the reputation, such as it might be, which they would bring to me, should give me any occasion to lose the time which I meant to set apart for my own instruction. For although it is true that each man is obliged to procure, as much as in him lies, the good of others, and that to be useful to nobody is popularly speaking to be worthless, it is at the same time true that our cares should extend further than the present time, and that it is good to set aside those things which may possibly be adapted to bring profit to the living, when we have in view the accomplishment of other ends which will bring much more advantage to our descendants. In the same way I should much like that men should know that the little which I have learned hitherto is almost nothing in comparison with that of which I am ignorant, and with the knowledge of which I do not despair of being able to attain. For it is much the same with those

67

who little by little discover the truth in the sciences, as with those who, commencing to become rich, have less trouble in obtaining great acquisitions than they formerly experienced, when poorer, in arriving at those much smaller in amount. Or we might compare them to the generals of our armies, whose forces usually grow in proportion to their victories, and who require more leadership in order to hold together their troops after the loss of a battle, than is needed to take towns and provinces after having obtained a success. For he really gives battle who attempts to conquer all the difficulties and errors which prevent him from arriving at a knowledge of the truth, and it is to lose a battle to admit a false opinion touching a matter of any generality and importance. Much more skill is required in order to recover the position that one beforehand held, than is necessary to make great progress when one already possesses principles which are assured. For myself, if I have succeeded in discovering certain truths in the sciences (and I hope that the matters contained in this volume will show that I have discovered some), I may say that they are resultant from, and dependent on, five or six principal difficulties which I have surmounted, and my encounter with these I look upon as so many battles in which I have had fortune on my side. I will not even hesitate to say that I think I shall have no need to win more than two or three other victories similar in kind in order to reach the accomplishment of my plans. And my age is not so advanced but that, in the ordinary course of nature, I may still have sufficient leisure for this end. But I believe myself to be so much the more bound to make the most of the time which remains, as I have the greater hope of being able to employ it well. And without doubt I should have many chances of being robbed of it, were I to publish the foundations of my physics; for though these are nearly all so evident that it is only necessary to understand them in order to accept them, and although there are none of them as to which I do not believe myself capable of giving demonstration, yet because it is impossible that they should accord with all the various opinions of other men, I foresee that I should often be diverted from my main design by the opposition which they would bring to birth.

We may say that these contradictions might be useful both in making me aware of my errors, and, supposing that I had reached some satisfactory conclusion, in bringing others to a fuller understanding of my speculations; and, as many can see more than can a single man, they might help in leading others who from the present time may begin to avail themselves of my system, to assist me likewise with their discoveries. But though I recognise that I am extremely liable to err, and though I almost never trust the first reflections that I arrive at, the experience which I have had of the objections which may be made to my system prevents my having any hope of deriving profit from them. For I have often had experience of the judgments both of those whom I have esteemed as my friends, and of some others to whom I believed myself to be indifferent, and even, too, of some whose ill-feeling and envy would, I felt sure, make them endeavour to reveal what affection concealed from the eyes of my friends. But rarely has it happened that any objection has been made which I did not in some sort foresee, unless where it was something very far removed from my subject. In this way hardly ever have I encountered any censor of my opinions who did not appear to me to be either less rigorous or less judicial than myself. And I certainly never remarked that by means of disputations employed by the schools any truth has been discovered of which we were formerly ignorant. And so long as each side attempts to vanquish his opponent, there is a much more serious attempt to establish probability than to weigh the reasons on either side; and those who have for long been excellent pleaders are not for that reason the best judges.

As to the advantage which others may receive from the communication of my reflections, it could not be very great, inasmuch as I have not yet carried them so far as that it is not necessary to add many things before they can be brought into practice. And I think I can without vanity say that if anyone is capable of doing this, it should be myself rather than another – not indeed that there may not be in the world many minds incomparably superior to my own, but because no one can so well understand a thing and make it his own when learnt from another as when it is discovered for himself. As regards the matter in hand there is so much truth in this, that although I have often explained some of my opinions to persons of very good intelligence, who, while I talked to them appeared to understand them very clearly, yet when they recounted them I remarked that they had almost always altered them in such a manner that I could no longer acknowledge them as mine. On this account I am very glad to have the opportunity here of begging my descendants never to believe that what is told to them proceeded from myself unless I have myself divulged it. And I do not in the least wonder at the extravagances attributed to all the ancient philosophers whose writings we do not possess, nor do I judge from these that their thoughts were very unreasonable, considering that theirs were the best minds of the time they lived in, but only that they have been imperfectly represented to us. We see, too, that it hardly ever happens that any of their disciples surpassed them, and I am sure that those who most passionately follow Aristotle nowadays would think themselves happy if they had as much knowledge of nature as he had, even if this were on the condition that they should never attain to any more. They are like the ivy that never tries to mount above the trees which give it support, and which often even descends again after it has reached their summit; for it appears to me that such men also sink again – that is to say, somehow render themselves more ignorant than they would have been had they abstained from study altogether. For, not content with knowing all that is intelligibly explained in their author, they wish in addition to find in him the solution of many difficulties of which he says nothing, and in regard to which he possibly had no thought at all. At the same time their mode of philosophising is very convenient for those who have abilities of a very mediocre kind, for the obscurity of the distinctions and principles of which they make use, is the reason of their being able to talk of all things as boldly as though they really knew about them, and defend all that they say against the most subtle and acute, without any one having the means of convincing them to the contrary. In this they seem to me like a blind man who, in order to fight on equal terms with one who sees, would have the latter to come into the bottom of a very dark cave. I may say, too, that it is in the interest of such people that I should abstain from publishing the principles of philosophy of which I make use, for, being so simple and evident as they are, I should, in publishing them, do the same as though I threw open the windows and caused daylight to enter the cave into which they have descended in order to fight. But even the best minds have no reason to desire to be acquainted with these principles, for if they wish to be able to talk of everything and acquire a reputation for learning, they will more readily attain their end by contenting themselves with the appearance of truth which may be found in all sorts of things without much trouble, than in seeking for truth which only reveals itself little by little in certain spheres, and which, when others come into question, obliges one to confess one's ignorance. If, however, they prefer the knowledge of some small amount of truth to the vanity of seeming to be ignorant of nothing, which knowledge is doubtless preferable, or if they desire to follow a course similar to my own, it is not necessary that I should say any more than what I have already said in this Discourse. For if they are capable of passing beyond the point I have reached, they will also so much the more be able to find by themselves all that I believe myself to have discovered; since, not having examined anything but in its order, it is certain that what remains for me to discover is in itself more difficult and more recondite than anything that I have hitherto been able to meet with, and they would have much less pleasure in learning from me than from themselves. Besides, the habit which they will acquire of seeking first things that are simple and then little by little and by degrees passing to others more difficult, will be of more use than could be all my instructions. For, as regards myself, I am persuaded that if from my youth up I had been taught all the truths of which I have since sought the demonstrations, or if I had not had any difficulty in learning them, I

71

72

should perhaps never have known any others, or at least I should never have acquired the habit or facility which I think I have obtained, of ever finding them anew, in proportion as I set myself to seek for them. And, in a word, if there is any work at all which cannot be so well achieved by another as by him who has begun it, it is that at which I labour.

It is true as regards the experiments which may conduce to this end, that one man could not possibly accomplish all of them. But yet he could not, to good advantage, employ other hands than his own, excepting those of artisans or persons of that kind whom he could pay, and whom the hope of gain – which is a very effectual incentive – might cause to perform with exactitude all the things they were directed to accomplish. As to those who, whether by curiosity or desire to learn, might possibly offer him their voluntary assistance, not only are they usually more ready with promises than with performance, planning out fine sounding projects, none of which are ever realised, but they will also infallibly demand payment for their trouble by requesting the explanation of certain difficulties, or at least by empty compliments and useless talk, which could not occupy any of the student's time without causing it to be lost. And as to the experiments already made by others, even if they desired to communicate these to him – which those who term them secrets would never do – they are for the most part accompanied by so many circumstances or superfluous matter, that it would be very difficult for him to disentangle the truth. In addition to this he would find nearly all so badly explained, or even so false (because those who carried them out were forced to make them appear to be in conformity with their principles), that if there had been some which might have been of use to him, they would hardly be worth the time that would be required in making the selection. So true is this, that if there were anywhere in the world a person whom one knew to be assuredly capable of discovering matters of the highest importance and those of the greatest possible utility to the public, and if for this reason all other men were eager by every means in their power to help him in reaching the end which he set before him, I do not see that they could do anything for him beyond contributing to defray the expenses of the experiments which might be requisite, or, for the rest, seeing that he was not deprived of his leisure by the importunities of anyone. But, in addition to the fact that I neither esteem myself so highly as to be willing to promise anything extraordinary, nor give scope to an imagination so vain as to conceive that the public should interest itself greatly in my designs, I do not yet own a soul so base as to be willing to accept from anyone whatever a favour which it might be supposed I did not merit.   74

All those considerations taken together were, three years ago, the cause of my not desiring to publish the treatise which I had on hand, and the reason why I even formed the resolution of not bringing to light during my life any other of so general a kind, or one by which the foundations of physics could be understood. But since then two other reasons came into operation which compelled me to bring forward certain attempts, as I have done here, and to render to the public some account of my actions and designs. The first is that if I failed to do so, many who knew the intention I formerly had of publishing certain writings, might imagine that the causes for which I abstained from so doing were more to my disadvantage than they really were; for although I do not care immoderately for glory, or, if I dare say so, although I even hate it, inasmuch as I judge it to be antagonistic to the repose which I esteem above all other things, at the same time I never tried to conceal my actions as though they were crimes, nor have I used many precautions against being known, partly because I should have thought it damaging to myself, and partly because it would have given me a sort of disquietude which would again have militated against the perfect repose of spirit which I seek. And forasmuch as having in this way always held myself in a condition of indifference as regards whether I was known or was not known, I have not yet been able to prevent myself from acquiring some sort of reputation, I thought that I should do my best at least to prevent myself from acquiring an evil reputation. The other reason which obliged me to put this in   75 writing is that I am becoming every day more and more alive to the delay which is being suffered in the design which I have of instructing myself, because of the lack of an infinitude of experiments, which it is impossible that I should perform without the aid of others. and although I do not flatter myself so much as to hope that the public should to any large degree participate in my interest, I yet do not wish to be found wanting, both on my own account, and as one day giving occasion to those who will survive me of reproaching me for the fact that I might have left many matters in a much better condition than I have done, had I not too much neglected to make them understand in what way they could have contributed to the accomplishment of my designs.

And I thought that it was easy for me to select certain matters which would not be the occasion for many controversies, nor yet oblige me to propound more of my principles than I wish, and which yet would suffice to allow a pretty clear manifestation of what I can do and what I cannot do in the sciences. In this I cannot say whether I have succeeded or have not succeeded, and I do not wish to anticipate the judgment of any one by myself speaking of my writings; but I shall be very glad if they will examine them. And in order that they may have the better opportunity of so doing, I beg all those who have any objections to offer to take the trouble of sending them to my publishers, so that, being made aware of them, I may try at the same time to subjoin my reply. By this means, the reader, seeing objections and reply at the same time, will the more easily judge of the truth; for I do not promise in any instance to make lengthy replies, but just to avow my errors very frankly if I am convinced of them; or, if I cannot perceive them, to say simply what I think requisite for the defence of the matters I have written, without adding the exposition of any new matter, so that I may not be endlessly engaged in passing from one side to the other.

If some of the matters of which I spoke in the beginning of the *Dioptrics* and *Meteors* should at first sight give offence because I call them hypotheses and do not appear to care about their proof, let them have the patience to read these in entirety, and I hope that they will find themselves satisfied. For it appears to me that the reasonings are so mutually interwoven, that as the later ones are demonstrated by the earlier, which are their causes, the earlier are reciprocally demonstrated by the later which are their effects. And it must not be imagined that in this I commit the fallacy which logicians name arguing in a circle, for, since experience renders the greater part of these effects very certain, the causes from which I deduce them do not so much serve to prove their existence as to explain them; on the other hand, the causes are explained by the effects. And I have not named them hypotheses with any other object than that it may be known that while I consider myself able to deduce them from the primary truths which I explained above,

76

yet I particularly desired not to do so, in order that certain persons may not for this reason take occasion to build up some extravagant philosophic system on what they take to be my principles, and thus cause the blame to be put on me. I refer to those who imagine that in one day they may discover all that another has arrived at in twenty years of work, so soon as he has merely spoken to them two or three words on the subject; while they are really all the more subject to err, and less capable of perceiving the truth as they are the more subtle and lively. For as regards the opinions that are truly mine I do not apologise for them as being new, inasmuch as if we consider the reasons of them well, I assure myself that they will be found to be so simple and so conformable to common sense, as to appear less extraordinary and less paradoxical than any others which may be held on similar subjects. And I do not even boast of being the first discoverer of any of them, but only state that I have adopted them, not because they have been held by others, nor because they have not been so held, but only because reason has persuaded me of their truth.

Even if artisans are not at once able to carry out the invention[7] explained in the *Dioptrics,* I do not for that reason think that it can be said that it is to be condemned; for, inasmuch as great address and practice is required to make and adjust the mechanism which I have described without omitting any detail, I should not be less astonished at their succeeding at the first effort than I should be supposing some one were in one day to learn to play the guitar with skill, just because a good sheet of musical notation were set up before him. And if I write in French which is the language of my country, rather than in Latin which is that of my teachers, that is because I hope that those who avail themselves only of their natural reason in its purity may be better judges of my opinions than those who believe only in the writings of the ancients; and as to those who unite good sense with study, whom alone I crave for my judges, they will not, I feel sure, be so partial to Latin as to refuse to follow my reasoning because I expound it in a vulgar tongue.

For the rest, I do not desire to speak here more particularly of the progress which I hope in the future to make in the sciences, nor to

77

78

7 Doubtless the machine for the purpose of cutting lenses which Descartes so minutely described.

bind myself as regards the public with any promise which I shall not with certainty be able to fulfil. But I will just say that I have resolved not to employ the time which remains to me in life in any other matter than in endeavouring to acquire some knowledge of nature, which shall be of such a kind that it will enable us to arrive at rules for medicine more assured than those which have as yet been attained; and my inclination is so strongly opposed to any other kind of pursuit, more especially to those which can only be useful to some by being harmful to others, that if certain circumstances had constrained me to employ them, I do not think that I should have been capable of succeeding. In so saying I make a declaration that I know very well cannot help me to make myself of consideration in the world, but to this end I have no desire to attain; and I shall always hold myself to be more indebted to those by whose favour I may enjoy my leisure without hindrance, than I shall be to any who may offer me the most honourable position in all the world.

*To the most wise and illustrious the Dean and Doctors
of the Sacred Faculty of Theology in Paris*

The motive which induces me to present to you this treatise is so
excellent, and, when you become acquainted with its design, I am
convinced that you will also have so excellent a motive for taking it
under your protection, that I feel that I cannot do better, in order to
render it in some sort acceptable to you, than in a few words to state
what I have set myself to do.

I have always considered that the two questions respecting God
and the soul were the chief of those that ought to be demonstrated
by philosophical rather than theological argument. For although it is
quite enough for us faithful ones to accept by means of faith the fact   2
that the human soul does not perish with the body, and that God
exists, it certainly does not seem possible ever to persuade infidels of
any religion, indeed, we may almost say, of any moral virtue, unless,
to begin with, we prove these two facts by means of the natural
reason. And inasmuch as often in this life greater rewards are offered
for vice than for virtue, few people would prefer the right to the
useful, were they restrained neither by the fear of God nor the
expectation of another life; and although it is absolutely true that we
must believe that there is a God, because we are so taught in the
Holy Scriptures, and, on the other hand that we must believe the
Holy Scriptures because they come from God (the reason of this is,
that, faith being a gift of God, He who gives the grace to cause us to
believe other things can likewise give it to cause us to believe that
He exists), we nevertheless could not place this argument before
infidels, who might accuse us of reasoning in a circle. And, in truth, I
have noticed that you, along with all the theologians, did not only
affirm that the existence of God may be proved by the natural
reason, but also that it may be inferred from the Holy Scriptures, that
knowledge about Him is much clearer than that which we have of

many created things, and, as a matter of fact, is so easy to acquire, that those who have it not are culpable in their ignorance. This indeed appears from the Wisdom of Solomon, chapter xiii, where it is said 'Howbeit they are not to be excused; for if their understanding was so great that they could discern the world and the creatures, why did they not rather find out the Lord thereof?' and in Romans, chapter i, it is said that they are 'without excuse', and again in the same place, by these words 'that which may be known of God is manifest in them', it seems as though we were shown that all that which can be known of God may be made manifest by means which are not derived from anywhere but from ourselves, and from the simple consideration of the nature of our minds. Hence I thought it not beside my purpose to inquire how this is so, and how God may be more easily and certainly known than the things of the world.

3   And as regards the soul, although many have considered that it is not easy to know its nature, and some have even dared to say that human reasons have convinced us that it would perish with the body, and that faith alone could believe the contrary, nevertheless, inasmuch as the Lateran Council held under Leo X (in the eighth session) condemns these tenets, and as Leo expressly ordains Christian philosophers to refute their arguments and to employ all their powers in making known the truth, I have ventured in this treatise to undertake the same task.

More than that, I am aware that the principal reason which causes many impious persons not to desire to believe that there is a God, and that the human soul is distinct from the body, is that they declare that hitherto no one has been able to demonstrate these two facts; and although I am not of their opinion but, on the contrary, hold that the greater part of the reasons which have been brought forward concerning these two questions by so many great men are, when they are rightly understood, equal to so many demonstrations, and that it is almost impossible to invent new ones, it is yet in my opinion the case that nothing more useful can be accomplished in philosophy than once for all to seek with care for the best of these reasons, and to set them forth in so clear and exact a manner, that it will henceforth be evident to everybody that they are veritable demonstrations. And, finally, inasmuch as it was desired that I should undertake this task by many who were aware that I had cultivated a certain method for the resolution of difficulties of every kind in the sciences – a method which it is true is not novel, since there is nothing more ancient than the truth, but of which they were aware that I had made use successfully enough in other matters of difficulty – I have thought that it was my duty also to make trial of it in the present matter.

Now all that I could accomplish in the matter is contained in this treatise. Not that I have here drawn together all the different reasons which might be brought forward to serve as proofs of this subject: for that never seemed to be necessary excepting when there was no one single proof that was certain. But I have treated the first and principal ones in such a manner that I can venture to bring them forward as very evident and very certain demonstrations. And more than that, I will say that these proofs are such that I do not think that there is any way open to the human mind by which it can ever succeed in discovering better. For the importance of the subject, and the glory of God to which all this relates, constrain me to speak here somewhat more freely of myself than is my habit. Nevertheless, whatever certainty and evidence I find in my reasons, I cannot persuade myself that all the world is capable of understanding them. Still, just as in geometry there are many demonstrations that have been left to us by Archimedes, by Apollonius, by Pappus, and others, which are accepted by everyone as perfectly certain and evident (because they clearly contain nothing which, considered by itself, is not very easy to understand, and as all through that which follows has an exact connection with, and dependence on that which precedes), nevertheless, because they are somewhat lengthy, and demand a mind wholly devoted to their consideration, they are only taken in and understood by a very limited number of persons. Similarly, although I judge that those of which I here make use are equal to, or even surpass in certainty and evidence, the demonstrations of geometry, I yet apprehend that they cannot be adequately understood by many, both because they are also a little lengthy and dependent the one on the other, and principally because they demand a mind wholly free of prejudices, and one which can be easily detached from the affairs of the senses. And, truth to say, there are not so many in the world who are fitted for metaphysical speculations as there are for those of geometry. And more than that; there is still this difference, that in geometry, since each one is persuaded that nothing must be advanced of which there is not a certain demonstration, those who are not entirely adepts more frequently err in approving what is false, in order to give the impression that they understand it, than in refuting the true. But the case is different in philosophy where everyone believes that all is problematical, and few give themselves to the search after truth; and the greater number, in their desire to acquire a reputation for boldness of thought, arrogantly combat the most important of truths.[1]

That is why, whatever force there may be in my reasonings, seeing they belong to philosophy, I cannot hope that they will have much effect on the minds of men, unless you extend to them your protection. But the estimation in which your company is universally held is so great, and the name of Sorbonne carries with it so much authority, that, next to the Sacred Councils, never has such deference been paid to the judgment of any body, not only in what concerns the faith, but also in what regards human philosophy as well: everyone indeed believes that it is not possible to discover elsewhere more perspicacity and solidity, or more integrity and wisdom in pronouncing judgment. For this reason I have no doubt that if you deign to take the trouble in the first place of correcting this work (for being conscious not only of my infirmity, but also of my ignorance, I should not dare to state that it was free from errors), and then, after adding to it these things that are lacking to it, completing those which are imperfect, and yourselves taking the trouble to give a more ample explanation of those things which have need of it, or at least making me aware of the defects so that I may apply myself to remedy them[1] – when this is done and when finally the reasonings by which I prove that there is a God, and that the human soul differs from the body, shall be carried to that point of perspicuity to which I am sure they can be carried in order that they may be esteemed as perfectly exact demonstrations, if you deign to authorise your approbation and to render public testimony to their truth and certainty, I do not doubt, I say, that henceforward all the errors and false opinions which have ever existed regarding these two questions will soon be effaced from the minds of men. For the truth itself will easily cause all men of mind and learning to subscribe to your judgment; and

1 The French version is followed here.

your authority will cause the atheists, who are usually more arrogant than learned or judicious, to rid themselves of their spirit of contradiction or lead them possibly themselves to defend the reasonings which they find being received as demonstrations by all persons of consideration, lest they appear not to understand them. And, finally, all others will easily yield to such a mass of evidence, and there will be none who dares to doubt the existence of God and the real and true distinction between the human soul and the body. It is for you now in your singular wisdom to judge of the importance of the establishment of such beliefs [you who see the disorders produced by the doubt of them].[2] But it would not become me to say more in consideration of the cause of God and religion to those who have always been the most worthy supports of the Catholic Church.

Preface to the Reader

I have already slightly touched on these two questions of God and the human soul in the *Discourse on the Method of rightly conducting the reason and seeking truth in the sciences*, published in French in the year 1637. Not that I had the design of treating these with any thoroughness, but only so to speak in passing, and in order to ascertain by the judgment of the readers how I should treat them later on. For these questions have always appeared to me to be of such importance that I judged it suitable to speak of them more than once; and the road which I follow in the explanation of them is so little trodden, and so far removed from the ordinary path, that I did not judge it to be expedient to set it forth at length in French and in a Discourse which might be read by everyone, in case the feebler minds should believe that it was permitted to them to attempt to follow the same path.

But, having in this *Discourse on Method* begged all those who have found in my writings somewhat deserving of censure to do me the favour of acquainting me with the grounds of it, nothing worthy of remark has been objected to in them beyond two matters: to these two I wish here to reply in a few words before undertaking their more detailed discussion.

7

2 When it is thought desirable to insert additional readings from the French version this will be indicated by the use of square brackets.

8   The first objection is that it does not follow from the fact that the human mind reflecting on itself does not perceive itself to be other than a thing that thinks, that its nature or its essence consists only in its being a thing that thinks, in the sense that this word *only* excludes all other things which might also be supposed to pertain to the nature of the soul. To this objection I reply that it was not my intention in that place to exclude these in accordance with the order that looks to the truth of the matter (as to which I was not then dealing), but only in accordance with the order of my thought [perception]; thus my meaning was that so far as I was aware, I knew nothing clearly as belonging to my essence, excepting that I was a thing that thinks, or a thing that has in itself the faculty of thinking. But I shall show hereafter how from the fact that I know no other thing which pertains to my essence, it follows that there is no other thing which really does belong to it.

The second objection is that it does not follow from the fact that I have in myself the idea of something more perfect than I am, that this idea is more perfect than I, and much less that what is represented by this idea exists. But I reply that in this term *idea* there is here something equivocal, for it may either be taken materially, as an act of my understanding, and in this sense it cannot be said that it is more perfect than I; or it may be taken objectively, as the thing which is represented by this act, which, although we do not suppose it to exist outside of my understanding, may, none the less, be more perfect than I, because of its essence. And in following out this treatise I shall show more fully how, from the sole fact that I have in myself the idea of a thing more perfect than myself, it follows that this thing truly exists.

9   In addition to these two objections I have also seen two fairly lengthy works on this subject, which, however, did not so much impugn my reasonings as my conclusions, and this by arguments drawn from the ordinary atheistic sources. But, because such arguments cannot make any impression on the minds of those who really understand my reasonings, and as the judgments of many are so feeble and irrational that they very often allow themselves to be persuaded by the opinions which they have first formed, however false and far removed from reason they may be, rather than by a true and solid but subsequently received refutation of these opinions, I do not desire to reply here to their criticisms in case of

being first of all obliged to state them. I shall only say in general that all that is said by the atheist against the existence of God, always depends either on the fact that we ascribe to God affections which are human, or that we attribute so much strength and wisdom to our minds that we even have the presumption to desire to determine and understand that which God can and ought to do. In this way all that they allege will cause us no difficulty, provided only we remember that we must consider our minds as things which are finite and limited, and God as a Being who is incomprehensible and infinite.

Now that I have once for all recognised and acknowledged the opinions of men, I at once begin to treat of God and the human soul, and at the same time to treat of the whole of the First Philosophy, without however expecting any praise from the vulgar and without the hope that my book will have many readers. On the contrary, I should never advise anyone to read it excepting those who desire to meditate seriously with me, and who can detach their minds from affairs of sense, and deliver themselves entirely from every sort of prejudice. I know too well that such men exist in a very small number. But for those who, without caring to comprehend the order and connections of my reasonings, form their criticisms on detached portions arbitrarily selected, as is the custom with many, these, I say, will not obtain much profit from reading this treatise. And although they perhaps in several parts find occasion of cavilling, they can for all their pains make no objection which is urgent or deserving of reply.

And inasmuch as I make no promise to others to satisfy them at once, and as I do not presume so much on my own powers as to believe myself capable of foreseeing all that can cause difficulty to anyone, I shall first of all set forth in these Meditations the very considerations by which I persuade myself that I have reached a certain and evident knowledge of the truth, in order to see if, by the same reasons which persuaded me, I can also persuade others. And, after that, I shall reply to the objections which have been made to me by persons of genius and learning to whom I have sent my Meditations for examination, before submitting them to the press. For they have made so many objections and these so different, that I venture to promise that it will be difficult for anyone to bring to mind criticisms of any consequence which have not been already touched upon. This is why I beg those who read these Meditations to form no judgment upon them unless they have given themselves the trouble to read all the objections as well as the replies which I have made to them.[3]

Synopsis of the six following Meditations

In the first Meditation I set forth the reasons for which we may, generally speaking, doubt about all things and especially about material things, at least so long as we have no other foundations for the sciences than those which we have hitherto possessed. But although the utility of a doubt which is so general does not at first appear, it is at the same time very great, inasmuch as it delivers us from every kind of prejudice, and sets out for us a very simple way by which the mind may detach itself from the senses; and finally it makes it impossible for us ever to doubt those things which we have once discovered to be true.

In the second Meditation, mind, which making use of the liberty which pertains to it, takes for granted that all those things of whose existence it has the least doubt, are non-existent, recognises that it is however absolutely impossible that it does not itself exist. This point is likewise of the greatest moment, inasmuch as by this means a distinction is easily drawn between the things which pertain to mind – that it to say to the intellectual nature – and those which pertain to body.

But because it may be that some expect from me in this place a statement of the reasons establishing the immortality of the soul, I feel that I should here make known to them that having aimed at writing nothing in all this treatise of which I do not posses very exact demonstrations, I am obliged to follow a similar order to that made use of by the geometers, which is to begin by putting forward as premises all those things upon which the proposition that we seek depends, before coming to any conclusion regarding it. Now the first and principal matter which is requisite for

3 Between the *Praefatio ad Lectorem* and the *Synopsis,* the Paris edition (1st edition) interpolates an *Index* which is not found in the Amsterdam edition (2nd edition). Since Descartes did not reproduce it, he was doubtless not its author. Mersenne probably composed it himself, adjusting it to the paging of the first edition.

thoroughly understanding the immortality of the soul is to form the clearest possible conception of it, and one which will be entirely distinct from all the conceptions which we may have of body; and in this Meditation this has been done. In addition to this it is requisite that we may be assured that all the things which we conceive clearly and distinctly are true in the very way in which we think them; and this could be proved previously to the fourth Meditation. Further we must have a distinct conception of corporeal nature, which is given partly in this second, and partly in the fifth and sixth Meditations. And finally we should conclude from all this, that those things which we conceive clearly and distinctly as being diverse substances, as we regard mind and body to be, are really substances essentially distinct one from the other; and this is the conclusion of the sixth Meditation. This is further confirmed in this same Meditation by the fact that we cannot conceive of body excepting in so far as it is divisible, while the mind cannot be conceived of excepting as indivisible. For we are not able to conceive of the half of a mind as we can do of the smallest of all bodies; so that we see that not only are their natures different but even in some respects contrary to one another. I have not however dealt further with this matter in this treatise, both because what I have said is sufficient to show clearly enough that the extinction of the mind does not follow from the corruption of the body, and also to give men the hope of another life after death, as also because the premises from which the immortality of the soul may be deduced depend on an elucidation of a complete system of physics. This would mean to establish in the first place that all substances generally – that is to say all things which cannot exist without being created by God – are in their nature incorruptible, and that they can never cease to exist unless God, in denying to them his concurrence, reduce them to nought; and secondly that body, regarded generally, is a substance, which is the reason why it also cannot perish, but that the human body, inasmuch as it differs from other bodies, is composed only of a certain configuration of members and of other similar accidents, while the human mind is not similarly composed of any accidents, but is a pure substance. For although all the accidents of mind be changed, although, for instance, it think certain things, will others, perceive others, etc., despite all this it does not emerge from these changes another mind:

14

the human body on the other hand becomes a different thing from the sole fact that the figure or form of any of its portions is found to be changed. From this it follows that the human body may indeed easily enough perish, but the mind [or soul of man (I make no distinction between them)] is owing to its nature immortal.

In the third Meditation it seems to me that I have explained at sufficient length the principal argument of which I make use in order to prove the existence of God. But none the less, because I did not wish in that place to make use of any comparisons derived from corporeal things, so as to withdraw as much as I could the minds of readers from the senses, there may perhaps have remained many obscurities which, however, will, I hope, be entirely removed by the Replies which I have made to the Objections which have been set before me. Amongst others there is, for example, this one, 'How the idea in us of a being supremely perfect possesses so much objective reality [that is to say participates by representation in so many degrees of being and perfection] that it necessarily proceeds from a cause which is absolutely perfect. This is illustrated in these Replies by the comparison of a very perfect machine, the idea of which is found in the mind of some workman. For as the objective contrivance of this idea must have some cause, i.e. either the science of the workman of that of some other from whom he has received the idea, it is similarly impossible that the idea of God which is in us should not have God himself as its cause.

In the Fourth Meditation it is shown that all these things which we very clearly and distinctly perceive are true, and at the same time it is explained in what the nature of error or falsity consists. This must of necessity be known but for the confirmation of the preceding truths and for the better comprehension of those that follow. (But it must meanwhile be remarked that I do not in any way there treat of sin – that is to say of the error which is committed in the pursuit of good and evil, but only of that which arises in the deciding between the true and the false. And I do not intend to speak of matters pertaining to the Faith or the conduct of life, but only of those which concern speculative truths, and which may be known by the sole aid of the light of nature.)

In the fifth Meditation corporeal nature generally is explained, and in addition to this the existence of God is demonstrated by a new proof in which there may possibly be certain difficulties also,

15

but the solution of these will be seen in the Replies to the
Objections. And further I show in what sense it is true to say that
the certainty of geometrical demonstrations is itself dependent on
the knowledge of God.

Finally in the sixth I distinguish the action of the understanding[4]
from that of the imagination;[5] the marks by which this distinction is
made are described. I here show that the mind of man is really
distinct from the body, and at the same time that the two are so
closely joined together that they form, so to speak, a single thing. All
the errors which proceed from the senses are then surveyed, while
the means of avoiding them are demonstrated, and finally all the
reasons from which we may deduce the existence of material things
are set forth. Not that I judge them to be very useful in establishing
that which they prove, to wit, that there is in truth a world, that
men possess bodies, and other such things which never have been
doubted by anyone of sense; but because in considering these
closely we come to see that they are neither so strong nor so evident
as those arguments which lead us to the knowledge of our mind and
of God; so that these last must be the most certain and most evident
facts which can fall within the cognisance of the human mind. And
this is the whole matter that I have tried to prove in these
Meditations, for which reason I here omit to speak of many other
questions with which I dealt incidentally in this discussion.

16

4 *intellectio*.   5 *imaginatio*.

17

MEDITATIONS ON THE FIRST PHILOSOPHY
IN WHICH THE EXISTENCE OF GOD AND
THE DISTINCTION BETWEEN MIND
AND BODY ARE DEMONSTRATED[1]

First Meditation *Of the things which may be brought within the sphere of the doubtful.*

It is now some years since I detected how many were the false beliefs that I had from my earliest youth admitted as true, and how doubtful was everything I had since constructed on this basis; and from that time I was convinced that I must once for all seriously undertake to rid myself of all the opinions which I had formerly accepted, and commence to build anew from the foundation, if I wanted to establish any firm and permanent structure in the sciences. But as this enterprise appeared to be a very great one, I waited until I had attained an age so mature that I could not hope that at any later date I should be better fitted to execute my design. This reason caused

me to delay so long that I should feel that I was doing wrong were I to occupy in deliberation the time that yet remains to me for action. Today, then, since very opportunely for the plan I have in view I have delivered my mind from every care [and am happily agitated by no passions] and since I have procured for myself an assured leisure in a peaceable retirement, I shall at last seriously and freely address myself to the general upheaval of all my former opinions.

Now for this object it is not necessary that I should show that all of these are false − I shall perhaps never arrive at this end. But inasmuch as reason already persuades me that I ought no less carefully to withhold my assent from matters which are not entirely certain and indubitable than from those which appear to me manifestly to be false, if I am able to find in each one some reason to

1 In place of this long title at the head of the page the first edition had immediately after the synopsis, and on the same page 7, simply 'First Meditation'.

doubt, this will suffice to justify my rejecting the whole. And for that end it will not be requisite that I should examine each in particular, which would be an endless undertaking; for owing to the fact that the destruction of the foundations of necessity brings with it the downfall of the rest of the edifice, I shall only in the first place attack those principles upon which all my former opinions rested.

All that up to the present time I have accepted as most true and certain I have learned either from the senses or through the senses; but it is sometimes proved to me that these senses are deceptive, and it is wiser not to trust entirely to any thing by which we have once been deceived.

But it may be that although the senses sometimes deceive us concerning things which are hardly perceptible, or very far away, there are yet many others to be met with as to which we cannot reasonably have any doubt, although we recognise them by their means. For example, there is the fact that I am here, seated by the fire, attired in a dressing gown, having this paper in my hands and other similar matters. And how could I deny that these hands and this body are mine, were it not perhaps that I compare myself to certain 19 persons, devoid of sense, whose cerebella are so troubled and clouded by the violent vapours of black bile, that they constantly assure us that they think they are kings when they are really quite poor, or that they are clothed in purple when they are really without covering, or who imagine that they have an earthenware head or are nothing but pumpkins or are made of glass. But they are mad, and I should not be any the less insane were I to follow examples so extravagant.

At the same time I must remember that I am a man, and that consequently I am in the habit of sleeping, and in my dreams representing to myself the same thing or even less probable things, than do those who are insane in their waking moments. How often has it happened to me that in the night I dreamt that I found myself in this particular place, that I was dressed and seated near the fire, whilst in reality I was lying undressed in bed! At this moment it does indeed seem to me that it is with eyes awake that I am looking at this paper; that this head which I move is not asleep, that it is deliberately and of set purpose that I extend my hand and perceive it; what happens in sleep does not appear so clear nor so distinct as does all this. But in thinking over this I remind myself that on many occasions I have in sleep been deceived by similar illusions, and in dwelling carefully on this reflection I see so manifestly that there are no certain indications by which we may clearly distinguish wakefulness from sleep that I am lost in astonishment. And my astonishment is such that it is almost capable of persuading me that I now dream.

Now let us assume that we are asleep and that all these particulars, e.g. that we open our eyes, shake our head, extend our hands, and so on, are but false delusions; and let us reflect that possibly neither our hands nor our whole body are such as they appear to us to be. At the same time we must at least confess that the things which are represented to us in sleep are like painted representations which can only have been formed as the counterparts of something real and true, and that in this way those general things at least, i.e. eyes, a head, hands, and a whole body, are not imaginary things, but things really existent. For, as a matter of fact, painters, even when they study with the greatest skill to represent sirens and satyrs by forms the most strange and extraordinary, cannot give them natures which are entirely new, but merely make a certain medley of the members of different animals; or if their imagination is extravagant enough to invent something so novel that nothing similar has ever before been seen, and that then their work represents a thing purely fictitious and absolutely false, it is certain all the same that the colours of which this is composed are necessarily real. And for the same reason, although these general things, to wit, [a body], eyes, a head, hands, and such like, may be imaginary, we are bound at the same time to confess that there are at least some other objects yet more simple and more universal, which are real and true; and of these just in the same way as with certain real colours, all these images of things which dwell in our thoughts, whether true and real or false and fantastic, are formed.

To such a class of things pertains corporeal nature in general, and its extension, the figure of extended things, their quantity or magnitude and number, as also the place in which they are, the time which measures their duration, and so on.

That is possibly why our reasoning is not unjust when we conclude from this that physics, astronomy, medicine and all other sciences which have as their end the consideration of composite things, are very dubious and uncertain; but that arithmetic, geometry and other sciences of that kind which only treat of things that are very simple and very general, without taking great trouble to ascertain whether they are actually existent or not, contain some measure of certainty and an element of the indubitable. For whether I am awake or asleep, two and three together always form five, and the square can never have more than four sides, and it does not seem possible that truths so clear and apparent can be suspected of any falsity [or uncertainty].

Nevertheless I have long had fixed in my mind the belief that an all-powerful God existed by whom I have been created such as I am. But how do I know that He has not brought it to pass that there is no earth, no heaven, no extended body, no magnitude, no place, and that nevertheless [I possess the perceptions of all these things and that] they seem to me to exist just exactly as I now see them? And, besides, as I sometimes imagine that others deceive themselves in the things which they think they know best, how do I know that I am not deceived every time that I add two and three, or count the sides of a square, or judge of things yet simpler, if anything simpler can be imagined? But possibly God has not desired that I should be thus deceived, for He is said to be supremely good. If, however, it is contrary to His goodness to have made me such that I constantly deceive myself, it would also appear to be contrary to His goodness to permit me to be sometimes deceived, and nevertheless I cannot doubt that He does permit this.

There may indeed be those who would prefer to deny the existence of a God so powerful, rather than believe that all other things are uncertain. But let us not oppose them for the present, and grant that all that is here said of a God is a fable; nevertheless in whatever way they suppose that I have arrived at the state of being that I have reached – whether they attribute it to fate or to accident, or make out that it is by a continual succession of antecedents, or by some other method – since to err and deceive oneself is a defect, it is clear that the greater will be the probability of my being so imperfect as to deceive myself ever, as is the Author to whom they assign my origin the less powerful. To these reasons I have certainly nothing to reply, but at the end I feel constrained to confess that there is nothing in all that I formerly believed to be true, of which I cannot in some measure doubt, and that not merely through want of thought or through levity, but for reasons which are very powerful and maturely considered; so that henceforth I ought not the less carefully to refrain from giving credence to these opinions

21

22

than to that which is manifestly false, if I desire to arrive at any certainty [in the sciences].

But it is not sufficient to have made these remarks, we must also be careful to keep them in mind. For these ancient and commonly held opinions still revert frequently to my mind, long and familiar custom having given them the right to occupy my mind against my inclination and rendered them almost masters of my belief; nor will I ever lose the habit of deferring to them or of placing my confidence in them, so long as I consider them as they really are, i.e. opinions in some measure doubtful, as I have just shown, and at the same time highly probable, so that there is much more reason to believe in than to deny them. That is why I consider that I shall not be acting amiss, if, taking of set purpose a contrary belief, I allow myself to be deceived, and for a certain time pretend that all these opinions are entirely false and imaginary, until at last, having thus balanced my former prejudices with my latter [so that they cannot divert my opinions more to one side than to the other], my judgment will no longer be dominated by bad usage or turned away from the right knowledge of the truth. For I am assured that there can be neither peril nor error in this course, and that I cannot at present yield too much to distrust, since I am not considering the question of action, but only of knowledge.

I shall then suppose, not that God who is supremely good and the fountain of truth, but some evil genius not less powerful than deceitful, has employed his whole energies in deceiving me; I shall consider that the heavens, the earth, colours, figures, sound, and all other external things are nought but the illusions and dreams of which this genius has availed himself in order to lay traps for my credulity; I shall consider myself as having no hands, no eyes, no flesh, no blood, nor any senses, yet falsely believing myself to possess all these things; I shall remain obstinately attached to this idea, and if by this means it is not in my power to arrive at the knowledge of any truth, I may at least do what is in my power [i.e. suspend my judgment], and with firm purpose avoid giving credence to any false thing, or being imposed upon by this arch deceiver, however powerful and deceptive he may be. But this task is a laborious one, and insensibly a certain lassitude leads me into the course of my ordinary life. And just as a captive who in sleep enjoys an imaginary liberty, when he begins to suspect that his liberty is but a dream, fears to awaken, and conspires with these agreeable illusions that the deception may be prolonged, so insensibly of my own accord I fall back into my former opinions, and I dread awakening from this slumber, lest the laborious wakefulness which would follow the tranquillity of this repose should have to be spent not in daylight, but in the excessive darkness of the difficulties which have just been discussed.

Second Meditation *Of the nature of the human mind; and that it is more easily known than the body.*

The Meditation of yesterday filled my mind with so many doubts that it is no longer in my power to forget them. And yet I do not see in what manner I can resolve them; and, just as if I had all of a sudden fallen into very deep water, I am so disconcerted that I can neither make certain of setting my feet on the bottom, nor can I swim and so support myself on the surface. I shall nevertheless make an effort and follow anew the same path as that on which I yesterday entered, i.e. I shall proceed by setting aside all that in which the least doubt could be supposed to exist, just as if I had discovered that it was absolutely false; and I shall ever follow in this road until I have met with something which is certain, or at least, if I can do nothing else, until I have learned for certain that there is nothing in the world that is certain. Archimedes, in order that he might draw the terrestrial globe out of its place, and transport it elsewhere, demanded only that one point should be fixed and immoveable; in the same way I shall have the right to conceive high hopes if I am happy enough to discover one thing only which is certain and indubitable.

I suppose, then, that all the things that I see are false; I persuade myself that nothing has ever existed of all that my fallacious memory represents to me. I consider that I possess no senses; I imagine that body, figure, extension, movement and place are but the fictions of my mind. What, then, can be esteemed as true? Perhaps nothing at all, unless that there is nothing in the world that is certain.

But how can I know there is not something different from those things that I have just considered, of which one cannot have the slightest doubt? Is there not some God, or some other being by whatever name we call it, who puts these reflections into my mind?

24

That is not necessary, for is it not possible that I am capable of producing them myself? I myself, am I not at least something? But I have already denied that I had senses and body. Yet I hesitate, for what follows from that? Am I so dependent on body and senses that I cannot exist without these? But I was persuaded that there was nothing in all the world, that there was no heaven, no earth, that there were no minds, nor any bodies: was I not then likewise persuaded that I did not exist? Not at all; of a surety I myself did exist since I persuaded myself of something [or merely because I thought of something]. But there is some deceiver or other, very powerful and very cunning, who ever employs his ingenuity in deceiving me. Then without doubt I exist also if he deceives me, and let him deceive me as much as he will, he can never cause me to be nothing so long as I think that I am something. So that after having reflected well and carefully examined all things, we must come to the definite conclusion that this proposition: I am, I exist, is necessarily true each time that I pronounce it, or that I mentally conceive it.

But I do not yet know clearly enough what I am, I who am certain that I am; and hence I must be careful to see that I do not imprudently take some other object in place of myself, and thus that I do not go astray in respect of this knowledge that I hold to be the most certain and most evident of all that I have formerly learned. That is why I shall now consider anew what I believed myself to be before I embarked upon these last reflections; and of my former opinions I shall withdraw all that might even in a small degree be invalidated by the reasons which I have just brought forward, in order that there may be nothing at all left beyond what is absolutely certain and indubitable.

What then did I formerly believe myself to be? Undoubtedly I believed myself to be a man. But what is a man? Shall I say a reasonable animal? Certainly not; for then I should have to inquire what an animal is, and what is reasonable; and thus from a single question I should insensibly fall into an infinitude of others more difficult; and I should not wish to waste the little time and leisure remaining to me in trying to unravel subtleties like these. But I shall rather stop here to consider the thoughts which of themselves spring up in my mind, and which were not inspired by anything beyond my own nature alone when I applied myself to the consideration of my being. In the first place, then, I considered myself as having a face, hands, arms, and all that system of members composed of bones and flesh as seen in a corpse which I designated by the name of body. In addition to this I considered that I was nourished, that I walked, that I felt, and that I thought, and I referred all these actions to the soul: but I did not stop to consider what the soul was, or if I did stop, I imagined that it was something extremely rare and subtle like a wind, a flame, or an ether, which was spread throughout my grosser parts. As to body I had no manner of doubt about its nature, but thought I had a very clear knowledge of it; and if I had desired to explain it according to the notions that I had then formed of it, I should have described it thus: By the body I understand all that which can be defined by a certain figure: something which can be confined in a certain place, and which can fill a given space in such a way that every other body will be excluded from it; which can be perceived either by touch, or by sight, or by hearing, or by taste, or by smell: which can be moved in many ways not, in truth, by itself, but by something which is foreign to it, by which it is touched [and from which it receives impressions]: for to have the power of self-movement, as also of feeling or of thinking, I did not consider to appertain to the nature of body: on the contrary, I was rather astonished to find that faculties similar to them existed in some bodies.

But what am I, now that I suppose that there is a certain genius which is extremely powerful, and, if I may say so, malicious, who employs all his powers in deceiving me? Can I affirm that I possess the least of all those things which I have just said pertain to the nature of body? I pause to consider, I revolve all these things in my mind, and I find none of which I can say that it pertains to me. It would be tedious to stop to enumerate them. Let us pass to the attributes of soul and see if there is any one which is in me? What of nutrition or walking [the first mentioned]? But if it is so that I have no body it is also true that I can neither walk nor take nourishment. Another attribute is sensation. But one cannot feel without body, and besides I have thought I perceived many things during sleep that I recognised in my waking moments as not having been experienced at all. What of thinking? I find here that thought is an attribute that belongs to me; it alone cannot be separated from me. I am, I exist, that is certain. But how often? Just when I think; for it

27

might possibly be the case if I ceased entirely to think, that I should likewise cease altogether to exist. I do not now admit anything which is not necessarily true: to speak accurately I am not more than a thing which thinks, that is to say a mind or a soul, or an understanding, or a reason, which are terms whose significance was formerly unknown to me. I am, however, a real thing and really exist; but what thing? I have answered: a thing which thinks.

And what more? I shall exercise my imagination [in order to see if I am not something more]. I am not a collection of members which we call the human body: I am not a subtle air distributed through these members, I am not a wind, a fire, a vapour, a breath, nor anything at all which I can imagine or conceive; because I have assumed that all these were nothing. Without changing that supposition I find that I only leave myself certain of the fact that I am somewhat. But perhaps it is true that these same things which I supposed were non-existent because they are unknown to me, are really not different from the self which I know. I am not sure about this, I shall not dispute about it now; I can only give judgment on things that are known to me. I know that I exist, and I inquire what I am, I whom I know to exist. But it is very certain that the knowledge of my existence taken in its precise significance does not depend on things whose existence is not yet known to me; consequently it does not depend on those which I can feign in imagination. And indeed the very term *feign* in imagination[2] proves to me my error, for I really do this if I imagine myself a something, since to imagine is nothing else than to contemplate the figure or image of a corporeal thing. But I already know for certain that I am, and that it may be that all these images, and, speaking generally, all things that relate to the nature of body are nothing but dreams [and chimeras]. For this reason I see clearly that I have as little reason to say, 'I shall stimulate my imagination in order to know more distinctly what I am,' as if I were to say, 'I am now awake, and I perceive somewhat that is real and true: but because I do not yet perceive it distinctly enough, I shall go to sleep of express purpose, so that my dreams may represent the perception with greatest truth and evidence.' And, thus, I know for certain that nothing of all that I can understand by means of my imagination belongs to this

28

2 Or 'form an image' (*effingo*).

knowledge which I have of myself, and that it is necessary to recall the mind from this mode of thought with the utmost diligence in order that it may be able to know its own nature with perfect distinctness.

But what then am I? A thing which thinks. What is a thing which thinks? It is a thing which doubts, understands, [conceives,] affirms, denies, wills, refuses, which also imagines and feels.

Certainly it is no small matter if all these things pertain to my nature. But why should they not so pertain? Am I not that being who now doubts nearly everything, who nevertheless understands certain things, who affirms that one only is true, who denies all the others, who desires to know more, is averse from being deceived, who imagines many things, sometimes indeed despite his will, and who perceives many likewise, as by the intervention of the bodily organs? Is there nothing in all this which is as true as it is certain that I exist, even though I should always sleep and though he who has given me being employed all his ingenuity in deceiving me? Is there likewise any one of these attributes which can be distinguished from my thought, or which might be said to be separated from myself? For it is so evident of itself that it is I who doubts, who understands, and who desires, that there is no reason here to add anything to explain it. And I have certainly the power of imagining likewise; for although it may happen (as I formerly supposed) that none of the things which I imagine are true, nevertheless this power of imagining does not cease to be really in use, and it forms part of my thought. Finally, I am the same who feels, that is to say, who perceives certain things, as by the organs of sense, since in truth I see light, I hear noise, I feel heat. But it will be said that these phenomena are false and that I am dreaming. Let it be so; still it is at least quite certain that it seems to me that I see light, that I hear noise and that I feel heat. That cannot be false; properly speaking it is what is in me called feeling;[3] and used in this precise sense that is no other thing than thinking.

From this time I begin to know what I am with a little more clearness and distinction than before; but nevertheless it still seems to me, and I cannot prevent myself from thinking, that corporeal things, whose images are framed by thought, which are tested by

29

3 *sentire*.

the senses, are much more distinctly known than that obscure part of me which does not come under the imagination. Although really it is very strange to say that I know and understand more distinctly these things whose existence seems to me dubious, which are unknown to me, and which do not belong to me, than others of the truth of which I am convinced, which are known to me and which pertain to my real nature, in a word, than myself. But I see clearly how the case stands: my mind loves to wander, and cannot yet suffer itself to be retained within the just limits of truth. Very good, let us once more give it the freest rein, so that, when afterwards we seize the proper occasion for pulling up, it may the more easily be regulated and controlled.

Let us begin by considering the commonest matters, those which we believe to be the most distinctly comprehended, to wit, the bodies which we touch and see; not indeed bodies in general, for these general ideas are usually a little more confused, but let us consider one body in particular. Let us take, for example, this piece of wax: it has been taken quite freshly from the hive, and it has not yet lost the sweetness of the honey which it contains; it still retains somewhat of the odour of the flowers from which it has been culled; its colour, its figure, its size are apparent; it is hard, cold, easily handled, and if you strike it with the finger, it will emit a sound. Finally all the things which are requisite to cause us distinctly to recognise a body, are met with in it. But notice that while I speak and approach the fire what remained of the taste is exhaled, the smell evaporates, the colour alters, the figure is destroyed, the size increases, it becomes liquid, it heats, scarcely can one handle it, and when one strikes it, no sound is emitted. Does the same wax remain after this change? We must confess that it remains; none would judge otherwise. What then did I know so distinctly in this piece of wax? It could certainly be nothing of all that the senses brought to my notice, since all these things which fall under taste, smell, sight, touch, and hearing, are found to be changed, and yet the same wax remains.

Perhaps it was what I now think, viz. that this wax was not that sweetness of honey, nor that agreeable scent of flowers, nor that particular whiteness, nor that figure, nor that sound, but simply a body which a little while before appeared to me as perceptible under these forms, and which is now perceptible under others. But what, precisely, is it that I imagine when I form such conceptions? Let us attentively consider this, and, abstracting from all that does not belong to the wax, let us see what remains. Certainly nothing remains excepting a certain extended thing which is flexible and movable. But what is the meaning of flexible and movable? Is it not that I imagine that this piece of wax being round is capable of becoming square and of passing from a square to a triangular figure? No, certainly it is not that, since I imagine it admits of an infinitude of similar changes, and I nevertheless do not know how to compass the infinitude by my imagination, and consequently this conception which I have of the wax is not brought about by the faculty of imagination. What now is this extension? Is it not also unknown? For it becomes greater when the wax is melted, greater when it is boiled, and greater still when the heat increases; and I should not conceive [clearly] according to truth what wax is, if I did not think that even this piece that we are considering is capable of receiving more variations in extension than I have ever imagined. We must then grant that I could not even understand through the imagination what this piece of wax is, and that it is my mind[4] alone which perceives it. I say this piece of wax in particular, for as to wax in general it is yet clearer. But what is this piece of wax which cannot be understood excepting by the [understanding or] mind? It is certainly the same that I see, touch, imagine, and finally it is the same which I have always believed it to be from the beginning. But what must particularly be observed is that its perception is neither an act of vision, nor of touch, nor of imagination, and has never been such although it may have appeared formerly to be so, but only an intuition[5] of the mind, which may be imperfect and confused as it was formerly, or clear and distinct as it is at present, according as my attention is more or less directed to the elements which are found in it, and of which it is composed.

Yet in the meantime I am greatly astonished when I consider [the great feebleness of mind] and its proneness to fall [insensibly] into error; for although without giving expression to my thoughts I consider all this in my own mind, words often impede me and I am almost deceived by the terms of ordinary language. For we say that we see the same wax, if it is present, and not that we simply judge

4 *entendement*, French; *mens*, Latin.   5 *inspectio*.

that it is the same from its having the same colour and figure. From this I should conclude that I knew the wax by means of vision and not simply by the intuition of the mind; unless by chance I remember that, when looking from a window and saying I see men who pass in the street, I really do not see them, but infer that what I see is men, just as I say that I see wax. And yet what do I see from the window but hats and coats which may cover automatic machines? Yet I judge these to be men. And similarly solely by the faculty of judgment which rests in my mind, I comprehend that which I believed I saw with my eyes.

A man who makes it his aim to raise his knowledge above the common should be ashamed to derive the occasion for doubting from the forms of speech invented by the vulgar; I prefer to pass on and consider whether I had a more evident and perfect conception of what the wax was when I first perceived it, and when I believed I knew it by means of the external senses or at least by the common sense[6] as it is called, that is to say by the imaginative faculty, or whether my present conception is clearer now that I have most carefully examined what it is, and in what way it can be known. It would certainly be absurd to doubt as to this. For what was there in this first perception which was distinct? What was there which might not as well have been perceived by any of the animals? But when I distinguish the wax from its external forms, and when, just as if I had taken from it its vestments, I consider it quite naked, it is certain that although some error may still be found in my judgment, I can nevertheless not perceive it thus without a human mind.

33   But finally what shall I say of this mind, that is, of myself, for up to this point I do not admit in myself anything but mind? What then, I who seem to perceive this piece of wax so distinctly, do I not know myself, not only with much more truth and certainty, but also with much more distinctness and clearness? For if I judge that the wax is or exists from the fact that I see it, it certainly follows much more clearly that I am or that I exist myself from the fact that I see it. For it may be that what I see is not really wax, it may also be that I do not possess eyes with which to see anything; but it cannot be that when I see, or (for I no longer take account of the distinction) when

6 *sensus communis.*

I think I see, that I myself who think am nought. So if I judge that the wax exists from the fact that I touch it, the same thing will follow, to wit, that I am; and if I judge that my imagination, or some other cause, whatever it is, persuades me that the wax exists, I shall still conclude the same. And what I have here remarked of wax may be applied to all other things which are external to me [and which are met with outside of me]. And further, if the [notion or] perception of wax has seemed to me clearer and more distinct, not only after the sight or the touch, but also after many other causes have rendered it quite manifest to me, with how much more [evidence] and distinctness must it be said that I now know myself, since all the reasons which contribute to the knowledge of wax, or any other body whatever, are yet better proofs of the nature of my mind! And there are so many other things in the mind itself which may contribute to the elucidation of its nature, that those which depend on body such as these just mentioned, hardly merit being taken into account.

But finally here I am, having insensibly reverted to the point I desired, for, since it is now manifest to me that even bodies are not properly speaking known by the senses or by the faculty of imagination, but by the understanding only, and since they are not known from the fact that they are seen or touched, but only because they are understood, I see clearly that there is nothing which is easier for me to know than my mind. But because it is difficult to rid oneself so promptly of an opinion to which one was accustomed for so long, it will be well that I should halt a little at this point, so that by the length of my meditation I may more deeply imprint on my memory this new knowledge.

34

Third Meditation *Of God: that He exists.*

I shall now close my eyes, I shall stop my ears, I shall call away all my senses, I shall efface even from my thoughts all the images of corporeal things, or at least (for that is hardly possible) I shall esteem them as vain and false; and thus holding converse only with myself and considering my own nature, I shall try little by little to reach a better knowledge of and a more familiar acquaintanceship with myself. I am a thing that thinks, that is to say, that doubts, affirms, denies, that knows a few things, that is ignorant of many [that loves,

that hates], that wills, that desires, that also imagines and perceives;
for as I remarked before, although the things which I perceive and
imagine are perhaps nothing at all apart from me and in themselves,
I am nevertheless assured that these modes of thought that I call
perceptions and imaginations, inasmuch only as they are modes of
thought, certainly reside [and are met with] in me.

And in the little that I have just said, I think I have summed up all
that I really know, or at least all that hitherto I was aware that I
knew. In order to try to extend my knowledge further, I shall now
look around more carefully and see whether I cannot still discover
in myself some other things which I have not hitherto perceived. I
am certain that I am a thing which thinks; but do I not then likewise
know what is requisite to render me certain of a truth? Certainly in
this first knowledge there is nothing that assures me of its truth,
excepting the clear and distinct perception of that which I state,
which would not indeed suffice to assure me that what I say is true,
if it could ever happen that a thing which I conceived so clearly and
distinctly could be false; and accordingly it seems to me that already
I can establish as a general rule that all things which I perceive[7] very
clearly and very distinctly are true.

At the same time I have before received and admitted many
things to be very certain and manifest, which yet I afterwards
recognised as being dubious. What then were these things? They
were the earth, sky, stars and all other objects which I apprehended
by means of the senses. But what did I clearly [and distinctly]
perceive in them? Nothing more than that the ideas or thoughts of
these things were presented to my mind. And not even now do I
deny that these ideas are met with in me. But there was yet another
thing which I affirmed, and which, owing to the habit which I had
formed of believing it, I thought I perceived very clearly, although
in truth I did not perceive it at all, to wit, that there were objects
outside of me from which these ideas proceeded, and to which they
were entirely similar. And it was in this that I erred, or, if perchance
my judgment was correct, this was not due to any knowledge
arising from my perception.

But when I took anything very simple and easy in the sphere of
arithmetic or geometry into consideration, e.g. that two and three

7 *percipio;* French, *nous concevons.*

together made five, and other things of the sort, were not these present to my mind so clearly as to enable me to affirm that they were true? Certainly if I judged that since such matters could be doubted, this would not have been so for any other reason than that it came into my mind that perhaps a God might have endowed me with such a nature that I may have been deceived even concerning things which seemed to me most manifest. But every time that this preconceived opinion of the sovereign power of a God presents itself to my thought, I am constrained to confess that it is easy to Him, if He wishes it, to cause me to err, even in matters in which I believe myself to have the best evidence. And, on the other hand, always when I direct my attention to things which I believe myself to perceive very clearly, I am so persuaded of their truth that I let myself break out into words such as these: Let who will deceive me, He can never cause me to be nothing while I think that I am, or some day cause it to be true to say that I have never been, it being true now to say that I am, or that two and three make more or less than five, or any such thing in which I see a manifest contradiction. And, certainly, since I have no reason to believe that there is a God who is a deceiver, and as I have not yet satisfied myself that there is a God at all, the reason for doubt which depends on this opinion alone is very slight, and so to speak metaphysical. But in order to be able altogether to remove it, I must inquire whether there is a God as soon as the occasion presents itself; and if I find that there is a God, I must also inquire whether He may be a deceiver; for without a knowledge of these two truths I do not see that I can ever be certain of anything.

And in order that I may have an opportunity of inquiring into this in an orderly way [without interrupting the order of meditation which I have proposed to myself, and which is little by little to pass from the notions which I find first of all in my mind to those which I shall later on discover in it] it is requisite that I should here divide my thoughts into certain kinds, and that I should consider in which of these kinds there is, properly speaking, truth or error to be found. Of my thoughts some are, so to speak, images of the things, and to these alone is the title 'idea' properly applied; examples are my thought of a man or of a chimera, of heaven, of an angel, or [even] of God. But other thoughts possess other forms as well. For example in willing, fearing, approving, denying, though I always perceive

37

something as the subject of the action of my mind,[8] yet by this action I always add something else to the idea[9] which I have of that thing; and of the thoughts of this kind some are called volitions or affections, and others judgments.

Now as to what concerns ideas, if we consider them only in themselves and do not relate them to anything else beyond themselves, they cannot properly speaking be false; for whether I imagine a goat or a chimera, it is not less true that I imagine the one than the other. We must not fear likewise that falsity can enter into will and into affections, for although I may desire evil things, or even things that never existed, it is not the less true that I desire them. Thus there remains no more than the judgments which we make, in which I must take the greatest care not to deceive myself. But the principal error and the commonest which we may meet with in them, consists in my judging that the ideas which are in me are similar or conformable to the things which are outside me; for without doubt if I considered the ideas only as certain modes of my thoughts, without trying to relate them to anything beyond, they could scarcely give me material for error.

But among these ideas, some appear to me to be innate, some adventitious, and others to be formed [or invented] by myself; for, as I have the power of understanding what is called a thing, or a truth, or a thought, it appears to me that I hold this power from no other source than my own nature. But if I now hear some sound, if I see the sun, or feel heat, I have hitherto judged that these sensations proceeded from certain things that exist outside of me; and finally it appears to me that sirens, hippogryphs, and the like, are formed out of my own mind. But again I may possibly persuade myself that all these ideas are of the nature of those which I term adventitious, or else that they are all innate, or all fictitious: for I have not yet clearly discovered their true origin.

And my principal task in this place is to consider, in respect to those ideas which appear to me to proceed from certain objects that are outside me, what are the reasons which cause me to think them similar to these objects. It seems indeed in the first place that I am

8 The French version is followed here as being more explicit. In it *action de mon esprit* replaces *mea cogitatio*.
9 In the Latin version *similitudinem*.

taught this lesson by nature; and, secondly, I experience in myself that these ideas do not depend on my will nor therefore on myself – for they often present themselves to my mind in spite of my will. Just now, for instance, whether I will or whether I do not will, I feel heat, and thus I persuade myself that this feeling, or at least this idea of heat, is produced in me by something which is different from me, i.e. by the heat of the fire near which I sit. And nothing seems to me more obvious than to judge that this object imprints its likeness rather than anything else upon me.

Now I must discover whether these proofs are sufficiently strong and convincing. When I say that I am so instructed by nature, I merely mean a certain spontaneous inclination which impels me to believe in this connection, and not a natural light which makes me recognise that it is true. But these two things are very different; for I cannot doubt that which the natural light causes me to believe to be true, as, for example, it has shown me that I am from the fact that I doubt, or other facts of the same kind. And I possess no other faculty whereby to distinguish truth from falsehood, which can teach me that what this light shows me to be true is not really true, and no other faculty that is equally trustworthy. But as far as [apparently] natural impulses are concerned, I have frequently remarked, when I had to make active choice between virtue and vice, that they often enough led me to the part that was worse; and this is why I do not see any reason for following them in what regards truth and error.

And as to the other reason, which is that these ideas must proceed from objects outside me, since they do not depend on my will, I do not find it any the more convincing. For just as these impulses of which I have spoken are found in me, notwithstanding that they do not always concur with my will, so perhaps there is in me some faculty fitted to produce these ideas without the assistance of any external things, even though it is not yet known by me; just as, apparently, they have hitherto always been found in me during sleep without the aid of any external objects.

And finally, though they did proceed from objects different from myself, it is not a necessary consequence that they should resemble these. On the contrary, I have noticed that in many cases there was a great difference between the object and its idea. I find, for example, two completely diverse ideas of the sun in my mind; the

39

one derives its origin from the senses, and should be placed in the category of adventitious ideas; according to this idea the sun seems to be extremely small; but the other is derived from astronomical reasonings, i.e. is elicited from certain notions that are innate in me, or else it is formed by me in some other manner; in accordance with it the sun appears to be several times greater than the earth. These two ideas cannot, indeed, both resemble the same sun, and reason makes me believe that the one which seems to have originated directly from the sun itself, is the one which is most dissimilar to it.

40 All this causes me to believe that until the present time it has not been by a judgment that was certain [or premeditated], but only by a sort of blind impulse that I believed that things existed outside of, and different from me, which, by the organs of my senses, or by some other method whatever it might be, conveyed these ideas or images to me [and imprinted on me their similitudes].

But there is yet another method of inquiring whether any of the objects of which I have ideas within me exist outside of me. If ideas are only taken as certain modes of thought, I recognise amongst them no difference or inequality, and all appear to proceed from me in the same manner; but when we consider them as images, one representing one thing and the other another, it is clear that they are very different one from the other. There is no doubt that those which represent to me substances are something more, and contain so to speak more objective reality within them [that is to say, by representation participate in a higher degree of being or perfection] than those that simply represent modes or accidents; and that idea again by which I understand a supreme God, eternal, infinite, [immutable], omniscient, omnipotent, and Creator of all things which are outside of Himself, has certainly more objective reality in itself than those ideas by which finite substances are represented.

Now it is manifest by the natural light that there must at least be as much reality in the efficient and total cause as in its effect. For, pray, whence can the effect derive its reality, if not from its cause? And in what way can this cause communicate this reality to it, unless it possessed it in itself? And from this it follows, not only that

41 something cannot proceed from nothing, but likewise that what is more perfect — that is to say, which has more reality within itself — cannot proceed from the less perfect. And this is not only evidently true of those effects which possess actual or formal reality, but also of

the ideas in which we consider merely what is termed objective reality. To take an example, the stone which has not yet existed not only cannot now commence to be unless it has been produced by something which possesses within itself, either formally or eminently, all that enters into the composition of the stone [i.e. it must possess the same things or other more excellent things than those which exist in the stone] and heat can only be produced in a subject in which it did not previously exist by a cause that is of an order [degree or kind] at least as perfect as heat, and so in all other cases. But further, the idea of heat, or of a stone, cannot exist in me unless it has been placed within me by some cause which possesses within it at least as much reality as that which I conceive to exist in the heat or the stone. For although this cause does not transmit anything of its actual or formal reality to my idea, we must not for that reason imagine that it is necessarily a less real cause; we must remember that [since every idea is a work of the mind] its nature is such that it demands of itself no other formal reality than that which it borrows from my thought, of which it is only a mode [i.e. a manner or way of thinking]. But in order that an idea should contain some one certain objective reality rather than another, it must without doubt derive it from some cause in which there is at least as much formal reality as this idea contains of objective reality. For if we imagine that something is found in an idea which is not found in the cause, it must then have been derived from nought; but however imperfect may be this mode of being by which a thing is objectively [or by representation] in the understanding by its idea, we cannot certainly say that this mode of being is nothing, nor, consequently, that the idea derives its origin from nothing.

Nor must I imagine that, since the reality that I consider in these ideas is only objective, it is not essential that this reality should be formally in the causes of my ideas, but that it is sufficient that it should be found objectively. For just as this mode of objective existence pertains to ideas by their proper nature, so does the mode of formal existence pertain to the causes of those ideas (this is at least true of the first and principal by the nature peculiar to them. And although it may be the case that one idea gives birth to another idea, that cannot continue to be so indefinitely; for in the end we must reach an idea whose cause shall be so to speak an archetype, in which the sole reality [or perfection] which is so to speak

42

objectively [or by representation] in these ideas is contained formally [and really]. Thus the light of nature causes me to know clearly that the ideas in me are like [pictures or] images which can, in truth, easily fall short of the perfection of the objects from which they have been derived, but which can never contain anything greater or more perfect.

And the longer and the more carefully that I investigate these matters, the more clearly and distinctly do I recognise their truth. But what am I to conclude from it all in the end? It is this, that if the objective reality of any one of my ideas is of such a nature as clearly to make me recognise that it is not in me either formally or eminently, and that consequently I cannot myself be the cause of it, it follows of necessity that I am not alone in the world, but that there is another being which exists, or which is the cause of this idea. On the other hand, had no such an idea existed in me, I should have had no sufficient argument to convince me of the existence of any being beyond myself; for I have made very careful investigation everywhere and up to the present time have been able to find no other ground.

But of my ideas, beyond that which represents me to myself, as to which there can here be no difficulty, there is another which represents a God, and there are others representing corporeal and inanimate things, others angels, others animals, and others again which represent to me men similar to myself.

As regards the ideas which represent to me other men or animals, or angels, I can however easily conceive that they might be formed by an admixture of the other ideas which I have of myself, of corporeal things, and of God, even although there were apart from me neither men nor animals, nor angels, in all the world.

And in regard to the ideas of corporeal objects, I do not recognise in them anything so great or so excellent that they might not have possibly proceeded from myself; for if I consider them more closely, and examine them individually, as I yesterday examined the idea of wax, I find that there is very little in them which I perceive clearly and distinctly. Magnitude or extension in length, breadth, or depth, I do so perceive; also figure which results from a termination of this extension, the situation which bodies of different figure preserve in relation to one another, and movement or change of situation; to which we may also add substance, duration and number. As to other things such as light, colours, sounds, scents, tastes, heat, cold and the other tactile qualities, they are thought by me with so much obscurity and confusion that I do not even know if they are true or false, i.e. whether the ideas which I form of these qualities are actually the ideas of real objects or not [or whether they only represent chimeras which cannot exist in fact]. For although I have before remarked that it is only in judgments that falsity, properly speaking, or formal falsity, can be met with, a certain material falsity may nevertheless be found in ideas, i.e. when these ideas represent what is nothing as though it were something. For example, the ideas which I have of cold and heat are so far   44 from clear and distinct that by their means I cannot tell whether cold is merely a privation of heat, or heat a privation of cold, or whether both are real qualities, or are not such. And inasmuch as [since ideas resemble images] there cannot be any ideas which do not appear to represent some things, if it is correct to say that cold is merely a privation of heat, the idea which represents it to me as something real and positive will not be improperly termed false, and the same holds good of other similar ideas.

To these it is certainly not necessary that I should attribute any author other than myself. For if they are false, i.e. if they represent things which do not exist, the light of nature shows me that they issue from nought, that is to say, that they are only in me in so far as something is lacking to the perfection of my nature. But if they are true, nevertheless because they exhibit so little reality to me that I cannot even clearly distinguish the thing represented from non-being, I do not see any reason why they should not be produced by myself.

As to the clear and distinct idea which I have of corporeal things, some of them seem as though I might have derived them from the idea which I possess of myself, as those which I have of substance, duration, number, and such like. For [even] when I think that a stone is a substance, or at least a thing capable of existing of itself, and that I am a substance also, although I conceive that I am a thing that thinks and not one that is extended, and that the stone on the other hand is an extended thing which does not think, and that thus there is a notable difference between the two conceptions – they seem, nevertheless, to agree in this, that both represent substances. In the same way, when I perceive that I now exist and further recollect that I have in former times existed, and when I remember that I have various thoughts of which I can recognise the number, I acquire ideas of duration and number which I can afterwards transfer to any object that I please. But as to all the other qualities of which the ideas of corporeal things are composed, to wit, extension, figure, situation and motion, it is true that they are not formally in me, since I am only a thing that thinks; but because they are merely certain modes of substance [and so to speak the vestments under which corporeal substance appears to us] and because I myself am also a substance, it would seem that they might be contained in me eminently.

Hence there remains only the idea of God, concerning which we must consider whether it is something which cannot have proceeded from me myself. By the name God I understand a substance that is infinite [eternal, immutable], independent, all-knowing, all-powerful, and by which I myself and everything else, if anything else does exist, have been created. Now all these characteristics are such that the more diligently I attend to them, the less do they appear capable of proceeding from me alone; hence, from what has been already said, we must conclude that God necessarily exists.

For although the idea of substance is within me owing to the fact that I am substance, nevertheless I should not have the idea of an infinite substance – since I am finite – if it had not proceeded from some substance which was veritably infinite.

Nor should I imagine that I do not perceive the infinite by a true idea, but only by the negation of the finite, just as I perceive repose and darkness by the negation of movement and of light; for, on the contrary, I see that there is manifestly more reality in infinite substance than in finite, and therefore that in some way I have in me the notion of the infinite earlier than the finite – to wit, the notion of God before that of myself. For how would it be possible that I should know that I doubt and desire, that is to say, that something is lacking to me, and that I am not quite perfect, unless I had within me some idea of a Being more perfect than myself, in comparison with which I should recognise the deficiencies of my nature?

And we cannot say that this idea of God is perhaps materially false and that consequently I can derive it from nought [i.e. that possibly it exists in me because I am imperfect], as I have just said is the case with ideas of heat, cold and other such things; for, on the contrary, as this idea is very clear and distinct and contains within it more objective reality than any other, there can be none which is of itself more true, nor any in which there can be less suspicion of falsehood. The idea, I say, of this Being who is absolutely perfect and infinite, is entirely true; for although, perhaps, we can imagine that such a Being does not exist, we cannot nevertheless imagine that His idea represents nothing real to me, as I have said of the idea of cold. This idea is also very clear and distinct; since all that I conceive clearly and distinctly of the real and the true, and of what conveys some perfection, is in its entirety contained in this idea. And this does not cease to be true although I do not comprehend the infinite, or though in God there is an infinitude of things which I cannot comprehend, nor possibly even reach in any way by thought; for it is of the nature of the infinite that my nature, which is finite and limited, should not comprehend it; and it is sufficient that I should understand this, and that I should judge that all things which I clearly perceive and in which I know that there is some perfection, and possibly likewise an infinitude of properties of which I am ignorant, are in God formally or eminently, so that the idea which I have of Him may become the most true, most clear, and most distinct of all the ideas that are in my mind.

But possibly I am something more than I suppose myself to be, and perhaps all those perfections which I attribute to God are in some way potentially in me, although they do not yet disclose themselves, or issue in action. As a matter of fact I am already sensible that my knowledge increases [and perfects itself] little by little, and I see nothing which can prevent it from increasing more and more into infinitude; nor do I see, after it has thus been increased [or perfected], anything to prevent my being able to acquire by its means all the other perfections of the Divine nature; nor finally why the power I have of acquiring these perfections, if it really exists in me, shall not suffice to produce the ideas of them.

At the same time I recognise that this cannot be. For, in the first place, although it were true that every day my knowledge acquired new degrees of perfection, and that there were in my nature many things potentially which are not yet there actually, nevertheless these excellences do not pertain to [or make the smallest approach to] the idea which I have of God in whom there is nothing merely potential [but in whom all is present really and actually]; for it is an infallible token of imperfection in my knowledge that it increases little by little. And further, although my knowledge grows more and more, nevertheless I do not for that reason believe that it can ever be actually infinite, since it can never reach a point so high that it will be unable to attain to any greater increase. But I understand God to be actually infinite, so that He can add nothing to His supreme perfection. And finally I perceive that the objective being of an idea cannot be produced by a being that exists potentially only, which properly speaking is nothing, but only by a being which is formal or actual.

To speak the truth, I see nothing in all that I have just said which by the light of nature is not manifest to anyone who desires to think attentively on the subject; but when I slightly relax my attention, my mind, finding its vision somewhat obscured and so to speak blinded by the images of sensible objects, I do not easily recollect the reason why the idea that I possess of a being more perfect than I, must necessarily have been placed in me by a being which is really more perfect; and this is why I wish here to go on to inquire whether I, who have this idea, can exist if no such being exists.

And I ask, from whom do I then derive my existence? Perhaps from myself or from my parents, or from some other source less perfect than God; for we can imagine nothing more perfect than God, or even as perfect as He is.

But [were I independent of every other and] were I myself the author of my being, I should doubt nothing and I should desire nothing, and finally no perfection would be lacking to me; for I should have bestowed on myself every perfection of which I possessed any idea and should thus be God. And it must not be imagined that those things that are lacking to me are perhaps more difficult of attainment than those which I already possess; for, on the contrary, it is quite evident that it was a matter of much greater difficulty to bring to pass that I, that is to say, a thing or a substance that thinks, should emerge out of nothing, than it would be to attain to the knowledge of many things of which I am ignorant, and which are only the accidents of this thinking substance. But it is clear that if I had of myself possessed this greater perfection of which I have just spoken [that is to say, if I had been the author of my own existence], I should not at least have denied myself the things which are the more easy to acquire [to wit, many branches of knowledge

48

of which my nature is destitute]; nor should I have deprived myself of any of the things contained in the idea which I form of God, because there are none of them which seem to me specially difficult to acquire: and if there were any that were more difficult to acquire, they would certainly appear to me to be such (supposing I myself were the origin of the other things which I possess) since I should discover in them that my powers were limited.

But though I assume that perhaps I have always existed just as I am at present, neither can I escape the force of this reasoning and imagine that the conclusion to be drawn from this is, that I need not seek for any author of my existence. For all the course of my life may be divided into an infinite number of parts, none of which is in any way dependent on the other; and thus from the fact that I was in existence a short time ago it does not follow that I must be in existence now, unless some cause at this instant, so to speak, produces me anew, that is to say, conserves me. It is as a matter of fact perfectly clear and evident to all those who consider with attention the nature of time, that, in order to be conserved in each moment in which it endures, a substance has need of the same power and action as would be necessary to produce and create it anew, supposing it did not yet exist, so that the light of nature shows us clearly that the distinction between creation and conservation is solely a distinction of the reason.

49

All that I thus require here is that I should interrogate myself, if I wish to know whether I possess a power which is capable of bringing it to pass that I who now am shall still be in the future; for since I am nothing but a thinking thing, or at least since thus far it is only this portion of myself which is precisely in question at present, if such a power did reside in me, I should certainly be conscious of it. But I am conscious of nothing of the kind, and by this I know clearly that I depend on some being different from myself.

Possibly, however, this being on which I depend is not that which I call God, and I am created either by my parents or by some other cause less perfect than God. This cannot be, because, as I have just said, it is perfectly evident that there must be at least as much reality in the cause as in the effect; and thus since I am a thinking thing, and possess an idea of God within me, whatever in the end be the cause assigned to my existence, it must be allowed that it is likewise a thinking thing and that it possesses in itself the idea of all the perfections which I attribute to God. We may again inquire whether this cause derives its origin from itself or from some other thing. For if from itself, it follows by the reasons before brought forward, that this cause must itself be God; for since it possesses the virtue of self-existence, it must also without doubt have the power of actually possessing all the perfections of which it has the idea, that is, all those which I conceive as existing in God. But if it derives its existence from some other cause than itself, we shall again ask, for the same reason, whether this second cause exists by itself or through another, until from one step to another, we finally arrive at an ultimate cause, which will be God.

And it is perfectly manifest that in this there can be no regression into infinity, since what is in question is not so much the cause which formerly created me, as that which conserves me at the present time.

Nor can we suppose that several causes may have concurred in my production, and that from one I have received the idea of one of the perfections which I attribute to God, and from another the idea of some other, so that all these perfections indeed exist somewhere in the universe, but not as complete in one unity which is God. On the contrary, the unity, the simplicity or the inseparability of all things which are in God is one of the principal perfections which I conceive to be in Him. And certainly the idea of this unity of all Divine perfections cannot have been placed in me by any cause from which I have not likewise received the ideas of all the other perfections; for this cause could not make me able to comprehend them as joined together in an inseparable unity without having at the same time caused me in some measure to know what they are [and in some way to recognise each one of them].

Finally, so far as my parents [from whom it appears I have sprung] are concerned, although all that I have ever been able to believe of them were true, that does not make it follow that it is they who conserve me, nor are they even the authors of my being in any sense, in so far as I am a thinking being; since what they did was merely to implant certain dispositions in that matter in which the self – i.e. the mind, which alone I at present identify with myself – is by me deemed to exist. And thus there can be no difficulty in their regard, but we must of necessity conclude from the fact alone that I exist, or that the idea of a Being supremely perfect – that is of God –

is in me, that the proof of God's existence is grounded on the highest evidence.

It only remains to me to examine into the manner in which I have acquired this idea from God; for I have not received it through the senses, and it is never presented to me unexpectedly, as is usual with the ideas of sensible things when these things present themselves, or seem to present themselves, to the external organs of my senses; nor is it likewise a fiction of my mind, for it is not in my power to take from or to add anything to it; and consequently the only alternative is that it is innate in me, just as the idea of myself is innate in me.

And one certainly ought not to find it strange that God, in creating me, placed this idea within me to be like the mark of the workman imprinted on his work; and it is likewise not essential that the mark shall be something different from the work itself. For from the sole fact that God created me it is most probable that in some way he has placed his image and similitude upon me, and that I perceive this similitude (in which the idea of God is contained) by means of the same faculty by which I perceive myself – that is to say, when I reflect on myself I not only know that I am something [imperfect], incomplete and dependent on another, which incessantly aspires after something which is better and greater than myself, but I also know that He on whom I depend possesses in Himself all the great things towards which I aspire [and the ideas of which I find within myself], and that not indefinitely or potentially alone, but really, actually and infinitely; and that thus He is God. And the whole strength of the argument which I have here made use of to prove the existence of God consists in this, that I recognise that it is not possible that my nature should be what it is, and indeed that I should have in myself the idea of a God, if God did not veritably exist – a God, I say, whose idea is in me, i.e. who possesses all those supreme perfections of which our mind may indeed have some idea but without understanding them all, who is liable to no errors or defect [and who has none of all those marks which denote imperfection]. From this it is manifest that He cannot be a deceiver, since the light of nature teaches us that fraud and deception necessarily proceed from some defect.

But before I examine this matter with more care, and pass on to the consideration of other truths which may be derived from it, it

52

seems to me right to pause for a while in order to contemplate God Himself, to ponder at leisure His marvellous attributes, to consider, and admire, and adore, the beauty of this light so resplendent, at least as far as the strength of my mind, which is in some measure dazzled by the sight, will allow me to do so. For just as faith teaches us that the supreme felicity of the other life consists only in this contemplation of the Divine Majesty, so we continue to learn by experience that a similar meditation, though incomparably less perfect, causes us to enjoy the greatest satisfaction of which we are capable in this life.

Fourth Meditation   *Of the true and the false.*

I have been well accustomed these past days to detach my mind from my senses, and I have accurately observed that there are very few things that one knows with certainty respecting corporeal objects, that there are many more which are known to us respecting the human mind, and yet more still regarding God Himself; so that I shall now without any difficulty abstract my thoughts from the consideration of [sensible or] imaginable objects, and carry them to those which, being withdrawn from all contact with matter, are purely intelligible. And certainly the idea which I possess of the human mind inasmuch as it is a thinking thing, and not extended in length, width and depth, nor participating in anything pertaining to body, is incomparably more distinct than is the idea of any corporeal thing. And when I consider that I doubt, that is to say, that I am an incomplete and dependent being, the idea of a being that is complete and independent, that is of God, presents itself to my mind with so much distinctness and clearness – and from the fact alone that this idea is found in me, or that I who possess this idea exist, I conclude so certainly that God exists, and that my existence depends entirely on Him in every moment of my life – that I do not think that the human mind is capable of knowing anything with more evidence and certitude. And it seems to me that I now have before me a road which will lead us from the contemplation of the true God (in whom all the treasures of science and wisdom are contained) to the knowledge of the other objects of the universe.

For, first of all, I recognise it to be impossible that He should ever deceive me; for in all fraud and deception some imperfection is to be found, and although it may appear that the power of deception is a mark of subtlety or power, yet the desire to deceive without doubt testifies to malice or feebleness, and accordingly cannot be found in God.

In the next place I experienced in myself a certain capacity for judging which I have doubtless received from God, like all the other things that I possess; and as He could not desire to deceive me, it is clear that He has not given me a faculty that will lead me to err if I use it aright.

And no doubt respecting this matter could remain, if it were not that the consequence would seem to follow that I can thus never be deceived; for if I hold all that I possess from God, and if He has not placed in me the capacity for error, it seems as though I could never fall into error. And it is true that when I think only of God [and direct my mind wholly to Him],[10] I discover [in myself] no cause of error, or falsity; yet directly afterwards, when recurring to myself, experience shows me that I am nevertheless subject to an infinitude of errors, as to which, when we come to investigate them more closely, I notice that not only is there a real and positive idea of God or of a Being of supreme perfection present to my mind, but also, so to speak, a certain negative idea of nothing, that is, of that which is infinitely removed from any kind of perfection; and that I am in a sense something intermediate between God and nought, i.e. placed in such a manner between the supreme Being and non-being, that there is in truth nothing in me that can lead to error in so far as a sovereign Being has formed me; but that, as I in some degree participate likewise in nought or in non-being, i.e. in so far as I am not myself the supreme Being, and as I find myself subject to an infinitude of imperfections, I ought not to be astonished if I should fall into error. Thus do I recognise that error, in so far as it is such, is not a real thing depending on God, but simply a defect; and therefore, in order to fall into it, that I have no need to possess a special faculty given me by God for this very purpose, but that I fall into error from the fact that the power given me by God for the purpose of distinguishing truth from error is not infinite.

Nevertheless this does not quite satisfy me; for error is not a pure negation [i.e. is not the simple defect or want of some perfection which ought not to be mine], but it is a lack of some knowledge

10 not in the French version.

which it seems that I ought to possess. And on considering the nature of God it does not appear to me possible that He should have given me a faculty which is not perfect of its kind, that is, which is wanting in some perfection due to it. For if it is true that the more skilful the artisan, the more perfect is the work of his hands, what can have been produced by this supreme Creator of all things that is not in all its parts perfect? And certainly there is no doubt that God could have created me so that I could never have been subject to error; it is also certain that He ever wills what is best; is it then better that I should be subject to err than that I should not?

In considering this more attentively, it occurs to me in the first place that I should not be astonished if my intelligence is not capable of comprehending why God acts as He does; and that there is thus no reason to doubt of His existence from the fact that I may perhaps find many other things besides this as to which I am able to understand neither for what reason nor how God has produced them. For, in the first place, knowing that my nature is extremely feeble and limited, and that the nature of God is on the contrary immense, incomprehensible, and infinite, I have no further difficulty in recognising that there is an infinitude of matters in His power, the causes of which transcend my knowledge; and this reason suffices to convince me that the species of cause termed final, finds no useful employment in physical [or natural] things; for it does not appear to me that I can without temerity seek to investigate the [inscrutable] ends of God.

It further occurs to me that we should not consider one single creature separately, when we inquire as to whether the works of God are perfect, but should regard all his creations together. For the same thing which might possibly seem very imperfect with some semblance of reason if regarded by itself, is found to be very perfect if regarded as part of the whole universe; and although, since I resolved to doubt all things, I as yet have only known certainly my own existence and that of God, nevertheless since I have recognised the infinite power of God, I cannot deny that He may have produced many other things, or at least that He has the power of producing them, so that I may obtain a place as a part of a great universe.

Whereupon, regarding myself more closely, and considering what are my errors (for they alone testify to there being any imperfection in me), I answer that they depend on a combination of two causes, to wit, on the faculty of knowledge that rests in me, and on the power of choice or of free will – that is to say, of the understanding and at the same time of the will. For by the understanding alone I [neither assert nor deny anything, but] apprehend[11] the ideas of things as to which I can form a judgment. But no error is properly speaking found in it, provided the word error is taken in its proper signification; and though there is possibly an infinitude of things in the world of which I have no idea in my understanding, we cannot for all that say that it is deprived of these ideas [as we might say of something which is required by its nature], but simply it does not possess these; because in truth there is no reason to prove that God should have given me a greater faculty of knowledge than He has given me; and however skilful a workman I represent Him to be, I should not for all that consider that He was bound to have placed in each of His works all the perfections which He may have been able to place in some. I likewise cannot complain that God has not given me a free choice or a will which is sufficient, ample and perfect, since as a matter of fact I am conscious of a will so extended as to be subject to no limits. And what seems to me very remarkable in this regard is that of all the qualities which I possess there is no one so perfect and so comprehensive that I do not very clearly recognise that it might be yet greater and more perfect. For, to take an example, if I consider the faculty of comprehension which I possess, I find that it is of very small extent and extremely limited, and at the same time I find the idea of another faculty much more ample and even infinite, and seeing that I can form the idea of it, I recognise from this very fact that it pertains to the nature of God. If in the same way I examine the memory, the imagination, or some other faculty, I do not find any which is not small and circumscribed, while in God it is immense [or infinite]. It is free-will alone or liberty of choice which I find to be so great in me that I can conceive no other idea to be more great; it is indeed the case that it is for the most part this will that causes me to know that in some manner I bear the image and similitude of God. For although the power of will is incomparably greater in God than in me, both by reason of the knowledge and the power which, conjoined with it, render it stronger and more efficacious, and by reason of its object, inasmuch as in God it extends to a great many

57

11 *percipio.*

things; it nevertheless does not seem to me greater if I consider it formally and precisely in itself: for the faculty of will consists alone in our having the power of choosing to do a thing or choosing not to do it (that is, to affirm or deny, to pursue or to shun it), or rather it consists alone in the fact that in order to affirm or deny, pursue or shun those things placed before us by the understanding, we act so that we are unconscious that any outside force constrains us in doing so. For in order that I should be free it is not necessary that I should be indifferent as to the choice of one or the other of two contraries; but contrariwise the more I lean to the one – whether I recognise clearly that the reasons of the good and true are to be found in it, or whether God so disposes my inward thought – the more freely do I choose and embrace it. And undoubtedly both divine grace and natural knowledge, far from diminishing my liberty, rather increase it and strengthen it. Hence this indifference which I feel, when I am not swayed to one side rather than to the other by lack of reason, is the lowest grade of liberty, and rather evinces a lack or negation in knowledge than a perfection of will: for if I always recognised clearly what was true and good, I should never have trouble in deliberating as to what judgment or choice I should make, and then I should be entirely free without ever being indifferent.

From all this I recognise that the power of will which I have received from God is not of itself the source of my errors – for it is very ample and very perfect of its kind – any more than is the power of understanding; for since I understand nothing but by the power which God has given me for understanding, there is no doubt that all that I understand, I understand as I ought, and it is not possible that I err in this. Whence then come my errors? They come from the sole fact that since the will is much wider in its range and compass than the understanding, I do not restrain it within the same bounds, but extend it also to things which I do not understand: and as the will is of itself indifferent to these, it easily falls into error and sin, and chooses the evil for the good, or the false for the true.

For example, when I lately examined whether anything existed in the world, and found that from the very fact that I considered this question it followed very clearly that I myself existed, I could not prevent myself from believing that a thing I so clearly conceived was true: not that I found myself compelled to do so by some external cause, but simply because from great clearness in my mind there followed a great inclination of my will; and I believed this with so much the greater freedom or spontaneity as I possessed the less indifference towards it. Now, on the contrary, I not only know that I exist, inasmuch as I am a thinking thing, but a certain representation of corporeal nature is also presented to my mind; and it comes to pass that I doubt whether this thinking nature which is in me, or rather by which I am what I am, differs from this corporeal nature, or whether both are not simply the same thing; and I here suppose that I do not yet know any reason to persuade me to adopt the one belief rather than the other. From this it follows that I am entirely indifferent as to which of the two I affirm or deny, or even whether I abstain from forming any judgment in the matter.

And this indifference does not only extend to matters as to which the understanding has no knowledge, but also in general to all those which are not apprehended with perfect clearness at the moment when the will is deliberating upon them: for, however probable are the conjectures which render me disposed to form a judgment respecting anything, the simple knowledge that I have that those are conjectures alone and not certain and indubitable reasons, suffices to occasion me to judge the contrary. Of this I have had great experience of late when I set aside as false all that I had formerly held to be absolutely true, for the sole reason that I remarked that it might in some measure be doubted.

But if I abstain from giving my judgment on any thing when I do not perceive it with sufficient clearness and distinctness, it is plain that I act rightly and am not deceived. But if I determine to deny or affirm, I no longer make use as I should of my free will, and if I affirm what is not true, it is evident that I deceive myself; even though I judge according to truth, this comes about only by chance, and I do not escape the blame of misusing my freedom; for the light of nature teaches us that the knowledge of the understanding should always precede the determination of the will. And it is in the misuse of the free will that the privation which constitutes the characteristic nature of error is met with. Privation, I say, is found in the act, in so far as it proceeds from me, but it is not found in the faculty which I have received from God, nor even in the act in so far as it depends on Him.

For I have certainly no cause to complain that God has not given me an intelligence which is more powerful, or a natural light which

60

is stronger than that which I have received from Him, since it is proper to the finite understanding not to comprehend a multitude of things, and it is proper to a created understanding to be finite; on the contrary, I have every reason to render thanks to God who owes me nothing and who has given me all the perfections I possess, and I should be far from charging Him with injustice, and with having deprived me of, or wrongfully withheld from me, these perfections which He has not bestowed upon me.

I have further no reason to complain that He has given me a will more ample than my understanding, for since the will consists only of one single element, and is so to speak indivisible, it appears that its nature is such that nothing can be abstracted from it [without destroying it]; and certainly the more comprehensive it is found to be, the more reason I have to render gratitude to the giver.

And, finally, I must also not complain that God concurs with me in forming the acts of the will, that is the judgment in which I go astray, because these acts are entirely true and good, inasmuch as they depend on God; and in a certain sense more perfection accrues to my nature from the fact that I can form them, than if I could not do so. As to the privation in which alone the formal reason of error or sin consists, it has no need of any concurrence from God, since it is not a thing [or an existence], and since it is not related to God as to a cause, but should be termed merely a negation [according to the significance given to these words in the schools]. For in fact it is not an imperfection in God that He has given me the liberty to give or withhold my assent from certain things as to which He has not placed a clear and distinct knowledge in my understanding; but it is without doubt an imperfection in me not to make a good use of my freedom, and to give my judgment readily on matters which I only understand obscurely. I nevertheless perceive that God could easily have created me so that I never should err, although I still remained free, and endowed with a limited knowledge, viz. by giving to my understanding a clear and distinct intelligence of all things as to which I should ever have to deliberate; or simply by His engraving deeply in my memory the resolution never to form a judgment on anything without having a clear and distinct understanding of it, so that I could never forget it. And it is easy for me to understand that, in so far as I consider myself alone, and as if there were only myself in the world, I should have been much more perfect than I am, if God had created me so that I could never err. Nevertheless I cannot deny that in some sense it is a greater perfection in the whole universe that certain parts should not be exempt from error as others are than that all parts should be exactly similar. And I have no right to complain if God, having placed me in the world, has not called upon me to play a part that excels all others in distinction and perfection.

And further I have reason to be glad on the ground that if He has not given me the power of never going astray by the first means pointed out above, which depends on a clear and evident knowledge of all the things regarding which I can deliberate, He has at least left within my power the other means, which is firmly to adhere to the resolution never to give judgment on matters whose truth is not clearly known to me; for although I notice a certain weakness in my nature in that I cannot continually concentrate my mind on one single thought, I can yet, by attentive and frequently repeated meditation, impress it so forcibly on my memory that I shall never fail to recollect it whenever I have need of it, and thus acquire the habit of never going astray.

62

And inasmuch as it is in this that the greatest and principal perfection of man consists, it seems to me that I have not gained little by this day's Meditation, since I have discovered the source of falsity and error. And certainly there can be no other source than that which I have explained; for as often as I so restrain my will within the limits of my knowledge that it forms no judgment except on matters which are clearly and distinctly represented to it by the understanding, I can never be deceived; for every clear and distinct conception[12] is without doubt something, and hence cannot derive its origin from what is nought, but must of necessity have God as its author – God, I say, who being supremely perfect, cannot be the cause of any error; and consequently we must conclude that such a conception [or such a judgment] is true. Nor have I only learned today what I should avoid in order that I may not err, but also how I should act in order to arrive at a knowledge of the truth; for without doubt I shall arrive at this end if I devote my attention sufficiently to those things which I perfectly understand; and if I separate from these that which I only understand confusedly and with obscurity. To these I shall henceforth diligently give heed.

12 *perceptio.*

63   **Fifth Meditation** *Of the essence of material things, and, again, of God, that He exists.*

Many other matters respecting the attributes of God and my own nature or mind remain for consideration; but I shall possibly on another occasion resume the investigation of these. Now (after first noting what must be done or avoided, in order to arrive at a knowledge of the truth) my principal task is to endeavour to emerge from the state of doubt into which I have these last days fallen, and to see whether nothing certain can be known regarding material things.

But before examining whether any such objects as I conceive exist outside of me, I must consider the ideas of them in so far as they are in my thought, and see which of them are distinct and which confused.

In the first place, I am able distinctly to imagine that quantity which philosophers commonly call continuous, or the extension in length, breadth, or depth, that is in this quantity, or rather in the object to which it is attributed. Further, I can number in it many different parts, and attribute to each of its parts many sorts of size, figure, situation and local movement, and, finally, I can assign to each of these movements all degrees of duration.

And not only do I know these things with distinctness when I consider them in general, but, likewise [however little I apply my attention to the matter], I discover an infinitude of particulars respecting numbers, figures, movements, and other such things,

64   whose truth is so manifest, and so well accords with my nature, that when I begin to discover them, it seems to me that I learn nothing new, or recollect what I formerly knew – that is to say, that I for the first time perceive things which were already present to my mind, although I had not as yet applied my mind to them.

And what I here find to be most important is that I discover in myself an infinitude of ideas of certain things which cannot be esteemed as pure negations, although they may possibly have no existence outside of my thought, and which are not framed by me, although it is within my power either to think or not to think them, but which possess natures which are true and immutable. For example, when I imagine a triangle, although there may nowhere in the world be such a figure outside my thought, or ever have been, there is nevertheless in this figure a certain determinate nature, form, or essence, which is immutable and eternal, which I have not invented, and which in no wise depends on my mind, as appears from the fact that diverse properties of that triangle can be demonstrated, viz. that its three angles are equal to two right angles, that the greatest side is subtended by the greatest angle, and the like, which now, whether I wish it or do not wish it, I recognise very clearly as pertaining to it, although I never thought of the matter at all when I imagined a triangle for the first time, and which therefore cannot be said to have been invented by me.

Nor does the objection hold good that possibly this idea of a triangle has reached my mind through the medium of my senses, since I have sometimes seen bodies triangular in shape; because I can form in my mind an infinitude of other figures regarding which we cannot have the least conception of their ever having been objects of sense, and I can nevertheless demonstrate various properties pertaining to their nature as well as to that of the triangle, and these must certainly all be true since I conceive them clearly. Hence they are something, and not pure negation; for it is perfectly clear that all that is true is something, and I have already fully demonstrated that all that I know clearly is true. And even although I had not demonstrated this, the nature of my mind is such that I could not prevent myself from holding them to be true so long as I conceive them clearly; and I recollect that even when I was still strongly attached to the objects of sense, I counted as the most certain those truths which I conceived clearly as regards figures, numbers, and the other matters which pertain to arithmetic and geometry, and, in general, to pure and abstract mathematics.

But now, if just because I can draw the idea of something from my thought, it follows that all which I know clearly and distinctly as pertaining to this object does really belong to it, may I not derive from this an argument demonstrating the existence of God? It is certain that I no less find the idea of God, that is to say, the idea of a supremely perfect Being, in me, than that of any figure or number whatever it is; and I do not know any less clearly and distinctly that an [actual and] eternal existence pertains to this nature than I know that all that which I am able to demonstrate of some figure or number truly pertains to the nature of this figure or number, and therefore, although all that I concluded in the preceding Meditations were found to be false, the existence of God would pass with me as at least as certain as I have ever held the truths of

65

66

mathematics (which concern only numbers and figures) to be.

This indeed is not at first manifest, since it would seem to present some appearance of being a sophism. For being accustomed in all other things to make a distinction between existence and essence, I easily persuade myself that the existence can be separated from the essence of God, and that we can thus conceive God as not actually existing. But, nevertheless, when I think of it with more attention, I clearly see that existence can no more be separated from the essence of God than can its having its three angles equal to two right angles be separated from the essence of a [rectilinear] triangle, or the idea of a mountain from the idea of a valley; and so there is not any less repugnance to our conceiving a God (that is, a Being supremely perfect) to whom existence is lacking (that is to say, to whom a certain perfection is lacking), than to conceive of a mountain which has no valley.

But although I cannot really conceive of a God without existence any more than a mountain without a valley, still from the fact that I conceive of a mountain with a valley, it does not follow that there is such a mountain in the world; similarly although I conceive of God as possessing existence, it would seem that it does not follow that there is a God which exists; for my thought does not impose any necessity upon things, and just as I may imagine a winged horse, although no horse with wings exists, so I could perhaps attribute existence to God, although no God existed.

But a sophism is concealed in this objection; for from the fact that I cannot conceive a mountain without a valley, it does not follow that there is any mountain or any valley in existence, but only that the mountain and the valley, whether they exist or do not exist, cannot in any way be separated one from the other. While from the fact that I cannot conceive God without existence, it follows that existence is inseparable from Him, and hence that He really exists; not that my thought can bring this to pass, or impose any necessity on things, but, on the contrary, because the necessity which lies in the thing itself, i.e. the necessity of the existence of God determines me to think in this way. For it is not within my power to think of God without existence (that is of a supremely perfect Being devoid of a supreme perfection) though it is in my power to imagine a horse either with wings or without wings.

And we must not here object that it is in truth necessary for me to assert that God exists after having presupposed that He possesses every sort of perfection, since existence is one of these, but that as a matter of fact my original supposition was not necessary, just as it is not necessary to consider that all quadrilateral figures can be inscribed in the circle; for supposing I thought this, I should be constrained to admit that the rhombus might be inscribed in the circle since it is a quadrilateral figure, which, however, is manifestly false. [We must not, I say, make any such allegations because] although it is not necessary that I should at any time entertain the notion of God, nevertheless whenever it happens that I think of a first and a sovereign Being, and, so to speak, derive the idea of Him from the storehouse of my mind, it is necessary that I should attribute to Him every sort of perfection, although I do not get so far as to enumerate them all, or to apply my mind to each one in particular. And this necessity suffices to make me conclude (after having recognised that existence is a perfection) that this first and sovereign Being really exists; just as though it is not necessary for me ever to imagine any triangle, yet, whenever I wish to consider a rectilinear figure composed only of three angles, it is absolutely essential that I should attribute to it all those properties which serve to bring about the conclusion that its three angles are not greater than two right angles, even although I may not then be considering this point in particular. But when I consider which figures are capable of being inscribed in the circle, it is in no wise necessary that I should think that all quadrilateral figures are of this number; on the contrary, I cannot even pretend that this is the case, so long as I do not desire to accept anything which I cannot conceive clearly and distinctly. And in consequence there is a great difference between the false suppositions such as this, and the true ideas born within me, the first and principal of which is that of God. For really I discern in many ways that this idea is not something factitious, and depending solely on my thought, but that it is the image of a true and immutable nature; first of all, because I cannot conceive anything but God himself to whose essence existence [necessarily] pertains; in the second place because it is not possible for me to conceive two or more Gods in this same position; and, granted that there is one such God who now exists, I see clearly that it is necessary that He should have existed from all eternity, and that He must exist eternally; and finally, because I know an infinitude of

68

other properties in God, none of which I can either diminish or change.

For the rest, whatever proof or argument I avail myself of, we must always return to the point that it is only those things which we conceive clearly and distinctly that have the power of persuading me entirely. And although amongst the matters which I conceive of in this way, some indeed are manifestly obvious to all, while others only manifest themselves to those who consider them closely and examine them attentively; still, after they have once been discovered, the latter are not esteemed as any less certain than the former. For example, in the case of every right-angled triangle, although it does not so manifestly appear that the square of the base is equal to the squares of the two other sides as that this base is opposite to the greatest angle; still, when this has once been apprehended, we are just as certain of its truth as of the truth of the other. And as regards God, if my mind were not preoccupied with prejudices, and if my thought did not find itself on all hands diverted by the continual pressure of sensible things, there would be nothing which I could know more immediately and more easily than Him. For is there anything more manifest than that there is a God, that is to say, a Supreme Being, to whose essence alone existence pertains?[13]

And although for a firm grasp of this truth I have need of a strenuous application of mind, at present I not only feel myself to be as assured of it as of all that I hold as most certain, but I also remark that the certainty of all other things depends on it so absolutely, that without this knowledge it is impossible ever to know anything perfectly.

For although I am of such a nature that as long as[14] I understand anything very clearly and distinctly, I am naturally impelled to believe it to be true, yet because I am also of such a nature that I cannot have my mind constantly fixed on the same object in order to perceive it clearly, and as I often recollect having formed a past judgment without at the same time properly recollecting the reasons that led me to make it, it may happen meanwhile that other reasons present themselves to me, which would easily cause me to change

13 'in the idea of whom alone necessary or eternal existence is comprised', French version.
14 'from the moment that', French version.

my opinion, if I were ignorant of the facts of the existence of God, and thus I should have no true and certain knowledge, but only vague and vacillating opinions. Thus, for example, when I consider the nature of a [rectilinear] triangle, I who have some little knowledge of the principles of geometry recognise quite clearly that the three angles are equal to two right angles, and it is not possible for me not to believe this so long as I apply my mind to its demonstration; but so soon as I abstain from attending to the proof, although I still recollect having clearly comprehended it, it may easily occur that I come to doubt its truth, if I am ignorant of there being a God. For I can persuade myself of having been so constituted by nature that I can easily deceive myself even in those matters which I believe myself to apprehend with the greatest evidence and certainty, especially when I recollect that I have frequently judged matters to be true and certain which other reasons have afterwards impelled me to judge to be altogether false.

But after I have recognised that there is a God – because at the same time I have also recognised that all things depend upon Him, and that He is not a deceiver, and from that have inferred that what I perceive clearly and distinctly cannot fail to be true – although I no longer pay attention to the reasons for which I have judged this to be true, provided that I recollect having clearly and distinctly perceived it no contrary reason can be brought forward which could ever cause me to doubt of its truth; and thus I have a true and certain knowledge of it. And this same knowledge extends likewise to all other things which I recollect having formerly demonstrated, such as the truths of geometry and the like; for what can be alleged against them to cause me to place them in doubt? Will it be said that my nature is such as to cause me to be frequently deceived? But I already know that I cannot be deceived in the judgment whose grounds I know clearly. Will it be said that I formerly held many things to be true and certain which I have afterwards recognised to be false? But I had not had any clear and distinct knowledge of these things, and not as yet knowing the rule whereby I assure myself of the truth, I had been impelled to give my assent from reasons which I have since recognised to be less strong than I had at the time imagined them to be. What further objection can then be raised? That possibly I am dreaming (an objection I myself made a little while ago), or that all the thoughts which I now have are no more true than the fantasies

70

71

of my dreams? But even though I slept the case would be the same, for all that is clearly present to my mind is absolutely true.

And so I very clearly recognise that the certainty and truth of all knowledge depends alone on the knowledge of the true God, in so much that, before I knew Him, I could not have a perfect knowledge of any other thing. And now that I know Him I have the means of acquiring a perfect knowledge of an infinitude of things, not only of those which relate to God Himself and other intellectual matters, but also of those which pertain to corporeal nature in so far as it is the object of pure mathematics [which have no concern with whether it exists or not].

Sixth Meditation *Of the existence of material things, and of the real distinction between the soul and body of man.*

Nothing further now remains but to inquire whether material things exist. And certainly I at least know that these may exist in so far as they are considered as the objects of pure mathematics, since in this aspect I perceive them clearly and distinctly. For there is no doubt that God possesses the power to produce everything that I am capable of perceiving with distinctness, and I have never deemed that anything was impossible for Him, unless I found a contradiction in attempting to conceive it clearly. Further, the faculty of imagination which I possess, and of which, experience tells me, I make use when I apply myself to the consideration of material things, is capable of persuading me of their existence; for when I attentively consider what imagination is, I find that it is nothing but a certain application of the faculty of knowledge to the body which is immediately present to it, and which therefore exists.

And to render this quite clear, I remark in the first place the difference that exists between the imagination and pure intellection [or conception].[15] For example, when I imagine a triangle, I do not conceive it only as a figure comprehended by three lines, but I also apprehend[16] these three lines as present by the power and inward vision of my mind,[17] and this is what I call imagining. But if I desire to think of a chiliagon, I certainly conceive truly that it is a figure composed of a thousand sides, just as easily as I conceive of a triangle

15 *conception*, French version; *intellectionem*, Latin version.
16 *intueor.*   17 *acie mentis.*

that it is a figure of three sides only; but I cannot in any way imagine the thousand sides of a chiliagon [as I do the three sides of a triangle], nor do I, so to speak, regard them as present [with the eyes of my mind]. And although in accordance with the habit I have formed of always employing the aid of my imagination when I think of corporeal things, it may happen that in imagining a chiliagon I confusedly represent to myself some figure, yet it is very evident that this figure is not a chiliagon, since it in no way differs from that which I represent to myself when I think of a myriagon or any other many-sided figure; nor does it serve my purpose in discovering the properties which go to form the distinction between a chiliagon and other polygons. But if the question turns upon a pentagon, it is quite true that I can conceive its figure as well as that of a chiliagon without the help of my imagination; but I can also imagine it by applying the attention of my mind to each of its five sides, and at the same time to the space which they enclose. And thus I clearly recognise that I have need of a particular effort of mind in order to effect the act of imagination, such as I do not require in order to understand, and this particular effort of mind clearly manifests the difference which exists between imagination and pure intellection.[18]

I remark besides that this power of imagination which is in one, inasmuch as it differs from the power of understanding, is in no wise a necessary element in my nature, or in [my essence, that is to say, in] the essence of my mind; for although I did not possess it I should doubtless ever remain the same as I now am, from which it appears that we might conclude that it depends on something which differs from me. And I easily conceive that if some body exists with which my mind is conjoined and united in such a way that it can apply itself to consider it when it pleases, it may be that by this means it can imagine corporeal objects; so that this mode of thinking differs from pure intellection only inasmuch as mind in its intellectual activity in some manner turns on itself, and considers some of the ideas which it possesses in itself; while in imagining it turns towards the body, and there beholds in it something conformable to the idea which it has either conceived of itself or perceived by the senses. I easily understand, I say, that the imagination could be thus constituted if it is true that body exists; and because I can discover

18 *intellectionem*.

no other convenient mode of explaining it, I conjecture with probability that body does exist; but this is only with probability, and although I examine all things with care, I nevertheless do not find that from this distinct idea of corporeal nature, which I have in my imagination, I can derive any argument from which there will necessarily be deduced the existence of body.

74   But I am in the habit of imagining many other things besides this corporeal nature which is the object of pure mathematics, to wit, the colours, sounds, scents, pain, and other such things, although less distinctly. And inasmuch as I perceive these things much better through the senses, by the meaning of which, and by the memory, they seem to have reached my imagination, I believe that, in order to examine them more conveniently, it is right that I should at the same time investigate the nature of sense perception, and that I should see if from the ideas which I apprehend by this mode of thought, which I call feeling, I cannot derive some certain proof of the existence of corporeal objects.

And first of all I shall recall to my memory those matters which I hitherto held to be true, as having perceived them through the senses, and the foundations on which my belief has rested; in the next place I shall examine the reasons which have since obliged me to place them in doubt; in the last place I shall consider which of them I must now believe.

First of all, then, I perceived that I had a head, hands, feet, and all other members of which this body – which I considered as a part, or possibly even as the whole, of myself – is composed. Further I was sensible that this body was placed amidst many others, from which it was capable of being affected in many different ways, beneficial and hurtful, and I remarked that a certain feeling of pleasure accompanied those that were beneficial, and pain those which were harmful. And in addition to this pleasure and pain, I also experienced hunger, thirst, and other similar appetites, as also certain corporeal inclinations towards joy, sadness, anger, and other similar passions. And outside

75   myself, in addition to extension, figure, and motions of bodies, I remarked in them hardness, heat, and all other tactile qualities, and, further, light and colour, and scents and sounds, the variety of which gave me the means of distinguishing the sky, the earth, the sea, and generally all the other bodies, one from the other. And certainly, considering the ideas of all these qualities which presented themselves

to my mind, and which alone I perceived properly or immediately, it was not without reason that I believed myself to perceive objects quite different from my thought, to wit, bodies from which those ideas proceeded; for I found by experience that these ideas presented themselves to me without my consent being requisite, so that I could not perceive any object, however desirous I might be, unless it were present to the organs of sense; and it was not in my power not to perceive it, when it was present. And because the ideas which I received through the senses were much more lively, more clear, and even, in their own way, more distinct than any of those which I could of myself frame in meditation, or than those I found impressed on my memory, it appeared as though they could not have proceeded from my mind, so that they must necessarily have been produced in me by some other things. And having no knowledge of those objects excepting the knowledge which the ideas themselves gave me, nothing was more likely to occur to my mind than that the objects were similar to the ideas which were caused. And because I likewise remembered that I had formerly made use of my senses rather than my reason, and recognised that the ideas which I formed of myself were not so distinct as those which I perceived through the senses, and that they were most frequently even composed of portions of these last, I persuaded myself easily that I had no idea in my mind which had not formerly come to me through the senses. Nor was it without some reason that I believed that this body (which by a certain special right I call my own) belonged to me more properly and more strictly than any other; for in fact I could never be separated from it as from other bodies; I experienced in it and on account of it all my appetites and affections, and finally I was touched by the feeling of pain and the titillation of pleasure in its parts, and not in the parts of other bodies which were separated from it. But when I inquired, why, from some, I know not what, painful sensation, there follows sadness of mind, and from the pleasurable sensation there arises joy, or why this mysterious pinching of the stomach which I call hunger causes me to desire to eat, and dryness of throat causes a desire to drink, and so on, I could give no reason excepting that nature taught me so; for there is certainly no affinity (that I at least can understand) between the craving of the stomach and the desire to eat, any more than between the perception of whatever causes pain and the thought of sadness which arises from

76

this perception. And in the same way it appeared to me that I had learned from nature all the other judgments which I formed regarding the objects of my senses, since I remarked that these judgments were formed in me before I had the leisure to weigh and consider any reasons which might oblige me to make them.

But afterwards many experiences little by little destroyed all the faith which I had rested in my senses; for I from time to time observed that those towers which from afar appeared to me to be round, more closely observed seemed square, and that colossal statues raised on the summit of these towers, appeared as quite tiny statues when viewed from the bottom; and so in an infinitude of other cases I found error in judgments founded on the external senses. And not only in those founded on the external senses, but even in those founded on the internal as well; for is there anything more intimate or more internal than pain? And yet I have learned from some persons whose arms or legs have been cut off, that they sometimes seemed to feel pain in the part which had been amputated, which made me think that I could not be quite certain that it was a certain member which pained me, even although I felt pain in it. And to those grounds of doubt I have lately added two others, which are very general; the first is that I never have believed myself to feel anything in waking moments which I cannot also sometimes believe myself to feel when I sleep, and as I do not think that these things which I seem to feel in sleep, proceed from objects outside of me, I do not see any reason why I should have this belief regarding objects which I seem to perceive while awake. The other was that being still ignorant, or rather supposing myself to be ignorant, of the author of my being, I saw nothing to prevent me from having been so constituted by nature that I might be deceived even in matters which seemed to me to be most certain. And as to the grounds on which I was formerly persuaded of the truth of sensible objects, I had not much trouble in replying to them. For since nature seemed to cause me to lean towards many things from which reason repelled me, I did not believe that I should trust much to the teachings of nature. And although the ideas which I receive by the senses do not depend on my will, I did not think that one should for that reason conclude that they proceeded from things different from myself, since possibly some faculty might be discovered in me – though hitherto unknown to me – which produced them.

But now that I begin to know myself better, and to discover more clearly the author of my being, I do not in truth think that I should rashly admit all the matters which the senses seem to teach us, but, on the other hand, I do not think that I should doubt them all universally.

And first of all, because I know that all things which I apprehend clearly and distinctly can be created by God as I apprehend them, it suffices that I am able to apprehend one thing apart from another clearly and distinctly in order to be certain that the one is different from the other, since they may be made to exist in separation at least by the omnipotence of God; and it does not signify by what power this separation is made in order to compel me to judge them to be different: and, therefore, just because I know certainly that I exist, and that meanwhile I do not remark that any other thing necessarily pertains to my nature or essence, excepting that I am a thinking thing, I rightly conclude that my essence consists solely in the fact that I am a thinking thing [or a substance whose whole essence or nature is to think]. And although possibly (or rather certainly, as I shall say in a moment) I possess a body with which I am very intimately conjoined, yet because, on the one side, I have a clear and distinct idea of myself inasmuch as I am only a thinking and unextended thing, and as, on the other, I possess a distinct idea of body, inasmuch as it is only an extended and unthinking thing, it is certain that this I [that is to say, my soul by which I am what I am], is entirely and absolutely distinct from my body, and can exist without it.

I further find in myself faculties employing modes of thinking peculiar to themselves, to wit, the faculties of imagination and feeling, without which I can easily conceive myself clearly and distinctly as a complete being; while, on the other hand, they cannot be so conceived apart from me, that is without an intelligent substance in which they reside, for [in the notion we have of these faculties, or, to use the language of the schools] in their formal concept, some kind of intellection is comprised, from which I infer that they are distinct from me as its modes are from a thing. I observe also in me some other faculties such as that of change of position, the assumption of different figures and such like, which cannot be conceived, any more than can the preceding, apart from some substance to which they are attached, and consequently cannot exist without it; but it is very clear that these faculties, if it be true that

78

79

they exist, must be attached to some corporeal or extended substance, and not to an intelligent substance, since in the clear and distinct conception of these there is some sort of extension found to be present, but no intellection at all. There is certainly further in me a certain passive faculty of perception, that is, of receiving and recognising the ideas of sensible things, but this would be useless to me [and I could in no way avail myself of it], if there were not either in me or in some other thing another active faculty capable of forming and producing these ideas. But this active faculty cannot exist in me [inasmuch as I am a thing that thinks] seeing that it does not presuppose thought, and also that those ideas are often produced in me without my contributing in any way to the same, and often even against my will; it is thus necessarily the case that the faculty resides in some substance different from me in which all the reality which is objectively in the ideas that are produced by this faculty is formally or eminently contained, as I remarked before. And this substance is either a body, that is, a corporeal nature in which there is contained formally [and really] all that which is objectively [and by representation] in those ideas, or it is God Himself, or some other creature more noble than body in which that same is contained eminently. But, since God is no deceiver, it is very manifest that He does not communicate to me these ideas immediately and by Himself, nor yet by the intervention of some creature in which their reality is not formally, but only eminently, contained. For since He has given me no faculty to recognise that this is the case, but, on the other hand, a very great inclination to believe [that they are sent to me or] that they are conveyed to me by corporeal objects, I do not see how He could be defended from the accusation of deceit if these ideas were produced by causes other than corporeal objects. Hence we must allow that corporeal things exist. However, they are perhaps not exactly what we perceive by the senses, since this comprehension by the senses is in many instances very obscure and confused; but we must at least admit that all things which I conceive in them clearly and distinctly, that is to say, all things which, speaking generally, are comprehended in the object of pure mathematics, are truly to be recognised as external objects.

As to other things, however, which are either particular only, as, for example, that the sun is of such and such a figure, etc., or which are less clearly and distinctly conceived, such as light, sound, pain

80

and the like, it is certain that although they are very dubious and uncertain, yet on the sole ground that God is not a deceiver, and that consequently He has not permitted any falsity to exist in my opinion which He has not likewise given me the faculty of correcting, I may assuredly hope to conclude that I have within me the means of arriving at the truth even here. And first of all there is no doubt that in all things which nature teaches me there is some truth contained; for by nature, considered in general, I now understand no other thing than either God Himself or else the order and disposition which God has established in created things; and by my nature in particular I understand no other thing than the complexus of all the things which God has given me.

But there is nothing which this nature teaches me more expressly [nor more sensibly] than that I have a body which is adversely affected when I feel pain, which has need of food or drink when I experience the feelings of hunger and thirst, and so on; nor can I doubt there being some truth in all this.

Nature also teaches me by these sensations of pain, hunger, thirst, etc., that I am not only lodged in my body as a pilot in a vessel, but that I am very closely united to it, and so to speak so intermingled with it that I seem to compose with it one whole. For if that were not the case, when my body is hurt, I, who am merely a thinking thing, should not feel pain, for I should perceive this wound by the understanding only, just as the sailor perceives by sight when something is damaged in his vessel; and when my body has need of drink or food, I should clearly understand the fact without being warned of it by confused feelings of hunger and thirst. For all these sensations of hunger, thirst, pain, etc. are in truth none other than certain confused modes of thought which are produced by the union and apparent intermingling of mind and body.

Moreover, nature teaches me that many other bodies exist around mine, of which some are to be avoided, and others sought after. And certainly from the fact that I am sensible of different sorts of colours, sounds, scents, tastes, heat, hardness, etc., I very easily conclude that there are in the bodies from which all these diverse sense-perceptions proceed certain variations which answer to them, although possibly these are not really at all similar to them. And also from the fact that amongst these different sense-perceptions some are very agreeable to me and others disagreeable, it is quite certain that my body (or rather myself in my entirety, inasmuch as I am formed of body and sole) may receive different impressions agreeable and disagreeable from the other bodies which surround it.

82   But there are many other things which nature seems to have taught me, but which at the same time I have never really received from her, but which have been brought about in my mind by a certain habit which I have of forming inconsiderate judgments on things; and thus it may easily happen that these judgments contain some error. Take, for example, the opinion which I hold that all space in which there is nothing that affects [or makes an impression on] my senses is void; that in a body which is warm there is something entirely similar to the idea of heat which is in me; that in a white or green body there is the same whiteness or greenness that I perceive; that in a bitter or sweet body there is the same taste, and so on in other instances; that the stars, the towers, and all other distant bodies are of the same figure and size as they appear from far off to our eyes, etc. But in order that in this there should be nothing which I do not conceive distinctly, I should define exactly what I really understand when I say that I am taught somewhat by nature. For here I take nature in a more limited signification than when I term it the sum of all the things given me by God, since in this sum many things are comprehended which only pertain to mind (and to these I do not refer in speaking of nature) such as the notion which I have of the fact that what has once been done cannot ever be undone and an infinitude of such things which I know by the light of nature [without the help of the body]; and seeing that it comprehends many other matters besides which only pertain to body, and are no longer here contained under the name of nature, such as the quality of weight which it possesses and the like, with which I also do not deal; for in talking of nature I only treat of those things given by God to me as a being composed of mind and body. But the nature here described truly teaches me to flee from things which cause the sensation of pain, and seek after the things which communicate to me the sentiment of pleasure and so forth; but I do not see that beyond this it teaches me that from those diverse sense-perceptions we should ever form any conclusion regarding things outside of us, without having [carefully and maturely] mentally examined them beforehand. For it seems to me that it is mind alone, and not mind

83   and body in conjunction, that is requisite to a knowledge of the

truth in regard to such things. Thus, although a star makes no larger an impression on my eye than the flame of a little candle there is yet in me no real or positive propensity impelling me to believe that it is not greater than that flame; but I have judged it to be so from my earliest years, without any rational foundation. And although in approaching fire I feel heat, and in approaching it a little too near I even feel pain, there is at the same time no reason in this which could persuade me that there is in the fire something resembling this heat any more than there is in it something resembling the pain; all that I have any reason to believe from this is, that there is something in it, whatever it may be, which excites in me these sensations of heat or of pain. So also, although there are spaces in which I find nothing which excites my senses, I must not from that conclude that these spaces contain no body; for I see in this, as in other similar things, that I have been in the habit of perverting the order of nature, because these perceptions of sense having been placed within me by nature merely for the purpose of signifying to my mind what things are beneficial or hurtful to the composite whole of which it forms a part, and being up to that point sufficiently clear and distinct, I yet avail myself of them as though they were absolute rules by which I might immediately determine the essence of the bodies which are outside me, as to which, in fact, they can teach me nothing but what is most obscure and confused.

But I have already sufficiently considered how, notwithstanding the supreme goodness of God, falsity enters into the judgments I make. Only here a new difficulty is presented – one respecting those things the pursuit or avoidance of which is taught me by nature, and also respecting the internal sensations which I possess, and in which I seem to have sometimes detected error [and thus to be directly deceived by my own nature]. To take an example, the agreeable taste of some food in which poison has been intermingled may induce me to partake of the poison, and thus deceive me. It is true, at the same time, that in this case nature may be excused, for it only induces me to desire food in which I find a pleasant taste, and not to desire the poison which is unknown to it; and thus I can infer nothing from this fact, except that my nature is not omniscient, at which there is certainly no reason to be astonished, since man, being finite in nature, can only have knowledge the perfectness of which is limited.

But we not unfrequently deceive ourselves even in those things to which we are directly impelled by nature, as happens with those who when they are sick desire to drink or eat things hurtful to them. It will perhaps be said here that the cause of their deceptiveness is that their nature is corrupt, but that does not remove the difficulty, because a sick man is none the less truly God's creature than he who is in health; and it is therefore as repugnant to God's goodness for the one to have a deceitful nature as it is for the other. And as a clock composed of wheels and counter-weights no less exactly observes the laws of nature when it is badly made, and does not show the time properly, than when it entirely satisfies the wishes of its maker, and as, if I consider the body of a man as being a sort of machine so built up and composed of nerves, muscles, veins, blood and skin, that though there were no mind in it at all, it would not cease to have the same motions as at present, exception being made of those movements which are due to the direction of the will, and in consequence depend upon the mind [as opposed to those which operate by the disposition of its organs], I easily recognise that it would be as natural to this body, supposing it to be, for example, dropsical, to suffer the parchedness of the throat which usually signifies to the mind the feeling of thirst, and to be disposed by this parched feeling to move the nerves and other parts in the way requisite for drinking, and thus to augment its malady and do harm to itself, as it is natural to it, when it has no indisposition, to be impelled to drink for its good by a similar cause. And although, considering the use to which the clock has been destined by its maker, I may say that it deflects from the order of its nature when it does not indicate the hours correctly; and as, in the same way, considering the machine of the human body as having been formed by God in order to have in itself all the movements usually manifested there, I have reason for thinking that it does not follow the order of nature when, if the throat is dry, drinking does harm to the conservation of health, nevertheless I recognise at the same time that this last mode of explaining nature is very different from the other. For this is but a purely verbal characterisation depending entirely on my thought, which compares a sick man and a badly constructed clock with the idea which I have of a healthy man and a well made clock, and it is hence extrinsic to the things to which it is applied; but according to the other interpretation of the term nature I understand something which is truly found in things and which is therefore not without some truth.

85

But certainly although in regard to the dropsical body it is only so to speak to apply an extrinsic term when we say that its nature is corrupted, inasmuch as apart from the need to drink, the throat is parched; yet in regard to the composite whole, that is to say, to the mind or soul united to this body, it is not a purely verbal predicate, but a real error of nature, for it to have thirst when drinking would be hurtful to it. And thus it still remains to inquire how the goodness of God does not prevent the nature of man so regarded from being fallacious.

In order to begin this examination, then, I here say, in the first place, that there is a great difference between mind and body, inasmuch as body is by nature always divisible and the mind is entirely indivisible. For, as a matter of fact, when I consider the mind, that is to say, myself inasmuch as I am only a thinking thing, I cannot distinguish in myself any parts, but apprehend myself to be clearly one and entire; and although the whole mind seems to be united to the whole body, yet if a foot, or an arm, or some other part, is separated from my body, I am aware that nothing has been taken away from my mind. And the faculties of willing, feeling, conceiving, etc. cannot be properly speaking said to be its parts, for it is one and the same mind which employs itself in willing and in feeling and understanding. But it is quite otherwise with corporeal or extended objects, for there is not one of these imaginable by me which my mind cannot easily divide into parts, and which consequently I do not recognise as being divisible; this would be sufficient to teach me that the mind or soul of man is entirely different from the body, if I had not already learned it from other sources.

I further notice that the mind does not receive the impressions from all parts of the body immediately, but only from the brain, or perhaps even from one of its smallest parts, to wit, from that in which the common sense[19] is said to reside, which, whenever it is disposed in the same particular way, conveys the same thing to the mind, although meanwhile the other portions of the body may be differently disposed, as is testified by innumerable experiments which it is unnecessary here to recount.

I notice, also, that the nature of body is such that none of its parts can be moved by another part a little way off which cannot also be

86

19 *sensus communis*.

moved in the same way by each one of the parts which are between the two, although this more remote part does not act at all. As, for example, in the cord ABCD [which is in tension] if we pull the last part D, the first part A will not be moved in any way differently from what would be the case if one of the intervening parts B or C were pulled, and the last part D were to remain unmoved. And in the same way, when I feel pain in my foot, my knowledge of physics teaches me that this sensation is communicated by means of nerves dispersed through the foot, which, being extended like cords from there to the brain, when they are contracted in the foot, at the same time contract the inmost portions of the brain which is their extremity and place of origin, and then excite a certain movement which nature has established in order to cause the mind to be affected by a sensation of pain represented as existing in the foot. But because these nerves must pass through the tibia, the thigh, the loins, the back and the neck, in order to reach from the leg to the brain, it may happen that although their extremities which are in the foot are not affected, but only certain ones of their intervening parts [which pass by the loins or the neck], this action will excite the same movement in the brain that might have been excited there by a hurt received in the foot, in consequence of which the mind will necessarily feel in the foot the same pain as if it had received a hurt. And the same holds good of all the other perceptions of our senses.

I notice finally that since each of the movements which are in the portion of the brain by which the mind is immediately affected brings about one particular sensation only, we cannot under the circumstances imagine anything more likely than that this movement, amongst all the sensations which it is capable of impressing on it, causes mind to be affected by that one which is best fitted and most generally useful for the conservation of the human body when it is in health. But experience makes us aware that all the feelings with which nature inspires us are such as I have just spoken of; and there is therefore nothing in them which does not give testimony to the power and goodness of the God [who has produced them[20]]. Thus, for example, when the nerves which are in the feet are violently or more than usually moved, their movement, passing through the medulla of the spine[21] to the inmost parts of the brain,

20 Latin version only.   21 *spini dorsae medullam.*

gives a sign to the mind which makes it feel somewhat, to wit, pain, as though in the foot, by which the mind is excited to do its utmost to remove the cause of the evil as dangerous and hurtful to the foot. It is true that God could have constituted the nature of man in such a way that this same movement in the brain would have conveyed something quite different to the mind; for example, it might have produced consciousness of itself either in so far as it is in the brain, or as it is in the foot, or as it is in some other place between the foot and the brain, or it might finally have produced consciousness of anything else whatsoever; but none of all this would have contributed so well to the conservation of the body. Similarly, when we desire to drink, a certain dryness of the throat is produced which moves its nerves, and by their means the internal portions of the brain; and this movement causes in the mind the sensation of thirst, because in this case there is nothing more useful to us than to become aware that we have need to drink for the conservation of our health; and the same holds good in other instances.

From this it is quite clear that, notwithstanding the supreme goodness of God, the nature of man, inasmuch as it is composed of mind and body, cannot be otherwise than sometimes a source of deception. For if there is any cause which excites, not in the foot but in some part of the nerves which are extended between the foot and the brain, or even in the brain itself, the same movement which usually is produced when the foot is detrimentally affected, pain will be experienced as though it were in the foot, and the sense will thus naturally be deceived; for since the same movement in the brain is capable of causing but one sensation in the mind, and this sensation is much more frequently excited by a cause which hurts the foot than by another existing in some other quarter, it is reasonable that it should convey to the mind pain in the foot rather than in any other part of the body. And although the parchedness of the throat does not always proceed, as it usually does, from the fact that drinking is necessary for the health of the body, but sometimes comes from quite a different cause, as is the case with dropsical patients, it is yet much better that it should mislead on this occasion than if, on the other hand, it were always to deceive us when the body is in good health; and so on in similar cases.

89

And certainly this consideration is of great service to me, not only in enabling me to recognise all the errors to which my nature is subject, but also in enabling me to avoid them or to correct them more easily. For knowing that all my senses more frequently indicate to me truth than falsehood respecting the things which concern that which is beneficial to the body, and being able almost always to avail myself of many of them in order to examine one particular thing, and, besides that, being able to make use of my memory in order to connect the present with the past, and of my understanding which already has discovered all the causes of my errors, I ought no longer to fear that falsity may be found in matters every day presented to me by my senses. And I ought to set aside all the doubts of these past days as hyperbolical and ridiculous, particularly that very common uncertainty respecting sleep, which I could not distinguish from the waking state; for at present I find a very notable difference between the two, inasmuch as our memory can never connect our dreams one with the other, or with the whole course of our lives, as it unites events which happen to us while we are awake. And, as a matter of fact, if someone, while I was awake, quite suddenly appeared to me and disappeared as fast as do the images which I see in sleep, so that I could not know from whence the form came nor whither it went, it would not be without reason that I should deem it a spectre or a phantom formed by my brain [and similar to those which I form in sleep], rather than a real man. But when I perceive things as to which I know distinctly both the place from which they proceed, and that in which they are, and the time at which they appeared to me; and when, without any interruption, I can connect the perceptions which I have of them with the whole course of my life, I am perfectly assured that these perceptions occur while I am waking and not during sleep. And I ought in no wise to doubt the truth of such matters, if after having called up all my senses, my memory, and my understanding, to examine them, nothing is brought to evidence by any one of them which is repugnant to what is set forth by the others. For because God is in no wise a deceiver, it follows that I am not deceived in this. But because the exigencies of action often oblige us to make up our minds before having leisure to examine matters carefully, we must confess that the life of man is very frequently subject to error in respect to individual objects, and we must in the end acknowledge the infirmity of our nature.

[ON MEDITATION 1]

[On the Method of Doubt]

[I] admire the devices you employ, you who, in order to investigate   479
the certain, employ the doubtful; who in order to bring us into that
light bid us plunge into darkness. Do you want me to take heed of
what I formerly believed myself to be?

[SEVENTH OBJECTIONS]

Here I shall make use of a very homely example for the purpose of   481
explaining to him the rationale of my procedure, in order that in
future he may not misunderstand it or dare to pretend that he does
not understand it. Supposing he had a basket of applies and, fearing
that some of them were rotten, wanted to take those out lest they
might make the rest go wrong, how could he do that? Would he not
first turn the whole of the applies out of the basket and look them
over one by one, and then having selected those which he saw not
to be rotten, place them again in the basket and leave out the others?
It is therefore just in the same way that those who have never rightly
philosophised have in their mind a variety of opinions some of
which they justly fear not to be true, seeing that it was in their
earliest years that they began to amass those beliefs. They then try to
separate the false from the true lest the presence of the former should
produce a general uncertainty about all. Now there is no better way
of doing this than to reject all at once together as uncertain or false,
and then having inspected each singly and in order, to reinstate only
those which they know to be true and indubitable. Thus it was no
bad course to reject everything at the outset.

[SEVENTH REPLIES]

* * *

What there is wholly exempt from doubt?

[SEVENTH OBJECTIONS]

573   [The author of the Seventh Objections] has not objected to anything in me but that I carried doubt much too far, it is not necessary in order to show how unjust he is in blaming me for this, that I should here mention all the places in my Meditations in which I have diligently, and, if I mistake not, more accurately than any other who has written on the subject, successfully refuted that doubt; but it is sufficient that I should here make known to you what I have expressly written in the beginning of my reply to the third

574   Objection; for I set forth no reasons for doubt with the object of persuading others thereto, but on the contrary for the purpose of refuting them; in this matter I clearly followed the example of doctors who 'describe the illness in regard to which they wish to teach the cure.' And tell me, pray, who has been so audacious and impudent as to blame Hippocrates or Galen for having shown the causes which engender illness, and who has concluded therefrom that they neither of them taught anything but the method of falling ill?

Certainly those who know that the Reverend Father has had this audacity, would have difficulty in persuading themselves that in this matter he acted on his own account and following his own counsel, if I did not myself bear witness and make known, how it came about that his previous writings against me had not been approved by your Society, and his last Dissertation has been sent to me at your request. And as this could not be more conveniently done than in this letter, I think that it is not out of place that I cause it to be printed with the Annotations which I have made on his Dissertation.[1]

[LETTER TO FATHER DINET APPENDED TO THE SEVENTH REPLIES]

*   *   *

1 The *Notae* of Descartes, interpolated in the *Dissertatio* of Father Bourdin, appeared, as a matter of fact, under the title of *Objectiones septimae* etc. in the same volume as this letter to Father Dinet.

[On the Argument from the Senses]

Refraction makes a stick thrust into the water appear broken,   418
though nevertheless it is straight; what corrects the error? The
understanding? Not at all; it is the sense of touch.

[SIXTH OBJECTIONS]

I cannot grant what you here add, viz. that that error is corrected   439
not by the understanding but by the touch. For, although it is
owing to touch that we judge that the staff is straight, and that by
the mode of judging to which from infancy we are accustomed, and
which is hence called sense, this, nevertheless, does not suffice to
correct the error. Over and above this we need to have some reason
to show us why in this matter we ought to believe the tactual
judgment rather than that derived from vision; and this reason, not
having been possessed by us from the times of infancy, must be
attributed not to sense but to the understanding. Hence in this
instance it is the understanding solely which corrects the error of
sense; and no case can ever be adduced in which error results from
our trusting the operation of the mind more than sense.

[SIXTH REPLIES]

* * *

If there is deception or falsity, it is not in sense, which is merely   332
passive and has to do only with things that appear and must appear
in the way they do owing to their own appropriate causes; it resides
in the judgment or in the mind, which does not act with sufficient
circumspection, and does not notice that things at a distance, owing
to this and that cause appear more confused and smaller than they
really are when they are near at hand, and so in other cases.
Nevertheless, wherever deception does occur, we must not deny
that some error exists; only the difficulty is, whether the error is
always such that we can never be sure of the truth in the case of
anything perceived by the senses.   [FIFTH OBJECTIONS]

In this passage you show very clearly that you rely on prejudices   385
merely and never divest yourself of them, when you wish to make
out that we suspect no falsity in matters in which we have never
detected falsity; it is thus that, when we behold a tower close at

386   hand and touch it, we are sure that it is square, if it appear to be square; so too when we are really awake we cannot doubt whether we are awake or dreaming; and so forth. Now you have no reason to think that all the things in which error can reside have been noticed by you, and it could easily be proved that you sometimes are wrong about those things which you accept as certain.

[FIFTH REPLIES]

*   *   *

[On the Argument from Dreaming]

171   It is sufficiently obvious from what is said in this Meditation, that we have no criterion[2] for distinguishing dreaming from waking and from what the senses truly tell us; and that hence the images present to us when we are awake and using our senses are not accidents inhering in external objects, and fail to prove that such external objects do as a fact exist. And therefore, if we follow our senses without using any train of reasoning, we shall be justified in doubting whether or not anything exists. Hence we acknowledge the truth of this Meditation. But, since Plato and other ancient Philosophers have talked about this want of certitude in the matters of sense, and since the difficulty in distinguishing the waking state from dreams is a matter of common observation, I should have been glad if our author, so distinguished in the handling of modern speculations, had refrained from publishing those matters of ancient lore.

[THIRD OBJECTIONS]

171   The reasons for doubt here admitted as true by this philosopher were propounded by me only as possessing verisimilitude, and my reason for employing them was not that I might retail them as new,

172   but partly that I might prepare my readers' minds for the study of intellectual matters and for distinguishing them from matters corporeal, a purpose for which such arguments seem wholly necessary; in part also because I intended to reply to those very arguments in the subsequent Meditations; and partly in order to

2 Latin version uses the Greek word κριτήριον.

show the strength of the truths I afterwards propound, by the fact that such metaphysical doubts cannot shake them. Hence, while I have sought no praise from their rehearsal, I believe that it was impossible for me to omit them, as impossible as it would be for a medical writer to omit the description of a disease when trying to teach the method of curing it.

[THIRD REPLIES]

* * *

I ask whether it is really the case that one, who dreams he doubts   195
whether he dreams or no, is unable to dream that his dream is connected with the idea of a long series of past events. If he can, those things which to the dreamer appear to be the actions of his past life may be regarded as true just as though he had been awake. Besides, since, as M. Descartes himself asserts, all certitude and truth   196
in knowledge depend alone upon our knowing the true God, either it will be impossible for an atheist to infer from the memory of his previous life that he wakes, or it will be possible for a man to know that he is awake, apart from knowledge of the true God.

[THIRD OBJECTIONS]

One who dreams cannot effect a real connection between what he   196
dreams and the ideas of past events, though he can dream that he does connect them. For who denies that in his sleep a man may be deceived? But yet when he has awakened he will easily detect his error.

But an atheist is able to infer from the memory of his past life that he is awake; still he cannot know that this sign is sufficient to give him the certainty that he is not in error, unless he knows that it has been created by a God who does not deceive.

[THIRD REPLIES]

* * *

[On Meditation 2]

[The Cogito]

124
125
Since you are not yet certain of the aforesaid existence of God, and yet according to your statement, cannot be certain of anything or know anything clearly and distinctly unless previously you know certainly and clearly that God exists, it follows that you cannot clearly and distinctly know that you are a thinking thing, since, according to you, that knowledge depends on the clear knowledge of the existence of God, the proof of which you have not yet reached at that point where you draw the conclusion that you have a clear knowledge of what you are.

[SECOND OBJECTIONS]

140
When I said that we could know nothing with certainty unless we were first aware that God existed, I announced in express terms that I referred only to the science apprehending such conclusions as can recur in memory without attending further to the proofs which led me to make them.[3] Further, knowledge of first principles is not usually called science by dialecticians. But when we become aware that we are thinking beings, this is a primitive act of knowledge derived from no syllogistic reasoning. He who says, 'I think, hence I am, or exist,' does not deduce existence from thought by a syllogism, but, by a simple act of mental vision, recognises it as if it were a thing that is known *per se*. This is evident from the fact that if it were syllogistically deduced, the major premise, that everything that thinks is, or exists, would have to be known previously; but yet that has rather been learned from the experience of the individual –
141
that unless he exists he cannot think. For our mind is so constituted by nature that general propositions are formed out of the knowledge of particulars.

[SECOND REPLIES]

*   *   *

3 cf. Meditation 5, p. 170.

I am, I exist, is true each time that you pronounce it, or that you   258
mentally conceive it.[4] But I don't see that you needed all this   259
mechanism, when you had other grounds for being sure, and it was
true, that you existed. You might have inferred that from any other
activity, since our natural light informs us that whatever acts also
exists.

[FIFTH OBJECTIONS]

When you say that I could have inferred the same conclusion from   352
any of my other actions, you wander far from the truth, because
there is none of my activities of which I am wholly certain (in the
sense of having metaphysical certitude, which alone is here involved), save thinking alone. For example you have no right to
make the inference: I walk, hence I exist, except in so far as our
awareness of walking is a thought; it is of this alone that the
inference holds good, not of the motion of the body, which
sometimes does not exist, as in dreams, when nevertheless I appear
to walk. Hence from the fact that I think that I walk I can very well
infer the existence of the mind which so thinks, but not that of the
body which walks. So it is also in all other cases.

[FIFTH REPLIES]

* * *

It does not appear altogether certain that we exist, from the fact that   413
we think. For in order to be sure that you think, you ought to know
what to think, or what thinking is, and what your existence is; but
since you do not yet know what these things are, how can you
know that you think or exist? Since, then, in saying 'I think', you do
not know what you are saying, and since in adding 'therefore I
exist', you are equally ignorant of the meaning of what you say, and
indeed do not know that you are saying or thinking anything, since
in order to do so it seems to be necessary for you to know that you
know what you are saying, and once more to know that you know
that you know what you say, and so on to infinity, it is clear that you
cannot know whether you exist, or even whether you think.

[SIXTH OBJECTIONS]

2 cf. Meditation 2, p. 140.

422   It is indeed true that no one can be sure that he knows or that he exists, unless he knows what thought is and what existence. Not that this requires a cognition formed by reflection or one acquired by demonstration; much less does it require a cognition of a reflective cognition, by which we know that we know, and again know that we know that we know and so *ad infinitum*. Such knowledge could never by obtained about anything. It is altogether enough for one to know it by means of that internal cognition which always precedes reflective knowledge, and which, when the object is thought and existence, is innate in all men; so that, however overwhelmed by prejudice and attentive to the words rather than their signification, though we may feign that we do not possess that knowledge, we cannot nevertheless really be without it. When, therefore, anyone perceives that he thinks and that it thence follows that he exists, although he chance never previously to have asked what thought is, nor what existence, he cannot nevertheless fail to have a knowledge of each sufficient to give him assurance on this score.

[SIXTH REPLIES]

[Of the Nature of the Human Mind]

172   I am a thing that thinks; quite correct. From the fact that I think, or have an image,[5] whether sleeping or waking, it is inferred that I am exercising thought;[6] for 'I think' and 'I am exercising thought' mean the same thing. From the fact that I am exercising thought it follows that I am, since that which thinks is not nothing. But, where it is added, this is the mind, the spirit, the understanding, the reason, a doubt arises. For it does not seem to be good reasoning to say: I am exercising thought, hence I am thought; or I am using my intellect, hence I am intellect. For in the same way I might say, I am walking; hence I am the walking.[7] It is hence an assumption on the part of M. Descartes that that which understands is the same as the exercise of understanding[8] which is an act of that which understands, or, at least, that that which understands is the same as the

5 *phantasma*, Latin version; *une idée*, French version.
6 *quod sum cogitans*.
7 *sum ambulans, ergo sum ambulatio*.
8 *intellectionem*.

understanding, which is a power possessed by that which thinks.   173
Yet all philosophers distinguish a subject from its faculties and
activities, i.e. from its properties and essences; for the entity itself is
one thing, its essence another. Hence it is possible for a thing that
thinks to be the subject of the mind, reason, or understanding, and
hence to be something corporeal; and the opposite of this has been
assumed, not proved. Yet this inference is the basis of the
conclusion that M. Descartes seems to wish to establish.

[THIRD OBJECTIONS]

Where I have said, this is the mind, the spirit, the intellect, or the   174
reason, I understood by these names not merely faculties, but rather
what is endowed with the faculty of thinking; and this sense the two
former terms commonly, the latter frequently bear. But I used them
in this sense so expressly and in so many places that I cannot see
what occasion there was for any doubt about their meaning.

Further, there is here no parity between walking[9] and thinking;
for walking is usually held to refer only to that action itself, while
thinking[10] applies now to the action, now to the faculty of
thinking, and again to that in which the faculty exists.

Again I do not assert that that which understands and the activity
of understanding are the same thing, nor indeed do I mean that the
thing that understands and the understanding are the same, if the
term understanding be taken to refer to the faculty of understanding; they are identical only when the understanding means the thing
itself that understands. I admit also quite gladly that, in order to
designate that thing or substance, which I wished to strip of
everything that did not belong to it, I employed the most highly
abstract terms I could; just as, on the contrary this philosopher uses
terms that are as concrete as possible, e.g. subject, matter, body, to
signify that which thinks, fearing to let it be sundered from the
body.

[THIRD REPLIES]

*   *   *

9   *ambulatio.*
10 *cogitatio.*

177   Perchance some one will answer the question thus – I, the very self
that thinks, am held to be distinct from my own thought; and,
though it is not really separate from me, my thought is held to be
diverse from me, just in the way (as has been said before) that
leaping[11] is distinguished from the leaper. But if M. Descartes shows
that he who understood and the understanding are identical we shall
lapse back into the scholastic mode of speaking. The understanding
understands, the vision sees, will wills, and by exact analogy, walking,
or at least the faculty of walking will walk. Now all this is obscure,
incorrect, and quite unworthy of M. Descartes' wonted clearness.

[THIRD OBJECTIONS]

177   I do not deny that I, the thinker, am distinct from my own thought,
in the way in which a thing is distinct from its mode. But when I
ask, what then is there distinct from my thought, this is to be taken
to refer to the various modes of thought there recounted, not to my
substance; and when I add, what can be said to be separate from me
myself, I mean only that these modes of thinking exist entirely in
me. I cannot see on what pretext the imputation here of doubt and
obscurity rests.

[THIRD REPLIES]

*   *   *

276   In saying that you are a thinking being, though you do assign a
predicate known to us, yet it was not previously unknown and was
not the object of your enquiry. Who doubts your thinking? That
which baffles us, that which we seek to discover is that inner
substance belonging to you, the property of which is to think.
Wherefore, your conclusion should correspond with your quest,
and that is to discover, not that you are a thinking thing, but of what
nature you, the thing which thinks, are. Is it not the case that it will
not be sufficient for you to say, when a knowledge of wine superior
to the vulgar is sought for: wine is a thing which is liquid, extracted
from grapes, is white or red, is sweet, intoxicating and so on?
Rather you will try to discover and to declare how that internal
substance, in accordance with that you have observed of its
fabrication, has been compounded out of a mixture of spirits,

11 walking, French version.

humour, tartar and other elements, in some or other particular quantity and proportion. Hence, similarly, since a knowledge of yourself superior to the vulgar, i.e. to what you previously possessed, is called for, you see quite clearly that it is not enough to inform us that you are a thing which thinks, doubts, understands, etc., but that you ought to scrutinise yourself, as it were, by a chemical method of procedure in order to be able to reveal and demonstrate to us your internal substance. If you accomplish this, we shall certainly ourselves discover by investigation whether you are better known than the body itself, of which anatomy, chemistry and many other sciences, many senses and numbers of experiments of all kinds tell us so much.

277

[FIFTH OBJECTIONS]

I am surprised that while here you confess that all those matters which I am aware of in wax, show indeed that I distinctly know that I exist, you maintain that they do not demonstrate what I am, since the one thing cannot be proved without the other. Nor do I see what else you expect the matter to yield, unless it be some revelation about the colour, odour or taste of the human mind, or the nature of the salt, sulphur, or mercury that go to its composition; for you wish us to examine it, as though it were a wine, by a sort of chemical analysis. This is really worthy of you, O flesh, and of all those who, conceiving nothing except what is wholly confused, are ignorant of the proper object of investigation in each inquiry. As for me, my belief has always been that nothing else is required in order to manifest the nature of substance except its various attributes, so that our comprehension of its nature is more perfect in proportion to the number of its attributes which we discern. Just as in wax we are able to distinguish many attributes, one that it is white, another that it is hard, a third that it can be liquefied, etc., so also in mind we can recognise as many – one that it has the power of being aware of the whiteness of wax, another that it possess the power of recognising its hardness, a third of knowing that it can be liquefied, i.e. that it can lose its hardness, etc.; for he can perceive its hardness who is not aware of its whiteness, viz. a man born blind; and so in the other cases. Whence it can be clearly inferred that nothing yields the knowledge of so many attributes as our mind, because as many can be enumerated in its

359

360

case as there are attributes in everything else, owing to the fact that it knows these; and hence its nature is best known of all.

[FIFTH REPLIES]

* * *

[On Animal Souls]

204   Since M. Descartes has undertaken to prove the immortality of souls, it is right to ask whether that follows evidently from this separateness of existence. According to the principles of the vulgar philosophy that conclusion by no means can be drawn, for the common opinion is that the souls of animals are distinct from their bodies, but nevertheless perish with them.

I had carried my criticism to this point and was intending to show how, according to our author's principles, which I believed I had gathered from his method of philosophical enquiry, the immortality of the soul[12] could be easily inferred from its distinctness from the body, when a new work,[13] a little treatise bearing the fruit of our author's reflections, came into my hands; and this work not only throws much light on the whole, but in connection with this passage brings forward exactly what I was to adduce with a view to the solution of the above problem.

205   For in the matter of the souls of animals, in other passages he lets us know sufficiently well that they have no soul, but merely a body disposed in a certain manner and so compounded of various organs that all the actions we see them perform can be effected in it and by its means.

But I fear that this belief will not carry persuasion into men's minds, unless supported by the strongest evidence. For at the first blush, it seems incredible that there is any way by which, without any intervention of the soul, it can come to pass that the light reflected from the body of a wolf into the eyes of a sheep should excite into motion the minute fibres of the optic nerves and by the penetration of this movement to the brain, discharge the animal spirits into the nerves in the manner requisite to make the sheep run off.

[FOURTH OBJECTIONS]

12 *mentis*.
13 The Synopsis of the *Meditations*.

I make no reply to M. Arnauld's additions about the immortality of the soul, because they are not in conflict with my doctrine. As for the matter of the souls of brutes, this is not the place to treat the subject, and I could not, without taking in the whole of physics, say more about them than in the explanations given in the fifth part of the Discourse on Method. Yet, not to pass over the matter altogether, I should point out that the chief thing to note appears to me to be that motion is impossible alike in our own bodies and in those of the brutes, unless all the organs or instruments are present, by means of which it can be effected in a machine. Hence in our very selves the mind [(or the soul)] by no means moves the external limbs immediately, but merely directs the subtle fluid styled the animal spirits,[14] that passes from the heart through the brain towards the muscles, and determines this fluid to perform definite motions, these animal spirits being in their own nature capable of being utilised with equal facility for many distinct actions. But the greater part of our motions do not depend on the mind at all. Such are the beating of the heart, the digestion of our food, nutrition, respiration when we are asleep, and even walking, singing and similar acts when we are awake, if performed without the mind attending to them. When a man in falling thrusts out his hand to save his head he does that without his reason counselling him so to act, but merely because the sight of the impending fall penetrating to his brain, drives the animal spirits into the nerves in the manner necessary for this motion, and for producing it without the mind's desiring it, and as though it were the working of a machine. Now, when we experience this as a fact in ourselves, why should we marvel so greatly if the light reflected from the body of a wolf into the eyes of a sheep should be equally capable of exciting in it the motion of flight?

But if we wish by reasoning to determine whether any of the motions of brutes are similar to those which we accomplish with the aid of the mind, or whether they resemble those that depend alone upon the *influxus* of the animal spirits and the disposition of the organs, we must pay heed to the differences that prevail between the two classes: viz. those differences explained in the fifth part of the Discourse on Method, for I have been able to discover no others. Then it will be seen that all the actions of brutes resemble only those

14 French version; *spiritus*, Latin version.

of ours that occur without the aid of the mind. Whence we are driven to conclude that we can recognise no principle of motion in them beyond the disposition of their organs and the continual discharge[15] of the animal spirits that are produced by the beat of the heart as it rarefies the blood. At the same time we shall perceive that we have had no cause for ascribing anything more to them, beyond that, not distinguishing these two principles of motion, when previously we have noted that the principle depending solely on the animal spirits and organs exists in ourselves and in the brutes alike, we have inadvisedly believed that the other principle, that consisting wholly of mind and thought, also existed in them. And it is true that a persuasion held from our earliest years, though afterwards shown by argument to be false, is not easily and only by long and frequent attention to these arguments expelled from our belief.[16]

[FOURTH REPLIES]

231

*   *   *

[On the Wax]

There is a great difference between imagining, i.e. having some idea, and conceiving with the mind, i.e. inferring, as the result of a train of reasoning, that something is, or exists. But M. Descartes has not explained to us the sense in which they differ. The ancient peripatetics also have taught clearly enough that substance is not perceived by the senses, but is known as a result of reasoning.

178

But what shall we now say, if reasoning chance to be nothing more than the uniting and stringing together of names or designations by the word 'is'? It will be a consequence of this that reason gives us no conclusion about the nature of things, but only about the terms that designate them, whether, indeed, or not there is a convention (arbitrarily made about their meanings) according to which we join these names together. If this be so, as is possible, reasoning will depend on names, names on the imagination, and imagination, perchance, as I think, on the motion of the corporeal organs. Thus mind will be nothing but the motions in certain parts of an organic body.

[THIRD OBJECTIONS]

15 *affluxus*.
15 The French version paraphrases this last sentence at considerable length.

I have here explained the difference between imagination and a   178
pure mental concept, as when in my illustration I enumerated the
features in wax that were given by the imagination and those solely
due to a conception of the mind. But elsewhere also I have
explained how it is that one and the same thing e.g. a pentagon, is in
one way an object of the understanding, in another way of the
imagination [for example how in order to imagine a pentagon a
particular mental act is required which gives us this figure (i.e. its
five sides and the space they enclose) which we dispense with
wholly in our conception]. Moreover, in reasoning we unite not
names but the things signified by the names; and I marvel that the
opposite can occur to anyone. For who doubts whether a French-
man and a German are able to reason in exactly the same way about   179
the same things, though they yet conceive the words in an entirely
diverse way? And has not my opponent condemned himself in
talking of conventions arbitrarily made above the meanings of
words? For, if he admits that words signify anything, why will he
not allow our reasonings to refer to this something that is signified,
rather than to the words alone? But, really, it will be as correct to
infer that earth is heaven or anything else that is desired, as to
conclude that mind is motion [for there are no other two things in
the world between which there is not as much agreement as there is
between motion and spirit, which are of two entirely different
natures].

[THIRD REPLIES]

* * *

[ON MEDITATION 3]

[On the Trademark Argument]

180   We have no image, no idea corresponding to it [i.e. God]. Hence
we are forbidden to worship God in the form of an image, lest we
should think we could conceive Him who is inconceivable.

[THIRD REPLIES]

181   Here the meaning assigned to the term idea is merely that of images
depicted in the corporeal imagination;[17] and, that being agreed on,
it is easy for my critic to prove that there is no proper idea of angel
or of God. But I have, everywhere, from time to time, and
principally in this place, shown that I take the term idea to stand for
whatever the mind directly perceives; and so when I will or when I
fear, since at the same time I perceive that I will and fear, that very
volition and apprehension are ranked among my ideas. I employed
this term because it was the term currently used by philosophers for
the forms of perception of the Divine mind, though we can
discover no imagery in God; besides I had no other more suitable
term. But I think I have sufficiently well explained what the idea of
God is for those who care to follow my meaning; those who prefer
to wrest my words from the sense I give then, I can never satisfy.

[THIRD OBJECTIONS]

*   *   *

124   How do you know that that idea [i.e., of God] would have come
before your mind if you had not been nurtured among men of
culture, but had passed all your life in some desert spot? Have you
not derived it from reflections previously entertained, from books,
from interchange of converse with your friends, etc., not from your
own mind alone or from a supreme being who exists? You must
therefore prove more clearly that that idea could not present itself to
you unless a supreme being did exist; though when you show this

17 *phantasia.*

we shall all confess ourselves vanquished. But it seems to be shown clearly that that idea springs from previous notions by the fact that the natives of Canada, the Hurons, and other savages, have no idea in their minds such as this, which is one that you can form from a previous survey of corporeal things, in such a way that your idea refers only to this corporeal world, which embraces all the perfections that you can imagine; hence you would have up to this point no grounds as yet for inferring more than an entirely perfect corporeal entity, unless you were to add something else conducting us to the [knowledge of the] incorporeal or spiritual. Let us add that you can construct the idea of an angel (just as you can form the notion of a supremely perfect being) without that idea being caused in you by a [really existing] angel; though the angel has more perfection than you have. But you do not possess the idea of God any more than that of an infinite number or of an infinite line; and though you did possess this, yet there could be no such number. Put along with this the contention that the idea of the unity and simplicity of a sole perfection which embraces all other perfections, is merely the product of the reasoning mind, and is formed in the same way as other universal unities, which do not exist in fact but merely in the understanding, as is illustrated by the cases of generic, transcendental and other unities.

[SECOND OBJECTIONS]

There is no force in your plea, that perchance the idea that conveys to me my knowledge of God has come from notions previously entertained, from books, from conversations with friends, etc., not from my own mind alone. For the argument takes the same course as it follows in my own case, if I raise the question whether those from whom I am said to have acquired the idea have derived it from themselves or from any one else; the conclusion will be always the same, that it is God from whom it first originated . . .   136

Those who maintain that they do not possess the idea of God, but in place of it form some image, etc., while they refuse the name concede the fact. I certainly do not think that that idea is of a nature akin to the images of material things depicted in the imagination, but that it is something that we are aware of by an apprehension or judgment or inference of the understanding alone. And I maintain that there is a necessary conclusion from the fact alone that,   139 howsoever it come about, by thought or understanding, I attain to the notion of a perfection that is higher than I; a result that may follow merely from the fact that in counting I cannot reach a highest of all numbers, and hence recognise that in enumeration there is something that exceeds my powers. And this conclusion is, not indeed to the effect that an infinite number does exist, nor yet that it implies a contradiction as you say, but that I have received the power of conceiving that a number is thinkable, that is higher than any that can ever be thought by me, and have received it not from myself but from some other entity more perfect than I.

It is of no account whether or not one gives the name idea to this concept of an indefinitely great number. But in order to understand what is that entity more perfect than I am, and to discover whether it is this very infinite number as an actually existing fact, or whether it is something else, we most take into account all the other attributes that can exist in the being from which the idea originates, over and above the power of giving me that idea; and the result is that it is found to be God.

Finally, when God is said to be unthinkable,[18] that applies to the thought that grasps him adequately, and does not hold good of that inadequate thought which we possess and which suffices to let us know that he exists. It likewise does not matter though the idea of the unity of all God's perfections is formed in the same way as 'Porphyrian'[19] universals. Though there is this important difference, that is designates a peculiar and positive perfection in God, while generic unity adds nothing real to the nature of the single individuals it unites.

[SECOND REPLIES]

*   *   *

18 *inconcevable*, French version.
19 e.g. generic unity.

If there is no idea of God (now it has not been proved that it exists),   183
as seems to be the case, the whole of this argument collapses.
Further (if it is my body that is being considered) the idea of my
own self proceeds [principally] from sight; but (if it is a question of
the soul) there is no idea of the soul. We only infer by means of the
reason that there is something internal in the human body, which
imparts to it its animal motion, and by means of which it feels and
moves; and this, whatever it be, we name the soul, without
employing any idea.

[THIRD OBJECTIONS]

If there is an idea of God (as it is manifest there is), the whole of this   183
objection collapses. When it is said further that we have no idea of
the soul but that we arrive at it by an inference of reason, that is the
same as saying that there is no image of the soul depicted in the
imagination, but that that which I have called its idea does,
nevertheless, exist.

[THIRD REPLIES]

*   *   *

It seems that at one and the same time the idea of the sun must be   184
single whether it is beheld by the eyes, or is given by our
intelligence as many times larger than it appears. For this latter
thought is not an idea of the sun, but an inference by argument that
the idea of the sun would be many times larger if we viewed the sun
from a much nearer distance.

But at different times the ideas of the sun may differ, e.g. when
one looks at it with the naked eye and through a telescope. But
astronomical reasonings do not increase or decrease the idea of the
sun; rather they show that the sensible idea is misleading.

[THIRD OBJECTIONS]

Here too what is said not to be an idea of the sun, but is,   184
nevertheless, described, is exactly what I call an idea. [But as long as
my critic refuses to come to terms with me about the meaning of
words, none of his objections can be other than frivolous].

[THIRD REPLIES]

*   *   *

[Innateness]

187   When M. Descartes says that the idea of God and that of the soul
188   are innate in us, I should like to know whether the minds of those
who are in a profound and dreamless sleep yet think. If not, they
have at that time no ideas. Whence no idea is innate, for what is
innate is always present.

[THIRD OBJECTIONS]

189   When I say that an idea is innate in us [or imprinted in our souls
by nature], I do not mean that it is always present to us. This would
make no idea innate. I mean merely that we possess the faculty of
summoning up this idea.

[THIRD REPLIES]

*   *   *

186   When I consider the attributes of God, in order to gather thence the
idea of God, and see whether there is anything contained in it that
cannot proceed from ourselves, I find, unless I am mistaken, that
what we assign in thought to the name of God neither proceeds
from ourselves nor needs to come from any other source than
external objects.

[THIRD OBJECTIONS]

188   Nothing that we attribute to God can come from external objects as
a copy proceeds from its exemplar, because in God there is nothing
similar to what is found in external things, i.e. in corporeal objects.
But whatever is unlike them in our thought [of God], must come
manifestly not from them, but from the cause of that diversity
existing in our thought [of God].

Further I ask how my critic derives the intellectual comprehension of God from external things. But I can easily explain the idea
which I have of it, by saying that by idea I mean whatever is the
form of any perception. For does anyone who understands something not perceive that he does so? and hence does he not possess
that form or idea of mental action? It is by extending this
indefinitely that we form the idea of the intellectual activity of God;
similarly also with God's other attributes.

But, since we have employed the idea of God existing in us for the purpose of proving His existence, and such mighty power is comprised in this idea, that we comprehend that it would be contradictory, if God exists, for anything besides Him to exist, unless it were created by Him; it clearly follows, from the fact that His existence has been demonstrated, that it has been also proved that the whole world, or whatever things other than God exist, have been created by Him.

[THIRD REPLIES]

* * *

Why one born blind has no idea of colour or one born deaf of   283
sound, if it is not because external things have not been able to convey from themselves any semblance of themselves into the mind of the afflicted individual? For the inlets have been closed since birth, and obstacles placed there for all time, which prevent anything from passing through them.

[FIFTH OBJECTIONS]

363

How do you know that one born blind has no idea of colour, when often enough in our case even when the eyes are closed the sense of light and colour is stimulated? And, though your contention be conceded, has not the man who denies the existence of material things as much ground for saying that one congenitally blind is destitute of ideas of colour because his mind lacks the faculty of forming them, as you have for asserting that their absence is due to his being without eyes to see?

[FIFTH REPLIES]

* * *

[Reality and its Degrees]

185   I pray M. Descartes to investigate the meaning of 'more reality'.
Does reality admit of more and less?

[THIRD OBJECTIONS]

185   I have explained how reality admits of more and less: viz. in the way
in which substance is greater than mode; and if there be real qualities
or incomplete substances, they are things to a greater extent than
modes are, but less than complete substances. Finally, if there be an
infinite and independent substance, it is more a thing than a substance
that is finite and dependent. Now all this is quite self-evident.

[THIRD REPLIES]

*   *   *

92   Explain what 'to be objectively in the understanding' is. As I was
taught, it is the determination of an act of mind by a modification
due to an object; but this is a merely external attribute of the thing
and nothing belonging to its reality. For, as 'being seen' is merely
the direction of the act of vision towards the percipient so 'being
thought' or 'being objectively in the understanding' is merely a
standing still of our thought within itself and ending there, which
can occur whether the thing is active or passive, indeed though it is
even non-existent. Hence, why should I ask for a cause of that
which is nothing actual, which is a mere name, a nonentity?

[FIRST OBJECTIONS]

102   I have written somewhere 'an idea is the thing thought of itself, in
so far as it is objectively in the understanding'. But these words he
evidently prefers to understand in a sense quite different from that in
which I use them, meaning to furnish me with an opportunity of
explaining them more clearly. 'Objective existence in the mind is,'
he says, 'the determination of the act of mind by a modification due
to an object, which is merely an extrinsic appellation and nothing
belonging to the object,' etc. Now, here it must be noticed firstly
that he refers to the thing itself, which is at it were placed outside
the understanding and respecting which it is certainly an extrinsic
attribute to be objectively in the understanding, and secondly, that
what I speak of is the idea, which at no time exists outside the mind,

and in the case of which 'objective existence' is indistinguishable from being in the understanding in that way in which objects are wont to be there. Thus, for example, if someone asks what feature in the sun's existence it is to exist in my mind, it will be quite right to reply that this is a merely extrinsic attribute which affects it, and to wit, one which determines an operation of the mind in the mode due to the object. But if the question be, what the idea of the sun is, and the reply is given, that it is the object thought of in so far as that exists objectively in the understanding, he will not understand that it is the sun itself, in so far as that extrinsic attribute is in it; neither will 'objective existence in the understanding' here signify that the mind's operation is here determined in the mode due to an object, but that it is in the mind in the way in which objectives are wont to exist there. Hence the idea of the sun will be the sun itself existing in the mind, not indeed formally, as it exists in the sky, but objectively, i.e. in the way in which objects are wont to exist in the mind; and this mode of being is truly much less perfect than that in which things exist outside the mind, but it is not on that account mere nothing, as I have already said.

103

[FIRST REPLIES]

* * *

[ON MEDITATION 4]

[On Error]

190   It is true that ignorance is merely a defect, and that we stand in need of no special positive faculty in order to be ignorant; but about error the case is not so clear. For it appears that stones and inanimate things are unable to err solely because they have no faculty of reasoning, or imagining. Hence it is a very direct inference that, in order to err, a faculty of reasoning, or at least of imagination is required; now both of these are positive faculties with which all beings that err, and only beings that err, have been endowed.

Further, M. Descartes says – I perceive that they (viz. my mistakes) depend upon the cooperation of two causes, viz. my faculty of cognition, and my faculty of choice, or the freedom of my will. But this seems to be contradictory to what went before. And we must note here also that the freedom of the will has been assumed without proof, and in opposition to the opinion of the Calvinists.

[THIRD OBJECTIONS]

190   Although in order to err the faculty of reasoning (or rather of judging, or affirming and denying) is required, because error is a lack of this power it does not hence follow that this defect is
191   anything real, just as it does not follow that blindness is anything real, although stones are not said to be blind merely because they are incapable of vision. I marvel that in these objections I have as yet found nothing that is properly argued out. Further I made no assumption concerning freedom which is not a matter of universal experience; our natural light makes this most evident and I cannot make out why it is said to be contradictory to previous statements.

But though there are many who, looking to the Divine fore-ordination, cannot conceive how that is compatible with liberty on our part, nevertheless no one, when he considers himself alone, fails to experience the fact that to will and to be free are the same thing [or rather that there is no difference between what is voluntary and what is free]. But this is no place for examining other people's opinions about this matter.

[THIRD REPLIES]

*   *   *

This term, 'great mental illumination', is metaphorical, and conse-   191
quently is not adapted to the purposes of argument. Moreover
everyone who is free from doubt claims to possess a similar   192
illumination, and in his will there is the same inclination to believe
that of which he does not doubt, as in that of one who truly knows.
Hence while this illumination may be the cause that makes a man
obstinately defend or hold some opinion, it is not the cause of his
knowing it to be true.

Further, not only to know a thing to be true, but also to believe it
or give assent to it, have nothing to do with the will. For, what is
proved by valid argument or is recounted as credible, is believed by
us whether we will or no. It is true that affirming and denying,
maintaining or refuting propositions, are acts of will; but it does not
follow on that account that internal assent depends upon the will.

Therefore the demonstration of the truth that follows is not
adequate – 'and it is in this misuse of our free-will, that this privation
consists that constitutes the form of error'.

[THIRD OBJECTIONS]

It does not at all matter whether or not this term 'great illumination'
is proper to argument, so long as it is serviceable for explanation, as
in fact it is. For no one can be unaware that by mental illumination
is meant clearness of cognition, which perhaps is not possessed by
everyone who thinks he possesses it. But this does not prevent it
from being very different from a bigoted opinion, to the formation
of which there goes no perceptual evidence.

Moreover when it is here said that when a thing is clearly
perceived[20] we give our assent whether we will or no, that is the
same as saying that we desire what we clearly know to be good
whether willing or unwilling; for the word 'unwilling' finds no
entrance in such circumstances, implying as it does that we will and
do not will the same thing.

[THIRD REPLIES]

*   *   *

20 *perspectis*; conceived, French version.

[On the Will]

416   A difficulty arises from the indifference of the judgment or liberty which you refuse to allow to the perfection of choice, but ascribe to an imperfect will alone, thus removing the indifference as often as the mind clearly perceives what ought to be believed or performed or left undone. But do you not see that by positing this you destroy

417   the liberty of God, from Whom you remove that indifference as to whether He will create this world rather than another or any world at all? Though yet it belongs to the faith to believe that God has from eternity been indifferent as to whether He would create one, or many, worlds, or no world. But who doubts that God has at all times had the clearest vision of all things that were to be done or left undone? Therefore the clearest vision and perception of things does not annul the indifference of choice; and if it cannot harmonise with human liberty, neither will it be compatible with the divine, since the essences of thing are, like numbers, indivisible and unchanging. Wherefore indifference is included no less in the divine than in human freedom of choice.

[SIXTH OBJECTIONS]

431   As to the freedom of the will, a very different account must be given of it as it exists in God and as it exists in us. For it is self-contradictory that the will of God should not have been from

432   eternity indifferent to all that has come to pass or that ever will occur, because we can form no conception of anything good or true, of anything to be believed or to be performed or to be omitted, the idea of which existed in the divine understanding before God's will determined Him so to act as to bring it to pass. Nor do I here speak of priority of time; I mean that it was not even prior to order, or in nature, or in reasoned relation,[21] as they say [in the schools], so that that idea of good impelled God to choose one thing rather than another. Thus, to illustrate, God did not will to create the world in time because he saw that it would be better thus than if he created it from all eternity; nor did he will the three angles of a triangle to be equal to two right angles because he knew that they could not be otherwise. On the contrary, because he worked to create the world in time it is for that reason better than if he had

21 *ratione ratiocinata.*

created it from all eternity; and it is because he willed the three angles of a triangle to be necessarily equal to two right angles that this is true and cannot be otherwise; and so in other cases. And though it may be said that it is the merit of the saints which is the cause of their obtaining eternal life, this causes no difficulty; for their merits are not causes of their obtaining this in the sense that they determine God to will anything; they are merely the cause of an effect of which God wished them from all eternity to be the cause. Thus that supreme indifference in God is the supreme proof of his omnipotence. But as to man, since he finds the nature of all goodness and truth already determined by God, and his will cannot bear upon anything else, it is evident that he embraces the true and the good the more willingly and hence the more freely in proportion as he sees the true and the good the more clearly, and that he is never indifferent save when he does not know what is the more true or the better, or at least when he does not see clearly enough to prevent him from doubting about it. Thus the indifference which attaches to human liberty is very different from that which belongs to the divine. Neither does it here matter that the essences of things are said to be indivisible: for firstly no essence can belong in a univocal sense both to God and His creature; and finally indifference does not belong to the essence of human liberty, since we are free not only when our ignorance of the right renders us indifferent, but also, and chiefly, when a clear perception impels us to prosecute some definite course.

433

[SIXTH REPLIES]

* * *

[ON MEDITATION 5]

[On the Ontological Argument]

99   Even though you have a distinct knowledge of a highest being, and
granted that a being of supreme perfection includes existence in the
concept of its essence, yet it does not follow that its existence is
anything actual, unless on the hypothesis that that highest being
does exist; for then indeed along with its other perfections it will in
actuality include this, its existence, also. Hence the proof of the
existence of this highest being must be drawn from some other
source.

[FIRST OBJECTIONS]

119   If we attentively consider whether existence is congruous with a
being of the highest perfection, and what sort of existence is so, we
shall be able clearly and distinctly to perceive in the first place that
possible existence is at least predicable of it, as it is of all other things
of which we have a distinct idea, even of those things which are
composed by a fiction of the mind. Further, because we cannot
think of God's existence as being possible, without at the same
time, and by taking heed of His immeasurable power, acknowledg-
ing that He can exist by His own might, we hence conclude that
He really exists and has existed from all eternity; for the light of
nature makes it most plain that what can exist by its own power
always exists. And thus we shall understand that necessary existence
is comprised in the idea of a being of the highest power, not by any
intellectual fiction, but because it belongs to the true and immutable nature of that being to exist. We shall at the same time easily
perceive that that all-powerful being must comprise in himself all
the other perfections that are contained in the idea of God, and
hence these by their own nature and without any mental fiction are
conjoined together and exist in God.

[FIRST REPLIES]

*   *   *

Though you properly enough compare essence with essence, in   322
your next step it is neither existence with essence, nor property with
property that you compare, but existence with property. Hence it
seems that you either ought to have said that God's omnipotence
can no more be separated from His essence than can that equality in   323
magnitude of the angles of a triangle from its essence; or at least, that
God's existence can no more be separated from His essence than the
existence from the essence of a triangle. Thus taken, each comparison would have proceeded on correct lines, and the truth would
have been conceded, not only of the former but of the latter,
although this would not be evidence that you had established your
conclusion that God necessarily exists, because neither does the
triangle necessarily exist, although its essence and its existence
cannot in reality be severed, howsoever much the mind separates
them or thinks of them apart, in the same way as the Divine essence
and existence may be thought of separately.

[FIFTH OBJECTIONS]

Here I do not see to what class of reality you wish to assign   382
existence, nor do I see why it may not be said to be a property as
well as omnipotence, taking the word property as equivalent to any   383
attribute or anything which can be predicated of a thing, as in the
present case it should be by all means regarded. Nay, necessary
existence in the case of God is also a true property in the strictest
sense of the word, because it belongs to Him and forms part of His
essence alone. Hence the existence of a triangle cannot be compared
with the existence of God, because existence manifestly has a
different relation to essence in the case of God and in the case of a
triangle.

Nor is it more a begging of the question, to enumerate existence
among the things belonging to the essence of God, than to reckon
the equality of the three angles of a triangle to two right angles
among the properties of the triangle.

Nor is it true that essence and existence can be thought, the one
apart from the other in God, as in a triangle, because God *is* His
existence, while a triangle is not its own existence. I do not,
nevertheless, deny that existence is a possible perfection in the idea
of a triangle, as it is a necessary one in the idea of God, for this fact
makes the idea of the triangle one of higher rank than the ideas of

those chimerical things whose existence can never be supposed. Hence you have not diminished the force of this argument of mine in the slightest, and you still remain deluded by that fallacy, which you say I could have exposed so easily.

[FIFTH REPLIES]

* * *

98   Though reason only and not authority is the arbiter in our discussion, yet, lest I be judged impertinent in gainsaying the contentions of such an illustrious philosopher, let me quote you what St Thomas says; it is an objection he urges against his own doctrine: As soon as the intellect grasps the signification of the name God, it knows that God exists; for the meaning of His name is an object nothing greater than which can be conceived.[22] Now that which exists in fact as well as in the mind is greater than what exists in the mind alone. Hence, since the name 'God' being understood, God consequently exists in the mind, it follows that He really exists. This argument formally expressed becomes – God is a being, a greater than which cannot be conceived; but that, a greater than which cannot be conceived, includes its existence; hence God by His very name or notion includes His existence, and as a direct consequence can neither be conceived as being, nor can be, devoid of existence. But now, kindly tell me is not this M. Descartes' own proof?

[FIRST OBJECTIONS]

115   My opponent here compares one of my arguments with another of St Thomas's, so, as it were to force me to show which of the two has the more force. This I seem to be able to do with a good enough grace, because neither did St Thomas use that argument as his own, nor does he draw the same conclusion from it; consequently there is nothing here in which I am at variance with the angelic Doctor. He himself asked whether the existence of God is in itself known to man, i.e. whether it is obvious to each single individual; he denies this, and I along with him.[23] Now the argument to which he puts himself in opposition can be thus

22 *significari*.
23 French version; *merito* Latin version.

propounded. 'When we understand what it is the word God signifies, we understand that it is that, than which nothing greater can be conceived;[24] but to exist in reality as well as in the mind is greater than to exist in the mind alone; hence, when the meaning of the word God is understood, it is understood that God exists in fact as well as in the understanding.' Here there is a manifest error in the form of the argument; for the only conclusion to be drawn is — hence, when we understand what the word God means, we understand that it means that God exists in fact as well as in the mind: but because a word implies something, that is no reason for this being true. My argument, however, was of the following kind — That which we clearly and distinctly understand to belong to the true and immutable nature of anything, its essence, or form, can be truly affirmed of that thing; but, after we have with sufficient accuracy investigated the nature of God, we clearly and distinctly understand that to exist belongs to His true and immutable nature; therefore we can with truth affirm of God that He exists. This is at least a legitimate conclusion. But besides this the major premise cannot be denied, because it was previously conceded that whatever we clearly and distinctly perceive is true. The minor alone remains, and in it there is, I confess, no little difficulty. This is firstly because we are so much accustomed to distinguish existence from essence in the case of other things, that we do not with sufficient readiness notice how existence belongs to the essence of God in a greater degree than in the case of other things. Further, because we do not distinguish that which belongs to the true and immutable nature of a thing from that which we by a mental fiction assign to it, even if we do fairly clearly perceive that existence belong to God's essence, we nevertheless do not conclude that God exists, because we do not know whether His essence is true and immutable or only a fiction we invent.

116

But, in order to remove the first part of this difficulty we must distinguish between possible and necessary existence, and note that in the concept or idea of everything that is clearly and distinctly conceived, possible existence is contained, but necessary existence never, except in the idea of God alone. For I am sure that all who diligently attend to this diversity between the idea of God and that

24 *significari*, Latin version.

117   of all other things, will perceive that, even though other things are indeed conceived[25] only as existing, yet it does not thence follow that they do exist, but only that they may exist, because we do not conceive that there is any necessity for actual existence being conjoined with their other properties; but, because we understand that actual existence is necessarily and at all times linked to God's other attributes, it follows certainly that God exists.

Further, to clear away the rest of the difficulty, we must observe that those ideas which do not contain a true and immutable nature, but only a fictitious one due to a mental synthesis, can be by that same mind analysed, not merely by abstraction (or restriction of the thought)[26] but by a clear and distinct mental operation; hence it will be clear that those things which the understanding cannot so analyse have not been put together by it. For example, when I think of a winged horse, or of a lion actually existing, or of a triangle inscribed in a square, I easily understand that I can on the contrary think of a horse without wings, of a lion as not existing and of a triangle apart from a square, and so forth, and that hence these things have no true and immutable nature. But if I think of the triangle or the square (I pass by for the present the lion and the horse, because their natures are not wholly intelligible to us), then certainly whatever I recognise as being contained in the idea of the triangle, as that its angles are equal to [two] right, etc., I shall truly affirm of the triangle; and similarly I shall affirm of the square whatsoever I find in the idea of it. For though I can think of the triangle, though stripping from it the equality of its angles to two right, yet I cannot deny that attribute of it

118   by any clear and distinct mental operation, i.e. when I myself rightly understand what I say. Besides, if I think of a triangle inscribed in a square, not meaning to ascribe to the square that which belongs to the triangle alone, or to assign to the triangle the properties of the square, but for the purpose only of examining that which arises from the conjunction of the two, the nature of that composite will be not less true and immutable than that of the square or triangle alone; and hence it will be right to affirm that the square cannot be less than double the inscribed triangle, together with the similar properties which belong to the nature of this composite figure.

25 *intelligamus*.
26 This phrase occurs only in the French version.

But if I think that existence is contained in the idea of a body of the highest perfection, because it is a greater perfection to exist in reality as well as in the mind than to exist in the intellect alone, I cannot then conclude that this utterly perfect body exists, but merely that it may exist; for I can well enough recognise that that idea has been put together by my mind uniting together all corporeal perfections, and that existence does not arise out of its other corporeal perfections, because it (existence) can be equally well affirmed and denied of them. Nay, because when I examine this idea of body I see in it no force by means of which it may produce or preserve itself, I rightly conclude that necessary existence, which alone is here in question, does not belong to the nature of a body, howsoever perfect it may be, any more than it belongs to the nature of a mountain not to have a valley, or any more than it pertains to the nature of a triangle to have its angles greater than two right angles. But now, if we ask not about a body but about a thing (of whatever sort this thing may turn out to be) which has all those perfections which can exist together, whether existence must be   119 included in the number of these perfections we shall at first be in doubt, because our mind, being finite, and not accustomed to consider them unless separately, will perchance not at first see how necessary is the bond between them.

[FIRST REPLIES]

* * *

[Cartesian Circle]

The only remaining scruple I have is an uncertainty as to how a   214 circular reasoning is to be avoided in saying: 'the only secure reason we have for believing that what we clearly and distinctly perceive is true, is the fact that God exists.'

But we can be sure that God exists, only because we clearly and evidently perceive that; therefore prior to being certain that God exists, we should be certain that whatever we clearly and evidently perceive is true.

[FOURTH OBJECTIONS]

245 To prove that I have not argued in a circle in saying, that the only
secure reason we have for believing that what we clearly and
distinctly perceive is true, is the fact that God exists; but that clearly
we can be sure that God exists only because we perceive that, I may
246 cite the explanations that I have already given at sufficient length in
my reply to the second set of Objections . . . There I distinguished
those matters that in actual truth we clearly perceive from those we
remember to have formerly perceived. For first, we are sure that
God exists because we have attended to the proofs that established
this fact; but afterwards it is enough for us to remember that we
have perceived something clearly, in order to be sure that it is true;
but this would not suffice, unless we knew that God existed and that
he did not deceive us.

[FOURTH REPLIES]

*   *   *

126 It is true that it is not necessary for God to contrive deception in
order for you to be deceived in the things which you think you
clearly and distinctly perceive, if the cause of the illusion may reside
in you yourself, provided only that you are unaware of the fact.
What if your nature be such as to be continually, or at least very
frequently, deceived? But what evidence is there that you are not
deceived and cannot be deceived in those matters whereof you have
clear and distinct knowledge? How often have we not experienced
the fact that a man has been deceived in those matters of which he
believed that he alone had clear knowledge? Hence we think that
this principle of clear and distinct knowledge should be explained so
clearly and distinctly that no one of sound mind may ever be
deceived in matters that he believes himself to know clearly and
distinctly; apart from this condition we cannot yet make out that
there is a possibility of certitude in any degree attaching to your
thinking or to the thoughts of the human race.

[SECOND OBJECTIONS]

143 In the case of our clearest and most accurate judgments which, if
false, could not be corrected by any that are clearer, or by any other
144 natural faculty, I clearly affirm that we cannot be deceived. For,
since God is the highest being He cannot be otherwise than the

highest good and highest truth, and hence it is contradictory that anything should proceed from Him that positively tends towards falsity. But yet since there is nothing real in us that is not given by God (as we proved along with His existence) and we have, as well, a real faculty of recognising truth, and distinguishing it from falsehood (as the mere existence in us of true and false ideas makes manifest), unless this faculty tended towards truth, at least when properly employed (i.e. when we give assent to none but clear and distinct perceptions, for no other correct use of this faculty can be imagined), God, who has given it to us, must justly be held to be a deceiver.

Thus you see that, after becoming aware of the existence of God, it is incumbent on us to imagine that he is a deceiver if we wish to cast doubt upon our clear and distinct perceptions; and since we cannot imagine that he is a deceiver, we must admit them all as true and certain.

But since I here perceive that you are still entangled in the difficulties which I brought forward in the first Meditation, and which I thought I had in the succeeding Meditations removed with sufficient care, I shall here a second time expound what seems to me the only basis on which human certitude can rest.

To begin with, directly we think that we rightly perceive something[27] we spontaneously persuade ourselves that it is true. Further, if this conviction is so strong that we have no reason to doubt concerning that of the truth of which we have persuaded ourselves, there is nothing more to enquire about; we have here all the certainty that can reasonably be desired. What is it to us, though perchance some one feigns that that, of the truth of which we are so firmly persuaded, appears false to God or to an angel, and hence is, absolutely speaking, false? What heed do we pay to the absolute falsity, when we by no means believe that it exists or even suspect its existence? We have assumed a conviction so strong that nothing can remove it, and this persuasion is clearly the same as perfect certitude.

145

But it may be doubted whether there is any such certitude, whether such firm and immutable conviction exists.

It is indeed clear that no one possesses such certainty in those cases where there is the very least confusion and obscurity in our

27 *concevoir clairement quelque verité*, French version.

perception; for this obscurity, of whatsoever sort it be, is sufficient to make us doubt here. In matters perceived by sense alone, however clearly, certainty does not exist, because we have often noted that error can occur in sensation, as in the instance of the thirst of the dropsical man, or when one who is jaundiced sees snow as yellow; for he sees it thus with no less clearness and distinctness than we see it as white. If, then, any certitude does exist, it remains that it must be found only in the clear perceptions of the intellect.

But of these there are some so evident and at the same time so simple, that in their case we never doubt about believing them true: e.g. that I, while I think, exist; that what is once done cannot be undone, and other similar truths, about which clearly we can possess this certainty. For we cannot doubt them unless we think of them; but we cannot think of them without at the same time believing them to be true, the position taken up.[28] Hence we can never doubt them without at the same time believing them to be true; i.e. we can never doubt them.

No difficulty is caused by the objection that we have often found that others have been deceived in matters which they believed they alone knew clearly. For we have never noticed that this has occurred, nor could anyone find it to occur with these persons who have sought to draw the clearness of their vision from the intellect alone, but only with those who have made either the senses or some erroneous preconception the source from which they derived that evidence.

Again there is no difficulty though some one feign that the truth appear false to God or to an angel, because the evidence of our perception does not allow us to pay any attention to such a fiction.

There are other matters that are indeed perceived very clearly by our intellect, when we attend sufficiently closely to the reasons on which our knowledge of them depends, and hence we cannot then by in doubt about them; but since we can forget those reasons, and yet remember the conclusions deduced from them, the question is raised whether we can entertain the same firm and immutable certainty as to these conclusions, during the time that we recollect that they have been deduced from first principles that are evident;

28 *ut assumptum est*, Latin version; *comme je viens de dire*, French version.

for this remembrance must be assumed in order that they may be called conclusions. My answer is that those possess it who, in virtue of their knowledge of God, are aware that the faculty of understanding given by Him must tend towards truth; but that this certainty is not shared by others. But the subject has been so clearly explained at the end of the fifth Meditation that there seems to be nothing to add here.

[SECOND REPLIES]

* * *

[ON MEDITATION 6]

[On the Existence of Material Things]

195   It is the common belief that no fault is committed by medical men who deceive sick people for their health's sake, nor by parents who mislead their children for their good; and that the evil in deception lies not in the falsity of what is said, but in the bad intent of those who practise it. M. Descartes must therefore look to this proposition, God can in no case deceive us, taken universally, and see whether it is true; for if it is not true, thus universally taken, the conclusion, hence corporeal things exist, does not follow.

[THIRD OBJECTIONS]

195   For the security of my conclusion we do not need to assume that we can never be deceived (for I have gladly admitted that we are often deceived), but that we are not deceived when that error of ours would argue an intention to deceive on the part of God, an intention it is contradictory to impute to Him. Once more this is bad reasoning on my critic's part.

[THIRD REPLIES]

*   *   *

[On the Real Distinction between Soul and Body]

198   Let us discover how we can demonstrate the fact that our mind is [distinct and] separate from our body.

I am able to doubt whether I have a body, nay, whether any body exists at all; yet I have no right to doubt whether I am, or exist, so long as I doubt or think.

Hence I, who doubt and think, am not a body; otherwise in entertaining doubt concerning body, I should doubt about myself.

Nay, even though I obstinately maintain that no body at all exists, the position taken up is unshaken: I am something, hence I am not a body.

This is really very acute, but someone could bring up the objection which our author urges against himself; the fact that I doubt about body or deny that body exists, does not bring it about that no body exists. Hence perhaps it happens that these very things which I suppose to be nothing, because they are unknown to me, yet do not in truth differ from that self which I do know. I know nothing about it, he says, I do not dispute this matter; [I can judge only about things that are known to me.] I know that I exist; I enquire who I, the known self, am; it is quite certain that the knowledge of this self thus precisely taken, does not depend on those things of the existence of which I am not yet acquainted.[29]

But he admits in consonance with the argument laid down in the method, that the proof has proceeded only so far as to exclude from the nature of the human mind whatsoever is corporeal, not from the point of view of the ultimate truth, but relatively only to his consciousness[30] (the meaning being that nothing at all was known to him to belong to his essential nature, beyond the fact that he was a thinking being).[31] Hence it is evident from this reply that the argument is exactly where it was, and that therefore the problem which it promises to solve remains entirely untouched. The problem is: how it follows, from the fact that one is unaware that anything else [(except the fact of being a thinking thing)] belongs to one's essence, that nothing else really belongs to one's essence.[31] But, not to conceal my dullness, I have been unable to discover in the whole of Meditation 2 where he has shown this. Yet so far as I can conjecture, he attempts this proof in Meditation 6, because he believes that it is dependent on the possession of the clear knowledge of God to which in Meditation 2 he has not yet attained. Here is his proof:

'Because I know that all the things I clearly and distinctly understand can be created by God just as I conceive them to exist, it is sufficient for me to be able to comprehend one thing clearly and distinctly apart from another, in order to be sure that the one is diverse from the other, because at least God can isolate them; and it does not matter by what power that isolation is effected, in order that I may be obliged to think them different from one another. Hence because, on the one hand, I have a clear and distinct idea of myself in so far as I am a thinking being, and not extended, and on

29 cf. Meditation 2.
30 *perceptionem*.
31 cf. Preface, p. 127.

200 the other hand, a distinct idea of body, in so far as it is only an extended thing, not one that thinks, it is certain that I am in reality distinct from my body and can exist apart from it.'

Here we must halt awhile; for on these few words the whole of the difficulty seems to hinge.

Firstly, in order to be true, the major premise of that syllogism must be held to refer to the adequate notion of a thing [(i.e. the notion which comprises everything which may be known of the thing)], not to any notion, even a clear and distinct one. For M. Descartes in his reply to his theological critic admits that it is sufficient to have a formal distinction and that a real one is not required, to cause one thing to be conceived separately and as distinct from another by the abstracting action of the mind when it conceives a thing inadequately. Whence in the same passage he draws the conclusion which he adds: But still I understand in a complete manner what body is [(i.e. I conceive body as a complete thing)], merely by thinking that it is extended, has figure, can move, etc., and by denying of it everything which belongs to the nature of mind. Conversely also, I understand that mind is something complete, which doubts, knows, wishes etc., although I deny that anything belongs to it which is contained in the idea of body. Hence there is a real distinction between mind and body.

But, if anyone casts doubt on the (minor) premise here assumed, and contends that it is merely that your conception is inadequate when you conceive yourself [(i.e. your mind)] as being a thinking but not an extended thing, and similarly when you conceive yourself [(i.e. your body)] as being an extended and not a thinking thing, we must look to its proof in the previous part of the argument. For I do not reckon a matter like this to be so clear as to warrant us in assuming it as an indemonstrable first principle and in dispensing with proof.

Now as to the first part of the statement, namely, that you
201 completely understand what body is, merely by thinking that it is extended, has figure, can move, etc., and by denying of it everything which belongs to the nature of mind, this is of little value. For one who contends that the human mind is corporeal does not on that account believe that every body is a mind. Hence body would be so related to mind as genus is to species. But the genus can be conceived without the species, even although one

deny of it whatsoever is proper and peculiar to the species; whence comes the common dictum of logicians, 'the negation of the species does not negate the genus.' Thus, I can conceive figure without conceiving any of the attributes proper to the circle. Therefore, we must prove over and above this that the mind can be completely and adequately conceived apart from the body.

I can discover no passage in the whole work capable of effecting this proof, save the proposition laid down at the outset: I can deny that there is any body or that any extended thing exists, but yet it is certain that I exist, so long as I make this denial, or think; hence I am a thing that thinks and not a body, and the body does not pertain to the knowledge of myself.

But the only result that I can see this to give, is that a certain knowledge of myself be obtained without a knowledge of the body. But it is not yet quite clear to me that this knowledge is complete and adequate, so as to make me sure that I am not in error in excluding the body from my essence. I shall explain by means of an example –

Let us assume that a certain man is quite sure that the angle in a semicircle is a right angle and that hence the triangle made by this angle and the diameter is right-angled; but suppose he questions and has not yet firmly apprehended, nay, let us imagine that, misled by some fallacy, he denies that the square on its base is equal to the squares on the sides of the right-angled triangle. Now, according to our author's reasoning, he will see himself confirmed in his false belief. For, he will argue, while I clearly and distinctly perceive that this triangle is right-angled, I yet doubt whether the square on its base is equal to the square on its sides. Hence the equality of the square on the base to those on the sides does not belong to its essence.

Further, even though I deny that the square on its base is equal to the squares on its sides, I yet remain certain that it is right-angled, and the knowledge that one of its angles is a right angle remains clear and distinct in my mind; and this remaining so, not God himself could cause it not to be right-angled.

Hence, that of which I doubt, or the removal of which leaves me with the idea still, cannot belong to its essence.

Besides, since I know that all things I clearly and distinctly understand can be created by God just as I conceive them to exist,

202

it is sufficient for me, in order to be sure that one thing is distinct from another, to be able to comprehend the one clearly and distinctly apart from the other, because it can be isolated by God. But I clearly and distinctly understand that this triangle is right-angled, without comprehending that the square on its base is equal to the squares on its sides. Hence God at least can create a right-angled triangle, the square on the base of which is not equal to the squares on its sides.

I do not see what reply can here be made, except that the man in question does not perceive clearly that the triangle is right-angled. But whence do I obtain any perception of the nature of my mind clearer than that which he has of the nature of the triangle? He is as sure that the triangle in a semicircle has one right angle (which is the notion of a right-angled triangle) as I am in believing that I exist because I think.

Hence, just as a man errs in not believing that the equality of the square on its base to the squares on its sides belongs to the nature of that triangle, which he clearly and distinctly knows to be right-angled, so why am I not perhaps in the wrong in thinking that nothing else belongs to my nature, which I clearly and distinctly know to be something that thinks, except the fact that I am this thinking being? Perhaps it also belongs to my essence to be something extended.

And certainly, some one will say it is no marvel if, in deducing my existence from the fact that I think, the idea that I form of the self, which is in this way an object of thought, represent me to my mind as merely a thinking being, since it has been derived from my thinking alone. And hence from this idea, no argument can be drawn to prove that nothing more belongs to my essence than what the idea contains.

[FOURTH OBJECTIONS]

I come first of all to the passage where my demonstration commences of how, from the fact that I know that nothing belongs to my essence (i.e. to the essence of the mind alone) beyond the fact that I am a thinking being, it follows that in actual truth nothing else does belong to it. That was, to be sure, the place where I proved that God exists, that God, to wit, who can accomplish whatever I clearly and distinctly know to be possible.

For although much exists in me of which I am not yet conscious (for example in that passage I did, as a fact, assume that I was not yet aware that my mind had the power of moving the body, and that it was substantially united with it), yet since that which I do perceive is adequate to allow of my existing with it as my sole possession, I am certain that God could have created me without putting me in possession of those other attributes of which I am unaware. Hence it was that those additional attributes were judged not to belong to the essence of the mind.

For in my opinion nothing without which a thing can still exist is comprised in its essence, and although mind belongs to the essence of man, to be united to a human body is in the proper sense no part of the essence of mind.

I must also explain what my meaning was in saying that a real distinction cannot be inferred from the fact that one thing is conceived apart from another by means of the abstracting action of the mind when it conceives a thing inadequately, but only from the fact that each of them is comprehended apart from the other in a complete manner, or as a complete thing. 220

For I do not think that an adequate knowledge of the thing is, in this case, required, as M. Arnauld assumes; nay, we have here the difference that if any knowledge is to be adequate, it must embrace all the properties which exist in the thing known. Hence, there is none but God who knows that He has adequate cognition of all things.

But a created mind actually possessed of adequate knowledge in many cases can never know that this is in its possession unless God give it a private revelation of the fact. But in order to have adequate knowledge of anything, it requires merely to have in itself a power of knowing what is adequate for that thing. And this can easily occur. But in order to know that he has this knowledge, or that God has put nothing in the thing in question over and above what he has knowledge of, a man's power of knowing would need to equal the infinite capacity of God – an obvious absurdity.

But now, in order to apprehend a real distinction between two things, we do not need to have adequate knowledge of them, unless we can be aware that it is adequate; but this being unattainable, as has just been said, it follows that an adequate knowledge is not required.

Hence, when I said that to apprehend one thing apart from

221   another by means of an act of abstraction on the part of the intellect when its conceptions are inadequate, is not sufficient, I did not think that it would be thence inferred that an adequate cognition was required for the purpose of inferring a real distinction, but merely a cognition which we had not, by an intellectual abstraction, rendered inadequate.

It is one thing for a cognition to be entirely adequate, of which fact we could never be sure unless it was revealed by God; it is quite another for our knowledge to have sufficient adequacy to let us see that we have not rendered it inadequate by an a intellectual abstraction.

Similarly, when I said that a thing must be comprehended in a complete manner, I meant not that the intellectual operation must be adequate, but merely that we must have a knowledge of the thing sufficient to let us know that it is complete.

I thought this had been sufficiently plain from previous and subsequent passages alike; for, shortly before I had distinguished incomplete from complete entities and had said that each single thing that has a really distinct existence, must be understood to be an entity in itself and diverse from every other.

But afterwards, preserving the same meaning as when I said that I understood in a complete manner what body is, I immediately added that I understood also that mind is something complete; I thus took 'to understand in a complete manner' and 'to understand that a thing is something complete' in one and the same sense.

But at this point a question may justly be raised as to what I understand by a complete thing, and how to prove that, understanding two things to be complete in isolation from one another is sufficient to establish a real distinction between them.

222   Therefore, to the first query I reply that by a complete thing I mean merely a substance endowed with those forms or attributes which suffice to let me recognise that it is a substance.

For we do not have immediate cognition of substances, as has been elsewhere noted; rather from the mere fact that we perceive certain forms or attributes which must inhere in something in order to have existence, we name the thing in which they exist a substance.

But if, afterwards, we desired to strip that substance of those attributes by which we apprehend it, we should utterly destroy our knowledge of it; and thus, while we might indeed apply words to it, they would not be words of the meaning of which we had a clear and distinct perception.

I do not ignore the fact that certain substances are popularly called incomplete substances. But if they are said to be incomplete, because they cannot exist by themselves [and unsupported by other things], I confess it seems to me to be a contradiction for them to be substances; i.e. for them to be things subsisting by themselves and at the same time incomplete, i.e. not capable of subsisting by themselves. But it is true that in another sense they can be called incomplete substances; viz. in a sense which allows that, in so far as they are substances, they have no lack of completeness, and merely asserts that they are incomplete in so far as they are referred to some other substance, in unison with which they form a single self-subsistent thing [distinct from everything else].

Thus, the hand is an incomplete substance, when taken in relation with the body, of which it is a part; but, regarded alone, it is a complete substance. Quite in the same way mind and body are incomplete substances viewed in relation to the man who is the unity which together they form; but, taken alone, they are complete.

For, as to be extended, divisible, possessed of figure, etc. are the forms or attributes by which I recognise that substance called body; so, to be a knowing, willing, doubting being, etc. are the forms by which I recognise the substance called mind; and I know that thinking substance is a complete thing, no less than that which is extended.   223

But it can nowise be maintained that, in the words of M. Arnauld, body is related to mind as genus is to species;[32] for, although the genus can be apprehended apart from this or that specific difference, the species can by no means be thought apart from the genus.

For, to illustrate, we easily apprehend figure, without thinking at all of a circle (although that mental act is not distinct unless we refer to some specific figure, and it does not give us a complete thing, unless it embraces the nature of the body); but we are cognisant of no specific difference belonging to the circle, unless at the same time we think of figure.

32 Above, p. 231.

But mind can be perceived clearly and distinctly, or sufficiently so to let it be considered to be a complete thing without any of those forms or attributes by which we recognise that body is a substance, as I think I have sufficiently shown in the second Meditation; and body is understood distinctly and as a complete thing apart from the attributes attaching to the mind.

Nevertheless M. Arnauld here urges that although a certain notion of myself an be obtained without a knowledge of the body, if yet does not thence result that this knowledge is complete and adequate, so as to make me sure that I am not in error in excluding the body from my essence. He elucidates his meaning by taking as an illustration the triangle inscribed in a semicircle, which we can clearly and distinctly know to be right-angled, though we do not know, or even deny, that the square on its base is equal to the squares on its sides; and nevertheless we cannot thence infer that we can have a [right-angled] triangle, the square on the base of which is not equal to the squares on the sides.

But, as to this illustration, the example differs in many respects from the case in hand.

For firstly, although perhaps a triangle may be taken in the concrete as a substance possessing triangular shape, certainly the property of having the square on the base equal to the squares on the sides is not a substance; so too, neither can either of these two things be understood to be a complete thing in the sense in which mind and body are; indeed, they cannot be called things in the sense in which I used the word when I said that I might comprehend one thing (i.e. one complete thing) apart from the other, etc. as is evident from the succeeding words – Besides, I discover in myself faculties, etc. For I did not assert these faculties to be things, but distinguished them accurately from things or substances.[33]

Secondly, although we can clearly and distinctly understand that the triangle in the semicircle is right-angled, without noting that the square on its base equals those on its sides, we yet cannot clearly apprehend a triangle in which the square on the base is equal to those on the sides, without at the same time perceiving that it is

33 For this last clause the French version has 'rather I wished to make a distinction between things, i.e. between substances, and the modes of these things, i.e. the faculties of these substances.'

right-angled. But we do clearly and distinctly perceive mind without body and body without mind.

Thirdly, although our concept of the triangle inscribed in the semicircle may be such as not to comprise the equality between the square on its base and those on its sides, it cannot be such that no ratio between the square on the base and those on the sides is held to prevail in the triangle in question; and hence, so long as we remain ignorant of what the ratio is, nothing can be denied of the triangle other than what we clearly know not to belong to it: but to know this in the case of the equality of the ratio is entirely impossible. Now, on the other hand, there is nothing included in the concept of body that belongs to the mind; and nothing in that of mind that belongs to the body.

Therefore, though I said that it was sufficient to be able to apprehend one thing clearly and distinctly apart from another, etc., we cannot go on to complete the argument thus: but I clearly and distinctly apprehend this triangle, etc. Firstly, because the ratio between the square on the base and those on the sides is not a complete thing. Secondly, because that ratio is clearly understood only in the case of the right-angled triangle. Thirdly, because the triangle itself cannot be distinctly apprehended if the ratio between the squares on the base and on the sides is denied.

But now I must explain how it is that, from the mere fact that I apprehend one substance clearly and distinctly apart from another, I am sure that the one excludes the other.

226

Really the notion of substance is just this – that which can exist by itself, without the aid of any other substance. No one who perceives two substances by means of two diverse concepts ever doubts that they are really distinct.

Consequently, if I had not been in search of a certitude greater that the vulgar, I should have been satisfied with showing in the second Meditation that mind was apprehended as a thing that subsists, although nothing belonging to the body be ascribed to it, and conversely that body was understood to be something subsistent without anything being attributed to it that pertains to the mind. And I should have added nothing more in order to prove that there was a real distinction between mind and body: because commonly we judge that all things stand to each other in respect to their actual relations in the same way as they are related in our consciousness.[34] But, since one of those hyperbolical doubts adduced in the first Meditation went so far as to prevent me from being sure of this very fact (viz. that things are in their true nature[35] exactly as we perceive them to be), so long as I supposed that I had not knowledge of the author of my being, all that I have said about God and about truth in the third, fourth and fifth Meditations serves to further the conclusion as to the real distinction between mind and body, which is finally completed in Meditation 6.

227   My opponent, however, says, I apprehend the triangle inscribed in the semicircle without knowing that the square on its base is equal to the squares on the sides. True, that triangle may indeed be apprehended although there is no thought of the ratio prevailing between the squares on the base and sides; but we can never think that this ratio must be denied. It is quite otherwise in the case of the mind where, not only do we understand that it exists apart from the body, but also that all the attributes of body may be denied of it; for reciprocal exclusion of one another belongs to the nature of substances.

There is no conflict between my theory and the point M. Arnauld next brings up, that it is no marvel if, in deducing my existence from the fact that I think, the idea I thus form of myself represents me merely as a thinking being. For, similarly when I examine the nature of body I find nothing at all in it that savours of thought; and there is no better proof of the distinctness of two things than if, when we study each separately, we find nothing in the one that does not differ from what we find in the other.

[FOURTH REPLIES]

*   *   *

204   The power of thinking seems to be attached to corporeal organs, since we can believe it to be asleep in infants, extinguished in the case of lunatics; and this is an objection strongly urged by those impious men whose aim is the soul's slaughter.

[FOURTH OBJECTIONS]

34 *perceptionem*, Latin version; *pensée*, French version.
35 *juxta veritatem*.

The fact that the power of thinking is asleep in infants and in 228
maniacs – though not indeed extinct, yet troubled – should not
make us believe that it is conjoined with the corporeal organs in
such a way as to be incapable of existing apart from them. The fact
that our thought is often in our experience impeded by them, does
not allow us to infer that it is produced by them; for this there is not
even the slightest proof.

I do not, however, deny that the close conjunction between soul
and body of which our senses constantly give us experience, is the 229
cause of our not perceiving their real distinction without attentive
reflection. But, in my judgment, those who frequently revolve in
their thought what was said in the second Meditation, will easily
persuade themselves that mind is distinguished from body not by a
mere fiction or intellectual abstraction, but is known as a distinct
thing because it is really distinct.

[FOURTH REPLIES]

* * *

Pray remember that it was not as an actual fact and in reality, but 122
merely by a mental fiction, that you so stoutly resisted the claim of
all bodies to be more than phantasms, in order that you might draw
the conclusion that you were merely a thinking being; for
otherwise there is perhaps a risk you might believe that you could
draw the conclusion that you were in truth nothing other than
mind, or thought, or a thinking being. This we find worthy of
mention only in connection with the first two Meditations, in
which you show clearly that it is at least certain that you, who
think, exist. But let us pause a little here. Up to this point you
know that you are a being that thinks; but you do not know what
this thinking thing is. What if that were a body which by its various
motions and encounters produces that which we call thought? For,
granted that you rejected the claim of every sort of body, you may
have been deceived in this, because you did not rule out yourself,
who are a body. For how will you prove that a body cannot think, 123
or that its bodily motions are not thought itself? Possibly even, the
whole bodily system, which you imagine you have rejected, or
some of its parts, say the parts composing the brain, can unite to
produce those motions which we call thoughts. 'I am a thinking

thing,' you say; but who knows but you are a corporeal motion, or a body in motion?

[SECOND OBJECTIONS]

129   You warn me to remember that it was not actually but merely by a mental fiction that I rejected the claim of bodies to be more than phantasms, in order to draw the conclusion that I was merely a thinking being, so as to avoid thinking that it was a consequence of this that I was really nothing more than mind. But in the second Meditation I have already shown that I bore this in mind sufficiently; here are the words: But perhaps it is the case that these very things, which I thus suppose to be non-existent because they are unknown to me, do not in very truth differ from that self which I know. I cannot tell; this is not the subject I am now discussing, etc. But these words I meant expressly to warn the reader that in that passage I did not as yet ask whether the mind was distinct from the body, but was merely investigating these properties of mind of which I am able to attain to sure and evident knowledge. And, since I discovered many such properties, I can only in a qualified sense admit what you subjoin, namely, That I am yet ignorant as to what a thinking thing is. For though I confess that as yet I have not discovered whether that thinking thing is the same as the body or something diverse from it, I do not, on that account, admit that I have no knowledge of the mind. Who has ever had such an acquaintance with anything as to know that there was absolutely nothing in it of which he was not aware? But in proportion as we perceive more in anything, the better do we say we know it; thus
130   we have more knowledge of those men with whom we have lived a long time, than of those whose face merely we have seen or whose name we have heard, even though they too are not said to be absolutely unknown. It is in this sense that I think I have demonstrated that the mind, considered apart from what is customarily attributed to the body, is better known than the body viewed as separate from the mind; and this alone was what I intended to maintain.

But I see what you hint at, namely, that since I have written only six Meditations on first Philosophy my readers will marvel that in the first two no further conclusion is reached than that I have just now mentioned, and that hence they will think the meditations to be too meagre, and unworthy of publication. To this I reply merely that I have no fear that anyone who reads with judgment what I have written should have occasion to suspect that my matter gave out; and moreover it appeared highly reasonable to confine to separate Meditations matters which demand a particular attention and must be considered apart from others.

Nothing conduces more to the obtaining of a secure knowledge of reality than a previous accustoming of ourselves to entertain doubts especially about corporeal things; and although I had long ago seen several books written by the academics and sceptics about this subject and felt some disgust in serving up again this stale dish, I could not for the above reasons refuse to allot to this subject one whole Meditation. I should be pleased also if my readers would expend not merely the little time which is required for reading it, in thinking over the matter of which the Meditation treats, but would give months, or at least weeks, to this, before going on further; for in this way the rest of the work will yield them a much richer harvest.

Further, since our previous ideas of what belongs to the mind have been wholly confused and mixed up with the ideas of sensible objects, and this was the first and chief reason why none of the propositions asserted of God and the soul could be understood with sufficient clearness, I thought I should perform something worth the doing if I showed how the properties or qualities of the soul are to be distinguished from those of the body. For although many have already maintained that, in order to understand the facts[36] of metaphysics, the mind must be abstracted from the senses, no one hitherto, so far as I know, has shown how this is to be done. The true, and in my judgment, the only way to do this is found in my second Meditation, but such is its nature that it is not enough to have once seen how it goes; much time and many repetitions are required if we would, by forming the contrary habit of distinguishing intellectual from corporeal matters, for at least a few days, obliterate the life-long custom of confounding them. This appeared to me to be a very sound reason for treating of nothing further in the said Meditation.

131

36 Latin version; *choses immaterielles ou metaphysiques*, French version.

But besides this you here ask how I prove that a body cannot think. Pardon me if I reply that I have not yet given ground for the raising of this question, for I first treat of it in the sixth Meditation. Here are the words: In order that I may be sure that one thing is diverse from another, it is sufficient that I should be able to conceive[37] the one apart from the other, etc., and shortly afterwards I say: Although I have a body very closely conjoined with me, yet since, on the one hand, I have a clear and distinct idea of myself, in so far as I am a thinking thing and not extended; and, on the other hand, I have a distinct idea of the body in so far as it is an extended, not a thinking thing, it is certain that I (that is the mind [or soul, by which I am what I am]) am really distinct from my body and can exist without it. It is easy from this to pass to the following: everything that can think is mind or is called mind, but, since mind and body are really distinct, no body is a mind; hence no body can think.

I do not here see what you are able to deny. Do you deny that in order to recognise a real distinctness between objects it is sufficient for us to conceive one of them clearly apart from the other? If so, offer us some surer token of real distinction. I believe that none such can be found. What will you say? That those things are really distinct each of which can exist apart from the other. But once more I ask how you will know that one thing can be apart from the other; this, in order to be a sign of the distinctness, should be known. Perhaps you will say that it is given to you by the senses, since you can see, touch, etc., the one thing while the other is absent. But the trustworthiness of the senses is inferior to that of the intellect, and it is in many ways possible for one and the same thing to appear under various guises or in several places or in different manners, and so to be taken to be two things. And finally if you bear in mind what was said at the end of the second Meditation about wax, you will see that properly speaking not even are bodies themselves perceived by sense, but that they are perceived by the intellect alone, so that there is no difference between perceiving by sense one thing apart from another, and having an idea of one thing and understanding that that idea is not

37 French version; *intelligere*, Latin verison.

the same as an idea of something else. Moreover, this knowledge can be drawn from no other source than the fact that the one thing is perceived apart from the other; nor can this be known with certainty unless the ideas in each case are clear and distinct. Hence that sign you offer of real distinctness must be reduced to my criterion in order to be infallible.

But if any people deny that they have distinct ideas of mind and body, I can do nothing further than ask them to give sufficient attention to what is said in the second Meditation. I beg them to note that the opinion they perchance hold, namely, that the parts of the brain join their forces[38] with the soul[39] to form thoughts, has not arisen from any positive ground, but only from the fact that they have never had experience of separation from the body, and have not seldom been hindered by it in their operations, and that similarly if anyone had from infancy continually worn irons on his legs, he would think that those irons were part of his own body and that he needed them in order to walk.

. [SECOND REPLIES]

* * *

I shall add but few words about the essence of the soul and the distinction between soul and body; for I confess that the speculations of this wonderful genius have so exhausted me that I can add but little more. If appears that the distinction between soul and body, if real, is proved by the fact that they can be conceived as distinct and as isolated from each other. Here I leave my opponent to contend with (Duns) Scotus, who says that — In so far as one thing can be conceived as distinct and separate from another, the adequate distinction to draw between them is what he calls a formal and objective one, which is intermediate between a real distinction and a distinction of reason. It is thus that he distinguishes between the Divine justice and the Divine pity. They have, he says, concepts formally diverse prior to any operation of the understanding, so that, even then, the one is not the other: yet it does not

100

---

38 *concurrant.*
39 This phrase is only in the French version.

follow that, because God's justice can be conceived apart from his pity, they can also exist apart.

[FIRST OBJECTIONS]

120   In the matter of the formal distinction which the learned theologian claims to draw from Scotus, my reply is briefly to the effect that this distinction in no way differs from a modal one, and applies only to incomplete entities, which I have accurately demarcated from complete beings. This is sufficient to cause one thing to be conceived separately and as distinct from another by the abstracting action of a mind when it conceives the thing inadequately, without sufficing to cause two things to be thought of so distinctly and separately that we understand each to be an entity in itself and diverse from every other; in order that we may do this a real distinction is absolutely necessary. Thus, for example, there is a formal distinction between the motion and the figure of the same body, and I can quite well think of the motion without the figure and of the figure apart from the motion and of either apart from the body; but nevertheless I cannot think of the motion in a complete

121   manner apart from the thing in which the motion exists nor of the figure in isolation from the object which has the figure; nor finally can I feign that anything incapable of having figure can possess motion, or that what is incapable of movement has figure. So it is also that neither can I understand justice apart from a just being, or compassion apart from the compassionate; nor may I imagine that the same being as is just cannot be compassionate. But yet I understand in a complete manner what body is [that is to say I conceive of body as a complete thing[40]], merely by thinking that it is extended, has figure, can move, etc., and by denying[41] of it everything which belongs to the nature of mind. Conversely also I understand that mind is something complete which doubts, knows, wishes, etc., although I deny that anything belongs to it which is contained in the idea of body. But this could not be unless there were a real distinction between mind and body.

This is my answer, gentlemen, to your friend's subtle and most serviceable criticisms. If it still is defective, I ask to be informed

40 This clause is found only in the French version.
41 Latin version; *encore que je nie*, French version.

about the omissions or the blunders it contains. To secure this from my critic through your good offices, would be to have a great kindness conferred upon me.

[FIRST REPLIES]

* * *

[Mind–Body Interaction]

In addition, it can be maintained that the argument[42] proves too much and conducts us to the Platonic doctrine (refuted nevertheless by our author) that nothing corporeal belongs to the essence of man, who is hence entirely spirit, while his body is merely the vehicle of spirit; whence follows the definition of man as a spirit that makes use of a body.

But if you reply that body is not absolutely excluded from my essence, but merely in so far precisely as I am a thinking being, the fear seems likely to arise that someone will entertain a suspicion that the knowledge of myself, in so far as I am a thinking being, is not the knowledge of anything fully and adequately conceived, but is known only inadequately and by a certain intellectual abstraction.

Hence, just as geometers conceive of a line as length without breadth, and of a surface as length and breadth together without depth, although there is no length apart from breadth, no breadth without depth, someone may perhaps doubt whether everything that thinks is not likewise something extended; a thing in which, nevertheless, over and above the attributes common to other extended things, e.g. the possession of figure, motion, etc., is found this unique[43] faculty of thinking. Whence it follows that while by an intellectual abstraction, it can be apprehended by means of this character alone and unaided as a thing that thinks, it is quite possible that in reality corporeal attributes are compatible with a thinking being; just as quantity can be mentally conceived by means of length alone, while it is possible that in reality breadth and depth go along with length in every quantity.

[FOURTH OBJECTIONS]

203

204

---

42 i.e. the argument for the real distinction between soul and body.
43 *peculiaris cogitandi virtus.*

227   I fail to see how this argument proves too much. For, in order to prove that one thing is really distinct from another, nothing less can be said, than that the divine power is able to separate one from the other. I thought I took sufficient care to prevent anyone thence

228   inferring that man was merely a spirit that makes use of a body; for in this very sixth Meditation in which I have dealt with the distinction between mind and body, I have at the same time proved that mind was substantially united with body; and I employed arguments, the efficacy of which in establishing this proof I cannot remember to have seen in any other case surpassed. Likewise, just as one who said that a man's arm was a substance really distinct from the rest of his body, would not therefore deny that it belonged to the nature of the complete man, and as in saying that the arm belongs to the nature of the complete man no suspicion is raised that it cannot subsist by itself, so I think that I have neither proved too much in showing that mind can exist apart from body, nor yet too little in saying that it is substantially united to the body, because that substantial union does not prevent the formation of a clear and distinct concept of the mind alone as of a complete thing. Hence this differs greatly from the concept of a superficies or of a line, which cannot be apprehended as complete things unless, in addition to length and breadth, depth be ascribed to them.

[FOURTH REPLIES]

*   *   *

343   It still remains to be explained, how that union [i.e., between mind and body] and apparent intermingling, or confusion, can be found in you, if you are incorporeal, unextended and indivisible. For if you are not greater than a point, how can you be united with the entire body, which is of such great magnitude? How, at least, can you be united with the brain, or some minute part in it, which (as has been said) must yet have some magnitude or extension,

344   however small it be? If you are wholly without parts, how can you mix or appear to mix with its minute subdivisions? For there is no mixture unless each of the things to be mixed has parts that can mix with one another. Further, if you are discrete, how could you be involved with and form one thing along with matter itself?

Again since conjunction or union exists between certain parts, ought there not to be a relation of similarity[44] between parts of this sort? But what must the union of the corporeal with the incorporeal be thought to be? Do we conceive how stone and air are fused together, as in pumice stone, so as to become a fusion of uniform character?[45] Yet the similarity between stone and air which itself is also a body, is greater than that between body and soul, or a wholly incorporeal mind. Further, ought not that union to take place by means of the closest contact? But how, as I said before, can that take place, apart from body? How will that which is corporeal seize upon that which is incorporeal, so to hold it conjoined with itself, or how will the incorporeal grasp the corporeal, so as reciprocally to keep it bound to itself, if in it, the incorporeal, there is nothing which it can use to grasp the other, or by which it can be grasped.

Hence, since you admit that you feel pain, I ask you how you think that you, if you are incorporeal and unextended, are capable of experiencing the sensation of pain. Thus the affection paid can only be understood as arising from some pulling asunder of bodily parts when something interferes and annuls their continuity. For example a state of pain is an unnatural state, but how can that be in an unnatural state or be affected contrary to nature, which by nature is of one sort, simple, indivisible and immutable? Again since pain is either alteration, or cannot occur without it, how can that be altered, which, being more devoid of parts than a point, cannot be altered nor can cease to be just as it is, unless it terms into nothing? I add also: since pain comes from the foot, the arm, and from other regions at the same time, ought there not to be in you various parts, in which you receive it in various ways, in order not to be confused and to regard it as being the pain of merely one part. But, in a word, the general difficulty always remains, viz. how the corporeal can have anything in common with the incorporeal, or what relationship may be established between the one and the other.

345

[FIFTH OBJECTIONS]

44 *proportio.*
45 *ut germana inde fiat compositio?*

390   What you say at this point relatively to the union of mind and
        body is similar to what precedes. At no place do you bring an
        objection to my arguments; you only set forth the doubts which
        you think follow from my conclusions, though they arise merely
        from your wishing to subject to the scrutiny of the imagination
        matters which, by their own nature, do not fall under it. Thus
        when you wish to compare the union of mind and body with the
        mixture of two bodies, it is enough for me to reply that no such
        comparison ought to be set up, because the two things are wholly
        diverse, and we must not imagine that there are parts in mind
        because it is aware of parts in body. Whence do you derive the
        conclusion that everything which mind knows must exist in mind?
        If that were so, then, when it was aware of the magnitude of the
        earth, it would be obliged to have that object within it, and
        consequently would not only be extended but greater in extent
        than the whole world.

                                                        [FIFTH REPLIES]

                             *   *   *

        How the soul moves the body if it is not material? and how it can
        receive the specific forms [*espèces*] of corporeal objects?
                        [FROM THE AUTHOR OF THE FIFTH OBJECTIONS]

AT IXA As for the two questions added at the end, viz. – how the soul
213   moves the body if it is not material? and how it can receive the
        specific forms of corporeal objects? these give me here merely the
        opportunity of declaring that our author had no right, under
        pretext of criticising me, to propound a mass of questions like this,
        the solution of which was not necessary for the proof of what I
        have written, questions of which the most ignorant man might
        raise more in a quarter of an hour than the wisest could solve in a
        lifetime. Thus I do not feel called upon to answer any of them.
        Likewise these objections, among other things, presuppose an
        explanation of the nature of the union between soul and body, a
        matter of which I have not yet treated. But to you, for your own
        benefit, I declare that the whole of the perplexity involved in these
        questions arises entirely from a false supposition that can by no
        manner of means by proved, viz. that if the soul and the body are

two substances of diverse nature, that prevents them from being capable of acting on one another; for, on the contrary, those who admit the existence of real accidents, like heat, weight, and so forth, do not doubt that these accidents have the power of acting on the body, and nevertheless there is more difference between them and it, i.e. between accidents and a substance, than there is between two substances.

[LETTER TO CLERSELIER APPENDED TO THE FIFTH REPLIES]

* * *

[On the Meditations]

AT VII
128

It would be well worth the doing if, hard upon your solution of the difficulties, you advanced as premises certain definitions, postulates and axioms, and thence drew conclusions, conducting the whole proof by the geometrical method, in the use of which you are so highly expert. Thus would you cause each reader to have everything in his mind, as it were at a single glance, and to be penetrated throughout with a sense of the Divine being.

[SECOND OBJECTIONS]

In the matter of the counsel you give me about propounding my arguments in geometrical fashion, in order that the reader may perceive them as it were with a single glance, it is worth while setting forth here the extent to which I have followed this method and that to which I intend in future to follow it. Now there are two things that I distinguish in the geometrical mode of writing, viz. the order and the method of proof.

155

The order consists merely in putting forward those things first that should be known without the aid of what comes subsequently, and arranging all other matters so that their proof depends solely on what precedes them. I certainly tried to follow this order as accurately as possible in my Meditations; and it was through keeping to this that I treated of the distinction between the mind and the body, not in the second Meditation, but finally in the sixth, and deliberately and consciously omitted much, because it required as explanation of much else besides.

Further, the method of proof is two-fold, one being analytic, the other synthetic.

Analysis shows the true way by which a thing was methodically discovered and derived, as it were effect from cause,[46] so that, if the reader care to follow it and give sufficient attention to everything, he understands the matter no less perfectly and makes it as much his own as if he had himself discovered it. But it contains nothing to incite belief in an inattentive or hostile reader; for if the very least thing brought forward escapes his notice, the necessity of the conclusions is lost; and on many matters which, nevertheless, should be specially noted, it often scarcely touches, because they are clear to anyone who gives sufficient attention to them.

Synthesis contrariwise employs an opposite procedure, one in which the search goes as it were from effect to cause[47] (though often here the proof itself is from cause to effect to a greater extent than in the former case). It does indeed clearly demonstrate its conclusions, and it employs a long series of definitions, postulates, axioms, theorems and problems so that if one of the conclusions that follow is denied, it may at once be shown to be contained in what has gone before. Thus the reader, however hostile and obstinate, is compelled to render his assent. Yet this method is not so satisfactory as the other and does not equally well content the eager learner, because it does not show the way in which the matter taught was discovered.

It was this synthesis alone that the ancient geometers employed in their writings, not because they were wholly ignorant of the analytic method, but, in my opinion, because they set so high a value on it that they wished to keep it to themselves as an important secret.

But I have used in my Meditations only analysis, which is the best and truest method of teaching. On the other hand synthesis, doubtless the method you here ask me to use, though it very suitably finds a place after analysis in the domain of geometry, nevertheless cannot so conveniently be applied to these metaphysical matters we are discussing.

For there is this difference between the two cases, viz. that the primary notions that are the presuppositions of geometrical proofs harmonise with the use of our senses, and are readily granted by all. Hence, no difficulty is involved in this case, except in the proper

46 *tanquam a priori.*
47 *tanquam a posteriori quaesitam.*

deduction of the consequences. But this may be performed by people of all sorts, even by the inattentive, if only they remember what has gone before; and the minute subdivisions of propositions is designed for the purpose of rendering citation easy and thus making people recollect even against their will.

On the contrary, nothing in metaphysics causes more trouble than the making the perception of its primary notions clear and distinct. For, though in their own nature they are as intelligible as, or even more intelligible than those the geometricians study, yet being contradicted by the many preconceptions of our senses to which we have since our earliest years been accustomed, they cannot be perfectly apprehended except by those who give strenuous attention and study to them, and withdraw their minds as far as possible from matters corporeal. Hence if they alone were brought forward it would be easy for anyone with a zeal for contradiction to deny them.

This is why my writing took the form of Meditations rather than that of philosophical disputations or the theorems and problems of a geometer; so that hence I might by this very fact testify that I had no dealings except with those who will not shrink from joining me in giving the matter attentive care and meditation. For from the very fact that anyone girds himself up for an attack upon the truth, he makes himself less capable of perceiving the truth itself, since he withdraws his mind from the consideration of those reasons that tend to convince him of it, in order to discover others that have the opposite effect.

But[48] perhaps someone will here raise the objection, that, while indeed a man ought not to seek for hostile arguments when he knows that it is the truth that is set before him, yet, so long as this is in doubt, it is right that he should fully explore all the arguments on either side, in order to find out which are the stronger. According to this objection it is unfair of me to want to have the truth of my contentions admitted before they have been fully scrutinised, while prohibiting any consideration of those reasons that oppose them.

This would certainly be a just criticism if any of the matters in

158

48 The French version here comes to an end, adding only a short paragraph of seven lines by way of formal conclusion.

which I desire attention and absence of hostility in my reader were capable of withdrawing him from the consideration of any others in which there was the least hope of finding greater truth than in mine. But consider that in what I bring forward you find the most extreme doubt about all matters, and that there is nothing I more strongly urge than that every single thing should be most carefully examined and that nothing should be admitted but what has been rendered so clear and distinct to our scrutiny that we cannot withhold our assent from it. Consider too that, on the other hand, there is nothing else from which I wish to divert the minds of my readers, save beliefs which they have never properly examined and which are derived from no sound reasoning, but from the senses alone. Therefore I hardly think that anyone will believe that there is much risk in confining his attention to my statement of the case; the danger will be precisely that of turning his gaze away from preconceptions in order to behold new truths that in some measure conflict with them, and dissipate the darkness of the prejudices[49] due to our senses.

Hence, in the first place, I rightly require singular attention on the part of my readers and have specially selected the style of writing which I thought would best secure it and which, I am convinced, will bring my readers more profit than they would acquire if I had used the synthetic method, one which would have made them appear to have learned more than they really had. But besides this I deem it quite fair to ignore wholly and to despise as of no account the criticisms of those who refuse to accompany me in my Meditations and cling to their preconceived opinions.

But I know how difficult it will be, even for one who does attend and seriously attempt to discover the truth, to have before his mind the entire bulk of what is contained in my Meditations, and at the same time to have distinct knowledge of each part of the argument; and yet, in my opinion, one who is to reap the full benefit from my work must know it both as a whole and in detail. Consequently I append here something in the synthetic style that may I hope be somewhat to my readers' profit. I should, however, like them kindly to notice that I have not cared to include here so much as

49 The Latin reads – *tenebrasque offundunt* (*hoc est ad praejudicia sensuum*). I propose to omit *ad*.

comes into my Meditations, for that would have caused me to be much more prolix than in the Meditations themselves, nor shall I explain in such accurate detail that which I do include; this is partly for brevity and partly to prevent anyone, believing that what is here written is sufficient, examining without adequate care the actual Meditations, a work from which, I am convinced, much more profit will be derived.

ARGUMENTS DEMONSTRATING THE EXISTENCE OF GOD AND THE DISTINCTION BETWEEN SOUL AND BODY, DRAWN UP IN GEOMETRICAL FASHION

160

Definitions

1 *Thought* is a word that covers everything that exists in us in such a way that we are immediately conscious of it. Thus all the operations of will, intellect, imagination, and of the senses are thoughts. But I have added *immediately*, for the purpose of excluding that which is a consequence of our thought; for example, voluntary movement, which, though indeed depending on thought as on a causal principle,[50] is yet itself not thought.

2 *Idea* is a word by which I understand the form of any thought, that form by the immediate awareness of which I am conscious of that said thought; in such a way that, when understanding what I say, I can express nothing in words, without that very fact making it certain that I possess the idea of that which these words signify. And thus it is not only images depicted in the imagination that I call ideas; nay, to such images I here decidedly refuse the title of ideas, in so far as they are pictures in the corporeal imagination, i.e. in some part of the brain. They are ideas only in so far as they constitute the form of the mind itself that is directed towards that part of the brain.

161

---

50 *cogitationem quidem pro principio habet*; '*volonté pour son principe*', French version, which is not so pointed.

3 By the *objective reality of an idea* I mean that in respect of which the thing represented in the idea is an entity,[51] in so far as that exists in the idea; and in the same way we can talk of objective perfection, objective device, etc. For whatever we perceive as being as it were in the objects of our ideas, exists in the ideas themselves objectively.

4 To exist *formally* is the term applied where the same thing exists in the object of an idea in such a manner that the way in which it exists in the object is exactly like what we know of it when aware of it; it exists *eminently* when, though not indeed of identical quality, it is yet of such amount as to be able to fulfil the function of an exact counterpart.

5 Everything in which there resides immediately, as in a subject, or by means of which there exists anything that we perceive, i.e. any property, quality, or attribute, of which we have a real idea, is called a *substance*; neither do we have any idea of substance itself, precisely taken, than that it is a thing in which this something that we perceive or which is present objectively in some of our ideas, exists formally or eminently. For by means of our natural light we know that a real attribute cannot be an attribute of nothing.

6 That substance in which thought immediately resides, I call *mind*[52]. I use the term 'mind' here rather than 'spirit', as 'spirit' is equivocal and is frequently applied to what is corporeal.

7 That substance, which is the immediate subject of extension in space[53], and of the accidents that presuppose extension, e.g. figure, situation, movement in space etc., is called *body*. But we must postpone till later on the inquiry as to whether it is one and the same substance or whether there are two diverse substances to which the names mind and body apply.

162

8 That substance which we understand to be supremely perfect and in which we conceive absolutely nothing involving defect or limitation of its perfection, is called *God*.

51 *entitatem rei representatae per ideam.*
52 The French cannot convey the distinction between *mens* and *anima.* Hence *esprit* has to do duty for both. The French version simply points out the ambiguity of the term.   53 *Extensionis localis.*

9 When we say that any attribute[54] is contained in the nature or concept of anything, that is precisely the same as saying that it is true of that thing or can be affirmed of it.

10 Two substances are said to be really distinct, when each of them can exist apart from the other.

Postulates

The first request I press upon my readers is a recognition of the weakness of the reasons on account of which they have hitherto trusted their senses, and the insecurity of all the judgments they have based upon them. I beg them to resolve this in their minds so long and so frequently that at length they will acquire the habit of no longer reposing too much trust in them. For I deem that this is necessary in order to attain to a perception of the certainty of metaphysical truths [not dependent on the senses].

Secondly, I ask them to make an object of study of their own mind and all the attributes attaching to it, of which they find they cannot doubt, notwithstanding it be supposed that whatever they have at any time derived from their senses is false; and I beg them not to desist from attending to it, until they have acquired the habit of perceiving it distinctly and of believing that it can be more readily known than any corporeal thing.

Thirdly, I bid them carefully rehearse those propositions, intelligible per se, which they find they possess, e.g. that the same thing cannot at the same time both be and not be; that nothing cannot be the efficient cause of anything, and so forth; and thus employ in its purity, and in freedom from the interference of the senses, that clarity of understanding that nature has implanted in them, but which sensuous objects are wont to disturb and obscure. For by this means the truth of the following axioms will easily become evident to them.

Fourthly, I postulate an examination of the ideas of those natures in which there is a complex of many coexistent attributes, such as e.g. the nature of the triangle or of the square, or of any other figure; and so too the nature of mind, the nature of body, and above all the nature of God, or of a supremely perfect entity. My

163

54 French version; *quid*, Latin version.

readers must also notice that everything which we perceive to be contained in these natures can be truly predicated of the things themselves. For example, because the equality of its three angles to two right angles is contained in the idea of the triangle, and divisibility is contained in the nature of body or of extended thing (for we can conceive nothing that is extended as being so small as not to be capable of being divided in thought at least), we constantly assert that in every triangle the angles are equal to two right angles, and that every body is divisible.

Fifthly, I require my readers to dwell long and much in contemplation of the nature of the supremely perfect Being. Among other things they must reflect that while possible existence indeed attaches to the ideas of all other natures, in the case of the idea of God that existence is not possible but wholly necessary. For from this alone and without any train of reasoning they will learn that God exists, and it will be not less self-evident to them than the fact that number two is even and number three odd, and similar truths. For there are certain truths evident to some people, without proof, that can be made intelligible to others only by a train of reasoning.

Sixthly, I ask people to go carefully over all the examples of clear and distinct perception, and likewise those that illustrate that which is obscure and confused, mentioned in my Meditations, and so accustom themselves to distinguish what is clearly known from what is obscure. For examples teach us better than rules how to do this; and I think that I have there either explained or at least to some extent touched upon all the instances of this subject.

Seventhly and finally, I require them, in virtue of their consciousness that falsity has never been found in matters of clear perception, while, on the contrary, amidst what is only obscurely comprehended they have never come upon the truth, except accidentally, to consider it wholly irrational to regard as doubtful matters that are perceived clearly and distinctly by the understanding in its purity, on account of mere prejudices of the senses and hypotheses in which there is an element of the unknown. By doing so they will readily admit the truth and certainty of the following axioms. Yet I admit that several of them might have been much better explained and should have been brought forward as theorems if I had wished to be more exact.

Axioms or common principles [55]

1 Nothing exists concerning which the question may not be raised – 'what is the cause of its existence?' For this question may be asked even concerning God. Not that He requires any cause in order to exist, but because in the very immensity of His being[56] lies the cause or reason why He needs no cause in order to exist. **165**

2 The present time has no causal dependence on the time immediately preceding it. Hence, in order to secure the continued existence[57] of a thing, no less a cause is required than that needed to produce it at the first.

3 A thing, and likewise an actually existing perfection belonging to anything, can never have nothing, or a non-existent thing, as the cause of its existence.

4 Whatever reality or perfection exists in a thing, exists formally or else eminently in its first and adequate[58] cause.

5 Whence it follows also that the objective reality of our ideas requires a cause in which the same reality is contained not indeed objectively, but formally or else eminently. We have to note that the admission of this axiom is highly necessary for the reason that we must account for our knowledge of all things, both of sensuous and of non-senuous objects, and do so by means of it alone. For whence, e.g., comes our knowledge that there is a heaven? Because we behold it? But that vision does not reach the mind, except in so far as it is an idea, an idea, I say, inhering in the mind itself, and not an image depicted in the fantasy. But neither can we, in virtue of this idea, assert that there is a heaven, except because every idea needs to have some really existing cause of its objective reality; and this cause we judge to be the heaven itself, and so in other cases.

6 There are diverse degrees of reality or (the quality of being an) entity. For substance has more reality than accident or mode; and infinite substance has more than finite substance. Hence there is more objective reality in the idea of substance than in that of accident; more in the idea of an infinite than in that of a finite substance. **166**

55 *notiones*.   56 *naturae*.
57 *ad rem conservandam*.   58 *totale*, French version

7 The will of a thinking being is borne, willingly indeed and freely (for that is of the essence of will), but none the less infallibly, towards the good that it clearly knows. Hence, if it knows certain perfections that it lacks, it will immediately give them to itself if they are in its power [for it will know that it is a greater good for it to possess them, than not to possess them].

8 That which can effect what is greater or more difficult, can also accomplish what is less.

9 It is a greater thing to create or conserve substance than the attributes or properties of substance; it is not, moreover, a greater thing to create that than to conserve its existence, as I have already said.

10 Existence is contained in the idea or concept of everything, because we can conceive nothing except as existent,[59] with this difference, that possible or contingent existence is contained in the concept of a limited thing, but necessary and perfect existence in the concept of a supremely perfect being.

Proposition 1

The knowledge of the existence of God proceeds from the mere consideration of his nature.

Demonstration: To say that something[60] is contained in the nature or concept of anything is the same as to say that it is true of that thing (definition 9). But necessary existence is contained in the concept of God (axiom 10). Hence it is true to affirm of God that necessary existence exists in Him, or that God Himself exists.

And this is the syllogism of which I made use above, in replying to the sixth objection. Its conclusion is self-evident to those who are free from prejudices, as was said in the fifth postulate. But, because it is not easy to arrive at such clearness of mind, we seek to establish it by other methods.

Proposition 2

A posteriori[61] *demonstration of God's existence from the mere fact that the idea of God exists in us.*

59 *nisi sub ratione existentis.*   60 *quelque attribut*, French version.
61 *par ses effets*, French version.

Demonstration: The objective reality of any of our ideas must have a cause, in which the very same reality is contained, not merely objectively but formally, or else eminently (axiom 5). But we do possess the idea of God (definitions 2 and 8), and the objective reality of this idea is contained in us neither formally nor eminently (axiom 6), nor can it be contained in anything other than God Himself (definition 8). Hence this idea of God, which exists in us, must have God as its cause, and hence God exists (axiom 3).

Proposition 3

168

The existence of God is proved by the fact that we, who possess this idea, ourselves exist.

Demonstration: If I had the power of conserving my own existence, I should have had a proportionately greater power of giving myself the perfections that I lack (axioms 8 and 9); for they are only attributes of substance, whereas I am a substance. But I do not have the power of giving myself these perfections; otherwise I should already possess them (axiom 7). Therefore I do not have the power of conserving myself.

Further, I cannot exist without being conserved, whilst I exist, either by myself, if I have that power, or by some other one who has that power (axioms 1 and 2); yet, though I do exist, I have not the power of conserving myself, as has just been proved. Consequently it is another being that conserves my existence.

Besides, He to whom my conservation is due contains within Himself formally or eminently everything that is in me (axiom 4). But there exists in me the perception of many perfections that I do not possess, as well as of the idea of God (definitions 2 and 8). Therefore the perception of the same perfections exists in Him by whom I am conserved.

Finally, this same Being cannot possess the perception of any perfections of which He is lacking, or which He does not possess within Himself either formally or eminently (axiom 7). For, since He has the power of conserving me, as has been already said, He would have the power of bestowing these upon Himself, if He lacked them (axioms 8 and 9). But He possesses the perception of all those that I lack, and which I conceive can exist in God alone, as has been lately proved. Therefore He possesses those formally or eminently within Himself, and hence is God.

169

Corollary

God has created the heaven and the earth and all that in them is. Moreover He can bring to pass whatever we clearly conceive, exactly as we conceive it.

Demonstration: This all follows clearly from the previous proposition. For in it we prove that God exists, from the fact that some one must exist in whom are formally or eminently all the perfections of which we have any idea. But we possess the idea of a power so great that by Him and Him alone, in whom this power is found, must heaven and earth be created, and a power such that likewise whatever else is apprehended by me as possible must be created by Him too. Hence concurrently with God's existence we have proved all this likewise about him.

Proposition 4

There is a real distinction between mind and body.

170   *Demonstration*:   God can effect whatever we clearly perceive just as we perceive it (preceding corollary). But we clearly perceive the mind, i.e. a thinking substance, apart from the body, i.e. apart from any extended substance (postulate 2); and vice versa we can (as all admit) perceive body apart from mind. Hence, at least through the instrumentality of the Divine power, mind can exist apart from body, and body apart from mind.

But now, substances that can exist apart from each other, are really distinct (definition 10). But mind and body are substances (definitions 5, 6 and 7), that can exist apart from each other (just proved). Hence there is a real distinction between mind and body.

Here it must be noted that I employed the Divine power as a means,[62] not because any extraordinary power was needed to effect the separation of mind and body, but because, treating as I did of God alone in what precedes, there was nothing else for me to use. But our knowledge of the real distinctness of two things is unaffected by any question as to the power that disunites them.

[SECOND REPLIES]

*   *   *

62 as a means for proving my point, French version.

PRINCIPLES OF PHILOSOPHY

Author's Letter to the Translator [1] of the
book, which may here serve as Preface

Sir – The version of my Principles which you have taken the
trouble to make is so polished and well-finished that it causes me to
hope that the work may be read by more persons in French than in
Latin, and that it will be better understood. My only apprehension is
that the title may repel certain people who have not been nourished
upon letters, or else who hold philosophy in evil esteem, because that
which has been taught them has not satisfied them; and this makes
me think that it would be a good thing to add a preface which would
expound the subject-matter of the book, the design I had in writing
it, and the use to be derived from it. But although it should be my
business to write this preface because I ought to know these things
better than anyone else, I can on my own account promise nothing
but a summary of the principal points which seem to me as though
they ought to be treated of in it; and I leave it to your discretion to
communicate to the public whatever you deem desirable.

I should have first of all desired to explain in it what philosophy is,
beginning with the most ordinary matters, such as that this word
philosophy signifies the study of wisdom, and that by wisdom we
not only understand prudence in affairs, but also a perfect knowledge of all things that man can know, both for the conduct of his
life and for the conservation of his health and the invention of all the
arts; and that in order that this knowledge should subserve these
ends, it is essential that it should be derived from first causes, so that
in order to study to acquire it (which is properly termed philosophising), we must begin with the investigation of these first causes,
i.e. of the Principles. It is also necessary that these Principles should
have two conditions attached to them; first of all they should be so
clear and evident that the mind of man cannot doubt their truth

1 i.e. the translator into French, the Abbé Claude Picot.

when it attentively applies itself to consider them: in the second place it is on them that the knowledge of other things depends, so that the Principles can be known without these last, but the other things cannot reciprocally be known without the Principles. We must accordingly try to so deduce from these Principles the knowledge of the things that depend on them, that there shall be nothing in the whole series of the deductions made from them which shall not be perfectly manifest. It is really only God alone who has Perfect Wisdom, that is to say, who has a complete knowledge of the truth of all things; but it may be said that men have more wisdom or less according as they have more or less knowledge of the most important truths. And I think that in this there is nothing regarding which all the learned do not concur.

I should in the next place have caused the utility of this philosophy to be considered, and shown that since it extends over the whole range of human knowledge, we are entitled to hold that it alone is what distinguishes us from savages and barbarians, and that the civilisation and refinement of each nation is proportionate to the superiority of its philosophy. In this way a state can have no greater good than the possession of true philosophy. And, in addition, it would have been pointed out that as regards the individual, it is not only useful to live with those who apply themselves to this study, but it is incomparably better to set about it oneself; just as it is doubtless much better to avail oneself of one's own eyes for the direction of one's steps, and by the same means to enjoy the beauty of colour and light, than to close these eyes and trust to the guidance of another. But this last is better than to hold them closed, and not have any but oneself to act as guide. Speaking accurately, living without philosophy is just having the eyes closed without trying to open them; and the pleasure of seeing everything that is revealed to our sight, is not comparable to the satisfaction which is given by the knowledge of those things which are opened up to us by philosophy. And finally, this study is more necessary for the regulation of our manners and for our conduct in life, than is the use of our eyes in the guidance of our steps. The brute beasts who have only their bodies to preserve, devote their constant attention to the search for the sources of their nourishment; but men, in whom the principal part is the mind, ought to make their principal care the search after wisdom, which is its true source of nutriment. And I am likewise able to assure myself that there are many who would not fail to make the search if they had any hope of success in so doing, and knew to what an extent they were capable of it. There does not exist the soul so ignoble, so firmly attached to objects of sense, that it does not sometimes turn away from these to aspire after some other greater good, even although it is frequently ignorant as to wherein that good consists. Those most favoured by fortune, those who have abundance of health, honour and riches, are not exempt from this desire any more than others; on the contrary, I am persuaded that it is those very people who yearn most ardently after another good more perfect and supreme than all those that they possess already. And this sovereign good, considered by the natural reason without the light of faith, is none other than the knowledge of the truth through its first causes, i.e. the wisdom whose study is philosophy. And because all these things are absolutely true, it would not be difficult to persuade men of them, were they well argued and expressed.

But since we are prevented from believing these doctrines by experience, which shows us that those who profess to be philosophers are frequently less wise and reasonable than others who have never applied themselves to the study, I should here have succinctly explained in what all the knowledge we now possess consists, and to what degrees of wisdom we have attained. The first of these contains only notions which are of themselves so clear that they may be acquired without any meditation. The second comprehends all that which the experience of the senses allows us. The third, what the conversation of other men teaches us. And for the fourth we may add to this the reading, not of all books, but especially of those which have been written by persons who are capable of conveying good instruction to us, for this is a species of conversation held with their authors. And it seems to me that all the wisdom that we usually possess is acquired by these four means only; for I do not place divine revelation in the same rank, because it does not lead us by degrees, but raises us at a stroke to an infallible belief. There have indeed from all time been great men who have tried to find a fifth road by which to arrive at wisdom, incomparably more elevated and assured than these other four. That road is to seek out the first causes and the true principles from which reasons may be deduced for all that which we are capable of knowing; and it is those who have made this their special work who have been called philosophers.

At the same time I do not know that up to the present day there have been any in whose case this plan has succeeded. The first and principal whose writings we possess, are Plato and Aristotle, between whom the only difference that exists is that the former, following the steps of his master Socrates, ingenuously confessed that he had never yet been able to discover anything for certain, and was content to set down the things that seemed to him to be probable, for this end adopting certain principles whereby he tried to account for other things. Aristotle, on the other hand, had less candour, and although he had been Plato's disciple for twenty years, and possessed no other principles than his master's, he entirely changed the method of stating them, and proposed them as true and certain although there was no appearance of his having ever held them to be such. But these two men had great minds and much wisdom acquired by the four methods mentioned before, and this gave them great authority, so that those who succeeded them were more bent on following their opinions than in forming better ones of their own. The main dispute between their disciples was as to whether every thing should be doubted, or whether there were some things which were certain. And this carried them, both on the one side and on the other, into extravagant errors; for certain of those who argued for doubt, extended it even to the actions of life, so that they omitted to exercise ordinary prudence in its conduct; and those who supported the doctrine of certainty, supposing it to depend on the senses, trusted to them entirely. To such a point was this carried that it is said that Epicurus ventured to affirm, contrary to all the reasonings of the astronomers, that the sun is no larger than it appears. A fault which may be observed in most disputes is that since the truth is a mean between the two opinions which are maintained, each disputant removes himself so much the further from it the greater his desire to contradict. But the error of those who tended too much to the side of doubt, was not followed for long, and that of the others has been in some degree corrected by the recognition of the fact that in many instances the senses deceive us. At the same time I do not know that it has been entirely removed by showing that certainty is not in the senses, but only in the understanding, when it has evident perceptions; and that while we only possess the knowledge which is acquired by the first four degrees of wisdom, we should not doubt those things that appear to

be true in what concerns the conduct of life, while yet we should
not hold them to be so certain that we may not change our minds
regarding them when obliged to do so by the evidence of reason.
From lack of having known this truth, or else, if there be those who
have known it, from neglecting it, the greater part of those in later
times who aspired to be philosophers, have blindly followed
Aristotle, so that frequently they have corrupted the sense of his
writings, attributing diverse opinions to him which he would not
recognise as his, were he to return to this world; and those who
have not followed him (amongst whom many of the best minds are
to be found) have yet been imbued with his teaching in their youth,
for it forms the sole teaching in the schools; and these minds were so
much occupied with this, that they were incapable of attaining to a
knowledge of true principles. And although I respect them all and
would never wish to incur the odium of denouncing them, I can
give a proof of my assertion which I do not think any one of them
will gainsay, and this is that all have taken for granted some
particular principle which they have not perfectly understood. For
example I have known none of them who did not presuppose
weight in terrestrial bodies, but although experiment proves to us
very clearly that the bodies we call weighty descend towards the
centre of the earth, we do not for all that know the nature of what is
called gravity, that is, the reason or principle which causes bodies to
descend thus, and we must derive it from elsewhere. The same may
be said of the vacuum and of atoms, of heat and cold, of dryness and
damp, and of salt, sulphur, mercury, and all other similar things
which have been adopted as their principles by some. And none of
the conclusions deduced from a principle which is not evident can
be evident even though they are deduced from them in a manner
which is evident and valid, and from this it follows that none of the
reasonings which they rested on principles such as these could give
them any certain knowledge of anything, nor in consequence cause
them to advance one step in the search after wisdom. And if they
have discovered any truth this has only come to pass by means of
certain of the four methods above mentioned. All the same I do not
desire one whit to detract from the honour to which each of them
may aspire, I am only obliged to say for the consolation of those
who have never studied, that just as in travelling while we turn our
backs on the place to which we desire to go, the longer and quicker

we walk the further we recede from the place we are making for, so that though we are afterwards put back into the right way, we cannot arrive at our destination as soon as if we had not walked in the wrong direction before; so when our principles are bad, the more we cultivate them and the more carefully we apply ourselves to derive from them various consequences, thinking that we are philosophising very well, the further we are moving from the knowledge of the truth and from wisdom. From this we must conclude that those who have learnt least about all that which has hitherto been named philosophy, are the most capable of apprehending the truth.

After having made these matters very clear, I should have desired to set forth the reasons which serve to prove that the true principles by which we may arrive at that highest point of wisdom in which the sovereign good of the life of man consists, are those which I have put forward in this book. And only two are requisite for that, the first that the principles must be very clear, and the second that from them we may deduce all other things; for there are but these two conditions that are essential in true principles. And I can easily prove that they are very clear, first of all by the manner in which I have found them, i.e. by rejecting all those propositions in respect to which I could find the slightest occasion for doubt; for it is certain that those which could not be rejected in this way when application was made to their consideration, are the most evident and clear of all that the human mind can know. Thus in considering that he who would doubt all things cannot yet doubt that he exists while he doubts, and that what reasons so in being unable to doubt of itself and yet doubting all else, is not what we call our body but what we call our soul or thought, I have taken the being or existence of this thought as the first principle from which I have very clearly deduced the following: viz. that there is a God who is the author of all that is in the world, or who, being the source of all truth, has not created in us an understanding liable to be deceived in the judgments that it forms on matters of which it has a very clear and distinct perception. These comprise the whole of the principles of which I make use respecting immaterial or metaphysical things, from which I very clearly deduce those of corporeal or physical things, to wit, that there are bodies extended in length, breadth and depth, which have diverse figures and move in diverse ways. These, in sum, are all the principles from which I deduce the truth of other things. The other reason which proves the clearness of the principles is that they have been known from all time, and even received as true and indubitable by all men, with the sole exception of the existence of God, which has been placed in doubt by certain people because they have ascribed too much to the perceptions of the senses, and because God can neither be seen nor touched. But although all the truths which I place in my Principles have been known from all time and by all men, nevertheless there has never yet been anyone, as far as I know, who has recognised them as the principles of philosophy, that is to say, as principles from which may be derived a knowledge of all things that are in the world: that is why it here remains to me to prove that they are such. And it appears to me that I cannot do better than cause this to be established by experience, that is to say, by inviting my readers to peruse this book. For although I have not treated of every thing, and although this is impossible, I consider that I have so explained all those matters with which I have had occasion to deal, that those who read them with attention will have reason to persuade themselves that there is no need to seek other principles than those I have brought forward, in order to arrive at all the most exalted knowledge of which the human mind is capable. And this will more especially be the case if, after having read my works, they take the trouble to consider how many diverse questions are therein explained, and if, perusing also the works of others, they observe how few are the probable reasons that can be given to explain the same questions by principles differing from mine. And in order that they may undertake this with greater ease, I should have been able to say to them that those who are imbued with my doctrines have much less trouble in under-standing the works of others and in recognising their true value than those who are not so imbued; and this is diametrically opposite to what I have just said of those who commenced with the ancient philosophy, i.e. that the more they have studied it the less are they fitted rightly to apprehend the truth.

I should also have here added a word of advice as regards the method of reading this book, which is that I should desire that it may first of all be run through in its entirety like a novel, without forcing the attention unduly upon it, or stopping at difficulties which may be met with, so that a general knowledge may be arrived at of the

11

12

matters of which I have treated; and after that, if it is found that they deserve to be examined more carefully, and if the reader has the curiosity to inquire about their causes, it may be read a second time in order to notice the sequence of my reasoning. But though the reader cannot follow the argument adequately throughout, or understand the whole of its bearing, he must not therefore immediately cast it aside. It is only necessary to mark with a pen the places where difficulty is found, and continue to read without interruption to the end. Then if the book is taken up for a third time, I venture to say that he will discover the solution of the greater part of the difficulties which have formerly been marked, and that if certain still remain, their solution will be discovered on a further perusal.

I have noticed on examining the nature of many different minds, that there are almost none of them so dull or slow of understanding that they are incapable of high feelings, and even of attaining to all the profoundest sciences, were they trained in the right way. And that may also be proved by reason. For since the principles are clear and nothing must be deduced from them but by very evident reasoning, we have all sufficient intelligence to comprehend the conclusions that depend on them. But in addition to the drawbacks of prejudice from which no one is entirely exempt, although it is those who have studied the false sciences most deeply whom they harm the most, it almost always happens that those of moderate intelligence neglect to study because they do not consider themselves capable of doing so, and that the others who are more eager, hasten on too quickly. And from this it comes that they often accept principles which are not really evident, and from them derive consequences which are uncertain. That is why I desire to assure those who too greatly disparage their powers, that there is nothing in my writings which they are not capable of completely understanding if they take the trouble to examine them; while I also warn the others that even the most superior understanding will require much time and attention to comprehend all the matters which I have designed to embrace in them.

Following on this, and in order to make very clear the end I have had in view in publishing them, I would like to explain here what seems to me to be the order which should be followed in our self-instruction. To begin with, a man who as yet has merely the common and imperfect knowledge which may be acquired by the

13

four methods before mentioned, should above all try to form for himself a code of morals sufficient to regulate the actions of his life, because this does not brook any delay, and we ought above all other things to endeavour to live well. After that he should likewise study logic – not that of the schools, because it properly speaking is only a dialectic which teaches how to make the things that we know understood by others, or even to repeat, without forming any judgment on them, many words respecting those that we do not know, thus corrupting rather than increasing good sense – but the logic that teaches us how best to direct our reason in order to discover those truths of which we are ignorant. And since this is very dependent on custom, it is good for him to practise the rules for a long time on easy and simple questions such as those of mathematics. Then when he has acquired a certain skill in discovering the truth in these questions he should begin seriously to apply himself to the true philosophy, the first part of which is metaphysics, which contains the principles of knowledge, amongst which is the explanation of the principal attributes of God, of the immateriality of our souls, and of all the clear and simple notions which are in us. The second is physics in which, after having found the true principles of material things, we examine generally how the whole universe is composed, and then in particular what is the nature of this earth and of all the bodies which are most commonly found in connection with it, like air, water and fire, the loadstone and other minerals. It is thereafter necessary to inquire individually into the nature of plants, animals, and above all of man, so that we may afterwards be able to discover the other sciences which are useful to man. Thus philosophy as a whole is like a tree whose roots are metaphysics, whose trunk is physics, and whose branches, which issue from this trunk, are all the other sciences. These reduce themselves to three principal ones, viz. medicine, mechanics and morals – I mean the highest and most perfect moral science which, presupposing a complete knowledge of the other sciences, is the last degree of wisdom.

14

But just as it is not from the roots or the trunk of the trees that one culls the fruit, but only from the extremities of their branches, so the main use of philosophy is dependent on those of its parts that we cannot learn till the end. Although, however, I am ignorant of almost all of these, the zeal which I have always shown in trying to

15

render service to the public is the reason of my causing to be printed ten or twelve years ago certain essays on things which I appeared to have learned. The first part of these essays was a *Discourse on the Method of rightly conducting one's Reason and seeking Truth in the Sciences,* where I summarised the principal rules of logic and of an imperfect system of morals which may be followed provisionally while we still know none better. The other parts were three treatises: the first *Of the Dioptric;* the second *Of Meteors,* and the last *Of Geometry.* In the *Dioptric* I intended it to be shown that we could make sufficient progress in philosophy to attain by its means a knowledge of those arts which are useful to life, because the invention of the telescope, which I there described, is one of the most difficult ever attempted. In the treatise on *Meteors* I endeavoured to make clear the difference which exists between the philosophy which I cultivate and that taught in the schools, where the same subject is usually treated. Finally in the *Geometry* I professed to show that I had found certain matters of which men were previously ignorant, and thus to afford occasion for believing that many more may yet be discovered, in order by this means to incite all men to the search after truth. From this time onwards, foreseeing the difficulty which would be felt by many in understanding the foundations of metaphysics, I tried to explain the principal points in a book of *Meditations* which is not very large, but whose volume has been increased, and whose matter has been much illuminated, by the Objections which many very learned persons have sent me in their regard, and by the replies which I have made to them. Then, finally, when it appeared to me that these preceding treatises had sufficiently prepared the mind of readers to accept the *Principles of Philosophy,* I likewise published them, and I divided the book containing them into four parts, the first of which contains the principles of knowledge, which is what may be called the first philosophy or Metaphysics. That is why it is better to read beforehand the Meditations which I have written on the same subject, in order that it may be properly understood. The other three parts contain all that is most general in physics, i.e. an explanation of the first laws or principles of nature, the manner in which the heavens and fixed stars, the planets, the comets, and generally all the universe is composed. Then the nature of this earth, and of the air, water, fire, and the loadstone, is dealt with more particularly, for these are the bodies which may most commonly be found everywhere about it, as also all the qualities observed in these bodies, such as light, heat, weight, and such like. By this means I believe myself to have commenced to expound the whole of philosophy in its order without having omitted anything which ought to precede the last of which I have written. But in order to carry this plan to a conclusion, I should afterwards in the same way explain in further detail the nature of each of the other bodies which are on the earth, i.e. minerals, plants, animals, and above all man; then finally treat exactly of medicine, morals and mechanics. All this I should have to do in order to give to mankind a body of philosophy which is complete; and I do not feel myself to be so old, I do not so much despair of my strength, I do not find myself so far removed from a knowledge of what remains, that I should not venture to endeavour to achieve this design, were I possessed of the means of making all the experiments necessary to me in order to support and justify my reasoning. But seeing that for this end great expense is requisite to which the resources of an individual like myself could not attain were he not given assistance by the public, and not seeing that I can expect that aid, I conceive it to be henceforward my duty to content myself with studying for my own private instruction, trusting that posterity will pardon me if I fail henceforward to work for its good.

In order, however, to show in how far I believe myself to have already been of service to my fellow men, I shall here state what are the fruits which I believe may be culled from my Principles. The first is the satisfaction which we must derive from discovering in them certain truths of which we have hitherto been ignorant; for although frequently the truth does not so much affect our imagination as does falsity and pretence, because it seems less wonderful and more simple, yet the satisfaction which it brings is always more lasting and solid. The second fruit is that in studying these Principles, we shall little by little accustom ourselves to judge better of all things with which we come in contact, and thus to become wiser. In this regard they will have an effect contrary to that of the ordinary philosophy, for it may easily be observed in those who are known as pedants, that it renders them less capable of reasoning than they would have been had they never learned it at all. The third fruit is that the truths which they contain, being perfectly clear and certain, will remove all subjects of dispute, and thus dispose men's minds to gentleness and concord. On the other hand the controversies of the schools, by insensibly making those who practise themselves in them more captious and self-sufficient, are possibly the chief causes of the heresies and dissensions which now exercise the world. The last and principal fruit of these Principles is that by cultivating them we may discover many truths which I have not expounded, and thus, passing little by little from one to the other, acquire in time a perfect knowledge of the whole of philosophy and attain to the highest degree of wisdom. For in all the arts we perceive how although at the first they are rude and imperfect, yet because they contain something that is true and whose effect is revealed by experience, they come little by little to perfection through practice. So, when we have true principles in philosophy we cannot fail, by following them, occasionally to meet with other truths; and there is no way in which we can better prove the falsity of those of Aristotle, than by pointing out that no progress has been attained by their means in all the centuries in which they have been followed.

I know very well that those who make such haste use so little circumspection in what they do, that even with quite solid foundations they cannot build anything that is firm and secure; and because it is commonly such men who are most ready to write books, they may in a short time spoil all that I have done, and if their writings are accepted as mine, or as representing my opinions, introduce uncertainty and doubt into my mode of philosophising, from which I have carefully tried to banish them. I have lately had experience as to this regarding one of them who might have been expected to have followed me most closely, and of whom I had even written 'that I was so assured of his intelligence that I did not believe him to have any opinion which I should not gladly have avowed as my own'; for he published a year ago a book entitled *Fundamenta Physicae*[2] in which, although he had apparently said nothing regarding physics and medicine which he had not derived from my writings – from those published as well as from another still imperfect regarding the nature of animals which fell into his hands – yet because he had transcribed badly, changed the order,

2 Henri Regii Ultrajectini, *Fundamenta Physicae*.

and denied certain truths of metaphysics upon which the whole of physics ought to rest, I am obliged entirely to disavow his work, and here to beg readers never to attribute to me any opinion unless they find it expressly stated in my works, and never to accept anything as true in my writings or elsewhere, unless they see it to be very clearly deduced from true principles.

20

I well know likewise that many centuries may pass until all the truths which may be deduced from these principles are so deduced, because the greater part of those which remain to be discovered depend on certain particular experiments which chance circumstances will never bring about, but which should be investigated with care and expense by the most intelligent of men, and because it will be unlikely that the same people who have the capacity of availing themselves of them will have the means of contriving them, and also because the majority of the best minds have formed such a bad conception of philosophy as a whole, owing to the defects which they have observed in that which has hitherto been in vogue, that they will not be able to discover a better. But finally, if the difference which is observable between these principles and those of all other men, and the great array of truths which may be deduced from them, causes them to perceive how important it is to continue in the search after these truths, and to observe to what a degree of wisdom, to what perfection of life, to what happiness they may lead us, I am convinced that no one will be found who will not attempt to occupy himself with so profitable a study, or at least will not favour and endeavour to assist with all his might those who employ themselves in this way with success. I trust that posterity may behold its happy issue.

DEDICATION

*To the most serene Princess Elizabeth, eldest daughter
of Frederick, King of Bohemia, Count Palatine and
Elector of the Holy Roman Empire*

MADAM — The great result which has accrued to me from the
works which I have already published, has been that through them I
have had the honour of coming under the notice of your Highness,
and of being able occasionally to have converse with one whose
qualities are so estimable that I conceive it to be a public service to
set them before posterity for its example. It would ill become me to
flatter, or even to write things as to which I have no certain
knowledge, above all in this place in which I shall try to set down
the principles of truth. And the generous modesty which is seen in
all the actions of your Highness suffices to assure me that the simple
and unaffected judgment of one who writes but what he believes,
will be more agreeable to you than the ornate praises of those who
have studied the art of compliment. That is why I shall put nothing
in this letter of which experience and reason has not rendered me
certain, and here in the exordium, I shall write philosophically, just
as in the rest of the book.

Great is the distinction between the apparent virtues and the true;
there is also a distinction between those true virtues which proceed
from an exact knowledge of the truth and others that are
accompanied by ignorance. The virtues which I call apparent, are
properly speaking but vices, which not being so frequent as other
vices which are contrary to them, and being further removed from
them than the virtues which occupy an intermediate position, are
usually held in greater esteem than they. Thus since there are many
more people who fear danger too much than those who fear it too
little, temerity is often opposed to timidity as a virtue to a vice, and
is more esteemed than true fortitude. Thus likewise the prodigal is
much more frequently praised than the liberal, and nothing is more
easy than for the superstitious and hypocritical to acquire a
reputation for great piety.

Many of the true virtues do not proceed from true knowledge, but there are some which likewise proceed from a sort of error: thus it is frequently the case that simplicity is the cause of kindness, fear of devotion, and despair of courage. And the virtues which are thus accompanied by some imperfection differ from one another and have likewise been given different names. But those pure and perfect virtues which proceed from the knowledge of good alone, are all of the same nature, and may be comprised under the name of wisdom. For whoever forms a firm and constant resolve always to make use of reason to the best of his power, and in all his actions to do what he believes to be best, is truly wise, so far as his nature allows him to be so; and by this alone he is just, courageous, moderate, and possesses all the other virtues; but these are so united together that none like the predominance over others; and this is why, although they are much more perfect than the virtues that the admixture of some defect causes to shine forth, yet because the ordinary man remarks them less, they are not accorded the same praise.

Further, of two things requisite to the wisdom thus described, i.e. the perception of the understanding and the disposition of the will, it is only that which consists in the will that all men may alike possess, inasmuch as the understanding of some is not as good as that of others. But although those who are inferior in mind may be as wise as their nature permits, and may render themselves acceptable to God by their virtue, if they only form a firm and constant resolution to do what they judge to be right, and spare no effort in learning that of which they are ignorant, yet those who while possessing a constant desire to do well, and taking very special care in reference to their self-instruction, are endowed with a highly perspicacious intellect, will doubtless attain to a higher point of wisdom than the others.

And these three things are found perfectly in your Royal Highness, since in your case no diversions of the Court nor that mode of education which ordinarily condemns princesses to ignorance, have been capable of preventing your study of all that is best in the arts and sciences. And the incomparable excellence of your intellect is evident in the fact that in a very short time you have mastered the secrets of the sciences, and obtained a perfect knowledge of them all. But I have yet another proof very special to myself, inasmuch as I have never met any one who understood so generally and thoroughly all that is contained in my writings. For there are many who find them most obscure, even amongst the most learned and intelligent; and I notice in almost all that those who grasp things which pertain to metaphysics with ease have a dislike to geometry, while those who cultivate geometry have no propensity for the study of first philosophy: and so true is this that I know of no mind but yours to which both studies are equally congenial, and which therefore merits to be termed incomparable. But what enhances my admiration most, is that so varied and perfect a knowledge of all the sciences does not reside in some ancient doctor who has for many years been given over to contemplation, but in a young Princess whose countenance and years would more fitly represent one of the Graces than a Muse or the sage Minerva.

Finally I not only remark in your Highness all that is requisite for a mind to attain to the highest and supremest wisdom, but also all that is requisite on the part of the will or the life. Benignity and gentleness are there so conjoined with majesty, that though fortune has perpetually attempted to injure you unjustly, it has failed to embitter you or cast you down. And this constrains me to accord such veneration that I consider this work not only due to you, since it treats of philosophy (which is just the study of wisdom), but I also have no greater pride in my reputation as a philosopher, than I have in subscribing myself as

The devoted servant
of your most Serene Highness,
DES-CARTES

First Part:
Of the Principles of Human Knowledge

1 *That in order to examine into the truth, it is necessary once in one's life to doubt of all things, so far as this is possible.*

As we have once on a time been children and have judged of the things presented to our senses in various ways, while as yet we had not the entire use of our reason, many judgments thus precipitately formed prevent us from arriving at the knowledge of the truth, and apparently there seems no way in which we can deliver ourselves from these, unless we undertake once in our lives to doubt all things in which the slightest trace of incertitude can be found.

2 *That we ought to consider as false all these things of which we may doubt.*

It will even be useful to reject as false all these things as to which we can imagine the least doubt to exist, so that we may discover with greater clearness which are absolutely true, and most easy to know.

3 *That we ought not to make use of this doubt for the conduct of our life meantime.*

But in the meantime it is to be observed that we are to make use of this doubt only when we are engaged in contemplating the truth. For, as regards the conduct of our life, we are frequently obliged to follow opinions which are merely probable, because the opportunities for action would in most cases pass away before we could deliver ourselves from our doubts. And when, as frequently happens with two courses of action, we do not perceive the probability of the one more than the other, we must yet select one of them.

4 *Why we may doubt of sensible things.*

But because we desire to apply ourselves only to the search after truth, we shall in the first place doubt if, of all sensible things, or things which we have imagined, there are any that really exist: in   6 the first place because we know that our senses have before deceived us, and that prudence directs us not to trust too much in what has even once deceived us: in the second place because in sleep we continually seem to feel or imagine innumerable things which have no existence. To those who thus resolve to doubt all, there is apparently no mark by which they can with certainty distinguish sleep from the waking state.[3]

5 *Why we may likewise doubt of the demonstration of mathematics.*

We shall also doubt of all the other things which have formerly seemed to us quite certain, even of the demonstrations of mathematics and of its principles which we formerly thought quite self-evident. One reason is that those who have fallen into error in reasoning on such matters, have held as perfectly certain and self-evident what we see to be false, but a yet more important reason is that we have been told that God who created us can do all that He desires. For we are still ignorant of whether He may not have desired to create us in such a way that we shall always be deceived, even in the things that we believe ourselves to know best; since this does not seem less possible than our being occasionally deceived, which experience tells us is the case. And if we think that an omnipotent God is not the author of our being, and that we subsist of ourselves, or through some other, yet the less perfect we suppose the author to be, the more reason have we to believe that we are not so perfect that we cannot be continually deceived.

6 *That we possess a free-will which causes us to abstain from giving assent to dubious things, and thus prevents our falling into error.*

But meanwhile whoever turns out to have created us, and even should he prove to be all-powerful and deceitful, we still experience a freedom through which we may abstain from accepting as true and indisputable those things of which we have not certain knowledge, and thus obviate our ever being deceived.

3 'whether the thoughts that come to us in sleep are as false as are the others.' French version.

7 *That we cannot doubt our existence without existing while we doubt; and this is the first knowledge that we obtain when we philosophise in an orderly way.*

While we thus reject all that of which we can possibly doubt, and feign that it is false, it is easy to suppose that there is no God, nor heaven, nor bodies, and that we possess neither hands, nor feet, nor indeed any body; but we cannot in the same way conceive that we who doubt these things are not; for there is a contradiction in conceiving that what thinks does not at the same time as it thinks, exist. And hence this conclusion *I think, therefore I am*, is the first and most certain of all that occurs to one who philosophises in an orderly way.

8 *This furnishes us with the distinction which exists between the soul and the body, or between that which thinks and that which is corporeal.*

This, then, is the best way to discover the nature of mind and the distinction between it and the body. For, in considering what we are who suppose that all things apart from ourselves [our thought] are false, we observe very clearly that there is no extension, figure, local motion, or any such thing which may be attributed to body, which pertains to our nature, but only thought alone; and consequently this notion of thought precedes that of all corporeal things and is the most certain; since we still doubt whether there are any other things in the world, while we already perceive that we think.

9 *What thought*[4] *is.*

By the word thought I understand all that of which we are conscious as operating in us. And that is why not alone understanding, willing, imagining, but also feeling, are here the same thing as thought. For if I say I see, or I walk, I therefore am, and if by seeing and walking I mean the action of my eyes or my legs, which is the work of my body, my conclusion is not absolutely certain; because it may be that, as often happens in sleep, I think I see or I walk, although I never open my eyes or move from my place, and the same thing perhaps might occur if I had not a body at all. But if I mean only to talk of my sensations,[5] or my consciously seeming to

4 *cogitatio.*   5 *sensu.*

see or to walk, it becomes quite true because my assertion now refers only to my mind, which alone is concerned with my feeling or thinking that I see and I walk.

10 *That conceptions which are perfectly simple and clear of themselves are obscured by the definitions of the schools, and that they are not to be numbered as amongst those capable of being acquired by study [but are inborn in us].*

I do not here explain various other terms of which I have availed myself or will afterwards avail myself, because they seem to me perfectly clear of themselves. And I have often noticed that philosophers err in trying to explain by definitions logically constructed, things which were perfectly simple in themselves; they thereby render them but more obscure. And when I stated that this proposition *I think, therefore I am* is the first and most certain which presents itself to those who philosophise in orderly fashion, I did not for all that deny that we must first of all know *what is knowledge, what is existence, and what is certainty,* and that *in order to think we must be,* and such like; but because these are notions of the simplest possible kind, which of themselves give us no knowledge of anything that exists, I did not think them worthy of being put on record.

11 *How we may know our mind better than our body.*

But in order to understand how the knowledge which we possess of our mind not only precedes that which we have of our body, but is also more evident, it must be observed that it is very manifest by the natural light which is in our souls, that no qualities or properties pertain to nothing; and that where some are perceived there must necessarily be some thing or substance on which they depend. And the same light shows us that we know a thing or substance so much the better the more properties we observe in it. And we certainly observe many more qualities in our mind than in any other thing, inasmuch as there is nothing that excites us to knowledge of whatever kind, which does not even much more certainly compel us to a consciousness of our thought. To take an example, if I persuade myself that there is an earth because I touch or see it, by that very same fact, and by a yet stronger reason, I should be persuaded that my thought exists; because it may be that I think I touch the earth even though there is possibly no earth existing at all, but it is not possible that I who form this judgment and my mind which judges thus, should be non-existent; and so in other cases.

12 *The reason why everyone does not comprehend this in the same way.*

Those who have not studied philosophy in an orderly way have held other opinions on this subject because they never distinguished their mind from their body with enough care. For although they had no difficulty in believing that they themselves existed, and that they had a greater assurance of this than of any other thing, yet because they did not observe that by themselves[6] they ought merely to understand their minds [when metaphysical certainty was in question], and since on the contrary they rather meant that it was their bodies which they saw with their eyes, touched with their hands, and to which they wrongly attributed the power of perception, they did not distinctly comprehend the nature of the mind.

13 *In what sense the knowledge of all other things depends on the knowledge of God.*

But when the mind which thus knows itself but still doubts all other things, looks around in order to try to extend its knowledge further, it first of all finds in itself the ideas of a multitude of things, and while it contemplates these simply and neither affirms nor denies that there is anything outside itself which corresponds to these ideas, it is beyond any danger of falling into error. The mind likewise discovers certain common ideas out of which it frames various demonstrations which absolutely convince us of their truth if we give attention to them. For example the mind has within itself the ideas of number and figure; it has also, amongst its ordinary conceptions this, that 'if equals are added to equals, the result is equal,' and so on. From this it is easy to demonstrate that the three angles of a triangle are equal to two right angles, etc. Now mind perceives these and other facts to be true so long as the premises from which they are derived are attended to. But since it cannot always devote this attention to them [when it remembers the conclusion and yet cannot recollect the order of its deduction], and conceives that it may have been created

6 *per se ipsos.*

of such a nature that it has been deceived even in what is most
evident, it sees clearly that it has great cause to doubt the truth of
such conclusions, and to realise that it can have no certain
knowledge until it is acquainted with its creator.

14 *That the existence of God may be rightly demonstrated from the fact that
the necessity of His existence is comprehended in the conception which we
have of Him.*

When mind afterwards considers the diverse conceptions which it
has and when it there discovers the idea of a Being who is
omniscient, omnipotent and absolutely perfect, which is far the
most important of all; in it it recognises not merely a possible and
contingent existence, as in all the other ideas it has of things which it
clearly perceives, but one which is absolutely necessary and eternal.
And just as it perceives that it is necessarily involved in the idea of
the triangle that it should have three angles which are equal to two
right angles, it is absolutely persuaded that the triangle has three
angles equal to two right angles. In the same way from the fact that
it perceives that necessary and eternal existence is comprised in the
idea which it has of an absolutely perfect Being, it has clearly to
conclude that this absolutely perfect Being exists.

15 *That necessary existence is not similarly included in the notion we have
of other things, but merely contingent existence.*

The mind will be the better assured of the truth of this conclusion if
it observes that it does not possess the idea of any other thing
wherein existence is necessarily contained. And from this it realises
that the idea of all absolutely perfect Being is not framed in it by
means of itself, nor does it represent a chimera, but that it is a true
and immutable nature, which cannot be non-existent, since in it
existence is necessarily contained.

16 *That prejudice prevents many from knowing clearly the necessity for the
existence of God.*

Our mind would have no trouble in persuading itself of this truth if
it were wholly free from prejudice to begin with; but inasmuch as
we are accustomed to distinguish essence from existence in all other
things, and as we can at will imagine many ideas of things which

neither are nor have been, it may easily occur that when we do not 11
steadily contemplate this absolutely perfect Being, we shall doubt
whether the idea which we form of Him is not one of those which
we frame at pleasure, or one to the essence of which existence does
not pertain.

17 *That the more objective perfection there is in our ideas the more should
its cause also be more perfect.*

Further, when we reflect on the various ideas that are in us, it is easy
to perceive that there is not much difference between them when
they are considered only as modes of thinking, but they are widely
different in another way, since the one represents one thing, and the
other another; and their cause must be more perfect as what they
represent of their objects is more perfect. For this is just the same as
in the case of someone said to have the idea of a machine in the
construction of which there is much skill displayed, we have reason
to ask how he obtained the idea, e.g. whether he saw somewhere a
similar machine made by another, or whether he had a thorough
knowledge of the science of mechanics, or whether he were
endowed with such force of mind that he was able of himself to
invent the machine without having seen anything similar anywhere
else. For the whole of the ingenuity involved in the idea which is
possessed by this man objectively, as in a picture, must exist in its
first and principal cause whatever that may be, not only objectively
or representatively, bat also formally or eminently.

18 *That we may thus demonstrate that there is a God.*

So, because we find within ourselves the idea of a God, or a
supremely perfect Being, we are able to investigate the cause which
produces this idea in us; but after, on considering the immensity of
the perfection it possesses, we are constrained to admit that we can
consider it only as emanating from an all-perfect Being, that is, from
a God who truly exists. For it is not only made manifest by the
natural light that nothing can be the cause of nothing whatever, and
that the more perfect cannot proceed from the less perfect so as to
be thus produced as by its efficient and total cause, but also that it is 12
impossible for us to have any idea of anything whatever, if there is
not within us or outside of us, an original, which as a matter of fact

comprehends all the perfections. But as we do not in any way possess all those absolute perfections of which we have the idea, we must conclude that they reside in some other nature different from ours, and that is, in God; or at least that they were once in Him; and it follows from this most manifestly that they are there still.

19 *That although we do not comprehend the whole nature of God, there is yet nothing which we know so clearly as His perfections.*

This is quite certain and manifest to those who have accustomed themselves to the contemplation of God and to turn their attention to His infinite perfections. For, though we do not comprehend them because the nature of the Infinite is such that we, being finite, cannot comprehend them, we yet conceive them more clearly and distinctly than any material thing, because, being more simple and not being limited by anything that may obscure them, they occupy our mind more fully.[7]

20 *That we are not the cause of ourselves, but that God is, and that consequently there is a God.*

But since everyone does not observe this, and because, when we have a notion of some machine in which there is much skill displayed, we sufficiently well know the manner in which we have acquired this knowledge, and because we cannot even recollect when the idea which we have of a God has been communicated to us by God, since it has always been present in us, we must yet inquire who then is the author of our Being, possessing as we do the idea of the infinite perfections which are in God. Because the light of nature makes it very clear that whoever knows something more perfect than himself cannot be the author of his being, because then he would have given himself all the perfections of which he had cognisance; and consequently he could not subsist by any other than by Him who possesses all these perfections in Himself, that is, by God.

7 *quia cogitationem nostram magis implent*, Latin. The French version is different, viz. 'being more simple and not being limited, what we do conceive of them is much less confused.' A sentence is added 'There is also no speculation which can better aid in perfecting our understanding, and which is more important, than this, inasmuch as the consideration of an object unlimited in its perfections fills us with satisfaction and assurance.'

21 *That the mere duration of our life suffices to prove the existence of God.*   13

We cannot doubt the truth of this demonstration so long as we observe the nature of time or of the duration of things; for this is of such a kind that its parts do not depend one upon the other, and never coexist; and from the fact that we now are, it does not follow that we shall be a moment afterwards, if some cause – the same that first produced us – does not continue so to produce us; that is to say, to conserve us. And we can easily recognise that there is no strength in us whereby we may conserve ourselves, but that He who has so much power that He can conserve us out of Himself must by so much the greater reason conserve Himself, or rather not require to be conserved by any other, for, in fine, He is God.

22 *That in recognising the existence of God in the manner here explained, we also recognise all His attributes, in so far as they may be known by the light of nature alone.*

We possess the great advantage in proving the existence of God in this way by His idea,[8] that we recognise at the same time what He is in so far as the weakness of our nature permits. For when we reflect on the idea of Him which is implanted in us, we perceive that He is eternal, omniscient, omnipotent, the source of all goodness and truth, creator of all things, and that in fine he has in Himself all that in which we can clearly recognise any infinite perfection or good that is not limited by some imperfection.

23 *That God is not corporeal, and does not perceive by means of the senses as we do, nor is He the originator of sin.*

For there are many things in the world which are in some respects imperfect, although we remark in them certain perfections; it is accordingly not possible that any of these exist in God. Thus in corporeal nature since divisibility is included in local extension, and divisibility indicates imperfection, it is certain that God is not body. And although it is of some advantage for us to have senses, yet because in all sensations there is passivity[9] and that indicates   14

8 *per ejus scilicet ideam.*
9 Latin *quia tamen in omni sensu passio est.* French 'yet because the sensations that are in us are there through impressions which proceed from elsewhere'.

dependence, we conclude that God is possessed of no senses, but that He understands and wills – not indeed as we do, by operations which are in some way distinct one from another, but ever by one identical and very simple action, and that He understands and wills and effects everything: that is, everything that really exists; for he does not will the evil of sin because that evil is nothing real.

24 *That in passing from the knowledge that God exists, to the knowledge of his creatures, we must recollect that our understanding is finite, and the power of God infinite.*

Being thus aware that God alone is the true cause of all that is or can be, we shall doubtless follow the best method of philosophising, if, from the knowledge which we possess of His nature, we pass to an explanation of the things which He has created, and if we try from the notions which exist naturally in our minds to deduce it, for in this way we shall obtain a perfect science, that is, a knowledge of the effects through their causes. But in order that we may undertake this task with most security from error, we must recollect that God, the creator of all things, is infinite and that we are altogether finite.

25 *And that we must believe all that God has revealed, even though it is above the range of our capacities.*

Thus if God reveals to us or to others certain things concerning Himself which surpass the range of our natural power of intelligence, such as the mysteries of the incarnation and the Trinity, we shall have no difficulty in believing them, although we may not clearly understand them. For we should not think it strange that in the immensity of His nature, as also in the objects of His creation, there are many things beyond the range of our comprehension.

26 *That we must not try to dispute about the infinite, but just consider that all that in which we find no limits is indefinite, such as the extension of the world, the divisibility of its parts, the number of the stars, etc.*

We will thus never hamper ourselves with disputes about the infinite, since it would be absurd that we who are finite should undertake to decide anything regarding it, and by this means in trying to comprehend it, so to speak regard it as finite. That is why we do not care to reply to those who demand whether the half of

15

an infinite line is infinite, and whether an infinite number is even or odd and so on, because it is only those who imagine their mind to be infinite who appear to find it necessary to investigate such questions. And for our part, while we regard things in which, in a certain sense, we observe no limits, we shall not for all that state that they are infinite, but merely hold them to be indefinite. Thus because we cannot imagine an extension so great that we cannot at the same time conceive that there may be one yet greater, we shall say that the magnitude of possible things is indefinite. And because we cannot divide a body into parts which are so small that each part cannot be divided into others yet smaller, we shall consider that the quantity may be divided into parts whose number is indefinite. And because we cannot imagine so many stars that it is impossible for God to create more, we shall suppose the number to be indefinite, and so in other cases.

27 *What is the difference between the indefinite and the infinite?*

And we shall name these things indefinite rather than infinite in order to reserve to God alone the name of infinite, first of all because in Him alone we observe no limitation whatever, and because we are quite certain that He can have none, and in the second place in regard to other things, because we do not in the same way positively understand them to be in every part unlimited, but merely negatively admit that their limits, if they exist, cannot be discovered by us.[10]

28 *That we must not inquire into the final, but only into the efficient causes of created things.*

Finally we shall not seek for the reason of natural things from the end which God or nature has set before him in their creation;[11] for

10 'As regards other things we know that they are not thus absolutely perfect because although we observe in them certain properties which appear to have no limit, we yet know that this proceeds from our lack of understanding and not from their natures.' (This, the French, translation is to obviate the use of the terms positive and negative.)
11 'We shall not stop to consider the ends which God has set before Himself in the creation of the world and we shall entirely set aside from our philosophy the search for final causes.' French version.

we should not take so much upon ourselves as to believe that God could take us into His counsels. But regarding Him as the efficient cause of all things, we shall merely try to discover by the light of nature that He has placed in us, applied to those attributes of which He has been willing we should have some knowledge, what must be concluded regarding the effects that we perceive by the senses; but we must keep in mind what has been said, that we must trust to this natural light only so long as nothing contrary to it is revealed by God Himself.

29 *That God is not the cause of our errors.*

The first of God's attributes which falls to be considered here is that He is absolutely true and the source of all light, so that it is evidently a contradiction that He should deceive us, that is to say that He should be properly and positively[12] the cause of the errors to which we are conscious of being subject. For although the capacity for deceit would seem to be a mark of subtlety of mind amongst men, yet the will to deceive proceeds only from malice, or fear, or weakness, and it cannot consequently be attributed to God.

30 *And consequently all that we perceive clearly is true, and this delivers us from the doubts put forward above.*

Whence it follows that the light of nature, or the faculty of knowledge which God has given us, can never disclose to us[13] any object which is not true, inasmuch us it comprehends it, that is, inasmuch as it apprehends it clearly and distinctly. Because we should have had reason to think God a deceiver if He had given us this faculty perverted, or such that we should take the false for the true [when using the faculty aright]. And this should deliver us from the supreme doubt which encompassed us when we did not know whether our nature had been such that we had been deceived in things that seemed most clear. It should also protect us against all the other reasons already mentioned which we had for doubting. The truths of mathematics should now be above suspicion, for they are of the clearest. And if we perceive anything by our senses, either

---

12 Latin *proprie ac positive.*
13 *attingere,* Latin; *n'apperçoit,* French; 'compass', Veitch's translation.

waking or sleeping, if it is clear and distinct, and if we separate it from what is obscure and confused, we shall easily assure ourselves of what is the truth. I do not require to say more on this particular subject here, since I have treated of it fully in the Meditations on metaphysics, and what I intend to say later will serve to explain it more accurately.

31 *That our errors in respect of God are but negations, while in respect of ourselves they are privations or defects.*

But as it happens that although God is not a deceiver we frequently fall into error, if we desire to investigate the origin and cause of our errors in order to guard against them, we must take care to observe that they do not depend so much on our intellect as on our will, and that they are not such as to require the actual assistance of God in order that they may be produced. In this way so far as He is concerned they are but negations, while in respect to us they are defects or privations.

32 *That in us there are but two modes of thought, the perception of the understanding and the action of the will.*

For all the modes of thinking that we observed in ourselves may be related to two general modes, the one of which consists in perception, or in the operation of the understanding, and the other in volition, or the operation of the will. Thus sense-perception,[14] imagining, and conceiving things that are purely intelligible, are just different methods of perceiving;[15] but desiring, holding in aversion, affirming, denying, doubting, all these are the different modes of willing.

33 *That we deceive ourselves only when we form judgments about anything insufficiently known to us.*

When we perceive anything, we are in no danger of misapprehending it, if we do not judge of it one way or the other; and even when we judge of it we should not fall into error, provided that we do not give our assent to what we do not know clearly and distinctly; but what usually misleads us is that we very frequently form a judgment 18

14 *sentire.*   15 *percipiendi.*

although we have no very exact knowledge regarding that of which we judge.

34   *That the will is requisite for judgment as well as the understanding.*

I admit that we can judge of nothing unless our understanding is made use of, because there is no reason to suppose we can judge of what we in no wise apprehend; but the will is absolutely essential for our giving our assent to what we have in some manner perceived. Nor, in order to form any judgment whatever, is it necessary that we should have a perfect and entire knowledge of a thing; for we often give our assent to things of which we have never had any but a very obscure and confused knowledge.

35   *That the will is more extended than the understanding, and that our errors proceed from this cause.*

Further, the perception of the understanding only extends to the few objects which present themselves to it, and is always very limited. The will, on the other hand, may in some measure be said to be the infinite, because we perceive nothing which may be the object of some other will, even of the immensity of the will that is in God, to which our will cannot also extend, so that we easily extend it beyond that which we apprehend clearly. And when we do this there is no wonder if it happens that we are deceived.

36   *Our errors cannot be imputed to God.*

And although God has not given us an understanding which is omnipotent, we must not for that reason consider that He is the originator of our errors. For all created understanding is finite, and it is of the nature of finite understanding not to embrace all things.

37   *That the principal perfection of man is to have the power of acting freely or by will, and that this is what renders him deserving of either praise or blame.*

That will should extend widely is in accordance with its nature, and it is the greatest perfection in man to be able to act by its means, that is freely, and by so doing we are in a peculiar way masters of our actions and thereby merit praise or blame. For we do not praise automatic machines although they respond exactly to the movements

which they were destined to produce, since their actions are
performed necessarily. We praise the workman who has made the
machines because he has formed them with accuracy and has done so
freely and not of necessity. And for the same reason when we choose
what is true, much more credit is due to us when the choice is made
freely, than when it is made of necessity.

38 *That our errors are the defects of our mode of action, but not of our
nature; and that the faults of subordinates may often be attributed to other
masters, but never to God.*

It is very true that whenever we err there is some fault in our
method of action, or in the manner in which we use our freedom;
but for all that there is no defect in our nature, because it is ever the
same whether our judgment be true or false. And even though God
could have given us so incisive an intellect that we should never
have fallen into error, we have no right for all that to demand this of
Him. For although amongst us men, he who could prevent an
impending evil and yet who does not so do, is judged to be its
cause, the case is not the same with regard to God, who is not to be
regarded as responsible for our errors though endowed with the
power to prevent them. For the power which some men possess
over others has been instituted for the purpose of their hindering
evil from being done by others, while the power held over the
universe by God is altogether absolute and free. This is why we
should be grateful for the good things He has granted us and not
complain that he does not bestow from His bounty all that we
knew He might have dispensed.

39 *That freedom of the will is self-evident.*

Finally it is so evident that we are possessed of a free will that can
give or withhold its assent, that this may be counted as one of the
first and most ordinary notions that are found innately in us. We had
before a very clear proof of this, for at the same time as we tried to
doubt all things and even supposed that He who created us
employed His unlimited powers in deceiving us in every way, we
perceived in ourselves a liberty such that we were able to abstain
from believing what was not perfectly certain and indubitable. But
that of which we could not doubt at such a time is as self-evident
and clear as anything we can ever know.

40 *That we likewise know certainly that everything is pre-ordained of God.*

But because that which we have already learnt about God proves to us that His power is so immense that it would be a crime for us to think ourselves ever capable of doing anything which He had not already pre-ordained, we should soon be involved in great difficulties if we undertook to make His pre-ordinances harmonise with the freedom of our will, and if we tried to comprehend them both at one time.

41 *How the freedom of the will may be reconciled with Divine pre-ordination.*

Instead of this, we shall have no trouble at all if we recollect that our thought is finite, and that the omnipotence of God, whereby He has not only known from all eternity that which is or can be, but also willed and pre-ordained it, is infinite. In this way we may have intelligence enough to come clearly and distinctly to know that this power is in God, but not enough to comprehend how He leaves the free action of man indeterminate; and, on the other hand, we are so conscious of the liberty and indifference which exists in us, that there is nothing that we comprehend more clearly and perfectly. For it would be absurd to doubt that of which we inwardly experience and perceive as existing within ourselves, just because we do not comprehend a matter which from its nature we know to be incomprehensible.

42 *How, although we do not will to err, we yet err by our will.*

But inasmuch as we know that all our errors depend on our will, and as no one desires to deceive himself we may wonder that we err at all. We must, however, observe that there is a great deal of difference between willing to be deceived and willing to give one's assent to opinions in which error is sometimes found. For although there is no one who expressly desires to err, there is hardly one who is not willing to give his assent to things in which unsuspected error is to be found. And it even frequently happens that it is the very desire for knowing the truth which causes those who are not fully aware of the order in which it should be sought for, to give judgment on things of which they have no real knowledge and thereby to fall into error.

43 *That we cannot err if we give our assent only to things that we know clearly and distinctly.*

But it is certain that we shall never take the false as the true if we only give our assent to things that we perceive clearly and distinctly. Because since God is no deceiver, the faculty of knowledge that He has given us cannot be fallacious, nor can the faculty of will, so long at least as we do not extend it beyond those things that we clearly perceive. And even if this truth could not be rationally demonstrated, we are by nature so disposed to give our assent to things that we clearly perceive, that we cannot possibly doubt of their truth.

44 *That we shall always judge ill when we assent to what we do not clearly perceive, although our judgment may be true; and that it frequently is our memory that deceives us by leading us to believe that certain things had been satisfactorily established by us.*

It is also quite certain that whenever we give our assent to some reason which we do not exactly understand, we either deceive ourselves, or, if we arrive at the truth, it is only by chance, and thus we cannot be certain that we are not in error. It is true that it happens but rarely that we judge of a matter at the same time as we observe that we do not apprehend it, because the light of nature teaches us that we must not judge of anything that we do not understand. But we frequently err when we presume we have known certain things as being stored up in our memory, to which on recollection we give our assent, and of which we have never possessed any knowledge at all

45 *What a clear and distinct perception is.*

There are even a number of people who throughout all their lives perceive nothing so correctly as to be capable of judging of it properly. For the knowledge upon which a certain and incontrovertible judgment can be formed, should not alone be clear but also distinct. I term that clear which is present and apparent to an attentive mind, in the same way as we assert that we see objects clearly when, being present to the regarding eye, they operate upon it with sufficient strength. But the distinct is that which is so precise and different from all other objects that it contains with itself nothing but what is clear.

22

46 *It is shown from the example of pain that a perception may be clear without being distinct, but it cannot be distinct unless it is clear.*

When, for instance, a severe pain is felt, the perception of this pain may be very clear, and yet for all that not distinct, because it is usually confused by the sufferers with the obscure [16] judgment that they form upon its nature, assuming as they do that something exists in the part affected, similar to the sensation of pain of which they are alone clearly conscious. In this way perception may be clear without being distinct, and cannot be distinct without being also clear.

47 *That in order to remove the prejudices of our youth, it must be considered what there is that is clear in each of our simple [17] notions.*

Indeed in our early years, our mind was so immersed in the body, that it knew nothing distinctly, although it perceived much sufficiently clearly; and because it even then formed many judgments, numerous prejudices were contracted from which the majority of us can hardly ever hope to become free. But in order that we may now free ourselves from them I shall here enumerate all these simple notions which constitute our reflections, and distinguish whatever is clear in each of them from what is obscure, or likely to cause us to err.

48 *That all the objects of our perceptions are to be considered either as things or the affections of things, or else as eternal truths; and the enumeration of things.*

I distinguish all the objects of our knowledge either into things or the affections of things,[18] or as eternal truths having no existence outside our thought. Of the things we consider as real, the most general are substance, duration, order, number, and possibly such other similar matters as range through all the classes of real things. I do not however observe more than two ultimate classes of real

---

16 'false', French version.   17 'first', French.
18 '*Le premier contient toutes les choses qui ont quelque existence, et l'autre toutes les veritez qui ne sont rien hors de notre pensée*', French version: 'I distinguish all the objects of our knowledge into two species; the first contains all things which have an existence; the second all the truths which have no existence outside our thought.'

things – the one is intellectual things, or those of the intelligence, that is, pertaining to the mind or to thinking substance, the other is material things, or that pertaining to extended substance, i.e. to body. Perception, volition, and every mode of knowing and willing, pertain to thinking substance; while to extended substance pertain magnitude or extension in length, breadth and depth, figure, movement, situation, divisibility into parts themselves divisible, and such like. Besides these, there are, however, certain things which we experience in ourselves and which should be attributed neither to mind nor body alone, but to the close and intimate union that exists between the body and mind as I shall later on explain in the proper place.[19] Such are the appetites of hunger, thirst, etc., and also the emotions or passions of the mind which do not subsist in mind or thought alone, as the emotions of anger, joy, sadness, love, etc.; and finally all the sensations such as pain, pleasure, light and colour, sounds, odours, tastes, heat, hardness, and all other tactile qualities.

49 *That eternal truths cannot be enumerated thus and that this is not requisite.*

What I have hitherto enumerated are regarded either as the qualities of things or their modes.

[We must now talk of what we know as eternal truths.]

When we apprehend that it is impossible that anything can be formed of nothing, the proposition *ex nihilo nihil fit* is not to be considered as an existing thing, or the mode of a thing, but as a certain eternal truth which has its seat in our mind, and is a common notion or axiom. Of the same nature are the following: 'It is impossible that the same thing can be and not be at the same time', and that 'what has been done cannot be undone', 'that he who thinks must exist while he thinks', and very many other propositions the whole of which it would not be easy to enumerate. But [this is not necessary since] we cannot fail to recognise them when the occasion presents itself for us to do so, and if we have no prejudices to blind us.

24

19 Part 4, articles 189, 190 and 191.

50 *That these eternal truths are clearly perceived, but not by all, by reason of prejudice.*

As regards the common notions, indeed, there is no doubt that they may be clearly and distinctly perceived, for otherwise they would not deserve to bear this name; but it is also true that there are some that do not in regard to all men deserve the name equally with others, because they are not equally perceived by all. Not, however, that I believe the faculty of knowledge to extend further with some men than with others; it is rather that these common opinions are opposed to the prejudices of some who are thereby prevented from easily perceiving them, although they are perfectly manifest to those who are free from these prejudices.

51 *What substance is, and that it is a name which we cannot attribute in the same sense to God and to His creatures.*

As regards these matters which we consider as being things or modes of things, it is necessary that we should examine them here one by one. By substance, we can understand nothing else than a thing which so exists that it needs no other thing in order to exist. And in fact only one single substance can be understood which clearly needs nothing else, namely, God. We perceive that all other things can exist only by the help of the concourse of God. That is why the word substance does not pertain *univoce* to God and to other things, as they say in the schools, that is, no common signification for this appellation which will apply equally to God and to them can be distinctly understood.

52 *That it may be attributed univocally to the soul and to body, and how we know substance.*

25   Created substances, however, whether corporeal or thinking, may be conceived under this common concept; for they are things which need only the concurrence of God in order to exist. But yet substance cannot be first discovered merely from the fact that it is a thing that exists, for that fact alone is not observed by us. We may, however, easily discover it by means of any one of its attributes because it is a common notion that nothing is possessed of no attributes, properties, or qualities. For this reason, when we perceive any attribute, we therefore conclude that some existing thing or substance to which it may be attributed, is necessarily present.

53 *That each substance has a principal attribute, and that the attribute of the mind is thought, while that of body is extension.*

But although any one attribute is sufficient to give us a knowledge of substance, there is always one principal property of substance which constitutes its nature and essence, and on which all the others depend. Thus extension in length, breadth and depth, constitutes the nature of corporeal substance; and thought constitutes the nature of thinking substance. For all else that may be attributed to body presupposes extension, and is but a mode of this extended thing; as everything that we find in mind is but so many diverse forms of thinking. Thus, for example, we cannot conceive figure but as an extended thing, nor movement but as in an extended space; so imagination, feeling, and will, only exist in a thinking thing. But, on the other hand, we can conceive extension without figure or action, and thinking without imagination or sensation, and so on with the rest; as is quite clear to anyone who attends to the matter.

54 *How we may have clear and distinct notions of thinking substance, of corporeal substance, and of God.*

We may thus easily have two clear and distinct notions or ideas, the one of created substance which thinks, the other of corporeal substance, provided we carefully separate all the attributes of thought from those of extension. We can also have a clear and distinct idea of an uncreated and independent thinking substance, that is to say, of God, provided that we do not suppose that this idea represents to us all that is exhibited in God, and that we do not mingle anything fictitious with it, but simply attend to what is evidently contained in the notion, and which we are aware pertains to the nature of an absolutely perfect Being. For no one can deny that such an idea of God exists in us, unless he groundlessly asserts that the mind of man cannot attain to a knowledge of God.

26

55 *How we can also have a distinct understanding of duration, order, and number.*

We shall likewise have a very distinct understanding of duration, order and number, if, in place of mingling with the idea that we have of them what properly speaking pertains to the conception of substance, we merely consider that the duration of each thing is a mode under which we shall consider this thing in so far as it continues to exist; and if in the same way we think that order and number are not really different from the things that are ordered and numbered, but that they are only the modes under which we consider these things.

56 *What are modes, qualities, and attributes.*

And, indeed, when we here speak of modes we mean nothing more than what elsewhere is termed attribute or quality. But when we consider substance as modified or diversified by them, I avail myself of the word *mode;* and when from the disposition or variation it can be named as of such and such a kind, we shall use the word *qualities* [to designate the different modes which cause it to be so termed]; and finally when we more generally consider that these modes or qualities are in substance we term them *attributes.* And because in God any variableness is incomprehensible, we cannot ascribe to Him modes or qualities; but simply attributes. And even in created things that which never exists in them in any diverse way, like existence and duration in the existing and enduring thing, should be called not qualities or modes, but attributes.

57 *That there are attributes which pertain to things and others to thought; and what duration and time are.*

Some of the attributes are in things themselves and others are only in our thought. Thus time, for example, which we distinguish from duration taken in its general sense and which we describe as the measure of movement, is only a mode of thinking; [20] for we do not indeed apprehend that the duration of things which are moved is different from that of the things which are not moved, as is evident from the fact that if two bodies are moved for the space of an hour, the one quickly, the other slowly, we do not count the time longer in one case than in the other, although there is much more movement in one of the two bodies than in the other. But in order to comprehend the duration of all things under the same measure, we usually compare their duration with the duration of the greatest and most regular motions, which are those that create years and days, and these we term time. Hence this adds nothing to the notion of duration, generally taken, but a mode of thinking.

20 'is only a mode of thinking that duration', French version.

58 *That number and all universals are simply modes of thought.*

Similarly number when we consider it abstractly or generally and not in created things, is but a mode of thinking; and the same is true of all that which [in the schools] is named universals.

59 *How universals are formed and what are the five common ones: genus, species, difference, property and accident.*

Universals arise solely from the fact that we avail ourselves of one and the same idea in order to think of all individual things which have a certain similitude; and when we comprehend under the same name all the objects represented by this idea, that name is universal. For example, when we see two stones, and without thinking further of their nature than to remark that there are two, we form in ourselves an idea of a certain number which we term the number of two; and when afterwards we see two birds or two trees, and we observe without further thinking about their nature, that there are two of them, we again take up the same idea which we had before, which idea is universal; and we give to this number the universal name 'two'. And in the same way when we consider a three-sided figure we form a certain idea which we call the idea of a triangle; and we afterwards make use of it as a universal in representing to ourselves all the figures having three sides. But when we notice more particularly that of three-sided figures some have a right angle and others have not, we form the universal idea of a rectangular triangle, which being related to the preceding as to a more general, may be termed *species;* and the right angle is the universal *difference* by which right-angled triangles are distinguished from all others. If we further observe that the square of the side which subtends the right-angle is equal to the squares of the two other sides, and that this property belongs only to this species of triangle, we may term it a [universal] *property* of the species. Finally if we suppose that certain of the triangles are moved, and others are not moved we should take that to be a universal *accident* of the same; and it is thus that we commonly enumerate the five universals, viz. genus, species, difference, property, accident.

28

60 *Of distinctions, and firstly of real distinction.*

But as to the number in things themselves, this proceeds from the distinction which exists between them; and distinction is of three sorts, viz. real, modal and of reason. The *real* is properly speaking found between two or more substances; and we can conclude that two substances are really distinct one from the other from the sole fact that we can conceive the one clearly and distinctly without the other. For in accordance with the knowledge which we have of God, we are certain that He can carry into effect all that of which we have a distinct idea. That is why from the fact that we now have, e.g. the idea of an extended or corporeal substance, although we do not yet know certainly whether such really exists at all, we may yet conclude that it may exist; and if it does exist, any one portion of it which we can demarcate in our thought must be distinct from every other part of the same substance. Similarly because each one of us is conscious that he thinks, and that in thinking he can shut off from himself all other substance, either thinking or extended, we may conclude that each of us, similarly regarded, is really distinct from every other thinking substance and from every corporeal substance. And even if we suppose that God had united a body to a soul so closely that it was impossible to bring them together more closely, and made a single thing out of the two, they would yet remain really distinct one from the other notwithstanding the union; because however closely God connected them He could not set aside the power which He possessed of separating them, or conserving them one apart from the other, and those things which God can separate, or conceive in separation, are really distinct.

61 *Of the modal distinction.*

There are two sorts of *modal* distinctions, i.e. the one between the mode properly speaking, and the substance of which it is the mode, and the other between two modes of the same substance. The former we recognise by the fact that we can clearly conceive substance without the mode which we say differs from it, while we cannot reciprocally have a perception of this mode without perceiving the substance. There is, for example, a modal distinction between figure or movement and the corporeal substance in which both exist: there is also a distinction between affirming or recollecting and the mind. As to the other kind of distinction, its characteristic is that we are able to recognise the one mode without the other and vice versa, but we can conceive neither the one nor the other without recognising that both subsist in one common substance. If, for example, a stone is moved and along with that is square, we are able to conceive the square figure without knowing that it is moved, and reciprocally, we may be aware that it is moved without knowing that it is square; but we cannot have a conception of this movement and figure unless we have a conception of the substance of the stone. As for the distinction whereby the mode of one substance is different from another substance, or from the mode of another substance, as the movement of one body is different from another body or from mind, or else as movement is different from duration; it appears to me that we should call it real rather than modal; because we cannot clearly conceive these modes apart from the substances of which they are the modes and which are really distinct.

30

62 *Of the distinction created by thought.*

Finally the distinction of *reason* is between substance and some one of its attributes without which it is not possible that we should have a distinct knowledge of it, or between two such attributes of the same substance. This distinction is made manifest from the fact that we cannot have a clear and distinct idea of such a substance if we exclude from it such an attribute; or we cannot have a clear idea of the one of the two attributes if we separate from it the other. For example, because there is no substance which does not cease to exist when it ceases to endure, duration is only distinct from substance by thought;[21] and all the modes of thinking which we consider as though they existed in the objects, differ only in thought both from the objects of which they are the thought and from each other in a common object.[22] I recollect having elsewhere conjoined this sort of distinction with modal distinction (near the end of the reply

21 *ratione.*
22 'And generally all the attributes which cause us to have diverse thoughts of the same thing, such as the extension of body and its property of divisibility, do not differ from the body which is to us the object of them, or the one from the other, excepting so far as we sometimes think confusedly of the one without the other.' French version.

made to the First Objection to the Meditations on the First Philosophy), but then it was not necessary to treat accurately of these distinctions, and it was sufficient for my purpose at the time simply to distinguish them both from the real.

63 *How we may have distinct conceptions of thought and extension, inasmuch as the one constitutes the nature of mind, and the other that of body.*

We may likewise consider thought and extension as constituting the natures of intelligence and corporeal substance; and then they must not be considered otherwise than as the very substances that think and are extended, i.e. as mind and body; for we know them in this way very clearly and distinctly. It is moreover more easy to know a substance that thinks, or an extended substance, than substance alone, without regarding whether it thinks or is extended. For we experience some difficulty in abstracting the notions that we have of substance from those of thought or extension, for they in truth do not differ but in thought,[23] and our conception is not more distinct because it comprehends fewer properties, but because we distinguish accurately that which it does comprehend from all other notions.

64 *How we may also conceive them as modes of substance.*

We may likewise consider thought and extension as the modes which are found in substance; that is, in as far as we consider that one and the same mind may have many different thoughts, and that one body, retaining the same size, may be extended in many different ways, sometimes being greater in length and less in breadth or depth, and sometimes on the contrary greater in breadth and less in length. We then distinguish them modally from substance, and they may be conceived not less clearly and distinctly, provided that we do not think of them as substance or things separate from others, but simply as modes of things. Because when we regard them as in the substances of which they are the modes, we distinguish them from these substances, and take them for what they actually are; while, on the contrary, if we wish to consider them apart from the substances in which they are, that will have the effect of our taking them as self-subsisting things and thus confounding the ideas of mode and substance.

23 *ratione.*

65 *How we may likewise know their diverse modes.*

We shall similarly best apprehend the diverse modes of thought such as understanding, imagining, recollecting, willing, etc., and the diverse modes of extension, or which pertain to extension, such as all figures, the situation of parts, and their movements, provided that we consider them simply as modes of the things in which they are; and as for motion we shall best understand it, if we inquire only about locomotion, without taking into account the force that produces it, which I shall nevertheless endeavour to set forth in its own place.

66 *That we also have a clear knowledge of our sensations, affections, and appetites, although we frequently err in the judgments we form of them.*

There remain our sensations, affections and appetites, as to which we may likewise have a clear knowledge, if we take care to include in the judgments we form of them that only which we know to be precisely contained in our perception of them, and of which we are intimately conscious. It is, however, most difficult to observe this condition, in regard to our senses at least, because we, everyone of us, have judged from our youth up that all things of which we have been accustomed to have sensation have had an existence outside our thoughts, and that they have been entirely similar to the sensation, that is the idea which we have formed of them. Thus, when, for example, we perceived a certain colour, we thought that we saw something which existed outside of us and which clearly resembled the idea of colour which we then experienced in ourselves, and from the habit of judging this way we seemed to see this so clearly and distinctly as to be convinced that it is certain and indubitable.

67 *That we frequently deceive ourselves in judging of pain itself.*

The same is true in regard to all our other sensations, even those which have to do with agreeable sensation and pain. For although we do not believe that these feelings exist outside of us, we are not wont to regard them as existing merely in our mind or our perception, but as being in our hands, feet, or some other part of our body. But there is no reason that we should be obliged to believe that the pain, for example, which we feel in our foot, is anything beyond our mind which exists in our foot, nor that the light which we imagine ourselves to see in the sun really is in the sun [as it is in us]; for both these are prejudices of our youth, as will clearly appear in what follows.

68 *How we may distinguish in such matters that which we know clearly from that in which we may err.*

But in order that we may here distinguish that which is clear from that which is obscure we ought to observe that we have a clear or distinct knowledge of pain, colour, and other things of the sort when we consider them simply as sensations or thoughts. But when we desire to judge of such matters as existing outside of our mind, we can in no wise conceive what sort of things they are. And when anyone says that he sees colour in a body or feels pain in one of his limbs, it is the same as if he told us that he there saw or felt something but was absolutely ignorant of its nature, or else that he did not know what he saw or felt. For although when he examines his thoughts with less attention he perhaps easily persuades himself that he has some knowledge of it, because he supposes that there is something resembling the sensation of colour or pain which he experiences, yet if he investigates what is represented to him by this sensation of colour or pain appearing as they do to exist in a coloured body or suffering part, he will find that he is really ignorant of it.

69 *That we know magnitude, figure, etc. quite differently from colour and pain, etc.*

This will be more especially evident if we consider that size in the body which is seen, or figure or movement (local movement at least, for philosophers by imagining other sorts of motion than this, have rendered its nature less intelligible to themselves), or situation, or duration, or number, and the like, which we clearly perceive in all bodies, as has been already described, are known by us in a quite different way from that in which colour is known in the same body, or pain, odour, taste, or any of the properties which, as hitherto mentioned, should be attributed to the senses. For although in observing a body we are not less assured of its existence from the colour which we perceive in its regard than from the figure which bounds it, we yet know this property in it which causes us to call it figured, with much greater clearness than what causes us to say that it is coloured.

70 *That we may judge in two ways of sensible things, by one of which we shall avoid error, while by the other we shall fall into error.*

It is thus evident when we say that we perceive colours in objects, that it is the same as though we said that we perceive something in the objects of whose nature we were ignorant, but which yet caused a very clear and vivid sensation in us, and which is termed the sensation of colours. But there is a great deal of difference in our manner of judging, for, so long as we believe that there is something in objects of which we have no knowledge (that is in things, such as they are, from which sensation comes to us), so far are we from falling into error that, on the contrary, we rather provide against it, for we are less likely to judge rashly of a thing which we have been forewarned we do not know. But when we think we perceive a certain colour in objects although we have no real knowledge of what the name colour signifies, and we can find no intelligible resemblance between the colour which we suppose to exist in objects and what we are conscious of in our senses, yet, because we do not observe this, or remark in these objects certain other qualities like magnitude, figure, number, etc., which we clearly know are or may be in objects, as our senses or understanding show us, it is easy to allow ourselves to fall into the error of holding that what we call colour in objects is something entirely resembling the colour we perceive, and then supposing that we have a clear perception of what we do not perceive at all.

71 *That the principal cause of error is found in the prejudices of childhood.*

It is here that the first and principal of our errors is to be found. For in the first years of life the mind was so closely allied to body that it applied itself to nothing but those thoughts alone by which it was aware of the things which affected the body; nor were these as yet referred to anything existing outside itself; but the fact was merely that pain was felt when the body was hurt, or pleasure experienced when the body received some good, or else if the body was so [slightly] affected that no great good nor evil was experienced, such sensations were encountered as we call tastes, smells, sound, heat, cold, light, colours, etc., which in truth represent nothing to us outside of our mind, but which vary in accordance with the diversities of the parts and modes in which the body is affected.[24] The mind at the same time also perceived magnitudes, figures, movements and the like, which were exhibited to it not as sensations but as things or the modes of things existing, or at least capable of existing, outside thought, although it did not yet observe this distinction between the two. And afterwards when the machine of the body which has been so constituted by nature that it can of its own inherent power turn here and there, by turning fortuitously this way and the other, followed after what was useful and avoided what was harmful, the mind which was closely allied to it, reflecting on the things which it followed after or avoided, remarked first of all that they existed outside itself, and attributed to them not alone magnitudes, figures, movements, and other such properties which it apprehended as things or modes of things, but also tastes, smells, and the like, the sensations of which it perceived that these things caused in it. And as all other things were only considered in as far as they served for the use of the body in which it was immersed, mind judged that there was more or less reality in each body, according as the impressions made on body were more or less strong. Hence came the belief that there was much more substance or corporeal reality in rocks or metals than in air or water, because the sensation of hardness and weight were much more strongly felt. And thus it was that air was only regarded as anything when it was agitated by some wind, and we experienced it to be either hot or cold. And because the stars would not give more light than tiny lighted candles, it did not hold them to be larger than such flames. Moreover because it did not as yet remark that the earth turned on its own axis, and that the superficies was curved like a sphere, it was more ready to apprehend that it was immovable and that the surface was flat. And we have in this way been imbued with a thousand other such prejudices from infancy, which in later youth we quite forgot we had accepted without sufficient examination, admitting them as though they were of perfect truth and certainty, and as if they had been known by means of our senses or implanted in us by nature.

24 'which vary according to the movements which pass from all parts of our body to the part of the brain to which it is closely united.' French version.

72 *That the second cause of our errors is that we cannot forget these prejudices.*

Though in coming to years of maturity, when the mind, being no longer wholly subject to the body, does not refer everything to it, but also inquires into the truth of things as they are in themselves, we find that much of the judgment that we before had formed is false, yet it is not easy to eradicate the false from our memory, and so long as it remains there it may be the cause of many errors. Thus, for example, since from our earliest years we imagined stars to be minute bodies, we have great difficulty in imagining anything different from this first conception, although astronomical reason tells us that they are amongst the largest – so greatly does prejudiced opinion affect our beliefs.

37

73 *The third cause is that our mind fatigues itself when it applies its attention to the objects which are not present to the senses; and that we are therefore in the habit of judging of these not from present perceptions, but from preconceived opinions.*

Further, since our mind cannot pause to consider any one thing with attention without difficulty and fatigue, and since of all objects it applies itself with the greatest difficulty to those which are present neither to the senses nor to the imagination, whether because it derives this nature from its union with the body, or because in the first years of our life we are so much occupied with feeling and imagining that we have acquired a greater facility for thinking in this way than in any other, besides acquiring the habit of so doing, it comes about that many men are unable to believe that there is any substance unless it is unavoidable and corporeal and even sensible. For they are ignorant that the only things that are imaginable are those that exist in extension, motion and figure, while there are many others that are intelligible; and they persuade themselves that there is nothing that can subsist but body, and finally, that there is no body which is not sensible. And since in truth we do not perceive any object as it is in itself by sense alone, as will be clearly shown later on, it comes to pass that most men in life perceive nothing but in a confused way.

74 *The fourth cause is that we attach our concepts to words which do not accurately answer to the reality.*

And finally, because we attach all our conceptions to words for the expression of them by speech, and as we commit to memory our thought in connection with these words; and as we more easily recall to memory words than things, we can scarcely conceive of anything so distinctly as to be able to separate completely that which we conceive from the words chosen to express the same. In this way most men apply their attention to words rather than things, and this is the cause of their frequently giving their assent to terms which they do not understand, either because they believe that they formerly understood them, or because they think that those who informed them correctly understood their signification. And although this is not the place in which to treat particularly of this matter, inasmuch as I have not yet dealt with the nature of the human body, nor even shown that any body exists at all, it yet appears to me that what I have already said may serve to enable us to distinguish those of our conceptions that are clear and distinct from those in which there is obscurity and confusion.

75 *A summary of all that has to be observed in order to philosophise correctly.*

That is why, if we desire to philosophise seriously, and apply ourselves to the research of all the truths we are capable of knowing, we must, in the first place, rid ourselves of our prejudices, and must take great care sedulously to set aside all the opinions which we formerly accepted, until, on applying to them further examination, we discover them to be true. We should afterwards hold an orderly review of the conceptions which we have within us, and accept as true those and only those which present themselves to our apprehension as clear and distinct. In this way we shall know, first of all that we exist, inasmuch as our nature is to think, and at the same time that there is a God on whom we depend; and after having considered His attributes we shall be in a position to inquire into the truth of all other things, since God is their cause. In addition to the notions we have of God and our thoughts, we shall likewise find within us a knowledge of many propositions which are eternally true, as, for example, that nothing cannot be the cause of anything, etc. We shall also find there the idea of a corporeal or extended nature which may be moved, divided, etc., and also of the sensations which affect us, such as those of pain, colour, taste, etc., although we do not as yet know the cause of our being so affected. And comparing this [what we now know by examining those things in their order] with our former confused knowledge, we shall acquire the custom of forming clear and distinct conceptions of all that we can know. And in these few precepts it appears to me that the principles of human knowledge are contained.

39

76 *That we ought to prefer the Divine authority to our perceptions,*[25] *but, excluding this, we should not assent to anything which we do not clearly perceive.*

Above all we should impress on our memory as an infallible rule that what God has revealed to us is incomparably more certain than anything else; and that we ought to submit to the Divine authority rather than to our own judgment even though the light of reason may seem to us to suggest, with the utmost clearness and evidence, something opposite. But in things in regard to which Divine authority reveals nothing to us, it would be unworthy of a philosopher to accept anything as true which he has not ascertained to be such, and to trust more to the senses, that is to judgments formed without consideration in childhood, than to the reasoning of maturity.

25 'reasonings' French version.

SECOND PART:

40   OF THE PRINCIPLES OF MATERIAL THINGS

1 *What are the reasons for our having a certain knowledge of material things?*
Although we are all persuaded that material things exist, yet because
we have doubted this before and have placed it in the rank of the
prejudices of our childhood, it is now requisite that we should
inquire into the reasons through which we may accept this truth
with certainty. To begin with we feel that without doubt all our
perceptions proceed from some thing which is different from our
mind. For it is not in our power to have one perception rather than
another, since each one is clearly dependent on the object which
affects our senses. It is true that we may inquire whether that object
is God, or some other different from God. But inasmuch as we
perceive, or rather are stimulated by sense to apprehend clearly and
distinctly a matter which is extended in length, breadth, and depth,
the various parts of which have various figures and motions, and
give rise to the sensations we have of colours, smells, pains, etc., if
41   God immediately and of Himself presented to our mind the idea of
this extended matter, or merely permitted it to be caused in us by
some other object which possessed no extension, figure, or motion,
there would be nothing to prevent Him from being regarded as a
deceiver. For we clearly apprehend this matter as different from
God, or ourselves, or our mind, and appear to discern very plainly
that the idea of it is due to objects outside of ourselves to which it is
absolutely similar. But God cannot deceive us, because deception is
repugnant to His nature, as has been explained. And hence we must
conclude that there is an object extended in length, breadth, and
depth, and possessing all those properties which we clearly perceive
to pertain to extended objects. And this extended object is called by
us either body or matter.

2 *How we likewise know that the body of man is closely united to the mind.*
It may be concluded also that a certain body is more closely united
to our mind than any other, from the fact that pain and other of our

sensations occur without our foreseeing them; and that mind is conscious that these do not arise from itself alone, nor pertain to it in so far as it is a thinking thing, but only in so far as it is united to another thing, extended and mobile, which is called the human body. But this is not the place to explain the matter further.

3 *That the perceptions of the senses do not teach us what is really in things, but merely that whereby they are useful or hurtful to man's composite nature.*

It will be sufficient for us to observe that the perceptions of the senses are related simply to the intimate union which exists between body and mind, and that while by their means we are made aware of what in external bodies can profit or hurt this union, they do not present them to us as they are in themselves unless occasionally and accidentally. For [after this observation] we shall without difficulty set aside all the prejudices of the senses and in this regard rely upon our understanding alone, by reflecting carefully on the ideas implanted therein by nature.

42

4 *That the nature of body consists not in weight, nor in hardness, nor colour and so on, but in extension alone.*

In this way we shall ascertain that the nature of matter or of body in its universal aspect, does not consist in its being hard, or heavy, or coloured, or one that affects our senses in some other way, but solely in the fact that it is a substance extended in length, breadth and depth. For as regards hardness we do not know anything of it by sense, excepting that the portions of the hard bodies resist the motion of our hands when they come in contact with them; but if, whenever we moved our hands in some direction, all the bodies in that part retreated with the same velocity as our hands approached them, we should never feel hardness; and yet we have no reason to believe that the bodies which recede in this way would on this account lose what makes them bodies. It follows from this that the nature of body does not consist in hardness. The same reason shows us that weight, colour, and all the other qualities of the kind that is perceived in corporeal matter, may be taken from it, it remaining meanwhile entire: it thus follows that the nature of body depends on none of these.

5 *That this truth regarding the nature of body is obscured by prejudices regarding rarefaction and the vacuum.*

There still remain two reasons which may cause us to doubt whether the true nature of body consists solely in extension. The first is that prevalent opinion that most bodies are capable of being rarefied and condensed, so that when rarefied they have greater extension than when condensed; and some have even subtilised to such an extent that they desire to distinguish the substance of a body from its quantity, and its quantity from its extension. The second reason is that when we conceive that there is extension in length, breadth and depth only, we are not in the habit of saying that there is a body, but only space and further empty space, which most people persuade themselves is a mere negation.

6   *In what way rarefaction takes place.*

But as regards rarefaction and condensation, whoever will examine his own thoughts and refuse to admit anything which he does not clearly perceive, will not allow that there is anything in these processes but a change of figure [in the body rarefied or condensed]: that is to say, rare bodies are those between whose parts there are many interstices filled with other bodies; and those are called dense bodies, on the other hand, whose parts, by approaching one another, either render these distances less than they were, or remove them altogether, in which case the body is rendered so dense that it cannot be denser. And yet it does not possess less extension than when the parts occupied a greater space, owing to their being further removed from one another. For we ought not to attribute to a body the extension of the pores or the interstices which its parts do not occupy [when it is rarefied], but to the other bodies which occupy these interstices. Just as when we see a sponge filled with water or some other fluid, we do not suppose that for this reason each part of the sponge is more extended than when it is compressed and dry, but only that its pores are wider, and that it is therefore distributed over a larger space.

7   *That rarefaction cannot be intelligibly explained in any other way.*

I am indeed unable to say why this rarefaction of bodies has been explained by some as the result of augmentation of quantity rather

than by the example of the sponge. For although when air or water
are rarefied we do not see any of the pores which are rendered large,   44
nor any new body that is added to occupy them, it is yet less
consonant with reason to suppose something that is unintelligible in
order to give a merely verbal explanation of how bodies are rarefied,
than to conclude in consequence of that rarefaction, that there are
pores or interstices which become greater, and which are filled with
some new body, although we do not perceive this new body with
the senses. For there is no reason which obliges us to believe that we
should perceive by our senses all the bodies which exist around us.
And we perceive that it is very easy to explain rarefaction in this
manner though not in any other. And finally it would be
undoubtedly contradictory to suppose that any body should be
increased by a fresh quantity or fresh extension, without the
addition to it of a new extended substance, i.e. a new body. Because
it is impossible to conceive any addition of extension or quantity,
without the addition of a substance having quantity or extension, as
will be more clearly shown below.

8 *That quantity and number differ only in thought* [26] *from what has
quantity and is numbered.*

For quantity differs from extended substance, or number from what
is numbered, not in reality but only in our conception. Thus, to
take an example, we may consider the whole nature of corporeal
substance which is comprised within a space of ten feet, although
we do not attend to this measure of ten feet; because it is clear that
the thing conceived is the same in any one part of that space as in
the whole. And vice versa, we can comprehend the number ten, as
also a continuous quantity of ten feet, without attending to any
particular determinate substance, because the conception of the
number of ten is plainly the same, whether considered in reference
to the measure of ten feet, or to any other ten; and we cannot
conceive a continuous quantity of ten feet without thinking of some   45
extended substance of which it is the quantity, but yet we can
conceive it without thinking of that determinate substance. In
reality it is however impossible that even the least part of such
quantity or extension can be taken away without taking away

26 *ratione.*

likewise an equal amount of substance; on the other hand, not the least part of the substance can be removed without our diminishing its quantity and extension by the same amount.

9 *That corporeal substance, when distinguished from its quantity, is confusedly conceived as something incorporeal.*

Although, however, some express themselves otherwise on this subject, I cannot think that they regard it otherwise than as I have just said; for when they distinguish substance from extension or quantity, they either mean nothing by the word substance, or they merely form in their minds a confused idea of incorporeal substance which they falsely attribute to corporeal, and leave to extension, which they nevertheless call an accident, that true idea of this corporeal substance, and thus it is easy to see that their words are not in harmony with their thoughts.

10 *What space or internal place is.*

Space or internal place and the corporeal substance which is contained in it, are not different otherwise than in the mode in which they are conceived of by us. For, in truth, the same extension in length, breadth, and depth, which constitutes space, constitutes body; and the difference between them consists only in the fact that in body we consider extension as particular and conceive it to change just as body changes; in space, on the contrary, we attribute to extension a generic unity, so that after having removed from a certain space the body which occupied it, we do not suppose that we have also removed the extension of that space, because it appears to us that the same extension remains so long as it is of the same magnitude and figure, and preserves the same position in relation to certain other bodies, whereby we determine this space.

46   **11** *In what sense it may be said that space is not different from corporeal substance.*

And it will be easy for us to recognise that the same extension which constitutes the nature of body likewise constitutes the nature of space, nor do the two mutually differ, excepting as the nature of the genus or species differs from the nature of the individual, provided that, in order to discern the idea that we have of any body, such as stone, we reject from it all that is not essential to the nature of body. In the first place, then, we may reject hardness, because if the stone were liquefied or reduced to powder, it would no longer possess hardness, and yet would not cease to be a body; let us in the next place reject colour, because we have often seen stones so transparent that they had no colour; again we reject weight, because we see that fire although very light is yet body; and finally we may reject cold, heat, and all the other qualities of the kind either because they are not considered as in the stone, or else because with the change of their qualities the stone is not for that reason considered to have lost its nature as body. After examination we shall find that there is nothing remaining in the idea of body excepting that it is extended in length, breadth, and depth; and this is comprised in our idea of space, not only of that which is full of body but also of that which is called a vacuum.

12 *How space is different from body in our mode of conceiving it.*

There is, however, some difference in our mode of conceiving them; for if we remove a stone from the space or place where it was, we conceive that the extension of this stone has also been removed from it, because we consider this to be singular, and inseparable from the stone itself. But meantime we suppose that the same extension of place occupied by the stone remains, though the place which it formerly occupied has been taken up with wood, water, air, and any other bodies, or even has been supposed to be empty, because we now consider extension in general, and it appears to us that the same is common to stones, wood, water, air, and all other bodies, and even to a vacuum, if there be such a thing, provided that it is of the same magnitude and figure as before, and preserves the same situation in regard to the external bodies which determine this space.

47

13 *What external place is.*

The reason of this is that the words place and space signify nothing different from the body which is said to be in a place, and merely designate its magnitude, figure, and situation as regards other bodies. For it is necessary in order to determine this situation to observe certain others which we consider to be immovable; and according as we regard different bodies we may find that the same thing at the same time changes its place, and does not change it. For example, if we consider a man seated at the stern of a vessel when it is carried out to sea, he may be said to be in one place if we regard the parts of the vessel with which he preserves the same situation: and yet he will be found continually to change his position, if regard be paid to the neighbouring shores in relation to which he is constantly receding from one, and approaching another. And further, if we suppose that the earth moves, and that it makes precisely the same way from west to east as the vessel does from east to west, it will again appear to us that he who is seated at the stern does not change his position, because that place is determined by certain immovable points which we imagine to be in the heavens. But if at length we are persuaded that there are no points in the universe that are really immovable, as will presently be shown to be probable, we shall conclude that there is nothing that has a permanent place except in so far as it is fixed by our thought.

14 Wherein place and space differ.

48

The terms place and space are however different, because place indicates situation more expressly than magnitude or figure; while, on the contrary, we more often think of the latter when we speak of space. For we frequently say that a thing has succeeded to the place of another, although it does not possess exactly either its magnitude or its figure; but we do not for all that mean that it occupies the same space as the other; and when the situation is changed, we say that the place also is changed, although the same magnitude and figure exist as before. And hence if we say that a thing is in a particular place, we simply mean that it is situated in a certain manner in reference to certain other things; and when we add that it occupies a certain space or place, we likewise mean that it is of a definite magnitude or figure [so as exactly to fill the space].

15 How external place is rightly taken to be the superficies of the surrounding body.

And thus we never distinguish space from extension in length, breadth and depth; but we sometimes consider place as in the thing placed, and sometimes as outside of it. Internal place is indeed in no way distinguished from space; but we sometimes regard external place as the superficies which immediately surrounds the thing placed in it. And it is to be observed that by superficies we do not here mean any portion of the surrounding body, but merely the extremity which is between the surrounding body and that surrounded, which is but a mode; or that we mean the common surface which is a surface that is not a part of one body rather than of the other, and that it is always considered the same, so long as it retains the same magnitude and figure. For although all the surrounding body with its superficies is changed, we should not imagine that the body which was surrounded by it had for all that changed its place, if it meanwhile preserved the same situation in regard to other bodies that are regarded as immovable. Thus if we suppose that a ship is carried along in one direction by the current of a stream, and is impelled by a contrary wind in another direction in an equal degree, so that its situation is not changed with regard to the banks, we are ready to admit that it remains in the same place although we see that the whole surrounding superficies is in a state of change.

49

16 *That it is contrary to reason to say that there is a vacuum or space in which there is absolutely nothing.*

As regards a vacuum in the philosophic sense of the word, i.e. a space in which there is no substance, it is evident that such cannot exist, because the extension of space or internal place, is not different from that of body. For, from the mere fact that a body is extended in length, breadth, or depth, we have reason to conclude that it is a substance, because it is absolutely inconceivable that nothing should possess extension, we ought to conclude also that the same is true of the space which is supposed to be void, i.e. that since there is in it extension, there is necessarily also substance.

17 *That a vacuum, in the ordinary sense, does not exclude all body.*

And when we take this word vacuum in its ordinary sense, we do not mean a place or space in which there is absolutely nothing, but only a place in which there are none of those things which we expected to find there. Thus because a pitcher is made to hold water, we say that it is empty when it contains nothing but air; or if there are no fish in a fishpond, we say that there is nothing in it, even though it be full of water; similarly we say a vessel is empty, when, in place of the merchandise which it was designed to carry, it is loaded only with sand, so that it may resist the impetuous violence of the wind; and finally we say in the same way that a space is empty when it contains nothing sensible, even though it contain created matter and self-existent substance; for we are not wont to consider things excepting those with which our senses succeed in presenting us.[27] And if, in place of keeping in mind what we should comprehend by these words – vacuum and nothing – we afterwards suppose that in the space which is termed vacuum there is not only nothing sensible, but nothing at all, we shall fall into the same error as if, because a pitcher is usually termed empty since it contains nothing but air, we were therefore to judge that the air contained in it is not a substantive thing.

18 *How the prejudice concerning the absolute vacuum is to be corrected.*

We have almost all lapsed into this error from the beginning of our lives, for, seeing that there is no necessary connection between the vessel and the body it contains, we thought that God at least could remove all the body contained in the vessel without its being necessary that any other body should take its place. But in order that we may be able to correct this error, it is necessary to remark that while there is no connection between the vessel and that particular body which it contains, there is an absolutely necessary one between the concave figure of the vessel and the extension considered generally which must be comprised in this cavity; so that there is not more contradiction in conceiving a mountain without a valley, than such a cavity without the extension which it contains, or this extension without the substance which is extended, because nothing, as has already been frequently remarked, cannot have extension. And therefore, if it is asked what would happen if God removed all the body contained in a vessel without permitting its place being occupied by another body, we shall answer that the sides of the vessel will thereby come into immediate contiguity with one another. For two bodies must touch when there is nothing between them, because it is manifestly contradictory for these two

27 'consider bodies near to us excepting in so far as they cause in our organs of sense impressions strong enough to enable us to perceive them.' French version.

bodies to be apart from one another, or that there should be a distance between them, and yet that this distance should be nothing; for distance is a mode of extension, and without extended substance it cannot therefore exist.

19 *That this confirms what was said of rarefaction.*   51

After we have thus remarked that the nature of material substance consists only in its being an extended thing, or that its extension is not different from what has been attributed to space however empty, it is easy to discover that it is impossible that any one of these parts should in any way occupy more space at one time than another, and thus that it may be rarefied otherwise than in the manner explained above; or again it is easy to perceive that there cannot be more matter or corporeal substance in a vessel when it is filled with gold or lead, or any other body that is heavy and hard, than when it only contains air and appears to be empty; for the quantity of the parts of matter does not depend on their weight or hardness, but only on the extension which is always equal in the same vessel.

20 *That from this may be demonstrated the non-existence of atoms.*

We also know that there cannot be any atoms or parts of matter which are indivisible of their own nature [as certain philosophers have imagined]. For however small the parts are supposed to be, yet because they are necessarily extended we are always able in thought to divide any one of them into two or more parts; and thus we know that they are divisible. For there is nothing which we can divide in thought, which we do not thereby recognise to be divisible; and therefore if we judged it to be indivisible, our judgment would be contrary to the knowledge we have of the matter. And even should we suppose that God had reduced some portion of matter to a smallness so extreme that it could not be divided into smaller, it would not for all that be properly termed indivisible. For though God had rendered the particle so small that it was beyond the power of any creature to divide it, He could not deprive Himself of His power of division, because it is absolutely   52
impossible that He should lessen His own omnipotence as was said before. And therefore, absolutely speaking, its divisibility remains [to the smallest extended particle] because from its nature it is such.

21 *That extension of the world is likewise indefinite.*

We likewise recognise that this world, or the totality of corporeal substance, is extended without limit, because wherever we imagine a limit we are not only still able to imagine beyond that limit spaces indefinitely extended, but we perceive these to be in reality such as we imagine them. That is to say that they contain in them corporeal substance indefinitely extended. For, as has been already shown very fully, the idea of extension that we perceive in any space whatever is quite evidently the same as the idea of corporeal substance.

22 *Thus the matter of the heavens and of the earth is one and the same, and there cannot be a plurality of worlds.*

It is thus not difficult to infer from all this, that the earth and heavens are formed of the same matter, and that even were there an infinitude of worlds, they would all be formed of this matter; from which it follows that there cannot be a plurality of worlds, because we clearly perceive that the matter whose nature consists in its being an extended substance only, now occupies all the imaginable spaces where these other worlds could alone be, and we cannot find in ourselves the idea of any other matter.

23 *That all the variety in matter, or all the diversity of its forms, depends on motion.*

There is therefore but one matter in the whole universe, and we know this by the simple fact of its being extended. All the properties which we clearly perceive in it may be reduced to the one, viz. that it can be divided, or moved according to its parts, and consequently is capable of all these affections which we perceive can arise from the motion of its parts. For its partition by thought alone makes no difference to it; but all the variation in matter, or diversity in its forms, depends on motion. This the philosophers have doubtless observed, inasmuch as they have said that nature was the principle of motion and rest, and by nature they understood that by which all corporeal things become such as they are experienced to be.

24 *What motion is in common parlance.*

But motion (i.e. local motion, for I can conceive no other kind, and do not consider that we ought to conceive any other in nature), in the vulgar sense, is nothing more than the action by which any body passes from one place to another. And just as we have remarked above that the same thing may be said to change and not to change its place at the same time, we can say that it moves and does not move at the same time. For he who is seated in a ship setting sail, thinks he is moving when he looks at the shore he has left, and considers it as fixed, but not if he regards the vessel he is on, because he does not change his position in reference to its parts. Likewise, because we are accustomed to think that there is no motion without action and that in rest there is cessation of action, the person thus seated may more properly be said to be in repose than in motion, since he is not conscious of any action in himself.

25 *What movement properly speaking is.*

But if, looking not to popular usage, but to the truth of the matter, let us consider what ought to be understood by motion according to the truth of the thing; we may say, in order to attribute a determinate nature to it, that it is the transference of one part of matter or one body from the vicinity of those bodies that are in immediate contact with it, and which we regard as in repose, into the vicinity of others. By *one body* or by a *part of matter* I understand all that which is transported together, although it may be composed of many parts which in themselves have other motions. And I say that it is the *transportation* and not either the force or the action which transports, in order to show that the motion is always in the mobile thing, not in that which moves; for these two do not seem to me to be accurately enough distinguished. Further, I understand that it is a mode of the mobile thing and not a substance, just as figure is a mode of the figured thing, and repose of that which is at rest.

54

The remaining Principles, 26–64, are here omitted. (Ed.)

80

THIRD PART:
OF THE VISIBLE WORLD

1 *That we cannot think too highly of the Works of God.*

Having now ascertained certain principles of material things which were derived, not from the prejudices of the senses, but from the light of reason, so that we cannot doubt of their truth, it is for us to examine whether from these alone we can explain all the phenomena of nature. And we shall commence with those which are the most general, and on which the others depend, such as the general structure of the visible world. But in order that we may philosophise correctly in this matter, two things are to be observed. The first is that we must ever keep before our minds the infinitude of the power and goodness of God, and not fear to fall into error by imagining His works to be too great, too beautiful, and too perfect, but that, on the contrary, we must take care lest, if we suppose any limits to exist in them of which we have no certain knowledge, we may seem to be insufficiently sensible of the greatness and power of the Creator.

2 *That we ought to beware lest we presume too much in supposing ourselves to understand the ends which God set before Himself in creating the world.*

The second is that we ought to beware lest we think too highly of ourselves. This we should appear to do if we supposed the universe to have certain limits not presented to our knowledge without at the same time being assured of the fact by divine revelation, which would be making our knowledge extend beyond that which God has made; but this would be even more so if we persuaded ourselves that it was only for us that all things were created by God, or even were we to suppose that by the powers of our mind we could comprehend the ends which He set before Himself in creating the universe.

81

3 *In what sense it can be said that all things were created for man.*

For although it may be a pious thought, as far as morals are concerned, to believe that God has created all things for us in as far as that incites us to a greater gratitude and affection toward Him, and although it is in some respect true, because there is nothing created from which we cannot derive some use, if it be but the exercise of our minds in considering it and the being incited to worship God by its means, it is yet not at all probable that all things have been created for us in such a manner that God has had no other end in creating them. And it seems to me that such a supposition would be certainly ridiculous and inept in reference to questions of physics, for we cannot doubt that an infinitude of things exist, or did exist, though now they have ceased to exist, which have never been beheld or comprehended by man and which have never been of any use to him.

The remaining Principles, 4–157, are here omitted. (Ed.)

Fourth Part: Of the Earth

The first 187 articles in Part 4 are here omitted. (Ed.)

315 **188** *Of what is to be borrowed from disquisitions on animals and man in order to advance the knowledge of material things.*

I should add no more to this fourth part of the Principles of Philosophy, did I (as I had formerly in my mind) purpose writing other sections, viz. a fifth and a sixth part, the fifth treating of living things, that is of animals and plants, and the sixth of man, But because I am not yet quite clear about all of the matters of which I should like to treat in these two last parts, and do not know whether I am likely to have sufficient leisure [or be able to make the experiments necessary] to complete them, I shall here add a little about the objects of the senses in order not to delay the earlier part too long to prevent [their lacking completeness or] anything being amissing which I should have reserved for the latter. For up to this point I have described the earth, and all the visible world, as if it were simply a machine in which there was nothing to consider but [the] figure and movements [of its parts], and yet our senses cause other things to be presented to us, such as colours, smells, sounds, and other such things, of which, if I did not speak, it might be thought that I had omitted the main part of the explanation of the objects of nature.

189 *What sensation* [28] *is, and how it operates.*

We must know, therefore, that although the mind of man informs[29] the whole body, it yet has its principal seat in the brain, and it is there that it not only understands and imagines, but also perceives; and this by means of the nerves which are extended like filaments from the brain to all the other members, with which they are so connected 316 that we can hardly touch any part of the human body without causing the extremities of some of the nerves spread over it to be moved; and this motion passes to the other extremities of those

28 *sensus*.   29 'is united with', French version.

nerves which are collected in the brain round the seat of the soul, as I have just explained quite fully enough in the fourth chapter of the Dioptrics. But the movements which are thus excited in the brain by the nerves, affect in diverse ways the soul or mind, which is intimately connected with the brain, according to the diversity of the motions themselves. And the diverse affections of our mind, or thoughts that immediately arise from these motions, are called perceptions of the senses, or, in common language, sensations.

190 *The different kinds of sensation; and firstly of the internal, that is, of the passions or affections* [30] *of the mind and of the natural appetites.*

The diversities of these sensations depend firstly on the diversity in the nerves themselves, and then on the diversities of the motions which occur in the individual nerves. We have not, however, so many individual senses as individual nerves; it is enough merely to distinguish seven chief different kinds, two of which belong to internal senses, and five to the external. The nerves which extend to the stomach, oesophagus, the fauces, and the other interior parts that serve for the satisfaction of our natural wants, constitute one of our internal senses, which is called the natural appetite. [31] The minute nerves, which extend to the heart and the neighbourhood of the heart, operate in the other internal sense which embraces all the emotions [32] of the mind or passions, and affections such as joy, sadness, love, hate and the like. For, to take an example, when the blood is pure and well-tempered, so that it dilates in the heart more readily and strongly than usual, this so enlarges and moves the little nerves scattered around the orifices, that there is thence a corresponding movement in the brain which affects the mind with a certain natural sense of cheerfulness; and as often as these same nerves are moved in the same way, even although it be from other causes, they excite in us this same feeling. [33] Thus the imagination of the fruition of some good does not contain in itself the sensation of joy, but it cause the animal spirits to pass from the brain to the muscles in which these nerves are inserted; and thus dilating the orifices of the heart, it causes these small nerves to move in the manner which necessarily produces the sensation of joy. Thus, when we are given

317

30 *affectibus.*   31 *appetitus naturalis.*   32 *commotiones.*
33 *sensus; sentiment de joye.*

news the mind first judges of it, and if it is good it rejoices with that intellectual joy which is independent of any emotion[34] of the body, and which the Stoics did not deny to their wise man [although they wished to regard him as free from all passion]. But as soon as this spiritual joy proceeds [from the understanding] to the imagination, the spirits flow from the brain to the muscles about the heart and these excite a movement in the small nerves by which another motion is excited in the brain which gives the soul the sensation of animal joy.[35] In the same way when the blood is so thick that it flows badly into the ventricles of the heart, and is not there sufficiently dilated, it excites in the same nerves a movement quite different from the preceding, which, communicated to the brain, gives a sensation of sadness to the mind, although it is itself perhaps ignorant of the cause of the sadness. And the other causes [which move these little nerves in the same way] may likewise give the same sensation to the soul. But the other movements of the same small nerves produce other affections, such as those of love, hate, fear, anger, etc. in as far as they are merely affections or passions of the mind, that is, in as far as they are confused thoughts which the mind does not have from itself alone, but because it is intimately united to the body, receiving its impressions therefrom. For there is the greatest difference between these passions and the distinct thoughts which we have of what ought to be loved, chosen, or shunned [although they are often found together]. The natural appetites such as hunger, thirst, etc., are likewise sensations excited in the mind by means of the nerves of the stomach, fauces, etc. and are entirely different from the will which we have to eat drink, etc. [and to do all that we think proper for the conservation of the body]; but because this will or appetition nearly always accompanies them, they are called appetites.

318

191 *Of the external senses and first of all of the sense of touch.*

As regards the external senses, everyone acknowledges five, because there are five different kinds of objects that stimulate the nerves which are organs, and because there is the same number of kinds of confused thoughts excited in the soul by these emotions in the nerves. In the first place there are nerves terminating in the skin all over the body. The skin serves as a medium by which the nerves

34 *commotio.*   35 *laetitia animalis.*

can come in contact with any material body whatever, and be moved by these wholes, in one way by their hardness, in another by their gravity, in another by their heat, in another by their humidity etc.; and these nerves excite as many different sensations in the mind as there are different modes by which they are moved, or their ordinary motion is prevented, and from this a corresponding number of tactile qualities derive their names. Besides this, when these nerves are moved a little more vehemently than usual, and yet in such a way that our body is in nowise injured, this causes a sense of gratification which is naturally agreeable to the mind, inasmuch as it gives evidence of the powers of the body to which it is closely joined. But if this action [be strong enough to] cause our body to be in some way hurt, that gives us the sensation of pain. And in this way we see why corporeal pleasure and pain, though absolutely contrary sensations, are almost similar in the objects causing them.

192 Of Taste.

In the next place the other nerves spread over the tongue and the neighbouring parts, are diversely moved by the particles of the bodies which are separated from one another and float in the saliva in the mouth, and thus cause the diverse tastes to be felt according to the diversity of their own figures.

193 Of Smell.

In the third place two nerves or appendages to the brain, for they do not go beyond the skull, are moved by the corporeal particles separated and flying in the air – not indeed by any particles whatsoever, but only by those which, when drawn into the nostrils, are subtle and lively enough to enter the pores of the bones we call the spongy, and thus to reach the nerves. And from the diverse motions of these particles, the diverse sensations of smell arise.

319

194 Of Hearing.

Fourthly, two other nerves hidden in the inward cavities of the ears receive the tremors and vibrations of the whole circumjacent air, for the air agitating the small membranes of the tympanum at the same time disturbs a chain of little bones which are attached, and to which these nerves adhere, and from the diversity of these movements the sensations of different sounds arise.

195 *Of Sight*.

Finally the extremities of the optic nerves, composing the covering of the eyes called the retina, are not moved by the air, nor by any other material object, but only by the globules of the second element, from which we derive the sense of light and colours, as I have already sufficiently explained in the *Dioptrics* and *Meteors*.

196 *That the soul does not perceive excepting in as far as it is in the brain*.

It is however easily proved that the soul feels those things that affect the body not in so far as it is in each member of the body, but only in so far as it is in the brain, where the nerves by their movements convey to it the diverse actions of the external objects which touch the parts of the body [in which they are inserted]. For, in the first place, there are many maladies which, though they affect the brain alone, yet either disorder or altogether take away from us the use of our senses; just like sleep itself which affects the brain alone, and yet every day takes from us during a great part of our time the faculty of perception, which is afterwards restored to us on awakening. Secondly, from the fact that though the brain be healthy [as well as the members in which the organs of the external senses are to be found], if the paths by which the nerves pass from the external parts to the brain are obstructed, that sensation is lost in these external parts of the body. And finally we sometimes feel pain as though it were in certain of our members, and yet its cause is not in these members where it is felt, but in others through which the nerves pass that extend to the brain from the parts where the pain is felt. And this I could prove by innumerable experiments; here, however, one will suffice. When a girl suffering from a serious affection of the hand was visited by the surgeon, her eyes were usually bandaged lest seeing the dressing should have a bad effect upon her. After some days, as gangrene set in, her arm had to be cut off from the elbow and several linen cloths tied together were substituted in place of the amputated limb, in such a way that she was quite ignorant of what had been done; meanwhile, however, she had various pains, sometimes in one of the fingers of the hand which was cut off, and sometimes in another. This could clearly only happen because the nerves which previously had been carried all the way from the brain to the hand, and afterwards terminated in the arm near the elbow, were there affected in the same way as it was their function to be

320

stimulated for the purpose of impressing on the mind residing in the brain the sensation of pain in this and that finger. [And this shows clearly that pain in the hand is not felt by the mind inasmuch as it is in the hand, but as it is in the brain.]

197 *That mind is of such a nature that from the motion of the body alone the various sensations can be excited in it.*

It may, in the next place, be [easily] proved that our mind is of such a nature that the motions which are in the body are alone sufficient to cause it to have all sorts of thoughts, which do not give us any image of any of the motions which give rise to them; and specially that there may be excited in it those confused thoughts called feelings or sensations.[36] For [first of all] we observe that words, whether uttered by the voice or merely written, excite in our minds all sorts of thoughts and emotions. On the same paper, with the same pen and ink, by moving the point of the pen ever so little over the paper in a certain way, we can trace letters which bring to the minds of our readers thoughts of battles, tempests or furies, and the emotions of indignation and sadness; while if the pen be moved in another way, hardly different, thoughts may be given of quite a different kind, viz. those of quietude, peace, pleasantness, and the quite opposite passions of love and joy. Someone will perhaps reply that writing and speech do not immediately excite any passions in the mind, or imaginations of things different from the letters and sounds, but simply so to speak various acts of the understanding; and from these the mind, making them the occasion,[37] then forms for itself the imaginations of a variety of things. But what shall we say of the sensations of what is painful and pleasurable? If a sword moved towards our body cuts it, from this alone pain results which is certainly not less different from the local movement of the sword or of the part of the body which is cut, than are colour or sound or smell or taste. And therefore, as we see clearly that the sensation of pain is easily excited in us from the fact alone that certain parts of our body are locally disturbed by the contact with certain other bodies, we may conclude that our mind is of such a nature that certain local motions can excite in it all the affections belonging to all the other senses.

321

36 *sensus, sive sensationes.*
37 'understanding the meaning of these words', French version.

198 *That there is nothing known of external objects by the senses but their figure, magnitude or motion.*

Besides this, we observe in the nerves no difference which may cause us to judge that some convey to the brain from the organs of the external sense any one thing rather than another, nor again that anything is conveyed there excepting the local motion of the nerves themselves. And we see that this local motion excites in us not alone the sensations of pleasure or pain, but also the sensations of sound and light. For if we receive a blow in the eye hard enough to cause the vibration to reach the retina, we see myriads of sparks which are yet not outside our eye; and when we place our finger on our ear to stop it, we hear a murmuring sound whose cause cannot be attributed to anything but the agitation of the air which is shut up within it. Finally we can likewise frequently observe that heat and the other sensible qualities, inasmuch as they are in objects, and also the forms of these bodies which are purely material, such as e.g. the forms of fire, are produced in them by the motions of certain other bodies, and that these again also produce other motions in other bodies. And we can very well conceive how the movement of one body can be caused by that of another, and diversified by the size, figure, and situation of its parts, but we can in nowise understand how these same things (viz. size, figure and motion) can produce something entirely different in nature from themselves, such as are those substantial forms and real qualities which many suppose to exist in bodies; nor likewise can we understand how these forms or qualities possess the force adequate to cause motion in other bodies. But since we know that our mind is of such a nature that the diverse motions of body suffice to produce in it all the diverse sensations that it has, and as we see by experience that some of the sensations are really caused by such motions, though we do not find anything but these movements to pass through the organs of the external senses to the brain, we may conclude that we in no way likewise apprehend that in external objects like light, colour, smell, taste, sound, heat, cold, and the other tactile qualities, or what we call their substantial forms, there is anything but the various dispositions of these objects which have the power of moving our nerves in various ways.

199 *That there is no phenomenon in nature which has not been dealt with in this treatise.*

And thus by a simple enumeration it may be deduced that there is no phenomenon in nature whose treatment has been omitted in this treatise. For there is nothing that can be counted as a phenomenon of nature, excepting what we are able to perceive by the senses. And with the exception of motion, magnitude and figure [or the situation of the parts of each body], which things I have explained as they exist in every body, we perceive nothing outside us by means of our senses, but light, colours, smells, tastes, sounds and the tactile qualities; and of all these I have just proved that they are nothing more, as far as is known to us, than certain dispositions of objects consisting of magnitude, figure, and motion [so well have I demonstrated that there is nothing in all the visible world, in as far as it is merely visible or sensible, but the things I have there explained].

200 *That there are no principles in this treatise which are not accepted by all men; and that this philosophy is not new, but is the most ancient and most common of all.*

But I likewise desire that it should be observed that although I have here tried to give an explanation of the whole nature of material things, I have nevertheless made use of no principle which has not been approved by Aristotle and by all the other philosophers of every time; so that this philosophy, instead of being new, is the most ancient and common of all. For I have only considered the figure, motion and magnitude of each body, and examined what must follow from their mutual concourse according to the laws of mechanics, confirmed as they are by certain and daily experience. But no one ever doubted that bodies were mixed and have diverse magnitudes and figures, according to the diversity of which their motions also vary, and that from mutual collision those that are larger are divided into many smaller, and thus change their figure. We have experience of this not alone by one single sense, but by several, e.g. by touch, sight and hearing; we also distinctly imagine and understand this. This cannot be said of other things that come under our senses, such as colours, sounds, and the like, which are perceived not by means of several senses, but by single ones; for their images are always confused in our minds, nor do we know what they are.

324

201 *That certain sensible bodies are composed of insensible particles.*

I consider that there are many particles in each body which cannot be perceived by our senses, and this will perhaps not be approved by those who take their senses as a measure of the things they can know. [But it seems to me to be doing great wrong to human reason if we do not consider that knowledge goes beyond the seen]; for no one can doubt that there are bodies so small that they cannot be perceived by any of our senses, if only we consider what is being added each moment to those bodies which increase little by little, and what is removed from those which diminish in the same fashion. We day by day see a tree grow, and it is impossible to comprehend how it becomes larger than it was before, unless by conceiving that some body is added to it. But who has ever observed by means of the senses what are the small bodies which are each day added to the plant that grows? Those at least who hold quantity to be finitely divisible should acknowledge that the particles may become so small as to be absolutely imperceptible. And indeed it should not be wondered at that we are unable to perceive very minute bodies, for the nerves, which must be moved by objects in order to cause us to perceive, are not very minute, but are like small cords which consist of a quantity of yet smaller fibres, and thus they cannot be moved by the minutest of bodies. Nor do I think that anyone who uses his reason will deny that we do much better to judge of what takes place in small bodies which their minuteness alone prevents us from perceiving, by what we see occurring in those that we do perceive [and thus explain all that is in nature, as I have tried to do in this treatise], than, in order to explain certain given things, to invent all sorts of novelties, that have no relation to those that we perceive [such as are first matter, substantial forms, and all the great array of qualities which many are in the habit of assuming, any of which it is more difficult to understand than all the things which we profess to explain by their means].

325

202 *That the philosophy of Democritus is not less different from ours than from the vulgar.*[38]

But Democritus also imagined that there were certain corpuscles that had various figures, sizes and motions, from the heaping together and mutual concourse of which all sensible bodies took their origin; and nevertheless his philosophy is by common consent universally rejected. To this I reply that it never was rejected by anyone because in it he considered bodies smaller than those that can be perceived by the senses, and attributed to them various sizes, figures and motions, for no one can doubt that there are in reality many such, as has been already shown. But this philosophy was rejected in the first place, because it presupposed certain indivisible corpuscles, which hypothesis I also completely reject; in the second place it was rejected because Democritus imagined a void about them, which I demonstrate to be an impossibility; in the third place because he attributed to them gravity, the existence of which I deny in any body in so far as it is considered by itself, because this is a quality depending on the relationship in respect of situation and motion which bodies bear to one another; and finally because he had not explained in detail how all things arose from the concourse of the corpuscles alone, or, if he explained it in regard to certain cases, his reasoning was not in all cases by any means coherent [or such as was capable of proving to us that all nature can be explained in the same way]. If we are to judge of his opinions from what has been preserved regarding his opinions, this at least is the verdict we must give on his philosophy. I leave it to others to judge as to whether what I have written in philosophy possesses sufficient coherence in itself [and whether it is fertile enough in yielding us conclusions. And inasmuch as because the consideration of figure, magnitude and motion has been admitted by Aristotle and all others, as well as by Democritus, and as I reject all that the latter has supposed with this one exception, while I reject practically all that has been supposed by the others, it is clear that this method of philosophising has no more affinity with that of Democritus than with any of the other particular sects.]

38 'from that of Aristotle and others'. French version.

203 *How we may arrive at a knowledge of the figures [magnitudes] and motions of the insensible particles of bodies.*

But since I assign determinate figures, magnitudes and motions to the insensible particles of bodies, as if I had seen them, whereas I admit that they do not fall under the senses, someone will perhaps demand how I have come to my knowledge of them. To this I reply that I first considered generally the most simple and best understood principles implanted in our understanding by nature, and examined the principal differences that could be found between the magnitudes, figures and situations of bodies insensible on account of their smallness alone, and what sensible effects could be produced by the various ways in which they impinge on one another.[39] And finally, when I found like effects in the bodies perceived by our senses, I considered that they might have been produced from a similar concourse of such bodies, especially as no other mode of explaining them could be suggested. And for this end the example of certain bodies made by art was of service to me, for I can see no difference between these and natural bodies, excepting that the effects of machines depend for the most part on the operation of certain instruments, which, since men necessarily make them, must always be large enough to be capable of being easily perceived by the senses. The effects of natural causes, on the other hand, almost always depend on certain organs minute enough to escape every sense. And it is certain that there are no rules in mechanics which do not hold good in physics, of which mechanics forms a part or species [so that all that is artificial is also natural]; for it is not less natural for a clock, made of the requisite number of wheels, to indicate the hours, than for a tree which has sprung from this or that seed, to produce a

39 The first clause of this sentence is amplified in the French version as follows: 'To this I reply that I first considered generally all the most clear and distinct notions of material things to be found in our understanding, and that finding none but those we possess of figures, magnitudes and motions, and the rules whereby these three things can be diversified by one another, which rules are the principles of geometry and mechanics, I judged that all the knowledge man can have of nature must be derived from this source alone, because all the notions that we have of sensible things, being confused and obscure, cannot serve to give us any acquaintanceship with anything outside ourselves, but may on the other hand serve to impede it.'

particular fruit. Accordingly, just as those who apply themselves to the consideration of automata, when they know the use of a certain machine and see some of its parts, easily infer from these the manner in which others which they have not seen are made, so from considering the sensible effects and parts of natural bodies, I have endeavoured to discover the nature of the imperceptible causes and insensible parts contained in them.

204 *That touching the things which our senses do not perceive, it is* 327 *sufficient to explain what the possibilities are about the nature of their existence, though perhaps they are not what we describe them to be [and this is all that Aristotle has tried to do].*

But here it may be said that although I have shown how all natural things can be formed, we have no right to conclude on this account that they were produced by these causes. For just as there may be two clocks made by the same workman, which though they indicate the time equally well and are externally in all respects similar yet in nowise resemble one another in the composition of their wheels, so doubtless there is an infinity of different ways in which all things that we see could be formed by the great Artificer [without it being possible for the mind of man to be aware of which of these means he has chosen to employ]. This I most freely admit; and I believe that I have done all that is required of me if the causes I have assigned are such that they correspond to all the phenomena manifested by nature [without inquiring whether it is by their means or by others that they are produced]. And it will be sufficient for the usages of life to know such causes, for medicine and mechanics and in general all these arts to which the knowledge of physics subserves, have for their end only those effects which are sensible, and which are accordingly to be reckoned among the phenomena of nature.[40] And lest it be supposed that Aristotle did, or desired to do, more than this, it must be recollected that he expressly says in the first book of the

40 'have for their end merely the application of certain sensible bodies to one another, so that by the operation of natural causes certain sensible effects are produced; and one will be able to accomplish this quite as well by considering the succession of certain causes thus imagined, although false, as if they were true, since this succession is supposed to be similar so far as sensible effects are concerned.' French version.

Meteorologics, in the beginning of the seventh chapter, that with regard to things not manifest to the senses, he considers that he supplies sufficient explanations and demonstrations of them, if he merely shows that they may be such as he explains them to be.

205 *That nevertheless there is a moral certainty that everything is such as it has been shown to be.*

But nevertheless that I may not injure the truth, we must consider [two kinds of uncertainty and] first of all what has moral certainty; that is, a certainty which suffices for the conduct of life, though if we regard the absolute power of God, what is morally certain may be uncertain. [So those who have never visited Rome do not doubt its being a city in Italy, although it may very well be that all those from whom they have heard about it have deceived them. Again,] if, for instance, anyone wishing to read a letter written in Latin characters that are not placed in their proper order, takes it into his head to read B wherever he finds A and C where he finds B, thus substituting for each letter the one following it in the alphabet, and if he in this way finds that there are certain Latin words composed of these, he will not doubt that the true meaning of the writing is contained in these words, though he may discover this by conjecture, and although it is possible that the writer did not arrange the letters in this order of succession, but on some other, and thus concealed another meaning in it: for this is so unlikely to occur [especially when the cipher contains many words] that it seems incredible. But they who observe how many things regarding the magnet, fire, and the fabric of the whole world, are here deduced from a very small number of principles, although they considered that I had taken up these principles at random and without good grounds, they will yet acknowledge that it could hardly happen that so much would be coherent if they were false.

206 *That we possess even more than a moral certainty.*

And further there are some, even among natural things, which we judge to be absolutely, and more than morally, certain.[41] This

41 'of which we judge that it is impossible that the thing should be other than as we think it.' French version.

certainty is founded on the metaphysical ground that as God is supremely good and cannot err, the faculty which He has given us of distinguishing truth from falsehood, cannot be fallacious so long as we use it aright, and distinctly perceive anything by it. Of this nature are mathematical demonstrations,[42] the knowledge that material things exist, and the evidence of all clear reasoning that is carried on about them. Amongst these truths it seems to me that there should be counted those conclusions which have been arrived at in this treatise, if it be considered that they are derived in a continual series from the first and most simple principles of human knowledge. And this is specially so, if it be sufficiently understood that we can perceive no external objects unless some local motion be excited by them in our nerves; and that such motion cannot be excited by the fixed stars, owing to their immense distance from us, unless a motion be also produced in them, and in the whole intervening heavens;[43] for these facts being admitted, all the others, at least the more general doctrines which I have advanced about the world and earth, appear to be the only possible explanations of the phenomena they present.

329

207 *Nevertheless all my opinions are submitted to the authority of the Church.*

At the same time, recalling my insignificance, I affirm nothing, but submit all these opinions to the authority of the Catholic Church, and to the judgment of the more sage; and I wish no one to believe anything I have written, unless he is personally persuaded by the force and evidence of reason.

42 'for we see clearly that it is impossible that two or three should together form less than five or that a square should not have four sides etc.' French version .
43 The French version states that the fluidity of the heavens follows from this.

NOTES DIRECTED AGAINST
A CERTAIN PROGRAMME

published in Belgium at the end of
the year 1647 under this title

An Explanation of the Human Mind or
Rational Soul: What it is and what it may be.

A few days ago I received two pamphlets attacking me, one openly and directly, the other only covertly and by implication. Of the first I make no account; indeed I am indebted to the author, for by the very fact that with all his inordinate labour he has succeeded in collecting nothing but groundless revilings and calumnies that none could credit, he has borne me witness that he could find nothing in my writings to which he could reasonably take exception, and thus has corroborated their truth better than he would have done by praising them, and moreover has effected this at the expense of his own reputation. The other pamphlet troubles me more, though I am not mentioned openly in the discussion, and it is published without the name of author or printer; for it contains opinions which I deem pernicious and erroneous and is issued in the shape of a programme which may be affixed to church doors, and exposed to the view of any chance reader. It is said, however, that it was previously printed in another form, with the name appended (purporting to be the author's),[1] of one whose doctrine is believed by many to be identical with my own. I am constrained to expose his errors, lest, perchance, they be attributed to me myself by those who happen to come across these papers, and have not read my writings.

1 Regius.

The following is the programme in the form in which it finally saw the light:

An Explanation of the Human Mind or Rational Soul: What it is, and what it may be.

1 The human mind is that wherein the processes of thought[2] are first accomplished by man; and it consists of the faculty of thinking alone, and the inward principle.

2 So far as the laws of nature are concerned, they seem to allow that the mind may be either a substance, or a mode of a corporeal substance, or, if we follow some other philosophers who state that extension and thought are attributes inherent in certain substances, as in subjects, then, as these attributes are not mutually opposed but diverse, there is no reason why mind should not be an attribute coexisting in the same subject with extension, though the one attribute is not comprised in the concept of the other. Whatever we can conceive can exist. But mind can be conceived, so that it can be any one of the aforesaid, for none of them involves a contradiction. Therefore it may be any one of these things.

3 Hence they are in error who assert that we conceive the human mind clearly and distinctly, as though it were necessarily[3] and really distinct from the body.

4 The fact that mind is in truth nothing other than a substance, or an entity really distinct from body, in actuality separable from it, and capable of existing apart and independently,[4] is revealed to us in Holy Scripture, in many places. And thus what in the view of some, the study of nature leaves doubtful[5] is already placed beyond all doubt for us through divine revelation in Scripture.

5 Nor is it any objection that we may have doubts about the body, but in nowise about the mind. For this only proves that, so long as we doubt about body, we cannot say that mind is a mode of body.

---

2 *actiones cogitivae.*   3 *sive actu* (note in the first edition).   4 *per se.*
5 *si accuratam et non moralem rerum veritatem et cognitionem quaeramus* (note in first edition).

344 **6** The human mind, though it is a substance really distinct from body, is nevertheless, so long as it is in the body, organic in all its activities. And therefore as there are diverse dispositions of the body, so there are correspondingly diverse processes [6] of the mind.

7 As mind is of a nature diverse from body, and from the disposition of body, and cannot arise from this disposition, therefore it is incorruptible.

8 As it has no parts and no extension in its concept, it is idle to speculate whether it exists as a whole in the whole, and is present as a whole in each individual part.

9 As mind can be affected in equal degree by things imaginary and by things real, hence the study of nature leaves us doubtful whether any material things are really perceived by us. But even this doubt is banished by divine revelation in Holy Writ, whereby it is beyond all doubt that God created heaven and earth, and all that in them is, and even now conserves them.

10 The bond which maintains body and soul in union is the law of the unchangeableness of nature whereby every individual thing persists in the state in which it is, until it is thrown out of that state by some other thing.

345 **11** As mind is a substance and is first brought into existence at the moment of generation, the most accurate opinion seems to be that of those who hold that the rational soul is brought into existence by God, at generation, by an immediate act of creation.

12 The mind has no need of innate ideas, or notions, or axioms, but of itself the faculty of thinking suffices for the accomplishment of its processes.[7]

13 Therefore all common notions, engraven on the mind, owe their origin to the observation of things or to tradition.

14 In fact the very idea of God which is implanted in the mind, is the outcome of divine revelation, or of tradition, or of observation.

15 Our concept of God, or the idea of God which exists in our mind, is not an argument strong enough to prove the existence of

6 *cogitationes.*   7 *actiones.*

God, since all things do not exist of which concepts are observed within us; and this idea, as conceived by us, and that imperfectly, does not, more than the concept of any other thing, transcend our proper powers of thought.

16 The thought of the mind is twofold: intellect and will.

17 Intellect is perception and judgment.

18 Perception is sense, memory, and imagination.

346

19 All sensation is the perception of some corporeal movement, which requires no intentional images[8] and it is effected, not in the outward channels of sense, but in the brain alone.

20 The will is free, and inclines indifferently to opposites in nature, as our self-consciousness bears us witness.

21 Will is self-determined, and is to be termed blind no more than vision to be termed deaf.

> '*No men more easily attain a great reputation for piety than the superstitious and the hypocrites.*'[9]

The following is an examination of the programme.

NOTES TO THE TITLE

I observe in the title a promise is made, not of bare assertions regarding the rational soul, but of an explanation of it, so that we must needs believe that in this programme are contained all, or at least, the principal arguments, which the author had, not only for proving his propositions, but also for unfolding them, and that no other arguments are to be expected from him. In that he terms the rational soul 'the human mind', he has my approbation, for thus he avoids the ambiguity of the word *soul*[10] and in this point follows me.

347

NOTES TO THE INDIVIDUAL ARTICLES

In the first article he seems to aim at a definition of the rational soul, with imperfect success, for he omits the genus (i.e. that it is a

8 *species intentionales*.
9 See *Principles*, Dedication, p. 275. This aphorism reproduced at the end of Regius' poster is a saying of Descartes.   10 *anima*.

substance, or a mode, or something else) and he expounds only the differentia, which he has borrowed from me, for no one before me, so far as I know, asserted that mind consisted in one thing alone, namely the faculty of thinking and the inward source (sc. of thinking).

In the second article he begins to speculate about its genus, and says that 'the laws of nature seem to allow that the human mind may be either a substance, or a mode of a corporeal substance.'

This assertion involves a contradiction, no less than if he had said, 'The laws of nature allow that a mountain can exist with or without a valley.' For a distinction must be drawn between things which from their nature can change, like the facts that I am at present either writing or not writing, that one man is prudent, another imprudent; and things which never change, such as are all the things that pertain to the essence of anything, as is generally acknowledged by philosophers. Of course there is no doubt that it can be said of contingent things that the laws of nature permit these things to be either one way or another – for instance, the fact that I am at present either writing or not writing. But when the point at issue is the essence of something, it is manifestly foolish and contradictory to say that the laws of nature allow that it may be after any fashion save the fashion after which it really is. Nor does it more pertain to the nature of a mountain that it cannot exist without a valley, than to the nature of the human mind that it is what it is, namely, that it is a substance, if substance it be, or, indeed, that it is a mode of a corporeal substance, if in truth it be such a mode. Of this our friend endeavours at this point to convince us, and to prove it throws in these words, 'or if we are to follow some other philosophers etc.', while by 'other philosophers' he obviously means myself; for I was the first to consider thought the predominant attribute of immaterial substance, and extension the predominant attribute of material substance. But I did not say that these attributes were inherent in the substances, as in subjects diverse from themselves. Here we must beware of understanding by the word 'attribute' nothing other than 'mode'. Whenever we see a quality assigned to anything by nature, whether it be a mode that can suffer change, or the very essence of that thing, manifestly unchangeable, we term that quality its attribute. Thus in God there are many attributes, but no modes. Thus too one of the attributes of any substance is this, that it exists *per se*. Thus the extension of any body can, within itself, admit diverse modes, for it is one mode of its extension, if that body be spherical, another if it be square; but extension itself, which is the subject of these modes, is not in itself a mode of material substance, but an attribute, because it constitutes the essence and nature of material substance. Thus, finally, the modes of thought are diverse, for affirmation is a different mode of thought from negation, and so on; but thought itself, being the inward source[11] from which these modes arise, and in which they are inherent, is not conceived as a mode, but as an attribute which constitutes the nature of a substance. Whether thought be material, or immaterial, is the question at present before us.

349

He adds that 'these attributes are not mutually opposed, but diverse.' In these words again there is a contradiction, for when the question concerns attributes that constitute the essence of substances, there can be no greater opposition between them than the fact that they are different. Once it is admitted that 'this is different from that', it is equivalent to saying that 'this is not that'; but to be and not to be are contraries. 'Since they are not mutually opposed,' he says, 'but different, there is no reason why mind should not be an attribute coexisting in the same subject with extension, though the one attribute is not comprised in the concept of the other.' In these words there is an obvious fallacy, for he comes to a conclusion with regard to every possible attribute, which can be valid only in the case of modes properly so called; and yet he nowhere proves that the mind, or inward principle of thought, is such a mode. On the contrary, from his own words in Article 5 I will soon demonstrate that it is not so. Of the other attributes which constitute the natures of things, it cannot be said that those which are different, and of which neither is contained in the concept if the other, are coexistent in one and the same subject, for that is equivalent to saying that one and the same subject has two different natures, and this involves a contradiction, at least so long as the subject in question is simple and not composite — as in the present case.

350

Three points are to be noted here, a sufficient grasp of which would have prevented this writer from falling into such obvious errors.

11 *principium*.

First: It belongs to the theory of modes that, though we can easily comprehend a substance apart from a mode, we cannot, conversely, clearly comprehend a mode unless at the same time we conceive the substance of which it is a mode (as I have explained in the first part of the Principles, Article 61),[12] and on this point all philosophers are agreed. That our friend however paid no respect to this rule, is manifest from his 5th Article. In that passage he admits that 'we can doubt about the existence of the body, while, at the same time, we do not doubt about the existence of the mind.' Hence it follows that the mind can be comprehended by us apart from the body, and, accordingly, is not a mode of the body.

The second point which I would note here is the difference between simple and composite entities.[13] A composite entity is one in which are found two or more attributes, any one of which can be comprehended distinctly apart from the other, for it is from the fact that one can be thus cognised without the other, that each of these constituent elements is seen to be, not a mode of the others, but a thing, or the attribute of a thing which can exist without that attribute. A simple entity is one in which such attributes are not found. Hence it is clear that that subject in which we understand extension only, with the various modes of extension, is a simple entity. So, too, is a subject in which we comprehend thought only, with the various modes of thought. But that in which we observe extension and thought coexistent is a composite entity, to wit, a man, who consists of soul and body. Our author seems to assume that man is body alone and that mind is but a mode of body.

Finally, we must note here that in subjects compounded of several substances there is frequently one substance predominant. This we contemplate in such a way as to treat any of the remaining substances which we connect with it as nothing more than a mode, Thus a man clad may be contemplated as a compound of man and clothes, but the being clad, in comparison with the man, is only a mode, although garments are substances. In the same way our author might, in the case of man, who is a compound of soul and body, consider body the predominant element, in relation to which the being animate, or the possessing of thought, is nothing other than a mode. But it is foolish to infer from that, that the mind itself,

12 p. 300.   13 *entia*.

or that through which the body thinks, is not a substance different from the body.

This dictum he endeavours to corroborate by means of the following syllogism: 'Whatever we can conceive can exist. But the mind can be conceived as one of the aforesaid (viz. a substance, or a mode of a corporeal substance); for none of these things involves a contradiction. Therefore etc.' Here it must be noted that though the rule, 'whatever we can conceive can exist,' is mine, and true, so long as the question concerns a clear and distinct concept, in which is contained the possibility of the thing to be realised[14] (because God can bring into being everything which we clearly perceive to be possible), nevertheless we must not make rash use of it. A man might quite easily imagine that he rightly understood something which in reality he did not understand, being utterly blinded by some sort of prejudice. This is the case of our author when he maintains that there is no contradiction involved in the statement that one and the same thing possesses either of two natures which are utterly incompatible, to wit, that it is a substance, or a mode. If he had only said that he perceived no reasons for believing the human mind to be an immaterial substance rather than a mode of a material substance, his ignorance might have been excused. If he had said that no reasons could be found by the brain of man to prove either alternative, his arrogance would certainly have been reprehensible, but his statement would have evinced no contradiction. But when he says that the 'laws of nature allow that the same thing may be a substance, or a mode,' his words are altogether self-contradictory and betray the irrationality of his brain.

In the third article he makes known his judgment concerning me. For it was I who wrote that ' the human mind can be clearly and distinctly perceived as a substance different from corporeal substance.' Our friend, however, though he relies on no other arguments than those self-contradictory ones which he has unfolded in the preceding article, proclaims that I am in error. Of that I make no account. Nor do I examine the words 'of necessity' or 'in actuality', which contain a certain ambiguity; for they are not of great moment.

Moreover, I scruple to examine the statements regarding Holy Writ in the fourth article, lest I should appear to assume the right of

352

353

14 *rei.*

investigating another man's religion. Thus much I will say: Here one must distinguish between three types of questions. Certain things are believed through faith alone. Such are the mystery of the Incarnation, the Trinity, and the like. Others, however, though they have a certain bearing on faith, can nevertheless be investigated by the natural reason. Among these are generally ranked by the orthodox theologians the existence of God, and the distinction of mind from body. Finally, there are others which belong in no wise to the sphere of faith, but only to the sphere of human reason, e.g. the question of the squaring of the circle or of making gold by the art of alchemy. And even as these men abuse the words of Holy Scripture, who, from a distorted interpretation of it presume to elicit these last questions, so do those others diminish its authority who undertake to solve the first type of question by arguments sought from philosophy alone. Nevertheless all theologians contend that these questions should be shown to be in nowise incompatible with the light of nature,[15] and to this end they direct their most jealous endeavours. As for questions of the second class, not only do they deem them in no way incompatible with the light of nature, but they even exhort philosophers to solve these questions, so far as in them lies, by theories evolved from the mind of man. But never have I seen anyone who would affirm that the laws of nature allow that anything should be otherwise than Holy Scripture teaches, unless he wished to show indirectly that he had no faith in Scripture. For as we were born men before we became Christians, it is beyond belief that any man should seriously embrace opinions which he thinks contrary to that right reason that constitutes a man, in order that he may cling to the faith through which he is a Christian.

354   But perhaps our author does not imply this, for his words are, 'Through study of nature some may find doubtful that which is already placed beyond all doubt for us by the Divine Revelation in Holy Writ.' In these words I find a two-fold contradiction. In the first place, in that he assumes the doctrine that the essence of one and the same thing, which must be assumed always to remain the same (because, if it be supposed to become different, it will be by this very fact a different thing, to be indicated by a different name), is nevertheless, so far as the study of nature goes, doubtful, and

15 *lumen naturale*.

accordingly changeable. The second contradiction is in the word 'some', because, as nature is the same for all men a thing that can be doubtful only to 'some' is not doubtful according to nature's showing.[16]

The fifth article is to be related to the second rather than to the fourth, for in it the author is concerned, not with Divine Revelation, but with the nature of mind – the question as to whether it is a substance or a mode. To prove the defensibility of the view that mind is nothing other than a mode, he attempts to refute an objection taken from my writings. I wrote that we could not doubt that our mind existed, because, from the very fact that we doubted, it followed that our mind existed, but that meantime we might doubt whether any material things existed; whence I deduced and demonstrated that mind was clearly perceived by us as an existence, or substance, even supposing we had no concept whatever of the body, and denied that any material things had existence; and, accordingly, that the concept of mind did not involve any concept of body. This argument he thinks to explode by saying that 'it only proves that, so long as we doubt about the body, we cannot term mind a mode of body'. Here he shows that he is utterly ignorant of what it is that philosophers term a 'mode'; for the nature of a mode consists in this, that it can by no means be comprehended, except it involve in its own concept the concept of the thing of which it is a mode – as I have explained above.[17] Our friend, however, admits that mind can sometimes be cognised apart from body, to wit, when there are doubts about the body; whence it assuredly follows that mind cannot be termed a mode of body. And what is sometimes true about the essence or nature of a thing is always true. Nevertheless he affirms that the laws of nature allow that mind may be only a mode of body. These two statements are manifestly irreconcilable.

In the sixth article I fail to apprehend his meaning. Certainly I remember hearing in the schools that the mind is an activity[18] of the organic body, but till this day I never heard the mind itself termed 'organic'. For this reason I crave our author's indulgence, to the end that, as I have nothing certain to base my remarks on at this point, I may expound my conjectures, not as though they were true

355

16 *per naturam.*   17 p. 343.   18 *actus.*

to fact, but simply as conjectures. I seem to observe two irreconcilable statements. One of these is to the effect that the human mind is
a substance really distinct from the body. This the author openly
states, but, so far as he can, waives argument on the point, and
contends that it can be proved only by the authority of Holy
Scripture. The other statement is that that same human mind, in all
its activities, is organic or instrumental, that is to say, such that it
does not act [19] of itself, but is used by the body as though it were
something that strengthened its members [20] and other corporeal
modes, and so he affirms in effect, if not in so many words, that the
mind is nothing other than a mode of body, as though he had
drawn up his whole artillery of argument to prove this point and
this alone. These two statements are so manifestly contraries that I
do not think the author wished them both, at one and the same
time, to find credence with readers, but deliberately coupled them
together, so that he might in some sort give satisfaction to the more
simple-minded, and to his friends the theologians, by his citation of
scriptural authority, and that, meantime, his more keen-witted
readers might realise that, when he said 'mind is distinct from body',
he was speaking in irony, and that he was heart and soul of the
opinion that mind is nothing but a mode.

In the seventh article again, and the eighth, he seems to be
speaking merely in irony. And he retains the same Socratic figure of
speech in the latter part of article 9. But in the first part he appends a
reason to his assertion, and thus, it would seem, is to be taken
seriously in this passage. He teaches that, so far as nature shows, it is
doubtful whether any material things are really perceived by us, and
submits as his reason the statement that 'the mind can be affected in
the same degree by things imaginary as by things real.' If this theory
is to be received as true, it must be granted that we have use of no
understanding [21] properly so called, but only of that faculty which is
usually termed the 'common sense' [22] whereby impressions are
received of things imaginary as much as of things real, so that they
affect the mind – a faculty which philosophers commonly allow
even to the brute creation. But surely those who have understanding,
and are not fashioned like the horse or mule, even although they are

19 *nihil agat.*   20 *membrorum suorum confirmatione.*
21 *intellectus.*   22 *sensus communis.*

356

affected not only by images of real things but also by those which   357
occur in the brain from other causes (as happens in sleep), can
distinguish the one kind of image from the other with the utmost
clearness, by the light of reason. The method in which this happens,
surely and infallibly, I have explained in my writings, so accurately
that I am convinced that no one who has read them throughout,
and is capable of understanding them, can be a sceptic.

In the tenth and eleventh articles it is still possible to suspect him
of irony. If the soul be believed to be a substance, it is foolish and
ridiculous to say 'the bond which maintains body and soul in union
is the law of the unchangeableness of nature, whereby every
individual thing persists in the state in which it is.' For it is equally
true of things disunited as of things united that they persist in the
same state so long as nothing changes that state. This is not at
present the point of issue. The question is, how it happens that the
mind is united with the body, and not dissevered from it. But if soul
be supposed to be a mode of body, it is rightly said that no bond of
union need be sought other than the fact that it persists in the state
in which it is, since modes have no other state than that present to
the things of which they are modes.

In article twelve he appears to dissent from me only in words, for
when he says that the mind has no need of innate ideas, or notions,
or axioms, and at the same time allows it the faculty of thinking (to
be considered natural or innate), he makes an affirmation in effect
identical with mine, but denies it in words. For I never wrote or
concluded that the mind required innate ideas which were in some
sort different from its faculty of thinking; but when I observed the   358
existence in me of certain thoughts which proceeded, not from
extraneous objects nor from the determination of my will, but solely
from the faculty of thinking which is within me, then, that I might
distinguish the ideas or notions (which are the forms of these
thoughts) from other thoughts adventitious or factitious, I termed
the former 'innate'. In the same sense we say that in some families
generosity is innate, in others certain diseases like gout or gravel, not
that on this account the babes of these families suffer from these
diseases in their mother's womb, but because they are born with a
certain disposition or propensity for contracting them.

The conclusion which he deduces in article 13 from the preceding
article is indeed wonderful. 'For this reason,' he says (i.e. because the

mind has no need of innate ideas, but the faculty of thinking of itself
is sufficient), 'all common notions, engraven on the mind, owe their
origin to the observation of things or to tradition' – as though the
faculty of thinking could of itself execute nothing, nor perceive nor
think anything save what it received from observation or tradition,
that is, from the senses. So far is this from being true, that, on the
contrary, any man who rightly observes the limitations of the senses,
and what precisely it is that can penetrate through this medium to
our faculty of thinking must needs admit that no ideas of things, in
the shape in which we envisage them by thought, are presented to us
by the senses. So much so that in our ideas there is nothing which
was not innate in the mind, or faculty of thinking, except only these
circumstances which point to experience – the fact, for instances,
that we judge that this or that idea, which we now have present to
our thought, is to be referred to a certain extraneous thing, not that
these extraneous things transmitted the ideas themselves to our
minds through the organs of sense, but because they transmitted
something which gave the mind occasion to form these ideas, by
means of an innate faculty, at this time rather than at another. For
nothing reaches our mind from external objects through the organs
of sense beyond certain corporeal movements, as our author himself
affirms, in article 19, taking the doctrine from my Principles; but
even these movements, and the figures which arise from them, are
not conceived by us in the shape they assume in the organs of sense,
as I have explained at great length in my Dioptrics. Hence it follows
that the ideas of the movements and figures are themselves innate in
us. So much the more must the ideas of pain, colour, sound and the
like be innate, that our mind may, on occasion of certain corporeal
movements, envisage these ideas, for they have no likeness to the
corporeal movements. Could anything be imagined more preposterous than that all common notions which are inherent in our mind
should arise from these movements, and should be incapable of
existing without them? I should like our friend to instruct me as to
what corporeal movement it is which can form in our mind any
common notion, e.g. the notion that 'things which are equal to the
same thing are equal to one another,' or any other he pleases; for all
these movements are particular, but notions are universal having no
affinity with movements and no relation to them.

360   He goes on to affirm in article 14, that even the idea of God which

is in us is the outcome, not of our faculty of thinking, as being native to it, but of Divine Revelation or tradition, or observation. The error of this assertion we shall the more readily realise if we reflect that anything can be said to be the outcome of another, either because this other is its proximate and primary cause, without which it could not exist, or only because it is a remote and accidental cause, which, certainly, gives the primary cause occasion to produce its effect at one time rather than at another. Thus all workmen are the primary and proximate causes of their works, but those who give them orders, or promise them reward, that they may perform these works, are accidental and remote causes, because, probably, they would not have performed the tasks unbidden. There is no doubt that tradition or observation is a remote cause, inviting us to bethink ourselves of the idea which we may have of God, and to present it vividly to our thought. But no one can maintain that this is the proximate and efficient[23] cause, except the man who thinks that we can apprehend nothing regarding God save this name 'God', and the corporeal figure which painters exhibit to us as a representation of God. For observation, if it takes place through the medium of sight, can of its own proper power present nothing to the mind beyond pictures, and pictures consisting only of a permutation of corporeal movements, as our author himself instructs us. If it takes place through the medium of hearing, it presents nothing beyond words and voices; if through the other sense, it has nothing in it which can have reference to God. And surely it is manifest to every man that sight, of itself and by its proper function, presents nothing beyond pictures, and hearing nothing beyond voices or sounds, so that all these things that we think of, beyond these voices or pictures, as being symbolised by them, are presented to us by means of ideas which come from no other source than our faculty of thinking, and are accordingly together with that faculty innate in us, that is, always existing in us potentially; for existence in any faculty is not actual but merely potential existence, since the very word 'faculty' designates nothing more or less than a potentiality. But that with regard to God we can comprehend nothing beyond a name or a bodily effigy, no one can affirm, save a man who openly professes himself an atheist, and moreover destitute of all intellect.

361

23 *effectrix*.

After expounding his opinion concerning God, our author, in article 15, thinks to refute all the arguments by which I have proved God's existence. At this point it occurs to one to marvel at the man's self-confidence, in that he imagines that he can so easily and in so few words overturn all that I have built up by dint of long and concentrated meditation, and to the explanation of which I have devoted a whole volume. But all the arguments which I have adduced in this matter can be subordinated to two. In the first place I have shown that we have a notion or idea of God such that, when we sufficiently attend to it and ponder the matter in the manner I have expounded,[24] we realise from this contemplation alone, that it cannot be but that God exists, since existence, not merely possible or contingent as in the ideas of all other things, but altogether necessary and actual, is contained in this concept. This argument, which is held as certainly and obviously proved, not only by myself but by several others, and these men pre-eminent in learning and genius who have sedulously investigated the matter – this argument, I say, the author of the programme thinks to refute in this fashion: 'Our concept of God or the idea of God which exists in our mind, is not an argument sufficiently strong to prove the existence of God, since all things do not exist of which concepts are observed within us.' By these words he shows that he has read my writings, but has in nowise had either the power or the will to understand them. For the point of my argument is, not the idea in general, but its peculiar property, a property which is evident in the highest degree in the idea we have of God, and which can be found in the concept of no other thing, namely, the necessity of existence, which is required as that crown of perfections without which we cannot comprehend God. The other argument by which I proved the existence of God, I deduced from my clear proof of the fact that we should not have had the faculty for conceiving all the perfections which we recognise in God, had it not been true that God existed, and that we were created by Him.[25] This argument our fried thinks he has more than exploded by saying that the idea we have of God does not, more than the concept of any other thing, transcend our proper powers of thinking. If by these words he only means that the concept which we have of God without the aid of supernatural

24 Meditation 5, p. 170.   25 Meditation 3, p. 147.

graces is no less natural than all the concepts we have of other things, he is at one with me; but on that basis nothing can be concluded against me. If, however, he thinks that that concept does not involve more objective perfections than all the others taken together, he is obviously wrong. I myself, on the other hand, have founded my argument entirely on this preponderance of perfections, in which our concept of God transcends other concepts.

363

In the six remaining articles there is nothing worthy of note except the fact that, when he wishes to distinguish the properties of the soul, he speaks of them confusedly and inappropriately. I have said that these are all to be subordinated to two predominant properties, one of which is the perception of the understanding, the other the determination of the will. These two our friend calls 'understanding' and 'will'. Then he subdivides what he calls 'understanding' into 'perception' and 'judgment'. In this point he differs from me, for when I saw that, over and above perception, which is required as a basis for judgment, there must needs be affirmation, or negation, to constitute the form of the judgment, and that it is frequently open to us to withhold our assent, even if we perceive a thing, I referred the act of judging, which consists in nothing but assent, i.e. affirmation or negation, not to the perception of the understanding, but to the determination of the will. Thereafter he enumerates, among the species of perception, nothing but sense, memory, and imagination; from which one may gather that he admits no pure intellection (i.e. intellection which deals with no corporeal images), and, accordingly, that he himself believes that no cognition is possessed of God, or of the human mind, or of other immaterial things. Of this I can imagine but one cause, namely, that the thoughts he has concerning these things are so confused that he never observes in himself a pure thought, different from every corporeal image.

364

Finally, in closing, he adds these words, taken from some portion of my writings: 'No men more easily attain a great reputation for piety, than the superstitious and the hypocrites.' What he means by these words I fail to see, unless perhaps he ascribes to hypocrisy the use he has made of irony, in many places, but I do not think that by that means he can attain a great reputation for piety.

For the rest, I am constrained to admit here, that I am covered with shame to think that in time past I lauded this author as a man of most penetrative genius, and wrote somewhere or other that 'I did not think he taught any doctrines which I should be unwilling to acknowledge as my own.'[26] But in truth when I wrote these words I had as yet seen no specimen of his work in which he was not a faithful copyist, except only on one occasion in one little phrase,[27] which brought such ill results to him, that I hoped he would make no further venture in that line; and, as I saw him in other matters embrace with a great show of zeal the opinions that I deemed nearest the truth, I attributed this to his genius and penetration. But now a manifold experience compels me to conclude that he is swayed not so much by love of truth as by love of novelty. As he holds all he has learned from others to be old-world and out-worn, thinking nothing sufficiently novel except what he has hammered out of his own brain; and, at the same time, is so unhappy in his inventions, that I have never noted a single word in his writings (excluding what he transcribed from other men), which I did not condemn as containing some error, I must therefore warn all those who are convinced that he is a champion of my opinions, that of these opinions – I speak, not only of those in the Metaphysics, on which he openly opposes me, but also of those in the physics, for he treats of this subject somewhere in his writings – there is none which he does not state awry and distort. Hence it causes me more indignation that such a Doctor should handle my writings and undertake to interpret, or in other words, to falsify them, than that other men should attack them with the utmost bitterness.

For I never yet saw one of these bitter critics who did not father on me opinions different from mine by a whole heaven, and so maundering and preposterous, that I had no fear that any man of intelligence could be persuaded that they were mine. Thus, even as I write these words, two new pamphlets are brought me – productions of an adversary of this type.[28] In the first of these it is stated that 'There are some Neoterics who deny all credibility to the senses, who contend that the philosophers deny God, and dare to doubt His existence, and who, meantime, admit that there are implanted by Nature in the human mind actual notions, species, and ideas of God.' In the second it is said that 'these Neoterics bare-facedly proclaim that God is, not only negatively, but positively, the efficient

26 Letter to Voetius.   27 *hominem esse ens per accidens*.
28 Jacques de Rives (Jacobus Revius).

cause of Himself.' In either pamphlet the only thing effected is the conglomeration of numerous arguments to prove, first, that we have no actual knowledge (*cognitio*) of God in our mother's womb, and accordingly that 'no actual species or idea of God is inborn in our mind'; secondly, that 'we must not deny God' and that 'they are atheists and punishable by law who deny Him'; and thirdly and finally that 'God is not the efficient cause of Himself.'

366

I might well suppose that all these dicta were not directed against me, because my name is not mentioned in the pamphlets, and of the opinions attacked in them there is none which I do not think absurd and erroneous. Nevertheless, as they are not dissimilar to those which have often ere now been slanderously imputed to me by men of that kidney, and as there are no other persons recognisable to whom these opinions could be attributed; as, finally, there are many who do not doubt that I am the object of attack in these pamphlets, I take this occasion to admonish their author to this effect:

First: By innate ideas I never understood anything other than that which he himself, on page 6 of his second pamphlet, affirms in so many words to be true, viz. that 'there is innate in us by nature a potentiality whereby we know God'; but that these ideas are actual, or that they are some kind of species different from the faculty of thought I never wrote nor concluded. On the contrary, I, more than any other man, am utterly averse to that empty stock of scholastic entities – so much so, that I cannot refrain from laughter when I see that mighty heap which our hero – a very inoffensive fellow no doubt – has laboriously brought together to prove that infants have no notion of God so long as they are in their mother's womb – as though in this fashion he was bringing a magnificent charge against me.

Secondly: I have never taught that God is to be denied, or that He can deceive us, or that one must doubt about everything, or that all credibility is to be denied to the senses, or that sleep cannot be distinguished from waking, or the like – doctrines which are sometimes thrown in my teeth by ignorant detractors. I have repudiated all these doctrines expressly and with the strongest arguments – stronger, I make bold to say, than any that have by any man before me been brought to the reputation of these doctrines. That I might the more fittingly and effectively compass this end, I proposed, at the beginning of my Meditations, to regard as doubtful

367

all the doctrines which did not owe their original discovery to me, but had been for long denounced by the sceptics.[29] What could be more unjust than to attribute to a writer opinions which he states only to the end that he may refute them? What more foolish than to imagine that, at least for the time being, while these false opinions are being propounded previous to their refutation, the author commits himself to them, and that, accordingly, the man who states the arguments of the atheists is an atheist for the time? What more childish than to say that, if he were to die meantime, before writing or evolving the hoped for refutation he would die an atheist – that he taught pernicious doctrine merely as a preliminary, but that 'evil should not be done that good may come of it' and so forth? Some one will say, perhaps, that I related these false opinions, not as the opinions of others, but as my own. But what of that? In the self-same book in which I related them I refuted them all. From the very title of the book it might be understood that I was altogether hostile to these beliefs, for it purports to give 'proofs of the existence of God.' Is there anyone obtuse enough to think that the man who compiled such a book was ignorant, so long as he was penning its first pages, of what he had undertaken to prove in the following? I enunciated the objections as though they were my own, to suit the exigencies of the style of 'meditations', which I judged the style best fitted for unfolding arguments. If this explanation does not satisfy our captious critics, I should like to know what they say of Holy Scripture – with which no human documents are to be compared – when they see in it some things that cannot be rightly understood unless they be supposed to be the utterance of impious men, or, at least, of others than the Holy Ghost and the prophets? Such are Ecclesiastes, chap. ii., these words 'There is nothing better for a man than that he should eat and drink, and that he should make his soul enjoy good in his labour. This also I saw that it was from the hand of God. For who can eat or who else can hasten thereunto more than I?' and, in the following chapter, 'I said in mine heart concerning the estate of the sons of men, that God might manifest them, and that they might see that they themselves are beasts; for that which befalleth the sons of men befalleth beasts; even one thing befalleth them: as the one dieth so dieth the other: yea they have all

29 Meditation 1, pp. 134ff.

one breath: so that a man hath no pre-eminence above a beast,' etc. Do they believe that here the Holy Spirit teaches us that we should indulge the belly, and have abundance of delights, and that our souls are no more immortal than the souls of beasts? I do not think they are so mad. Neither should they calumniate me because in writing I have not made use of the precautions which are observed by some other writers, but not by the Holy Spirit.

In the third place, and finally, I warn the author of these pamphlets that I never wrote that 'God should be said to be, not only negatively, but positively, the efficient cause of Himself,' as he affirms in a very rash and ill-considered manner in page 8 of his second pamphlet. Let him turn over, read, and thoroughly search my writings, he will find in them nothing like this, but the very reverse. The fact that I am far indeed from accepting such monstrous opinions is well known to all who have read my writings, or have any knowledge of myself, or, at any rate, do not think me utterly fatuous. On this account I am only moved to wonder what is the aim of these detractors; for if they wish to convince any one that I wrote things of which the very contrary is found in my writings, they should have taken the preliminary precaution of suppressing all my publications, and should even have wiped out the memory of them from the minds of those who had already read them; for so long as they fail to effect this they do themselves more harm than me. Moreover, I marvel that they should inveigh with such bitterness and such zeal against me, who have never troubled them, nor done them any hurt, though, perhaps, possessing the power to hurt them if they provoked me; and meantime should take no action against many other men who devote whole books to the refutation of their doctrine, and ridicule them as simpletons and blindfold gladiators.[30] But I am unwilling to add any word here that might make them renounce their habit of impugning me in their pamphlets. I am glad to see that they think me of so much importance. Meantime I pray Heaven to grant them sanity.

369

Written at Egmond, in Holland, towards the end of December 1647.

30 *simplicios et andabatas*. Andabatae were Roman gladiators whose masks had no opening for the eyes and who fought blind in order to amuse the spectators.

THE PASSIONS OF THE SOUL[1]

First Part

Of the passions in general, and incidentally of the whole nature of man

1 *That what in respect of a subject is passion, is in some other regard always action.*

There is nothing in which the defective nature of the sciences which we have received from the ancients appears more clearly than in what they have written on the passions; for, although this is a matter which has at all times been the object of much investigation, and though it would not appear to be one of the most difficult, inasmuch as since every one has experience of the passions within himself, there is no necessity to borrow one's observations from elsewhere in order to discover their nature; yet that which the ancients have taught regarding them is both so slight, and for the most part so far from credible, that I am unable to entertain any hope of approximating to the truth excepting by shunning the paths which they have followed. This is why I shall be here obliged to write just as though I were treating of a matter which no one had ever touched on before me; and, to begin with, I consider that all that which occurs or that happens anew, is by the philosophers, generally speaking, termed a passion, in as far as the subject to which it occurs is concerned, and an action in respect of him who causes it to occur. Thus although the agent and the recipient [patient] are frequently very different, the action and the passion are always one and the same thing, although having different names, because of the two diverse subjects to which it may be related.

1 The expression 'Passions' is in this Treatise of course used in its etymological significance.

2 *That in order to understand the passions of the soul its functions must be distinguished from those of the body.*

Next I note also that we do not observe the existence of any subject which more immediately acts upon our soul than the body to which it is joined, and that we must consequently consider that what in the soul is a passion is in the body commonly speaking an action; so that there is no better means of arriving at a knowledge of our passions than to examine the difference which exists between soul and body in order to know to which of the two we must attribute each one of the functions which are within us.

3 *What rule we must follow to bring about this result.* 329

As to this we shall not find much difficulty if we realise that all that we experience as being in us, and that to observation may exist in wholly inanimate bodies, must be attributed to our body alone; and, on the other hand, that all that which is in us and which we cannot in any way conceive as possibly pertaining to a body, must be attributed to our soul.

4 *That the heat and movement of the members proceed from the body, the thoughts from the soul.*

Thus because we have no conception of the body as thinking in any way, we have reason to believe that every kind of thought which exists in us belongs to the soul; and because we do not doubt there being inanimate bodies which can move in as many as or in more diverse modes than can ours, and which have as much heat or more (experience demonstrates this to us in flame, which of itself has much more heat and movement than any of our members), we must believe that all the heat and all the movements which are in us pertain only to body, inasmuch as they do not depend on thought at all.

5 *That it is an error to believe that the soul supplies the movement and heat to body.* 330

By this means we shall avoid a very considerable error into which many have fallen; so much so that I am of opinion that this is the primary cause which has prevented our being able hitherto satisfactorily to explain the passions and the other properties of the soul. It arises from the fact that from observing that all dead bodies are devoid of heat and consequently of movement, it has been thought that it was the absence of soul which caused these movements and this heat to cease; and thus, without any reason, it was thought that our natural heat and all the movements of our body depend on the soul: while in fact we ought on the contrary to believe that the soul quits us on death only because this heat ceases, and the organs which serve to move the body disintegrate.

6 *The difference that exists between a living body and a dead body.*

In order, then, that we may avoid this error, let us consider that death never comes to pass by reason of the soul, but only because some one of the principal parts of the body decays; and we may judge that the body of a living man differs from that of a dead man just as does a watch or other automaton (i.e. a machine that moves of itself), when it is wound up and contains in itself the corporeal principle of those movements for which it is designed along with all that is requisite for its action, from the same watch or other machine when it is broken and when the principle of its movement ceases to act.

7 *A brief explanation of the parts of the body and some of its functions.*

In order to render this more intelligible, I shall here explain in a few words the whole method in which the bodily machine is composed. There is no one who does not already know that there are in us a heart, a brain, a stomach, muscles, nerves, arteries, veins, and such things. We also know that the food that we eat descends into the stomach and bowels where its juice, passing into the liver and into all the veins, mingles with, and thereby increases the quantity of the blood which they contain. Those who have acquired even the minimum of medical knowledge further know how the heart is composed, and how all the blood in the veins can easily flow from the vena cava into its right side and from thence pass into the lung by the vessel which we term the arterial vein, and then return from the lung into the left side of the heart, by the vessel called the venous artery, and finally pass from there into the great artery, whose branches spread throughout all the body. Likewise all those whom the authority of the ancients has not entirely blinded, and who have chosen to open their eyes for the purpose of investigating the opinion of Harvey regarding the circulation of the blood, do not doubt that all the veins and arteries of the body are like streams by which the blood ceaselessly flows with great swiftness, taking its course from the right cavity of the heart by the arterial vein whose branches are spread over the whole of the lung, and joined to that of the venous artery by which it passes from the lung into the left side of the heart; from these, again, it goes into the great artery whose branches, spread throughout all the rest of the body, are united to the branches of the vein, which branches once more carry the same blood into the right cavity of the heart. Thus these two cavities are like sluices through each of which all the blood passes in the course of each circuit which it makes in the body. We further know that all the movements of the members depend on the muscles, and that these muscles are so mutually related one to another that when the one is contracted it draws toward itself the part of the body to which it is attached, which causes the opposite muscle at the same time to become elongated; then if at another time it happens that this last contracts, it causes the former to become elongated and it draws back to itself the part to which they are attached. We know finally that all these movements of the muscles, as also all the senses, depend on the nerves, which resemble small filaments, or little tubes, which all proceed from the brain, and thus contain like it a certain very subtle air or wind which is called the animal spirits.

8 *What is the principle of all these functions?*

But it is not usually known in what way these animal spirits and these nerves contribute to the movements and to the senses, nor what is the corporeal principle which causes them to act. That is why, although I have already made some mention of them in my other writings, I shall not here omit to say shortly that so long as we live there is a continual heat in our heart, which is a species of fire which the blood of the veins there maintains, and that this fire is the corporeal principle of all the movements of our members.

9 *How the movement of the heart is carried on.*

Its first effect is to dilate the blood with which the cavities of the heart are filled; that causes this blood, which requires a greater space for its occupation, to pass impetuously from the right cavity into the arterial vein, and from the left into the great artery; then when this dilation ceases, new blood immediately enters from the vena cava into the right cavity of the heart, and from the venous artery into the left; for there are little membranes at the entrances of these four vessels, disposed in such a manner that they do not allow the blood to enter the heart but by the two last, nor to issue from it but by the two others. The new blood which has entered into the heart is then immediately afterwards rarefied, in the same manner as that which preceded it; and it is just this which causes the pulse, or beating of the heart and arteries; so that this beating repeats itself as often as the new blood enters the heart. It is also just this which gives its motion to the blood, and causes it to flow ceaselessly and very quickly in all the arteries and veins, whereby it carries the heat which it acquires in the heart to every part of the body, and supplies them with nourishment.

10 *How the animal spirits are produced in the brain.*

But what is here most worthy of remark is that all the most animated and subtle portions of the blood which the heat has rarefied in the heart, enter ceaselessly in large quantities into the cavities of the brain. And the reason which causes them to go there rather than elsewhere, is that all the blood which issues from the heart by the great artery takes its course in a straight line towards that place, and not being able to enter it in its entirety, because there are only very narrow passages there, those of its parts which are the most agitated and the most subtle alone pass through, while the rest spreads abroad in all the other portions of the body. But these very subtle parts of the blood form the animal spirits and for this end they have no need to experience any other change in the brain, unless it be that they are separated from the other less subtle portions of the blood; for what I here name spirits are nothing but material bodies and their one peculiarity is that they are bodies of extreme minuteness and that they move very quickly like the particles of the flame which issues from a torch. Thus it is that they never remain at rest in any spot, and just as some of them enter into the cavities of the brain, others issue forth by the pores which are in its substance, which pores conduct them into the nerves, and from there into the muscles, by means of which they move the body in all the different ways in which it can be moved.

11 *How the movements of the muscles take place.*

For the sole cause of all the movements of the members is that certain muscles contract, and that those opposite to them elongate, as has already been said; and the sole cause of one muscle contracting rather than that set against it, is that there comes from the brain some additional amount of animal spirits, however little it may be, to it rather than to the other. Not that the spirits which proceed immediately from the brain suffice in themselves to move the muscles, but they determine the other spirits which are already in these two muscles, all to issue very quickly from the one of them and to pass into the other. By this means that from which they issue becomes longer and more flaccid, and that into which they enter, being rapidly distended by them, contracts, and pulls the member to which it is attached. This is easy to understand provided that we know that there are but very few animal spirits which continually proceed from the brain to each muscle, but that there are always a quantity of others enclosed in the same muscle, which move there very quickly, sometimes by only turning about in the place where they are, – that is, when they do not find any passage open from which to issue forth from it – and sometimes by flowing into the opposite muscle; and inasmuch as there are little openings in each of these muscles by which the spirits can flow from one to the other, and which are so arranged that when the spirits that come from the brain to one of them have ever so little more strength than those that proceed to the other, they open all the entrances by which the spirits of the other muscle can pass into this one, and at the same time close all those by which the spirits of this last can pass into the other. By this means all the spirits formerly contained in these two muscles very quickly collect in one of them and then distend and shorten it, while the other becomes elongated and flaccid.

336

12 *How outside objects act upon the organs of the senses.*

We have still to understand the reasons why the spirits do not flow always from the brain into the muscles in the same fashion, and why occasionally more flow towards some than towards others. For in addition to the action of the soul which is truly in our case one of these causes, as I shall subsequently explain, there are two others which depend only on the body, and of these we must speak. The first consists in the diversity of movements which are excited in the organs of sense by their objects, and this I have already explained fully enough in the Dioptric; but in order that those who see this work may not be necessitated to read others, I shall here repeat that there are three things to consider in respect of the nerves, i.e. first of all their marrow or interior substance, which extends in the form of little filaments from the brain, from which it originates, to the extremities of the other members to which these filaments are attached; secondly the membranes which surround them, and which, being conterminous with those which envelope the brain, form the little tubes in which these little filaments are enclosed; and finally the animal spirits which, being carried by these same tubes from the brain to the muscles, are the reason of these filaments remaining there perfectly free and extended, so that the least thing that moves the part of the body to which the extremity of any one of them is attached, causes by that same means the part of the brain from which it proceeds to move, just as when one draws one end of a cord the other end is made to move.

13 *That this action of outside objects may lead the spirits into the muscles in diverse ways.*

And I have explained in the Dioptric how all the objects of sight communicate themselves to us only through the fact that they move locally by the intermission of transparent bodies which are between them and us, the little filaments of the optic nerves which are at the back of our eyes, and then the parts of the brain from which these nerves proceed; I explained, I repeat, how they move them in as many diverse ways as the diversities which they cause us to see in things, and that it is not immediately the movements which occur in the eye, but those that occur in the brain which represent these objects to the soul. To follow this example it is easy to conceive

337

338

how sounds, scents, tastes, heat, pain, hunger, thirst and generally speaking all objects of our other external senses as well as of our internal appetites, also excite some movement in our nerves which by their means pass to the brain; and in addition to the fact that these diverse movements of the brain cause diverse perceptions to become evident to our soul, they can also without it cause the spirits to take their course towards certain muscles rather than towards others, and thus to move our limbs, which I shall prove here by one example only. If someone quickly thrusts his hand against our eyes as if to strike us, even though we know him to be our friend, that he only does it in fun, and that he will take great care not to hurt us, we have all the same trouble in preventing ourselves from closing them; and this shows that it is not by the intervention of our soul that they close, seeing that it is against our will, which is its only, or at least its principal activity; but it is because the machine of our body is so formed that the movement of this hand towards our eyes excites another movement in our brain, which conducts the animal spirits into the muscles which cause the eyelids to close.

339

14 *That the diversity which exists between the animal spirits may also cause a diversity in the course they take.*

The other cause which serves to conduct the animal spirits differently into the muscles, is the unequal agitation of these spirits and the diversity of their parts. For when some of their parts are more coarse and more agitated than others, they pass further forward in a straight line into the cavities and pores of the brain, and by this means are conducted into other muscles than those they would enter if they had less force.

15 *The causes of their diversity.*

340

And this inequality may proceed from the diverse matters of which they are composed, as we see in the case of those who have drunk much wine – that the vapours of this wine entering quickly into the blood, rise from the heart to the brain, where they become converted into animal spirits, which, being stronger and more abundant than those ordinarily there, are capable of moving the body in many strange fashions. This inequality of spirits may also proceed from diverse dispositions of the heart, liver, stomach, spleen, and all other parts which contribute to their production; for we must here notice principally certain little nerves inserted in the base of the heart, which serve to enlarge and diminish the entrances of its cavities, whereby the blood dilating there more or less forcibly, produces spirits disposed in diverse ways. We must also notice that although the blood which enters the heart comes there from all other parts of the body, it nevertheless often happens that it is more forcibly driven from some parts than from others, because the nerves and muscles which lead to these particular parts press or agitate it to a greater extent; and that, according to the diversity of the parts from which it comes the most, it dilates variously in the heart and then produces spirits which have different qualities. Thus, for example, that which comes from the lower part of the liver where is the gall, dilates in another fashion in the heart than that which comes from the spleen, and this one again differently from what comes from the veins of the arms or legs, and this finally quite otherwise than the juice of the food when, having newly issued from the stomach and bowels, it at once passes by the liver to the heart.

16 *How all the members may be moved by the objects of the senses and by the animal spirits without the aid of the soul.*

We must finally remark that the machine of our body is so formed that all the changes undergone by the movement of the spirits may cause them to open certain pores in the brain more than others, and reciprocally that when some one of the pores is opened more or less than usual (to however small a degree it may be) by the action of the nerves which are employed by the senses, that changes something in the movement of the spirits and causes them to be conducted into the muscles which serve to move the body in the way in which it is usually moved when such an action takes place. In this way all the movements which we make without our will contributing thereto (as frequently happens when we breathe, walk, eat, and in fact perform all those actions which are common to us and to the brutes), only depend on the conformation of our members, and on the course which the spirits, excited by the heat of the heart, follow naturally in the brain, nerves, and muscles, just as the movements of a watch are produced simply by the strength of the springs and the form of the wheels.

17 *What the functions of the soul are.*

After having thus considered all the functions which pertain to the body alone, it is easy to recognise that there is nothing in us which we ought to attribute to our soul excepting our thoughts, which are mainly of two sorts, the one being the actions of the soul, and the other its passions. Those which I call its actions are all our desires, because we find by experience that they proceed directly from our soul, and appear to depend on it alone: while, on the other hand, we may usually term one's passions all those kinds of perception or forms of knowledge which are found in us, because it is often not our soul which makes them what they are, and because it always receives them from the things which are represented by them.

18 *Of the will.*   343

Our desires, again, are of two sorts, of which the one consists of the actions of the soul which terminate in the soul itself, as when we desire to love God, or generally speaking, apply our thoughts to some object which is not material; and the other of the actions which terminate in our body, as when from the simple fact that we have the desire to take a walk, it follows that our legs move and that we walk.

19 *Of the perceptions.*

Our perceptions are also of two sorts, and the one have the soul as a cause and the other the body. Those which have the soul as a cause are the perceptions of our desires, and of all the imaginations or other thoughts which depend on them. For it is certain that we cannot desire anything without perceiving by the same means that we desire it; and, although in regard to our soul it is an action to desire something, we may say that it is also one of its passions to perceive that it desires. Yet because this perception and this will are really one and the same thing, the more noble always supplies the denomination, and thus we are not in the habit of calling it a passion, but only an action.

20 *Of the imaginations and other thoughts which are formed by the soul.*   344

When our soul applies itself to imagine something which does not exist, as when it represents to itself an enchanted palace or a chimera, and also when it applies itself to consider something which is only intelligible and not imaginable, e.g. to consider its own nature, the perceptions which it has of these things depend principally on the act of will which causes it to perceive them. That is why we consider them as actions rather than passions.

21 Of the imaginations which have the body only as a cause.

Amongst the perceptions which are caused by the body, the most part depend on the nerves; but there are also some which do not depend on them, and which we name imaginations, such as those of which I have just spoken, from which they yet differ inasmuch as our will has no part in forming them; and this brings it to pass that they cannot be placed in the number of the actions of the soul. And they only proceed from the fact that the spirits being agitated in diverse ways and meeting with traces of diverse preceding impressions which have been effected in the brain, take their course there fortuitously by certain pores rather than by others. Such are the illusions of our dreams, and also the daydreams which we often have when awake, and when our thought wanders aimlessly without applying itself to anything of its own accord. But, although some of these imaginations are the passions of the soul, taking this word in its most correct and perfect significance, and since they may all be thus termed if we take it in a more general significance, yet, because they have not a cause of so notable and determinate a description as the perceptions which the soul receives by the intermission of the nerves, and because they appear to be only a shadow and a picture, we must, before we can distinguish them very well, consider the difference prevailing among these others.

22 Of the difference which exists among the other perceptions.

All the perceptions which I have not yet explained come to the soul by the intermission of the nerves, and there is between them this difference, that we relate them in the one case to objects outside which strike our senses, in the other to our soul.

23 Of the perceptions which we relate to objects which are without us.

Those which we relate to the things which are without us, to wit to the objects of our senses, are caused, at least when our opinion is not false, by these objects which, exciting certain movements in the organs of the external senses, excite them also in the brain by the intermission of the nerves, which cause the soul to perceive them. Thus when we see the light of a torch, and hear the sound of a bell, this sound and this light are two different actions which, simply by the fact that they excite two different movements in certain of our nerves, and by these means in the brain, give two different sensations to the soul, which sensations we relate to the subjects which we suppose to be their causes in such a way that we think we see the torch itself and hear the bell, and do not perceive just the movements which proceed from them.

24 Of the perceptions which we relate to our body.

The perceptions which we relate to our body, or to some of its parts, are those which we have of hunger, thirst, and other natural appetites, to which we may unite pain, heat, and the other affections which we perceive as though they were in our members, and not as in objects which are outside us; we may thus perceive at the same time and by the intermission of the same nerves, the cold of our hand and the heat of the flame to which it approaches; or, on the other hand, the heat of the hand and the cold of the air to which it is exposed, without there being any difference between the actions which cause us to feel the heat or the cold which is in our hand, and those which make us perceive that which is without us, excepting that from the one of these actions following upon the other, we judge that the first is already in us, and what supervenes is not so yet, but is in the object which causes it.

347

25 Of the perceptions which we relate to our soul.

The perceptions which we relate solely to the soul are those whose effects we feel as though they were in the soul itself, and as to which we do not usually know any proximate cause to which we may relate them: such are the feelings of joy, anger, and other such sensations, which are sometimes excited in us by the objects which move our nerves and sometimes also by other causes. But, although all our perceptions, both those which we relate to objects which are outside us, and those which we relate to the diverse affections of our body, are truly passions in respect of our soul, when we use this

348   word in its most general significance, yet we are in the habit of restricting it to the signification of those alone which are related to soul itself; and it is only these last which I have here undertaken to explain under the name of the passions of the soul.

26 *That the imaginations which only depend on the fortuitous movements of the spirits, may be passions just as the perceptions which depend on the nerves.*

It remains for us to notice here that all the same things which the soul perceives by the intermission of the nerves, may also be represented by the fortuitous course of the animal spirits, without there being any other difference excepting that the impressions which come into the brain by the nerves are usually more lively or definite than those excited there by the spirits, which caused me to say in article 21 that the former resemble the shadow or picture of the latter. We must also notice that it sometimes happens that this picture is so similar to the thing which it represents that we may be mistaken therein regarding the perceptions which relate to objects which are outside us, or at least those which relate to certain parts of our body, but that we cannot be so deceived regarding the passions, inasmuch as they are so close to, and so entirely within our soul, that it is impossible for it to feel them without their being actually such

349   as it feels them to be. Thus often when we sleep, and sometimes even when we are awake, we imagine certain things so forcibly, that we think we see them before us, or feel them in our body, although they do not exist at all; but although we may be asleep, or dream, we cannot feel sad or moved by any other passion without its being very true that the soul actually has this passion within it.

27 *The definition of the passions of the soul.*

After having considered in what the passions of the soul differ from all its other thoughts, it seems to me that we may define them generally as the perceptions, feelings, or emotions of the soul which we relate specially to it, and which are caused, maintained, and fortified by some movement of the spirits.

28 *Explanation of the first part of this definition.*

We may call them perceptions when we make use of this word generally to signify all the thoughts which are not actions of the soul, or desires, but not when the term is used only to signify clear cognition; for experience shows us that those who are the most agitated by their passions, are not those who know them best; and that they are of the number of perceptions which the close alliance which exists between the soul and the body, renders confused and obscure. We may also call them feelings because they are received into the soul in the same way as are the objects of our outside senses, and are not otherwise known by it; but we can yet more accurately call them emotions of the soul, not only because the name may be attributed to all the changes which occur in it − that is, in all the diverse thoughts which come to it, but more especially because of all the kinds of thought which it may have; there are no others which so powerfully agitate and disturb it as do these passions.

350

29 *Explanation of the second part.*

I add that they particularly relate to the soul, in order to distinguish them from the other feelings which are related, the one to outside objects such as scents, sounds, and colours; the others to our body such as hunger, thirst, and pain. I also add that they are caused, maintained, and fortified by some movement of the spirits, in order to distinguish them from our desires, which we may call emotions of the soul which relate to it, but which are caused by itself; and also in order to explain their ultimate and most proximate cause, which plainly distinguishes them from the other feelings.

30 *That the soul is united to all the portions of the body conjointly.*

351

But in order to understand all these things more perfectly, we must know that the soul is really joined to the whole body, and that we cannot, properly speaking, say that it exists in any one of its parts to the exclusion of the others, because it is one and in some manner indivisible, owing to the disposition of its organs, which are so related to one another that when any one of them is removed, that renders the whole body defective; and because it is of a nature which has no relation to extension, nor dimensions, nor other properties of the matter of which the body is composed, but only to the whole conglomerate of its organs, as appears from the fact that we could not in any way conceive of the half or the third of a soul, nor of the space it occupies, and because it does not become smaller owing to the cutting off of some portion of the body, but separates itself from it entirely when the union of its assembled organs is dissolved.

31 *That there is a small gland in the brain in which the soul exercises its functions more particularly than in other parts.*

352   It is likewise necessary to know that although the soul is joined to the whole body, there is yet in that a certain part in which it exercises its functions more particularly than in all the others; and it is usually believed that this part is the brain, or possibly the heart: the brain, because it is with it that the organs of sense are connected, and the heart because it is apparently in it that we experience the passions. But, in examining the matter with care, it seems as though I had clearly ascertained that the part of the body in which the soul exercises its functions immediately is in nowise the heart, nor the whole of the brain, but merely the most inward of all its parts, to wit, a certain very small gland which is situated in the middle of its substance and so suspended above the duct whereby the animal spirits in its anterior cavities have communication with those in the posterior, that the slightest movements which take place in it may alter very greatly the course of these spirits; and reciprocally that the smallest changes which occur in the course of the spirits may do much to change the movements of this gland.

32 *How we know that this gland is the main seat of the soul.*

The reason which persuades me that the soul cannot have any other seat in all the body than this gland wherein to exercise its functions 353   immediately, is that I reflect that the other parts of our brain are all of them double, just as we have two eyes, two hands, two ears, and finally all the organs of our outside senses are double; and inasmuch as we have but one solitary and simple thought of one particular thing at one and the same moment, it must necessarily be the case that there must somewhere be a place where the two images which come to us by the two eyes, where the two other impressions which proceed from a single object by means of the double organs of the other senses, can unite before arriving at the soul, in order that they may not represent to it two objects instead of one. And it is easy to apprehend how these images or other impressions might unite in this gland by the intermission of the spirits which fill the cavities of the brain: but there is no other place in the body where they can be thus united unless they are so in this gland.

33 That the seat of the passions is not in the heart.

As to the opinion of those who think that the soul receives its passions in the heart, it is not of much consideration, for it is only founded on the fact that the passions cause us to feel some change taking place there; and it is easy to see that this change is not felt in the heart excepting through the medium of a small nerve which descends from the brain towards it, just as pain is felt as in the foot by means of the nerves of the foot, and the stars are perceived as in the heavens by means of their light and of the optic nerves; so that it is not more necessary that our soul should exercise its functions immediately in the heart, in order to feel its passions there, than it is necessary for the soul to be in the heavens in order to see the stars there.

354

34 How the soul and the body act on one another.

Let us then conceive here that the soul has its principal seat in the little gland which exists in the middle of the brain, from whence it radiates forth through all the remainder of the body by means of the animal spirits, nerves, and even the blood, which, participating in the impressions of the spirits, can carry them by the arteries into all the members. And recollecting what has been said above about the machine of our body, i.e. that the little filaments of our nerves are so distributed in all its parts, that on the occasions of the diverse movements which are there excited by sensible objects, they open in diverse ways the pores of the brain, which causes the animal spirits contained in these cavities to enter in diverse ways into the muscles, by which means they can move the members in all the different ways in which they are capable of being moved; and also that all the other causes which are capable of moving the spirits in diverse ways suffice to conduct them into diverse muscles; let us here add that the small gland which is the main seat of the soul is so suspended between the cavities which contain the spirits that it can be moved

355

by them in as many different ways as there are sensible diversities in the object, but that it may also be moved in diverse ways by the soul, whose nature is such that it receives in itself as many diverse impressions, that is to say, that it possesses as many diverse perceptions as there are diverse movements in this gland. Reciprocally, likewise, the machine of the body is so formed that from the simple fact that this gland is diversely moved by the soul, or by such other cause, whatever it is, it thrusts the spirits which surround it towards the pores of the brain, which conduct them by the nerves into the muscles, by which means it causes them to move the limbs.

35 *Example of the mode in which the impressions of the objects unite in the gland which is in the middle of the brain.*

Thus, for example, if we see some animal approach us, the light reflected from its body depicts two images of it, one in each of our eyes, and these two images form two others, by means of the optic nerves, in the interior surface of the brain which faces its cavities; then from there, by means of the animal spirits with which its cavities are filled, these images so radiate towards the little gland which is surrounded by these spirits, that the movement which forms each point of one of the images tends towards the same point of the gland towards which tends the movement which forms the point of the other image, which represents the same part of this animal. By this means the two images which are in the brain form but one upon the gland, which, acting immediately upon the soul, causes it to see the form of this animal.

36 *Example of the way in which the passions are excited in the soul.*

And, besides that, if this figure is very strange and frightful – that is, if it has a close relationship with the things which have been formerly hurtful to the body, that excites the passion of apprehension in the soul and then that of courage, or else that of fear and consternation according to the particular temperament of the body or the strength of the soul, and according as we have to begin with been secured by defence or by flight against the hurtful things to which the present impression is related. For in certain persons that disposes the brain in such a way that the spirits reflected from the image thus formed on the gland, proceed thence to take their places partly in the nerves which serve to turn the back and dispose the legs for flight, and partly in those which so increase or diminish the orifices of the heart, or at least which so agitate the other parts from whence the blood is sent to it, that this blood being there rarefied in a different manner from usual, sends to the brain the spirits which are adapted for the maintenance and strengthening of the passion of fear, i.e. which are adapted to the holding open, or at least reopening, of the pores of the brain which conduct them into the same nerves. For from the fact alone that these spirits enter into these pores, they excite a particular movement in this gland which is instituted by nature in order to cause the soul to be sensible of this passion; and because these pores are principally in relation with the little nerves which serve to contract or enlarge the orifices of the heart, that causes the soul to be sensible of it for the most part as in the heart.

357

37 *How it seems as though they are all caused by some movement of the spirits.*

And because the same occurs in all the other passions, to wit, that they are principally caused by the spirits which are contained in the cavities of the brain, inasmuch as they take their course towards the nerves which serve to enlarge or contract the orifices of the heart, or to drive in various ways to it the blood which is in the other parts, or, in whatever other fashion it may be, to carry on the same passion, we may from this clearly understand why I have placed in my definition of them above, that they are caused by some particular movement of the animal spirits.

38 *Example of the movements of the body which accompany the passions and do not depend on the soul.*

358

For the rest, in the same way as the course which these spirits take towards the nerves of the heart suffices to give the movement to the gland by which fear is placed in the soul, so, too, by the simple fact that certain spirits at the same time proceed towards the nerves which serve to move the legs in order to take flight, they cause another movement in the same gland, by means of which the soul is sensible of and perceives this flight, which in this way may be excited in the body by the disposition of the organs alone, and without the soul's contributing thereto.

39 *How one and the same cause may excite different passions in different men.*

The same impression which a terrifying object makes on the gland, and which causes fear in certain men, may excite in others courage and confidence; the reason of this is that all brains are not constituted in the same way, and that the same movement of the gland which in some excites fear, in others causes the spirits to enter into the pores of the brain which conduct them partly into the nerves which serve to move the hands for purposes of self-defence, and partly into those which agitate and drive the blood towards the heart in the manner requisite to produce the spirits proper for the continuance of this defence, and to retain the desire of it.

40 *The principal effect of the passions.*

For it is requisite to notice that the principal effect of all the passions in men is that they incite and dispose their soul to desire those things for which they prepare their body, so that the feeling of fear incites it to desire to fly, that of courage to desire to fight, and so on.

41 *The power of the soul in regard to the body.*

But the will is so free in its nature, that it can never be constrained; and of the two sorts of thoughts which I have distinguished in the soul (of which the first are its actions, i.e. its desires, the others its passions, taking this word in its most general significance, which comprises all kinds of perceptions), the former are absolutely in its power, and can only be indirectly changed by the body, while on the other hand the latter depend absolutely on the actions which govern and direct them, and they can only indirectly be altered by the soul, excepting when it is itself their cause. And the whole action of the soul consists in this, that solely because it desires something, it causes the little gland to which it is closely united to move in the way requisite to produce the effect which relates to this desire.

42 *How we find in the memory the things which we desire to remember.*

Thus when the soul desires to recollect something, this desire causes the gland, by inclining successively to different sides, to thrust the spirits towards different parts of the brain until they come across that part where the traces left there by the object which we wish to recollect are found; for these traces are none other than the fact that the pores of the brain, by which the spirits have formerly followed their course because of the presence of this object, have by that means acquired a greater facility than the others in being once more opened by the animal spirits which come towards them in the same way. Thus these spirits in coming in contact with these pores, enter into them more easily than into the others, by which means they excite a special movement in the gland which represents the same object to the soul, and causes it to know that it is this which it desired to remember.

43 *How the soul can imagine, be attentive, and move the body.* 361

Thus when we desire to imagine something we have never seen, this desire has the power of causing the gland to move in the manner requisite to drive the spirits towards the pores of the brain by the opening of which pores this particular thing may be represented; thus when we wish to apply our attention for some time to the consideration of one particular object, this desire holds the gland for the time being inclined to the same side. Thus, finally, when we desire to walk or to move our body in some special way, this desire causes the gland to thrust the spirits towards the muscles which serve to bring about this result.

44 *That each desire is naturally united to some movement of the gland; but that, by intentional effort or by custom, it may be united to others.*

At the same time it is not always the desire to excite in us some movement, or bring about some result which is able so to excite it, for this changes according as nature or custom have diversely united each movement of the gland to each particular thought. Thus, for example, if we wish to adjust our eyes so that they may look at an 362 object very far off, this desire causes their pupils to enlarge; and if we wish to set them to look at an object very near, this desire causes them to contract; but if we think only of enlarging the pupil of the eye we may have the desire indeed, but we cannot for all that enlarge it, because nature has not joined the movement of the gland which serves to thrust forth the spirits towards the optic nerve, in the manner requisite for enlarging or diminishing the pupil, with the desire to enlarge or diminish it, but with that of looking at objects which are far away or near. And when in speaking we think only of the sense of what we desire to say, that causes us to move the tongue and lips much more quickly and much better than if we thought of moving them in all the many ways requisite to utter the same words, inasmuch as the custom which we have acquired in learning to speak, caused us to join the action of the soul (which, by the intermission of the gland can move the tongue and lips), with the significance of words which follow these movements, rather than with the movements themselves.

45 *What is the power of the soul in reference to its passions.*

Our passions cannot likewise be directly excited or removed by the action of our will, but they can be so indirectly by the representation of things which are usually united to the passions which we desire to have, and which are contrary to those which we desire to set aside. Thus, in order to excite courage in oneself and remove fear, it is not sufficient to have the will to do so, but we must also apply ourselves to consider the reasons, the objects or examples which persuade us that the peril is not great; that there is always more security in defence than in flight; that we should have the glory and joy of having vanquished, while we could expect nothing but regret and shame for having fled, and so on.

363

46 *The reason which prevents the soul from being able wholly to control its passion.*

And there is a special reason which prevents the soul from being able at once to change or arrest its passions, which has caused me to say in defining them that they are not only caused, but are also maintained and strengthened by some particular movement of the spirits. This reason is that they are nearly all accompanied by some commotion which takes place in the heart, and in consequence also in the whole of the blood and the animal spirits, so that until this commotion has subsided, they remain present to our thought in the same manner as sensible objects are present there while they act upon the organs of our senses. And as the soul, in rendering itself very attentive to some other thing, may prevent itself from hearing a

364

slight noise or feeling a slight pain, but cannot prevent itself in the same way from hearing thunder or feeling the fire which burns the hand, it may similarly easily get the better of the lesser passions, but not the most violent and strongest, excepting after the commotion of the blood and spirits is appeased. The most that the will can do while this commotion is in its full strength is not to yield to its effects and to restrain many of the movements to which it disposes the body. For example, if anger causes us to lift our hand to strike, the will can usually hold it back; if fear incites our legs to flee, the will can arrest them, and so on in other similar cases.

47 *In what the strife consists which we imagine to exist between the lower and higher part of the soul.*

And it is only in the repugnance which exists between the movements which the body by its animal spirits, and the soul by its will, tend to excite in the gland at the same time, that all the strife which we are in the habit of conceiving to exist between the inferior part of the soul, which we call the sensuous, and the superior which is rational, or as we may say, between the natural appetites and the will, consists. For there is within us but one soul, and this soul has not in itself any diversity of parts; the same part that is subject to sense impressions is rational, and all the soul's appetites are acts of will. The error which has been committed in making it play the part of various personages, usually in opposition one to another, only proceeds from the fact that we have not properly distinguished its functions from those of the body, to which alone we must attribute every thing which can be observed in us that is opposed to our reason; so that there is here no strife, excepting that the small gland which exists in the middle of the brain, being capable of being thrust to one side by the soul, and to the other by the animal spirits, which are mere bodies, as I have said above, it often happens that these two impulses are contrary, and that the stronger prevents the other from taking effect. We may, however, distinguish two sorts of movement excited by the animal spirits in the gland – the one sort represents to the soul the objects which move the senses, or the impressions which are met with in the brain, and makes no attempt to affect its will; the others do make an effort to do so – i.e. those which cause the passions or the movements of the body which accompany the

365

passions. And as to the first, although they often hinder the actions of the soul, or else are hindered by them, yet, because they are not directly contrary to them, we do not notice any strife between them. We only notice the strife between the latter and the acts of will which conflict with them: e.g. between the effort with which the spirits impel the gland in order to cause a desire for something in the soul, and that with which the soul repels it again by the desire which it has to avoid the very same thing. And what causes this strife to come into evidence for the most part is that the will, not having the power to excite the passions directly, as has just been said, is constrained to use its best endeavours, and to apply itself to consider successively several things as to which, though it happens that one has the power to change for a moment the course taken by the spirits, it may come to pass that that which succeeds does not have it, and that they immediately afterwards revert to that same course because the disposition which has before held its place in the nerves, heart, and blood has not changed, and thus it comes about that the soul feels itself almost at the same time impelled to desire and not to desire the same thing. It is from this that occasion has been taken to imagine in the soul two powers which strive one with the other. At the same time we may still conceive a sort of strife to exist, inasmuch as often the same cause which excites some passion in the soul, also excites certain movements in the body to which the soul does not contribute, and which it stops, or tries to stop, directly it perceives them; as we see when what excites fear also causes the spirits to enter into the muscles which serve to move the legs with the object of flight, and when the wish which we have to be brave stops them from doing so.

48 *How we recognise the strength or infirmity of souls, and what is lacking in those that are most feeble.*

And it is by success in these combats that each individual can discover the strength or the weakness of his soul; for those in whom by nature the will can most easily conquer the passions and arrest the movements of the body which accompany them, without doubt possess the strongest souls. But there are those people who cannot bring their strength to the test, because they never cause their will to do battle with its proper arms, but only

366
367

with those with which certain passions furnish it in order to resist certain others. That which I call its proper arms consists of the firm and determinate judgments respecting the knowledge of good and evil, in pursuance of which it has resolved to conduct the actions of its life; and the most feeble souls of all are those whose will does not thus determine itself to follow certain judgments, but allows itself continually to be carried away by present passions, which, being frequently contrary to one another, draw the will first to one side, then to the other, and, by employing it in striving against itself, place the soul in the most deplorable possible condition. Thus when fear represents death as an extreme evil, and one which can only be avoided by flight, ambition on the other hand sets forth the infamy of this flight as an evil worse than death. These two passions agitate the will in diverse ways; and in first obeying one and then the other, it is in continual opposition to itself, and thus renders the soul enslaved and unhappy.

49 *That the strength of the soul does not suffice without the knowledge of the truth.*

It is true that there are very few men so weak and irresolute that they desire nothing except what their passion dictates to them. The most part have determinate judgments, in pursuance of which they regulate a part of their actions; and although often their judgments are false or even founded on certain passions by which the will formerly allowed itself to be vanquished or led astray, yet, because it continues to follow them when the passion which has caused them is absent, they may be considered as its proper arms, and we may reflect that souls are stronger or weaker by reason of the fact that they are able to follow these judgments more or less closely, and resist the present passions which are contrary to them. Yet there is a great difference between the resolutions which proceed from a false opinion, and those which are founded only on the knowledge of the truth, inasmuch as if we follow the latter we are assured that we shall never regret nor repent it, whereas we do so always when we have followed the first mentioned, and hence discovered our error in doing so.

368

50 *That there is no soul so feeble that it cannot, if well directed, acquire an absolute power over its passions.*

And it is useful here to know that, as has already been said above, although each movement of the gland seems to have been joined by nature to each one of our thoughts from the beginning of our life, we may at the same time join them to others by means of custom, as experience shows us in the case of words which excite movements in the gland, which, so far as the institution of nature is concerned, do not represent to the soul more than their sound when they are uttered by the voice, or the form of their letters when they are written, and which, nevertheless, by the custom which has been acquired in thinking of what they signify when their sound has been heard or their letters have been seen, usually make this signification to be understood rather than the form of their letters or the sound of their syllables. It is also useful to know that although the movements both of the gland and of the spirits of the brain, which represent certain objects to the soul, are naturally joined to those which excite in it certain passions, they can at the same time be separated from these by custom, and joined to others which are very different; and also that this custom can be acquired by a solitary action, and does not require long usage. Thus when we unexpectedly meet with something very foul in food that we are eating with relish, the surprise that this event gives us may so change the disposition of our brain, that we can no longer see any such food without horror, while we formerly ate it with pleasure. And the same thing is to be noticed in brutes, for although they have no reason, nor perhaps any thought, all the movements of the spirits and of the gland which excite the passions in us, are none the less in them, and in them serve in maintaining and strengthening not, as in our case, the passions, but the movements of the nerves and muscles which usually accompany them. So when a dog sees a partridge he is naturally disposed to run towards it, and when he hears a gun fired, this sound naturally incites him to flight. But nevertheless setters are usually so trained that the sight of a partridge causes them to stop, and the sound which they afterwards hear when a shot is fired over them, causes them to run up to us. And these things are useful in inciting each one of us to study to regard our passions; for since we can with a little industry change the movement of the brain in animals deprived of reason, it is evident that we can do so yet more in the case of men, and that even those who have the feeblest souls can acquire a very absolute dominion over all their passions if sufficient industry is applied in training and guiding them.

The remaining articles — Part 2, 51–148 and Part 3, 149–212 — are here omitted. (Ed.)

THE SEARCH AFTER TRUTH BY THE
LIGHT OF NATURE

The search after truth by means of the light of nature which alone, and without the assistance of religion or philosophy, determines what are the opinions which a good man should hold on all matters which may occupy his thoughts, and which penetrates into the secrets of the most curious of the sciences.

A good man has no need to have read every book, nor to have carefully learned all that which is taught in the schools; it would even be a defect in his education were he to have devoted too much of his time to the study of letters. There are many other things to do in life, and he has to direct that life in such a manner that the greater part of it still remain to him for the performance of good actions which his own reason ought to teach him, even supposing that he were to receive his lessons from it alone. But he comes into the world in ignorance, and as the knowledge of his earliest years rests only on the weakness of the senses and the authority of masters, he can scarcely avoid his imagination being filled with an infinite number of false ideas, before his reason has the power of taking his conduct into its own hands; in consequence he requires to have good natural endowments or else instruction from a wise man, both in order to rid himself of the false doctrines with which his mind is filled, and for building the first foundations of a solid knowledge, and discovering all the means by which he may carry his knowledge to the highest point to which it can possibly attain.

In this work I propose to show what these means are, and to bring to light the true riches of our souls, by opening to each one the road by which he can find in himself, and without borrowing from any, the whole knowledge which is essential to him in the direction of his life, and then by his study succeed in acquiring the most curious forms of knowledge that the human reason is capable of possessing.

But in order that the greatness of my scheme may not to begin with seize your minds with an astonishment so great that confidence in my works can no longer find therein a place, I warn you that what I undertake is not as difficult as might be imagined. Those branches of knowledge which do not extend beyond the capacities of the human mind are, as a matter of fact, united by a bond so marvellous, they are capable of being deduced from one another by sentences so necessary, that it is not essential to possess much art or address in order to discover them, provided that by commencing with those that are most simple we learn gradually to raise ourselves to the most sublime. That is what I shall try to show you here by a system of reasoning so clear and yet so simple, that every one will be able to judge for himself that if he has not observed the same things, it is solely because he has not cast his eyes in the right direction, nor fixed his thoughts on the same considerations as I, and that no more glory is due to me for having discovered them, than is due to a casual passer-by for having accidentally discovered under his feet a rich treasure which had for long successfully eluded the searches of many.

And certainly I am surprised that amongst so many distinguished minds which in a matter of this description should have succeeded much better than I, none have had the patience to find their way out of their difficulties; and that nearly all have followed in the footsteps of these travellers who, abandoning the main route in favour of a crossroad, find themselves lost amongst briars and precipices.

But I do not desire to examine into what others have known or have been ignorant of. It will suffice for me to note that even if all the knowledge which we can desire is to be found in books, that which they contain of good is mingled with so many futilities, and confusedly dispersed in such a mass of great volumes, that, in order to read them, more time would be requisite than human life can supply us with, and more talent in discovering the useful than would be required in ascertaining it for ourselves.

That is what makes me hope that the reader will not be vexed by here finding an easier path, and that the facts which I shall advance will not be the less well received, even although I do not borrow them from Plato or Aristotle, but show that they have current value in the world, just as has money which is in nowise of less value when it proceeds from the purse of a peasant than when it comes from the treasury. I have even made it my business to make them equally useful to all men; and I have not been able to discover a style better adapted to this end than that of genuine conversation, wherein each one familiarly explains to his friends the best of his thoughts. And under the names Eudoxus, Polyander, and Epistemon, I assume that a man endowed with ordinary mental gifts, but whose judgment is not spoiled by any false ideas, and who is in possession of his whole reason in all the purity of its nature, receives as his guests in the country house which he inhabits, two men the most distinguished and interesting of their time, one of whom has studied not at all, while the other is well acquainted with all that can be learnt in the schools. And there (in the midst of other discourse which each one can imagine for himself, as well as the local conditions and particular surroundings from which I shall frequently cause them to take examples in order to make their conceptions more clear), they thus introduce the subject of which they will afterwards treat to the end of these two books.

POLYANDER, EPISTEMON, EUDOXUS

Polyander. I consider you are so fortunate in having discovered all these wonderful things in the Greek and Latin books, that it seems to me that if I had studied as much as you, I should be as different from what I now am, as angels are from you. And I cannot excuse the folly of my parents who, being persuaded that the study of letters would enfeeble the mind, sent me to the court and camps at so early an age, that I should all my life have had to bewail my ignorance, had I not learned something from my association with you.

Epistemon. The best thing that you could be taught on this subject is that the desire for knowledge, which is common to all men, is an evil which cannot be cured, for curiosity increases with knowledge; and as the deficiencies that are present in our soul only trouble us in so far as we recognise them, you have a certain advantage over us, in that you do not see as we do, that many things are lacking to you.

Eudoxus. Can it be, Epistemon, that you who are so well instructed, can believe that there is in nature any evil so universal that there is no remedy to be applied to it? As for me, I consider that just as there are in each country sufficient fruits and rivers to appease the hunger and thirst of all men, so there are truths that can be known in every matter sufficient to satisfy fully the curiosity of healthy minds; and I think that the body of a dropsical patient is not further removed from its normal condition than the mind of those who are perpetually worked upon by an insatiable curiosity.

Epistemon. I have, it is true, heard in former times that our desires could not extend naturally to things that seemed to us impossible, and that it ought not to do so to those that are vicious or useless; but so many things can be known which appear possible to us, and which are not only good and agreeable, but also very necessary in the conduct of life, that I cannot believe that anyone ever knew enough of them not to have legitimate reasons always to desire to know more.

Eudoxus. What, then, would you say of me, if I tell you that I no longer feel any desire to learn anything at all, and that I am as happy with my small knowledge as Diogenes used to be with his tub, and all this without my having any need of his philosophy? For the knowledge of my neighbours is not the limit of my own, as are their fields which here surround the small piece of ground that I possess; and my mind at its own will disposing of all the truths which it comes across, does not dream that there are others to discover. For it enjoys the same repose that the king of an isolated country would have were he so separated from all others as to imagine that beyond his frontiers there was nothing but unfertile deserts and uninhabitable mountains.

Epistemon. If any other but you spoke to me thus, I should regard him as one whose mind was either very vain or else too little given to curiosity; but the retreat which you have chosen in this solitude, and the small amount of pains that you take to become known, removes from you the charge of vanity; and the time you have hitherto consecrated to journeyings, visiting learned men, and examining everything that is most difficult in each science, suffices to assure us that you are not lacking in curiosity. I can hence say nothing but that I consider you very happy and that I am convinced that you must be in the possession of a knowledge much more perfect than that of others.

Eudoxus. I thank you for the good opinion in which you hold me, but I do not desire to abuse your courtesy to the point of desiring that you should believe what I have just said, solely on the faith of my words. We must not advance opinions so far removed from vulgar beliefs, without at the same time being able to demonstrate

501

502

certain effects from so doing; that is why I beg you both to be good enough to spend this delightful season here, so that I may have the opportunity of openly showing you some part of the things that I know. For I venture to flatter myself that not alone will you recognise that I have some reason for being happy in this knowledge, but, in addition, that you yourselves will have much happiness from the things that you will have learned.

Epistemon. I would not wish to refuse a favour that already I so ardently desired of you.

Polyander. And I shall have great pleasure in being present at this discussion, not that I believe myself capable of deriving any good from it.

Eudoxus. On the contrary, Polyander, believe me it will be you who will derive advantage from it, because you are quite unprejudiced, and it will be easier for me to guide aright any one with an open mind than Epistemon, whom we shall often find in opposition to us. But in order to make you more easily understand the nature of the knowledge of which I am going to treat, I beg you to observe a difference which exists between the sciences and those simple forms of knowledge which can be acquired without the aid of reasoning, such as languages, history, geography, etc., or to speak generally, everything that depends on experience alone. I am ready to grant that the life of a man would not suffice to acquire a knowledge of all that the world contains; but I am also persuaded that it would be folly to desire that it should be so, and that it is no more the duty of an ordinary well-disposed man to know Greek and Latin than it is to know the languages of Switzerland or Brittany; or that the history of the Empire should be known any more than that of the smallest state in Europe. And I consider that such a one should consecrate his leisure to good and useful things alone, and occupy his memory only with those that are most necessary. As to those sciences which are nothing but the judgments which we base on some knowledge previously acquired, some are deduced from common objects of which every one is cognisant, and others from rare and well thought out experiments. And I confess likewise that it would be impossible for us to treat in detail each one of these last; for we should first of all have to examine all the herbs and stones brought to us from the Indies; we should have

503

to have beheld the phoenix, and in a word to be ignorant of none of the marvellous secrets of nature. But I shall believe myself to have sufficiently fulfilled my promise if, in explaining to you the truths which may be deduced from common things known to each one of us, I make you capable of discovering all the others when it pleases you to take the trouble to seek them.

Polyander. For my part I believe that this is likewise all that it is possible to desire, and I would have been satisfied if you had merely taught me a certain number of propositions which are so celebrated that no one can be ignorant of them, such as those that concern the Deity, the rational soul, the virtues, their reward, etc., propositions which I compare with those ancient families which every one recognises as the most illustrious, although the titles of their nobility are concealed under the ruins of antiquity. For I do not really doubt that those who first of all induced the human race to believe in all these things had excellent reasons for proving them; but their arguments have been so rarely repeated since, that no one knows them any longer: and yet they are truths so important, that the dictates of prudence tell us that we should believe them blindly at the risk of being deceived, rather than that we should await a future life in order to be further instructed in them.

Epistemon. As far as I am concerned I am a little more curious, and I should like you to explain to me certain particular difficulties which suggest themselves to me in each branch of knowledge, and principally in what concerns the secrets of the human arts, apparitions, illusions, and in a word all the wonderful effects attributed to magic. For I believe it to be useful to know all that, not in order to make use of the knowledge, but in order that one should not allow one's judgment to be beguiled by wonder at an unknown thing.

Eudoxus. I shall try to satisfy you in regard to both; and, in order to adopt an order which we may make use of to the end, I wish first of all, Polyander, to talk with you of all things that the world contains, considering them in themselves, on the understanding that Epistemon shall interrupt our talk as little as possible, because his observations would often force us to leave our subject. We shall finally consider all these things anew, though under another aspect, in so far as they are in relation with us, and as they may be termed true or false, good or evil; and it is here that Epistemon will find occasion to set forth

504

505

all the difficulties which will remain to him from the preceding discourses.

Polyander. Tell us, then, the order that you will follow in your explanations.

Eudoxus. We must commence with the human soul because all our knowledge depends on it; and after having considered its nature and effects, we shall reach its author; and when we come to know who He is and how He has created all things in the world, we shall observe what is most certain regarding other creatures; and we shall inquire how our senses perceive things, and how our reflections become false or true. Then I shall place before your eyes the works of man upon corporeal objects, and after having struck wonder into you by the sight of machines the most powerful, and automata the most rare, visions the most specious, and tricks the most subtle that artifice can invent, I shall reveal to you secrets which are so simple that you will henceforward wonder at nothing in the works of our hands. After that I shall reach the works of nature, and, after having shown you the cause of all its changes, the diversity of its qualities, and the reason why the soul of plants and animals differs from ours, I shall place under your consideration the whole building up of sensible things. The phenomena of the heavens, and those certain conclusions which we may derive from them being observed, I shall pass on to most sane conjectures regarding what man cannot determine positively, in order to try to give an account of the relation sensible things bear to intellectual, and both to the Creator, of the immortality of the creatures, and of their state after the end of time. Then we shall come to the second part of this discourse in which we shall treat in detail of all the sciences, selecting in each that which is most solid, and we shall support a method whereby they may be carried on much further, and find of ourselves, with a mind of ordinary ability, what those most subtle can discover. After having thus prepared our minds for judging perfectly of the truth, we must also apply ourselves to the direction of our wills in respect of distinguishing good from evil, and observing the true difference between virtue and vice. That being done, I trust that your desire for knowledge will not be so violent, and that all that I shall have said to you will seem so well established that you will come to believe that a man with a healthy mind, had he brought up in a desert and never received more than the light of nature to illumine him, could not if he carefully weighed all the same reasons, adopt an opinion different from ours. In order to begin this discourse we must inquire as to what is the first knowledge man arrives at, in what part of the soul it is to be found, and why it is so imperfect to begin with.

Epistemon. All that seems to me to explain itself very clearly if we compare the imagination of children to a *tabula rasa* on which our ideas, which resemble portraits of each object taken from nature, should depict themselves. The senses, the inclinations, our masters and our intelligence, are the various painters who have the power of executing this work; and amongst them, those who are least adapted to succeed in it, i.e. the imperfect senses, blind instinct, and foolish nurses, are the first to mingle themselves with it. There finally comes the best of all, intelligence, and yet it is still requisite for it to have an apprenticeship of several years, and to follow the example of its masters for long, before daring to rectify a single one of their errors. In my opinion this is one of the principal causes of the difficulty we experience in attaining to true knowledge. For our senses really perceive that alone which is most coarse and common; our natural instinct is entirely corrupted; and as to our masters, although there may no doubt be very perfect ones found amongst them, they yet cannot force our minds to accept their reasoning before our understanding has examined it, for the accomplishment of this end pertains to it alone. But it is like a clever painter who might have been called upon to put the last touches on a bad picture sketched out by prentice hands, and who would find it vain to employ all the rules of his art in correcting little by little first a trait here, then a trait there, and finally be required to add to it from his own hand all that was lacking, and who yet could not prevent great faults from remaining in it, because from the beginning the picture would have been badly conceived, the figures badly placed, and the proportions badly observed.

Eudoxus. Your comparison places perfectly under our eyes the first obstacle which stands in our way; but you do not show the means of which we must avail ourselves if we wish to avoid it. And according to me it is this, that just as your artist would have done much better, after having effaced by drawing over it a sponge all the features of the picture, to begin it entirely over again rather than lose

507

508

his time in correcting it, so each one who has reached a certain term of years known as the age of knowledge, should set himself once for all to remove from his imagination all the inexact ideas which have hitherto succeeded in engraving themselves upon it, and seriously begin to form new ones, applying thereto all the strength of his intelligence with such zeal that if he does not bring them to perfection, the fault will not at least be laid on the weakness of the senses, or on the errors of nature.

509

Epistemon. That would be an excellent remedy if we could easily employ it; but you are not ignorant that the opinions first received by our imagination remain so deeply imprinted there, that our will alone, if it did not employ the aid of certain strong reasons, could not arrive at effacing them.

Eudoxus. It is certain of these reasons that I hope to teach you; and if you wish to derive some fruit from this our intercourse, you must give me your whole attention, and allow me to converse a little with Polyander in order that I may begin by upsetting all the knowledge he has hitherto acquired. And as it is not sufficient to satisfy him, and it cannot but be bad, I may compare it to a badly constructed edifice whose foundations are not solid. I know no better remedy than absolutely to rase it to the ground, in order to raise a new one in its stead. For I do not wish to be placed amongst the number of these insignificant artisans, who apply themselves only to the restoration of old works, because they feel themselves incapable of achieving new. We can, however, Polyander, while we are busy destroying this edifice, at the same time form the foundations which may serve our purpose, and prepare the best and most solid materials that are necessary in order to succeed in our task; provided you are in any degree willing to examine with me

510

which of all the truths men can know, are those that are most certain and easy of knowledge.

Polyander. Is there anyone who can doubt that sensible things (I mean thereby those that can be seen and touched) are much more certain than the others? As for me I should be very much astonished if you would show me as clearly some of those things that are said of God and our soul.

Eudoxus. That, however, is what I hope to do, and it seems to me surprising that men are credulous enough to base their knowledge on the certitude of the senses, when there is no one who is unaware that they frequently deceive us, and that we have good reason for always mistrusting those that have once betrayed us.

Polyander. I am well aware that the senses sometimes deceive us when they are ill affected, just as a sick person thinks that all food is bitter; when they are too far from the object this is also so, just as when we look at the stars they never appear to us as large as they really are; and in general when they do not act freely according to the constitution of their nature. But all their errors are easily known, and do not prevent my being now perfectly persuaded that I see you, that we walk in a garden, that the sun gives light, and, in a word, that all that my senses usually offer to me is true.

Eudoxus. Since it is not sufficient for me to tell you that the senses deceive us in certain cases where you perceive it, in order to make you fear being deceived by them on other occasions when you are not aware of it, I shall go further and ask if you have ever seen a melancholic man of the nature of those who believe themselves to be vases, or who think some part of their body is of enormous size; they would swear that they see and touch that which they imagine they do. And it is true that any ordinary man would be indignant if anyone were to say to him that he could not have any more reason than they to be certain of his opinion, since it rests equally with theirs on what the senses and his imagination represent to him. But you cannot be annoyed if I ask you whether you are not like other men subject to sleep, and if you cannot think when you sleep that you see me, that you walk in this garden, that the sun gives light, in a word all these other things that you imagine yourself now to be certain of. Have you never heard in comedies this expression for astonishment, 'Am I awake or asleep?' How can you be certain that your life is not a perpetual dream and that all that you imagine you learn by means of your senses is not as false now as it is when you sleep? More particularly as you have learned that you have been created by a superior Being to whom as omnipotent it would not have been more difficult to make us such as I have described, than such as you believe yourself to be?

Polyander. Certainly these are reasons sufficient to upset all the knowledge of Epistemon if he is contemplative enough to give his attention to it; as for me, I should fear becoming in some degree crazy, if, never having applied my mind to study, or accustomed myself to turn my mind away from the things of the senses, I was going to apply myself to meditations which, as far as I am concerned, a little exceed my capacities.

Epistemon. I think it very dangerous to proceed too far in this mode of reasoning. General doubts of this kind lead us straight to the ignorance of Socrates, or the uncertainty of the Pyrrhonists, which resembles water so deep that one cannot find any footing in it.

Eudoxus. I confess that it is not without great danger that one ventures without a guide when one does not know the ford, and many have lost their way in doing so; but you have no reason to
513   fear if you follow after me. It is such fears, indeed, that have prevented many learned men from attaining to the knowledge of a doctrine which is solid and certain enough to deserve the name of science; when, imagining that there was nothing on which they could rest their faith more firm and solid than the things that we perceive by the senses, they built on this foundation of sand rather than by digging down further finding a firm substratum of rock or clay. It is not here that we must stop. There is more; even if you did not wish further to examine the reasons which I have just stated, they would yet already in their principal effect have attained to the goal I wished to reach, so long as they had so affected your imagination as to place you on your guard against them. That is an indication to show you that your knowledge is not so infallible that you may not fear to see its foundations shattered since they make you doubt all; and consequently you are made to doubt your very knowledge itself, and this proves that I have accomplished my end, which was to upset your knowledge by showing you its uncertainty. From fear, however, that you may lack more courage and refuse to follow me further, I declare to you that those doubts which alarmed you to begin with, are like those phantoms and vain images which appear in the night by the uncertain glimmer of a feeble light. Fear pursues you if you flee, but if you approach and touch them, you will find nought but wind and shadow, and you will ever after be better able to meet whatever may arrive.

514   *Polyander.* Convinced by your reasoning I desire then to set before myself all these difficulties in the strongest manner possible, and to apply myself to doubt whether I have not been dreaming all my life,

and whether even all those ideas that I thought could only enter into my mind by the door of the senses, might not have been formed of themselves, just as similar ideas are formed when I sleep, or when I am certain that my eyes are shut, my ears closed, and, in a word, that none of my senses are in operation. In this way I shall be uncertain not only as to whether you are in the world, if a world exists, if there be a sun, but also whether I have eyes, ears, a body, even whether I talk with you, whether you address me, in short I shall doubt all things.[1]

Eudoxus. There you are, well prepared, and this is the very point I wished to bring you to; but this is the very moment for your giving your attention to the consequences which I wish to derive from your argument. You see very well that you can reasonably doubt all things, the knowledge of which comes to you by the senses alone; but can you doubt of your doubt and remain uncertain whether you doubt or not?

Polyander. I confess that this astonishes me, and the little sagacity which a sufficiently small amount of common sense gives me brings it to pass that I do not without stupefaction find myself forced to confess that I know nothing with certainty, but that I doubt all things and am certain of nothing. But what conclusions do you wish to derive from this? I do not see to what use this universal astonishment can serve, nor by what reason a doubt of this kind can be a principle which is able to carry us very far. Quite on the contrary, you have made the end of this our converse relief from all our doubts, and the discovery of truths of which Epistemon, wise as he is, may very well have been ignorant.

515

Eudoxus. Just give me your attention; I am going to conduct you further than you think. For it is really from this universal doubt which is like a fixed and unchangeable point, that I have resolved to derive the knowledge of God, of yourself, and of all that the world contains.

Polyander. You certainly make great promises and provided you carry them out it would certainly be worth our while to grant what you ask for. Keep, then, your promises and we will keep those we made to you.

1 This completes the original French manuscript. The rest is taken from the Latin translation of the original.

Eudoxus. Since then, you cannot deny that you doubt, and that it is on the other hand certain that you doubt, and so certain that you cannot even doubt of that, it is likewise true that you are, you who doubt; and that is so true that you can no longer doubt of it any more.

Polyander. I agree with you, for if I did not exist I could not doubt.

Eudoxus. You are, then, and you know that you are, and you know it because you doubt.

Epistemon. All that is very true.

Eudoxus. But in order that you may not be turned aside from your plan, go on little by little, and as I have said to you, you will feel yourself drawn on further than you think. You are, and you know that you are, and you know that because you know that you doubt. But you, who doubt all and who cannot doubt of yourself, what are you?

Polyander. The reply is not difficult and I see very well that you have chosen me in place of Epistemon so that I may respond to your questions. You had no mind to put any question to which it is not quite easy to reply. I shall then tell you that I am a man.

Eudoxus. You pay no attention to my question, and the reply that you make to me, simple as it may appear to you, will bring us into a labyrinth of difficulties, if I try ever so little to press you. Were I for example to ask Epistemon himself what a man is, and were he to reply, as is done in the schools, that a man is a rational animal; and if, in addition, in order to explain these two terms which are not less obscure than the first, he were to conduct us by all the steps which are termed metaphysical, we should be dragged into a maze from which it would be impossible for us to emerge. As a matter of fact, from this question two others arise; the first is what is an animal? The second, what is reasonable? And further, if, to explain what an animal is he were to reply that it is a living thing possessed of sensations, that a living thing is an animate body, that a body is a corporeal substance, you see that the question, like the branches of a genealogical tree, would go on increasing and multiplying; and finally all these wonderful questions would finish in pure tautology, which would clear up nothing, and would leave us in our original ignorance.

Epistemon. I am sorry to see that you despise this tree of Porphyry which has always excited the admiration of the learned, and I am vexed that you wish to show Polyander what he is by another method than the one which for so long has been admitted by the schools. In fact until now no better means has been found, nor a means more calculated to teach us what we are, than that of placing in sequence under our eyeball the successive items which constitute the totality of our nature, so that by this means, by ascending and descending all the steps, we may be made aware of what we have in common with other beings, and of that in which we differ. That is the highest point to which our knowledge can attain.

Eudoxus. I neither have nor should I ever have any intention of condemning the method employed in the schools; it is to it that I am indebted for the little that I know, and it is of its assistance that I have availed myself, in order to become aware of the uncertainty of all that I have learned there. Therefore although my teachers taught me nothing that was certain, I yet owe to them my thanks for having been taught by them to acknowledge this; and I now owe them all the greater thanks in that the things they taught me were doubtful, than had they been more in conformity with reason; for in that latter case I might possibly have contented myself with the small amount of reason that I should have discovered there, and that would have rendered me less zealous in the search after truth. The admonition that I gave to Polyander serves less to dissipate the obscurity into which his reply cast you than to make him more attentive to my question. I return then to my subject, and in order that we may not digress further I ask him a second time what he is, he who can doubt all things and cannot doubt of himself.

517

Polyander. I thought I had satisfied you by saying to you that I was a man, but I now see that I did not calculate well. I see very well that this answer does not satisfy you, and, truth to say, I confess that it does not now satisfy myself, more especially since you have shown me the embarrassment and uncertainty into which it can throw us if we wish to get light upon it and understand it. As a matter of fact, whatever Epistemon may say, I observe great obscurity in all these metaphysical steps. If, for instance, we say that a body is a corporeal substance without saying what a corporeal substance is, these two words will not teach us more than the word body. In the same way if we say that what lives is an animate body without having first explained what body is, and what animate is, and if we likewise enquire into all the other metaphysical degrees, it may be to put forward words in a certain order, but it is to express nothing; for it indicates nothing that can be conceived or that can form a clear and distinct idea in our mind. Even when, in order to reply to your question, I said that I was a man, I did not think of all the scholastic entities of which I was ignorant, and of which I had never even heard, and which, as far as I am concerned, exist only in the imagination of those who have invented them. But I spoke of the things that we see, that we touch, that we feel, that we experience in ourselves, in a word, of the things that the simplest of men know as well as the greatest philosopher in the world, that is to say that I am a certain whole composed of two arms, two legs, a head, and all the parts which constitute what we call the human body, and which in addition is nourished, walks, feels, and thinks.

Eudoxus. I saw at once by your reply that you had not quite understood my question,, and that you replied to more things than I asked of you. But as you have just numbered in the things of which you doubt, the arms, legs, head, and all the other parts composing the human body, I did not wish to interrogate you on any of these things of whose existence you are not sure. Tell me, then, what you really are inasmuch as you doubt. It is on this point alone, the only one which you can know with certainty, that I desired to question you.

Polyander. I now see that I have been mistaken in my reply and that I have gone further than I should, inasmuch as I did not properly understand your idea. That will render me more circumspect in future and at the same time it causes me to marvel at the exactitude of your method, whereby you conduct us little by little by simple and easy paths to the knowledge of the things that you wish to teach us. I have however reason to call the error that I have committed happy, since, thanks to it, I know very well that what I am inasmuch as I doubt, is in no wise what I call my body. And more than that, I do not even know that I have a body, since you have shown me that I might doubt of it. In addition to this I may add that I cannot even absolutely deny that I have a body. Yet, while entirely setting aside all these suppositions, this will not prevent my being certain that I exist. On the contrary, they confirm me yet more in the certainty that I exist and that I am not a body; otherwise, doubting of my body I should at the same time doubt of myself, and this I cannot do; for I am absolutely convinced that I exist, and I am so much convinced of it, that I can in no wise doubt of it.

Eudoxus. That is beautifully expressed and you bring out the matter so well that I should not do better myself. I see very well that all that now remains is to leave you entirely to yourself, merely taking care to set you on the right road. Nay, further: I think that in order to find the most difficult truths, provided we are well guided, the only necessity is to have common sense, to put it vulgarly; and, as I find you very well provided with that, as I had hoped, all I have to do is to show you the road you should henceforward follow. Continue then to deduce by yourself the consequences which flow from this first principle.

Polyander. This principle seems to me so fertile, and it offers me so many things at once, that it seems as though I should want a great deal of work to reduce them to order. This one admonition that you have given me to consider who I who doubt am, and not to confound myself with what I formerly believed to be me, has thrown such a flood of light upon my mind, and so dissipated the mists, that by the light of this torch I see more accurately in myself what is not visible to the eyes, and that I am more persuaded that I possess what cannot be touched, than I ever have been of possessing a body.

Eudoxus. This warmth pleases me infinitely well although it may displease Epistemon who, because you have not shown him his error, or placed under his eyes a part of the things that you say are contained in this principle, will always believe, or will at least fear, that the torch offered to you is similar to those wandering fires that are extinguished and vanish away when they are approached, and that so you may fall into your original darkness, i.e. into your former ignorance. And it certainly would be marvellous if you who have never studied nor opened books of philosophy, should all at once gain wisdom at such a small cost. So we should not be astonished that Epistemon judges in this way.

Epistemon. Yes, I confess I took that to be the result of mere enthusiasm, and I thought that Polyander who has never meditated on the great truths which philosophy teaches, was so transported by the discovery of the least of them that he could not prevent himself from letting you know of it by his shouts of joy. But those who like you[2] have travelled this road for long, have expended much oil and trouble in reading and rereading the writings of the ancients, and in unravelling and expounding all that is most complicated in the philosophers, are no longer astonished by this enthusiasm, and make no more of it than they do of the vain hopes which frequently lay hold of one in commencing mathematics, when the threshold of the temple alone has so far been saluted. These novices have scarcely been given the line and the circle, and shown what is a straight line and a curved, when they believe that they are going to square the circle and duplicate the cube. But we have so frequently refuted the opinion of the Pyrrhonists, and they themselves have derived so little fruit from this method of philosophising, that they have been in error all their lives, and have not been able to get free of the doubts which they have introduced into philosophy. They thus seem never to have worked for anything but learning to doubt: that is why, with Polyander's permission, I shall doubt whether he himself can derive anything better from it.

Eudoxus. I see very clearly that you speak to Polyander in order to spare me; your pleasantries are all the same evidently directed against me; but let Polyander speak and after that we shall see which of us will laugh last.

Polyander. I will do so willingly; nay, I fear that this dispute will become hot between you two and that if you plunge into the matter too deeply, I shall end by understanding nothing at all. Thus shall I lose the fruit which I promise myself in returning to my original studies. I pray then that Epistemon may permit me to nourish this hope for so long as it pleases Eudoxus to lead me by the hand in the path in which he has placed me.

Eudoxus. You have already clearly recognised in considering yourself simply as doubting, that you are not body, and that as such you would not find within you any of the parts which constitute the human machine: that is to say, that you have neither arms, nor legs, nor head, nor eyes, nor ears, nor any organ which may serve for a sense of any kind. But notice whether in the same way you cannot reject all the things that you formerly understood by the

2 The French editors conjecture 'like me'.

description which you gave of the idea which in former times you had of man. For, as you judiciously remarked, that was a fortunate error that you committed in passing beyond the limits of my question. Thanks really to it, you can arrive at a knowledge of what you are by removing from you and rejecting all that you perceive clearly does not belong to you, and by simply admitting what so necessarily pertains to you that you are as certain of it as of your existence and doubt.

Polyander. I thank you for thus setting me on my way; I did not know any longer where I was. I said first of all that I was a whole formed of arms, legs, a head, and all the parts which form the human body, besides which I walk, am nourished, feel and think. It has been necessary for me, in order to consider myself simply as I know myself to be, to set aside all these parts or all these members which constitute the human machine; that is to say, I must consider myself as without arms, legs, head, and, in a word, without body. But it is true that what in me doubts is not what we call our body; so then it is also true that I, inasmuch as I doubt, do not eat or walk, for neither of these two things can be done without body. Further, I cannot even state that I, inasmuch as I doubt, can feel. As feet really serve for walking, so do eyes for seeing, and ears for hearing. But, as I have none of these organs because I have not body, I cannot say that I feel. In addition to that, I have often in dreaming thought I felt many things that I did not really feel at all, and as I resolved to admit nothing here but what was so true that I could not doubt of it, I cannot say that I am a perceiving thing, that is, one that sees with eyes and hears with ears. It might indeed be that I thought I perceived although none of these things happened.

Eudoxus. I cannot prevent myself from stopping you here, not to turn you aside, but to encourage you, and make you consider what common sense can do if it is well directed. As a matter of fact, is there anything in all this which is not exact, which is not legitimately argued, and well deduced from what precedes? And all that is said and done without logic, or rule, or a formula for the argument, but with the simple light of reason and with a just sense which, acting alone and of itself, is less exposed to error than when it anxiously tries to follow a thousand diverse routes which art and human idleness have discovered, less to bring it to perfection than to

521

corrupt it. Epistemon even seems to be in this matter of our opinion; for while saying nothing of the matter, he gives us to understand that he approves what we have said. Go on, then, Polyander, and show him how far good sense can carry us, and at the same time what consequences can be derived from our principle.

Polyander. Of all the attributes which I bestowed upon myself, only one remains for me to examine and that is thought; and I see that it is the only one that I cannot separate from myself. For if it is true that I doubt just because I cannot doubt that I do so, it is also equally true that I think; for what is doubting but thinking in a certain way? And in fact if I did not think, I could not know whether I doubt or exist. Yet I am, and I know that I am, and I know it because I doubt, that is to say because I think. And better, it might be that if I ceased for an instant to think I should cease at the same time to be. Likewise the sole thing that I cannot separate from me, that I know certainly to be me and that I can now affirm without fear of deception – that one thing, I repeat, is that I am a thinking thing.

522   *Eudoxus.* What, Epistemon, do you think of what Polyander has just said? Do you find his argument to be halting or inconsequent? Should you have thought that an unlettered man, and one who had not studied, would have reasoned so well and followed out his ideas so rigorously? Here, if I do not mistake, you must begin to see that he who knows how properly to avail himself of doubt can deduce from it absolutely certain knowledge, better, more certain, and more useful than that derived from this great principle which we usually establish as the basis or centre to which all other principles are referred and from which they start forth, viz. *it is impossible that one and the same thing should both be and not be.* I shall perhaps have occasion to demonstrate the utility of it to you. But let us not interrupt Polyander's discourse, or remove ourselves from our subject; as to you, see if you have anything to say or any objection to make.

Epistemon. Since you lay the blame on me and even exasperate me, I shall show you what logic can do when it is roused, and at the same time I shall raise difficulties and obstacles of such a nature that not only Polyander but you yourself will have much difficulty in getting free of them. Let us then go no further, but stop here and severely examine your principles and deductions. As a matter of fact with the aid of true logic, and after your own principles, I shall show that nothing of what Polyander has said rests on a legitimate foundation or brings about any conclusion. You say that you are and that you know that you are, that you know it because you doubt and because you think. But do you know what doubting or what thinking is? And as you do not desire to admit anything of which you are not certain and do not know perfectly, how can you be certain that you are by means of attributes so obscure and consequently so uncertain? It would have been better first of all to have taught Polyander what doubt is, what thought is, what existence is, so that his reasoning might have the strength of a demonstration, and that he might first of all understand himself before applying himself to make others comprehend.

Polyander. That is beyond me, so I give it up leaving you to unravel this knot with Epistemon.

Eudoxus. For this occasion I undertake it with pleasure, but on the condition that you will be judge of our differences; for I dare not hope that Epistemon will give way to my reasoning. He who is like him, full of opinions and prepossessed with a hundred prejudices, finds it difficult to hand himself over to the light of nature alone; for long he has been accustomed to yield to authority rather than to lend his ear to the dictates of his own reason. He likes better to interrogate others, to weigh what the ancients have written, than to consult himself on the judgment which he should form; and as from his childhood he has taken as reason what rested only on the authority of preceptors, now he gives his authority as a reason and desires that others should pay to him the tribute which he formerly paid them. But I shall have reason to be content and I shall believe myself to have sufficiently answered the objections which have been proposed to you by Epistemon, if you give your assent to what I shall say, and if your reason convinces you of it.

523

Epistemon. I am not so rebellious nor so difficult to persuade, nor is it so difficult to satisfy me as you think. And further, although I had reasons for mistrusting Polyander, I would willingly submit our case to his arbitration; and as soon as he favours you I promise you to confess myself vanquished. But he must guard himself from being deceived and falling into the error for which he reproaches others, that is to say, from taking as a motive for persuasion the esteem which he has formed for you.

Eudoxus. If he allowed himself to rest on so feeble a support he would look badly after his own interests and I presume that he will attend to them. But let us return to our subject matter. I am quite of your opinion, Epistemon, that we must know what doubt is, what thought is, before being fully convinced of the truth of this reasoning, *I doubt therefore I am;* or, what comes to the same, *I think therefore I am.* But do not go and imagine that in order to know this we must do violence to our mind and put it to torture in order to ascertain the *proximate species* and the *essential difference,* and form from it a definition by rule. All that must be left to him who is going to be a professor or to dispute in the schools. But whoever desires to examine things by himself and judge of them as he conceives them, cannot be so devoid of mental power not to see clearly whenever he is willing to give attention to it, what doubt is, or thought or existence, and to be required to learn their distinctions. Further I declare that there are certain things which we render more obscure by trying to define them, because, since they are very simple and clear, we cannot know and perceive them better than by themselves. Nay, we must place in the number of those chief errors that can be committed in the sciences, the mistakes committed by those who would try to define what ought only to be conceived, and who cannot distinguish the clear from the obscure, nor discriminate between what, in order to be known, requires and deserves to be defined, from what can be best known by itself. And in the number of the things which are clear in the way above explained and which can be known by themselves, we must place doubt, thought, and existence.

524

I do not think that anyone has ever existed who is stupid enough to have required to learn what existence is before being able to conclude and affirm that he is; the same holds true of thought and doubt. Indeed I add that one learns those things in no other way than by one's self and that nothing else persuades us of them except our own experience and this knowledge and internal testimony that each one finds within himself when he examines things. In vain shall we define what white is in order to make it comprehensible to him who sees absolutely nothing, while in order to know it, it is only requisite to open one's eyes and see the white; in the same way in order to know what doubt is, or thought, it is only requisite to doubt and think. That teaches us all that we can know of it, and explains more respecting it than even the most exact definitions. It is thus true that Polyander ought to have known these things, before being able to draw the conclusions which he has advanced; but since we have chosen him as judge, ask him if he has ever been ignorant of what is.

Polyander. I certainly confess that it is with the greatest pleasure that I have heard you disputing regarding a thing which you have not been able to know but from me, and it is not without some joy that I see, at least on this occasion, that it is necessary for me to be recognised as your master and for you to recognise yourselves as my pupils. Therefore in order to put both of you out of pain and quickly to resolve your difficulty (as a matter of fact we say that a thing is promptly done when it is done beyond all hope and expectation), I can state for certain that I never doubted what doubt is, although I never began to know it, or rather to think of it until the time which Epistemon desired to place it in doubt. You no sooner showed me the small amount of certainty which we have as to the existence of things which are only known to us by the evidence of the senses, than I commenced to doubt of them, and that sufficed to make me know doubt and at the same time my certainty of it, in such a way that I can affirm that as soon as I commenced to doubt I commenced to know with certainty. But my doubt and my certainty did not relate to the same object; my doubt regarded things only which existed outside me, my certainty concerned me and my doubt. Eudoxus then spoke truly when he asserted that there are things that we cannot know without seeing them; therefore to learn what doubt is, what thought is, it is necessary only that we ourselves should think and doubt. The same holds good of existence; it is only necessary to know what we understand by this word; we know at the very same moment what the thing is, at least in so far as we can know it, and there is no necessity here for a definition, which will more confuse than clear up the matter.

Epistemon. Since Polyander is satisfied I likewise give my assent, and I shall not push the dispute further. However I do not see that during the two hours that we have been here and that we have been arguing, he has advanced much. All that Polyander has learnt by the help of this wonderful method of which you so boast, consists solely of the fact that he doubts that he thinks and that he is a thinking thing. A wonderful knowledge in truth! Many words for small results'. As much could be said in four words and we should have all given our assent. As for me if I had to employ as many words and as much time in learning something of so small an importance, I confess I should not resign myself to it without regret. Those who are our instructors tell us much more about the matter; they are much more confident; nothing stops them; they take everything upon them and decide about all. Nothing turns them aside from their plan, nothing astonishes them, whatever happens; when they feel themselves pressed too hard, an equivocation or the *distinguo* saves them from all embarrassment. And more, be certain that their method will always be preferred to that of one like you who doubts all and who fears so much to trip that he keeps treading the same spot and thus makes no advance.

Eudoxus. I never intended to prescribe to anyone the method he ought to follow in the search after truth, but merely to expound that of which I have availed myself, so that if it were found bad it would be set aside; if it were found good and useful others would avail themselves of it in turn; and I always left full liberty to all to set it aside or to admit it. If it is now said that it has advanced me little, it is for experience to decide as to that; and I am certain, provided that you continue to lend me your attention, you will yourself confess that we cannot take too many precautions in the establishment of our bases, and that once they are well established we shall push the consequences further and with much more facility than we had dared to promise ourselves; so that I believe that all the errors which are found in the sciences come from the fact that we have in the beginning formed our judgments too precipitately by admitting as principles obscure things of which we had no clear and distinct notion. The truth of this is shown by the modicum of progress that we have made in the sciences whose principles are certain and known by all; for, on the other hand, in the others, whose principles are obscure or uncertain, those who desire sincerely to express their thought will be forced to confess that after having employed much time, and having read many great volumes, they have to recognise that they know nothing and have learnt nothing. It must not then appear astonishing to you, my dear Epistemon, if, desiring to lead Polyander in the way that is surer than that in which I was trained to walk, I am so careful and exact that I hold that only to be true of which I have a certainty equal to that with which I am aware that I am, I think, I am a thinking thing.

Epistemon. You seem to me to resemble these tumblers who always fall back on their feet, so ceaselessly do you return to your principle. Yet if you proceed by this path you will go neither far nor quickly. How, as a matter of fact, shall you always find truths of which you are as certain as of your existence?

Eudoxus. That is not as difficult as you think; for all the truths succeed one another and are united by a common bond; the whole secret consists simply in beginning with the first and most simple, and in rising little by little, and so to speak by gradations, to those more remote and complicated. Who now will doubt that what I have set forth as first principle is the first of the things which we might come to know with the help of a method? It is certain that we cannot doubt it, even were we to doubt of all things in the world. As then we are certain of having begun well, we must take pains not to deceive ourselves in what follows, we must apply our whole care not to admit that to be true which is liable to the smallest doubt. Pursuing this plan we must in my opinion allow Polyander to speak; for as he follows no guidance but that of his common sense, and as his reason is corrupted by no prejudices, it is difficult for him to be deceived, or at any rate he would easily perceive that this was so, and he would without any trouble return to the right road. Let him then speak, and set forth what he himself alleges he has seen in your principle.

Polyander. So many things are contained in the idea of a thinking thing that whole days would be required to develop them. We shall only treat of the principal ones and those that can make the notion clearer and hinder our confounding it with what bears no relationship to it. I mean by a thinking being . . . [3]

527

3 The Amsterdam Latin version here inserts 'The rest is wanting.'

WORDSWORTH CLASSICS
OF WORLD LITERATURE

APULEIUS
The Golden Ass

ARISTOTLE
The Nicomachean Ethics

MARCUS AURELIUS
Meditations

FRANCIS BACON
The Essays of Sir Francis Bacon

JOHN BUNYAN
The Pilgrim's Progress

KARL VON CLAUSEWITZ
On War (abridged)

CONFUCIUS
The Analects

CHARLES DARWIN
Voyage of the Beagle

DESCARTES
*Key Philosophical
Writings*

SIGMUND FREUD
The Interpretation of Dreams

EDWARD GIBBON
*The Decline and Fall of the
Roman Empire (abridged)*

KHALIL GIBRAN
The Prophet

HERODOTUS
Histories

HORACE
Selected Odes

LAO TZU
Tao te ching

T. E. LAWRENCE
Seven Pillars of Wisdom

SIR THOMAS MALORY
Le Morte Darthur

JOHN STUART MILL
*On Liberty & The Subjection
of Women*

SIR THOMAS MORE
Utopia

THOMAS PAINE
Rights of Man

MARCO POLO
The Travels

SAMUEL PEPYS
Selections from the Diary

PLATO
*The Symposium &
the Death of Socrates*

The Republic

LA ROCHEFOUCAULD
Maxims

JEAN-JACQUES ROUSSEAU
The Confessions

SUETONIUS
Lives of the Twelve Caesars

THUCYDIDES
*The History of the
Peloponnesian War*